How to Tell What People Are Thinking
(Revised and Expanded Edition)

Also by Peter Collett

Foreign Bodies: A Guide to European Mannerisms
Gestures: Their Origins and Distribution (co-author)
Driving Passion: The Psychology of the Car (co-author)
Social Psychology at Work (co-editor)

REVISED AND EXPANDED EDITION

How to Tell What People Are Thinking

FROM THE BEDROOM TO THE BOARDROOM

PETER COLLETT

Collins

Published by Collins, an imprint of HarperCollins Publishers Ltd

Originally published in Great Britain by Doubleday as *The Book of Tells*: 2003
First published in Canada by HarperCollins Publishers Ltd as *The Book of Tells*: 2004
First published in Canada as *How to Tell What People Are Thinking* by Collins, an imprint of HarperCollins
Publishers Ltd: 2009
First published in Canada as *How to Tell What People Are Thinking*
(Revised and Expanded Edition) by Collins: 2024

HarperCollins books may be purchased for educational, business, or sales
promotional use through our Special Markets Department.

HarperCollins Publishers Ltd
Bay Adelaide Centre, East Tower
22 Adelaide Street West, 41st Floor
Toronto, Ontario, Canada
M5H 4E3

www.harpercollins.ca

Library and Archives Canada Cataloguing in Publication

Title: How to tell what people are thinking : from the bedroom to the boardroom / Peter Collett.
Other titles: Book of tells
Names: Collett, Peter, 1945- author.
Description: Revised and expanded edition. | Originally published under title: The book of tells. |
Includes bibliographical references.
Identifiers: Canadiana (print) 20240360001 | Canadiana (ebook) 20240360028 | I
SBN 9781443472647 (softcover) | ISBN 9781443472654 (ebook)
Subjects: LCSH: Body language. | LCSH: Nonverbal communication.
Classification: LCC BF637.N66 C64 2024 | DDC 153.6/9—dc23

Printed and bound in the United States of America
24 25 26 27 28 LBC 5 4 3 2 1

For Jill, Katie and Clementine

Contents

How to Tell What People Are Thinking
(Revised and Expanded Edition)

1. Tells

In the game of poker a *tell* refers to any action made by a player—be it physical, verbal, or behavioural—that might provide a clue about the kinds of cards they may be holding, the mood they're in, or the move they're likely to make next. If you're a poker player, being able to spot your opponents' tells and figure out what they mean will almost certainly give you a winning advantage. These skills may be important in poker, but they're even more vital in our everyday lives.

Let's imagine that you're talking to an old friend about people you dated in the past. You casually ask him if he regrets breaking off with the attractive girl he was dating during his final year at school. "Oh, no," he replies. "I don't have any regrets, and it didn't upset me when we broke up either." As he's talking, your friend briefly wipes the skin under his right eye with his index finger. There's no reason why you should notice this tiny gesture, and if you did you'd probably think that he was just removing a bit of dust from his face. But he isn't. The gesture is in fact a *tell*, and it casts an entirely different light on your friend's true feelings. Although he says that the bust-up didn't disturb him, part of his brain knows otherwise, and it instructs his finger to wipe away an imaginary tear. So while the conscious part of his brain is saying "I wasn't upset," another part is producing a tell that says "Well, actually, I was upset!" Momentarily your friend might recognize his complicated feelings, but it's highly unlikely that he notices what his unruly finger is doing or what it reveals about his true feelings.

The friend who wipes away an imaginary tear produces an *autonomous tell*—in other words, a tell that has no purpose other than to reveal his true feelings. Because autonomous tells aren't intentional, they are hardly ever noticed by the people who produce them or the

1

people who witness them. That's not necessarily the case with *attached tells*, which are connected to some other activity. For example, when two people are introduced to each other, the fact that they shake hands may be less informative than *how* they actually do so. How tightly they grip each other's hand, how they position their palm, how much enthusiasm they show, how much control they try to exert, the actual words they use to greet each other—these are all attached tells. Within the greeting ritual they reveal what each person is really like, and what they're trying to achieve with the other person.

Whether a tell is an action or the way that an action is performed usually depends on how common the action is. Consider two societies: one where men regularly greet each other with a kiss on the cheek, and another where they hardly ever do so. When two men kiss each other in the first society, they are simply doing what all the other men do. The fact that they kiss each other is therefore not very informative—it doesn't tell us anything about their relationship. However, *how* they kiss each other does tell us about their relationship. The situation in the second society tends to be reversed. Here, when two men greet each other with a kiss on the cheek they are doing something unusual. Now it's the kiss itself, rather than the way it's performed, that tells us what kind of relationship the two men have.

Poker Tells

Poker tells are the signals that players unintentionally produce give when they're trying to conceal what kinds of cards they're holding or the strategy they're employing. There are two essential skills in poker: The first is the capacity to hide your feelings so that the other players have no idea whether you're holding a bad hand or a royal flush. This is the ability to keep a "poker face"—to remain completely enigmatic. The other essential skill is the ability to read people's behaviour—to work out what kind of cards they're holding simply by observing their actions and listening to what they say. While you, as a poker player, are looking for telltale signs in the other players' behaviour, the other players are busy doing everything they can to mislead you. The reverse is also true—while the other players are trying to figure out what you're up to, you're doing everything in your power to ensure that you don't give them anything to go on, or if you do that it sends them off in the wrong direction.

One of the ways that poker players can improve their game is by learning to recognize the links between their opponents' actions, the cards that they're holding and the moves they make. Players can start to pay attention to little things, like the way someone holds their cards or the way they look at them, the way they make a call, what they do with their hands, how they fiddle with their glasses—the list of potential tells is endless. Poker guru Mike Caro has made a lifelong study of poker tells and the ways that players give themselves away by sighing, humming, tapping their fingers, playing for time, checking their cards and trying to lay false trails.[1] Several films, like *House of Games*, *Casino Royale* and *Rounders*, have included scenes where the plot turns on someone discovering a poker tell. In *Rounders*, for example, there's a showdown game of poker between Mike, the hero (played by Matt Damon), and Teddy KGB, a Russian mobster (played by John Malkovich) who likes to break open Oreo cookies and eat them while he's playing poker. Mike eventually wins the game by working out the mobster's tell—when he splits the cookie beside his ear he's got a good hand, but when he splits it in front of his face it means that he's bluffing!

Poker players have lots to think about. Apart from deciding what to do next, they're constantly trying to undermine other players' attempts to understand them while doing everything possible to see past the defences erected by the other players. It all seems very confusing, but in fact it's no more complicated than the things that we all do every time we relate to other people. In our daily encounters we're constantly trying to project an image of ourselves, and so are other people, and while they're trying to work out what we are thinking, we're doing the same to them. Our chances of success, like those of the poker player, will always depend on how sensitive we are to other people, and whether we can recognize and understand their tells.

Surveying Tells

Everyday tells are highly informative. The way you stand when you're talking to someone—how you move your feet, hands, eyes and eyebrows—says a lot about your commitment to the conversation and your underlying attitude to the other person. It also affects how long you get to talk and how often you get interrupted. How you position your arms and legs when you're seated also provides a wealth of information about your mood and intentions, showing whether you feel dominant or submissive, preoccupied or bored, involved or detached. The way you smile—the facial muscles you use and how rapidly you recruit them—shows whether you're genuinely happy, faking it, lying or telling the truth, feeling anxious, miserable, superior or unsure of yourself. Speech disfluencies are also highly informative. The way you hesitate when you're speaking, how you *um* and *er*, provides important clues to your mood. While the words you choose, the phrases you select and the way you construct your utterances may convey an official message to other people, your linguistic choices also contain disguised messages that reveal your true intentions.

A tell needs to satisfy four conditions:

1. It has to be some kind of activity—a feature of someone's appearance, a movement of their body or something they say. Broadly speaking, tells fall into two categories: "attributes," like height or weight, and "actions," like folding the arms, smiling or using certain giveaway words and phrases.
2. The action needs to reveal something about the person that's not directly observable—it has to tell us about their background, their thoughts, their mood or their intentions. It follows that not every action is a tell; only those actions that convey information about someone are tells. Of course, there are some actions that we don't recognize as tells because we haven't yet discovered what they reveal about people. These are *undiscovered tells*. When we do learn how they are linked to people's internal states, they too will be added to the list of tells.

4

3. The action has to be noticed. One factor that decides whether an action gets noticed is its size. Large, expansive movements of the body, for example, are more likely to attract attention, especially when they're visible for a long time. Small, fleeting movements, on the other hand, often get ignored, either because they're not in view for long enough or because they're obscured by other actions. Although large actions are more visible, it doesn't mean that we automatically notice them or that we understand their significance. As Sherlock Holmes remarked to Dr. Watson, we may see but we don't always observe.

4. The significance of the action needs to be recognized. It's not enough for us to notice that someone has adopted a certain posture or used an unusual expression. We also need to recognize what that posture or that expression tells us about that person.

When we look at the evolution of tells we find that there's a tendency for some tells to get bigger, and a tendency for others to get smaller. In areas like dominance and courtship, where there's a lot of competition between individuals, there's a natural tendency for the anatomical features that signal strength and reproductive fitness to get bigger, and for the displays associated with those features to become bolder and more eye-catching. Good looks, a toned body, a healthy, youthful appearance—all of these features are designed to attract attention, to get the message across, to outclass the competition and ultimately to enable the individual to gain access to limited resources like food, shelter or sexual partners.

Micro-tells

There are two situations where signals get smaller. One is where there's a deliberate attempt to ensure secrecy, and the other is where there's unintended disclosure of what's going on in someone's head. By their very nature, secret signals are targeted at selected individuals—in order to remain secret it's essential that only certain people get the message and that everyone else doesn't. Very often this is achieved by using a miniature signal and by attaching it to an everyday action that doesn't attract attention. Lovers sometimes communicate in code, using special words or tiny signs when they're with other people—in this way they can exchange loving signals without anyone else knowing. In a similar fashion, members of secret societies often identify themselves to each other by the way they shake hands—for example, by scratching the palm or positioning the fingers so that the other person gets the message but nobody else can see what's happening. Detection is avoided by deliberately keeping the signal small. As a further safeguard, it's hidden inside an activity that's unlikely to arouse suspicion.

Miniature signals are also common when people are trying to hide what they're thinking. When people are lying, for example, or feeling anxious, the giveaway signs that expose their true feelings are often extremely small and short-lived. Unlike the signs exchanged by lovers or members of secret societies, these *micro-tells* are entirely unintentional. Psychologists have identified a special group of micro-tells called "micromomentary expressions" or "microexpressions," which are confined to the face.[2] They are very brief and usually appear for less than half a second, and sometimes no more than one-eighth of a second. When people are describing a painful experience while putting on a brave face, it's not uncommon for them to reveal their discomfort by briefly altering their facial expression. One moment they're smiling, giving the impression that the experience didn't bother them at all; the next moment their face is transformed into the briefest of grimaces. Then, before anyone notices anything, the smile is back, and all evidence of discomfort is erased from their face.

The distinguishing feature of facial micro-tells is their brevity—it's as though someone has opened the curtains, allowing passers-by to look into their home, and then immediately closed them again. The action is so rapid that people don't notice the curtains opening, let alone what's in the house. That's exactly how it is with micro-tells. When we're concealing our thoughts, or a particularly strong image enters our mind, it sometimes shows on our face or in our movements.

As soon as the wayward thought has managed to sneak onto our face, the processes that control our demeanour spring into action, remove it and reinstate the desired expression. In the meantime, however, the evidence is there for anyone to see—they just need to spot the micro-tell and be able to interpret it correctly.

In principle, micro-tells can appear anywhere on the body, but because of the fine-grained nature of the facial muscles, they're most likely to appear on the face. When a micro-tell does appear on our face, it shows that we're in a state of conflict—usually between a positive emotional state that we want other people to see and a negative emotional state that we're trying to conceal. When the negative emotional state momentarily gains the upper hand, our facial control breaks down and the micro-tell appears. Most of the time we're completely unaware of the conflict that's taking place in us, and the fact that we're revealing our inner thoughts to the outside world. But even when we are conscious of our conflicting emotions, we still don't realize that our facial micro-tells are giving us away.

Facial micro-tells usually expose the emotions that people would rather conceal—like fear, surprise, sadness and disgust. There are times, however, when people are trying to sustain a serious expression and a micro-tell in the shape of a smile breaks through.

Sometimes micro-tells appear on one side of the face; at other times they can be seen on both sides. Because they are so rapid, most micro-tells don't get noticed. When people are primed to look out for micro-tells, they're more likely to recognize them, although some people are much better at spotting them than others. Those who are good at it are generally more interested in other people, and they are better at identifying liars. However, everybody can be trained to be more sensitive to micro-tells.

Stealth Tells

Some tells are shy, giving the impression that they would rather not be noticed—they operate by stealth, pretending to be something other than what they really are. The *eye-wipe tell*, for example, tries to pass itself off as an innocent attempt to remove a flake of skin or a speck of dust from under the eye, but it's actually an unacknowledged sign that the person is feeling sad or regretful.

There are lots of other *stealth tells*. When people are lying, for example, they frequently feel an unconscious urge to stop themselves saying something that might give them away. They often respond to this impulse by touching their lips or by positioning a finger so that it stands guard over their mouth. These are unconscious gestures of self-restraint, and they would be quite easy to spot were it not for the fact that they manage to disguise themselves as other kinds of actions. Consequently, when we see people touching their lips we automatically think that they're just wiping them clean, and when we see people placing a finger beside their mouth we simply assume that they're being thoughtful or attentive. We don't recognize these actions as tells of self-restraint because the tells have succeeded in passing themselves off as something else.

It's the same with patting. If you watch people hugging, you'll sometimes see one or both parties patting the other on the back. To the observers, to the person who's being patted, and even to the person who's doing the patting, this appears to be a gesture of affection. But it's not—it's actually a signal to release! Although people don't realize it, they always respond to being patted on the back by bringing the hug to an abrupt close. Although the person who's been patted on the back has been silently instructed to let go, there isn't any feeling of rejection. That's because the release signal operates by stealth, pretending to be a gesture of affection while it's actually giving a command.

Genuine Tells

Genuine tells show what's really happening in people's heads. They often reveal things about people that they don't want others to know and, in some cases, are actively trying to conceal from others. However, there are some actions that pretend to be tells but aren't. These are not real tells—they're *false tells*. There are several differences between genuine tells and false tells. First of all, unintentional tells tend to be genuine. Blushing, sweating and pupil dilation, for example, operate outside conscious control. This means that there's no opportunity for bluffing—people cannot fake blushing or make themselves sweat or make their pupils dilate to order. Consequently, when someone's face reddens we can be sure that they're feeling self-conscious, and when we see someone sweating we can be certain that they're either hot or bothered, or both. Similarly, when we see someone's pupils expanding, we can reasonably assume it's because there's less light around or that the person is emotionally aroused.

Although blushing, sweating and pupil dilation are all outside conscious control, there are nevertheless differences between them. For example, when we're blushing we're fully aware that other people can see our embarrassment and there's nothing we can do about it. Also, the people who witness our embarrassment are fully aware that they're drawing inferences on the basis of our blushing. However, the situation is very different with pupil dilation. When our pupils dilate, we are totally unaware of the information that we're providing about our emotional state. What's equally interesting is that people who see us, and who recognize our heightened state of arousal, don't know how they came to that conclusion—they know there's something attractive about our face, but they can't identify what it is.[3] In other words, when our pupils dilate we produce a genuine tell, but we don't know that we're doing it. At the same time, other people may react to the tell but not know why.

Genuine tells often appear when people are being deceptive—when they're trying to pass themselves off as more dominant or confident than they really are, when they're lying, when they're trying to conceal their anxiety or cover up their real intentions. Imposters, professional con artists, expert liars and psychopaths often manage to produce convincing performances, with a minimum of revealing tells. Most people, however, feel awkward when they're being deceptive, and that's when they're betrayed by their tells. The pressure of trying to sustain a convincing performance is too much for them—their performance starts to fracture and very soon the tells are seeping out through the cracks. Paul Ekman and his colleagues at the University of California in San

Francisco have shown that people differ widely in their ability to produce convincing lies, and that those who find it easy to lie produce fewer cues to deception or "leakage."[4] Some experts believe that there is no such thing as a consummate liar, and that, regardless of their ability, people always leave telltale traces of their deception. Freud, for example, believed that people ultimately cannot conceal their internal states from others—in the end there is always some outward sign of what a person is thinking. As he put it, "He that has eyes to see or ears to hear may convince himself that no mortal can keep a secret. If his lips are silent, he chatters with his fingertips; betrayal oozes out of every pore."[5]

False Tells

A *false tell* appears to reveal something about someone but doesn't. This may occur for at least two reasons: 1) because the tell is unreliable, and 2) because the person is faking the tell (in other words, deliberately trying to get other people to draw the wrong conclusion about their thoughts or feelings). These are *counterfeit tells*. Tells are unreliable when they fail to give us an accurate reading of someone's internal state. Sweating palms, for example, are a good indicator of a person's anxiety. But they're not completely reliable because 5 percent of the population has hyperhidrosis, a genetic condition that produces chronic sweating and has nothing to do with anxiety.[6]

Counterfeit tells are everywhere. Every time someone puts on a jacket with padded shoulders or wears high-heel shoes, they are deliberately providing misleading information about how broad or tall they are, and doing so in full knowledge of the impression they're trying to create. In other situations they may be less aware of what they're trying to achieve. For example, when a man puffs out his chest or a woman walks on tiptoes, he seems broader and she appears taller, even though neither is fully aware why they are behaving in this way, if in fact they have noticed anything different about their own behaviour. In the animal world vocal pitch serves as a genuine signal of size. The depth of a toad's croak, for example, provides a very accurate prediction of how large the toad is. This enables individual toads to publicize how big they are, and to assess how big their competitors are, and it's very difficult for toads to fake. Among adult humans the relationship between pitch and body size isn't straightforward, although everyone assumes that large people have deep voices. What's more, people find it relatively easy to lower their voice, and to give the impression that they're bigger than they really are. For humans, therefore, pitch isn't a genuine tell of size.

A counterfeit tell occurs when someone simulates a tell without having the attribute or the state of mind that normally goes with that tell. Take crying, which of course is a tell of sadness and distress. When we're feeling this way we can either give in to the impulse to cry or we can try to hold back the tears. One way we can do this is by biting our lower lip. This sends two messages. Firstly, it shows that our feelings are so strong that they need to be brought under control. Secondly, it shows that we're capable of reining in our emotions. The act of biting our lower lip is not so much a tell as it is a *tell-suppressing tell*—in other words, a tell whose purpose is to mask other tells.

As any actor will tell you, it's much easier to bite one's lower lip than it is to produce a false display of crying. When people want to pretend that they're in the grip of strong emotions, it's much easier to produce a false version of a tell-suppressing tell than a false version of the tell itself. During his presidential campaign, Bill Clinton made a habit of biting his lower lip. He'd tell his audience that "people are hurting all over the country" and "you can see the pain in their faces," and then he'd bite his lip to show that he really meant it. Of course this could have been a genuine expression of Clinton's feelings, but it's much more likely that his lip-biting was a counterfeit tell, simply because it happened on more than one occasion and he stood to increase his popularity by giving the impression that he could be overwhelmed by feelings of compassion.

The whole point of Clinton's lip-bite is that it was deliberate and that it *pretended* to be an unconscious gesture of self-restraint, a way of keeping his powerful emotions under control. In 1998, when Clinton was accused of having an affair with Monica Lewinsky, his first response was to deny it ("I did not have sexual relations with that woman, Miss Lewinsky"). Later on, however, he decided to come clean. A so-called "Prayer Breakfast" was duly arranged, with assorted politicians and over a hundred religious leaders present, so that Clinton could deliver his public *mea culpa*. The brief apology he made for his wayward behaviour evidently convinced the assembled audience, but what really did the trick was Clinton's lip-bite. During the twelve minutes or so that he spoke, Clinton bit his lip no fewer than fifteen times! Even though he did it repeatedly, it's highly unlikely that his audience was consciously aware of what he was doing because his lip-bite was so discreet. This doesn't mean that they weren't affected by Clinton's lip-bite—they clearly were. They just didn't know it.

Signature Tells

Tells come in several varieties. Some tells are widespread, even universal. Others are restricted to groups of people, and some even appear to be unique to specific individuals. First there are *common tells*. These include blushing, shrugging and the genuine smile—wherever you go, blushing remains a sign of embarrassment, shrugging a sign of helplessness, and the genuine smile a sign of happiness. Next there are *local tells*. These are shaped by history and culture, and they are therefore confined to certain communities or groups of people. Local tells include different ways of standing, sitting, sleeping and eating. Then we have *signature tells* or *trademark tells*. These aren't necessarily unique, but because of their powerful association with certain individuals they appear to be unique to them, just like a signature or a trademark.

Several important historical figures have been identified with trademark tells. For example, the Roman writer Plutarch tells us that Julius Caesar had a habit of scratching his head with his index finger rather than with all the fingers of his hand.[7] This meant that he didn't have to disturb his carefully arranged coiffure any more than necessary, and it showed him up as a vain man. Adolf Hitler had a habit of standing with his hands clasped in front of his genitals. This is a defensive posture, and it's commonly used by people who feel socially or sexually insecure. In Hitler's case it even prompted the joke in Germany at the time that, with his hands neatly poised over his crotch, he was "hiding the last unemployed member of the Third Reich."

Whenever we think of Napoleon Bonaparte we imagine him with his right hand tucked into his waistcoat. In fact if you want to pretend that you're Napoleon, all you need to do is to slip your hand into an imaginary waistcoat and everyone will recognize you immediately. In spite of the universality of this image, there's very little evidence to show that this was Napoleon's favourite posture. Quite the contrary. It's said that his trademark tell was his habit of walking with his hands clasped behind his back, a practice that made him instantly recognizable to his troops, even at a great distance. The idea that Napoleon tucked his hand into his waistcoat comes from a famous painting by Jacques-Louis David, where Napoleon appears in his study in the Tuileries Palace, assuming this posture. What's interesting is that Napoleon didn't actually sit for this portrait—the artist did it from memory. It's quite likely that Napoleon's posture in the picture is a painterly conceit rather than a faithful depiction of how he actually stood. At the time it was customary for important men to be represented in paintings with their hand in their waistcoat, even when they didn't habitually adopt the posture. This convention was established in Europe and America long before Napoleon had come to power, and there's even a portrait of George Washington in which he's adopting this posture. Washington is remembered for many things but not for standing around with his hand in his waistcoat.

We all know people with signature tells—for example, the person who leans their head to one side when they're talking to you, or your friend who curls their hair around their fingers in an unusual way. Most people recognize the signature tells of famous people—like Donald Trump's "yank-shake," Vladimir Putin's lopsided way of walking or Angela Merkel's "steeple gesture," where she brings the tips of her fingers together—but they don't understand what these tells reveal about the person concerned. In the chapters that follow we'll take a close look at these tells and uncover their true meaning.

Adolf Hitler's trademark tell. The Nazi leader had a habit of standing with his hands clasped in front of his genitals, prompting Germans at the time to comment that he was "concealing the last unemployed member of the Third Reich."

Transposed Tells

When you see someone tapping their foot you can reasonably assume that they're feeling impatient at that moment, and not that they were impatient some time ago or that they anticipate being impatient in the future. Most tells relate to what's happening at that moment—in other words, they are "time-locked." There are two types of time-locked tells: one type reveals people's enduring traits, the other their current states. When someone who is chronically anxious bites their nails, it's because of their enduring traits, not because of any passing mood. On the other hand, when someone who's acutely anxious bites their nails, it's because of the current mood they're in, not because of their enduring condition. In each of these cases the nail-biting reveals what the person is feeling at that time, even though it's a permanent experience for the first person and a temporary one for the second.

A number of time-locked tells reveal people's enduring traits. Some, like nail-biting and hair-pulling, are voluntary, while others, like tics, sweating, and heavy or shallow breathing, are involuntary. Depending on their severity, some of these conditions may require medical or psychiatric treatment. A classic example of a chronic time-locked tell is hysterical paralysis, where, for example, the person is unable to use one of their arms, not because it's been physically damaged but because they have experienced a traumatic event that has placed their arm beyond voluntary control. In such cases paralysis can be cured only by psychological treatment, not by any medical intervention.

There are also states that lie dormant, as it were, waiting to reveal themselves in people's actions. Phobias are a good example. People who jump up at the sight of a spider aren't in a permanent state of fear—it's only the appearance of a spider that makes them frightened. It's the same with "memories in the muscles." People who have experienced traumatic events sometimes lock their memories of those events away in their muscles. The effects of these locked-up memories can sometimes be seen in the way that people hold their bodies. Sometimes there's no external evidence—it's only when the muscles that retain these memories become relaxed that the memories are released. When this happens the person is usually overwhelmed by very powerful emotions.

While some tells are time-locked, others are transposed in time. They are "time-shifted"—that is, they reveal what the person was feeling earlier, or will feel later, and not what they are feeling at that moment. There are many everyday examples of *time-shifted tells*. If you watch people's hands while they're talking, you'll notice that they often use illustrative gestures to trace out the shape of the physical object they're talking about. The interesting thing about these gestures is that they tend to occur *before* the person utters the word that refers to the object. For example, someone who's talking about a spiral staircase will perform a spiralling motion with his hand before he actually says "spiral staircase." John Bulwer, the seventeenth-century student of gesture, recognized this when he described how "the *Hand*, which is a ready Midwife, takes often-times the thoughts from the forestalled Tongue, making a more quicke dispatch by gesture; . . . For the gesture of the *Hand* many times gives a hint of our intention, and speakes out a good part of our meaning, before our words, which accompany or follow it, can put themselves into a vocall posture to be understood."[8] This pre-emptive property of gestures shows that our thoughts can influence our actions before they inspire what we say—or, more controversially, that our gestures may actually shape what we think and say. On those occasions when we have trouble remembering a word, it's often only by performing the appropriate gesture that we can recover the word from memory.

There are other, equally revealing examples of time-shifted tells. George Mahl, a clinical psychologist, described an interview with one of his patients in which the woman was playing with her wedding ring while she was describing her symptoms. During this time she made no mention of her husband. It was only after she had stopped fiddling with her wedding ring that she started to complain about her husband, saying that he didn't help her around the house and that he made her feel inadequate.[9] There are two ways to understand what's happening when the woman plays with her wedding ring—either she had an unconscious image of her husband at the time, or it was the act of playing with her ring that brought her husband to mind and prompted her to complain about him. Either way, it's clear that while she was playing with the ring she was not consciously thinking about her husband—that only came later. Her manipulation of the ring is therefore transposed in time—it's a time-shifted tell. On the other hand, if we were to regard her verbal complaint about her husband as a tell, we would consider it to be a time-locked tell, because it reveals what she was thinking about at that moment.

Predictive Tells

Some tells are predictive—they show what someone is about to do next or how a confrontation is likely to end. Imagine a situation where a young man and woman are talking to each other on a park bench, and she decides that it's time for her to take her leave. She doesn't just get to her feet, announce that she's leaving, and then disappear. Instead she does things by stages. To ensure that she doesn't upset the young man, she starts by producing a series of "intention movements," to show him that she's thinking of leaving. These may consist of tiny adjustments to her gaze or the way she arranges her arms and legs. The important point about these intention displays is that they aren't necessarily deliberate, and the woman may not even be aware that she's producing them. Although the woman's signals are very subtle, the man is likely to pick up on them and to alter his own posture accordingly. By responding to her displays and producing his own, he's able to show that he's understood her intentions. He may be unaware of the effect that her signals are having on him, and how he is responding—in fact the entire dialogue of *leaving tells* may be played out without either of them being conscious of what's happening.

There are other instances where people respond to tells without being aware of what's happening. When two people are talking to each other it's not uncommon for one or both of them to "mirror" the posture of the other. One person may, for example, cross her legs and then turn her face, and a few minutes later her friend may perform exactly the same actions.[10] When we mimic other people's actions in this way we are usually oblivious of our own actions—it's only when it's been pointed out to us that we notice what we've been doing. Yawning operates on similar principles. We all know that yawning is highly contagious, and that when one person yawns other people nearby are very likely to follow suit. Research has shown that it doesn't require a complete yawn for one person to copy another—the mere sight of an open mouth, or the sound of a yawn, is often enough to get other people yawning.[11]

Our ability to read other people's intention movements is highly developed. We don't need to think about it—it happens automatically, very quickly, and usually with remarkable accuracy. Like other animals, we need to know whether other individuals are favourably disposed toward us. Instead of waiting to see what they do, we rapidly scan their behaviour for signs of intention movements that will help us to decide what they're likely to do next.

Intention movements play a central role in the resolution of confrontations. In the animal world threat displays are used to scare off the competition—in this way individuals can get what they want without getting involved in a fight and risking injury. If threat displays don't work, physical attack may be necessary. It's generally assumed that individuals who produce threat displays are likely to attack. However, research with birds and fish shows that threat displays don't necessarily lead to attack—in some cases individuals are bluffing and in others a threat is enough to achieve what they want.[12] Threat displays, it turns out, are not a very good predictor of who's likely to win in a confrontation. However, signs of uncertainty are a good predictor because they show which individual does not want to take the confrontation to the next stage. So if you want to know which individual is most likely to win a contest you should look out for *hesitation tells* rather than *threat tells*. For example, a middle-distance track athlete who takes the lead in a race may or may not dishearten the other athletes by continuing to look ahead. However, if he turns around to see where the others are, he's likely to expose his uncertainty and to reduce his chances of winning.

Telling Tells

As we can see, tells are everywhere. If you watch people talking to each other you'll notice that they are constantly moving their eyes, face, hands and body while they're speaking, and that sometimes they are just as active while they're listening. Every posture they assume, even the fleeting, almost imperceptible, expressions that dash across their face, carry messages about their thoughts and feelings. But tells aren't confined to conversations—even when people are alone they are constantly shifting their body, touching their face and providing clues to their state of mind.

Tells sometimes tell us things about people that they don't even know themselves. Because certain tells are controlled by involuntary processes in the brain they are outside people's conscious control and therefore much more accurate indicators of people's emotions than the accounts that they might offer about their feelings. If you ever have to choose between believing what someone has to say about their feelings and what you can observe from their involuntary tells, you should always opt for the latter. In these instances the golden rule is always "Trust the tells" and not what people say about themselves, or what other people say about them.

Some tells are easily recognized and widely understood; for example, when someone blushes, we all know that they're feeling embarrassed or self-conscious. Other tells aren't understood. That's because they're not recognized as tells, or because it's not clear what they mean, or because they seldom even get noticed. Even when people do notice other people's tells it doesn't mean that they understand them. This is especially noticeable in relations between men and women. It's not unusual, for example, for a woman to make a friendly overture toward a man, and for the man to misinterpret her actions as a come-on. Equally, when we fail to notice the tells that other people produce, it doesn't mean that we aren't affected by them. It's still possible for their tells to slip under our radar, so to speak, and to influence us in ways that we don't fully understand. For example, psychologists have discovered that marriages are more likely to break down if one partner produces facial expressions of contempt, even if the other person is unaware that they're doing so.[13]

Tells are like the constituents of a language. But it's a very unusual language because, while we all speak it fluently, we often don't hear what other people are saying or understand what their tells are telling us about them. To become more proficient in the language of tells we need to be more observant—it's only by noticing what people say and do that we can begin to understand their thoughts and feelings. Concentrating on tells makes us more sensitive to other people, and ultimately it makes our dealings with them more rewarding. It also helps us to understand our own behaviour, and the impact that we have on others.

There are two ways of thinking about the relationship between brain and behaviour. The widely held view is that our attitudes, feelings and motivations—in a sense, what's inside us—determine how we behave, in other words, what's outside us. This is what we might call the "inside-out" approach to human behaviour. The contrasting, and far less common, view is the "outside-in" approach, which contends that our outer behaviour can shape and modify our inner attitudes, feelings and motivations.

Fanciful as it may seem, growing evidence supports the "outside-in" approach.

- The early research on what psychologists called "post-decision dissonance reduction" showed that when people get to own something—like a car or a house—they're inclined to rate it more positively than other things that they previously rated as being just as good.

- Gamblers at the racecourse who have just placed a bet are more confident that their horse is going to win than the people who are lining up to place their bets—in other words, doing something that can't be revised increases your commitment to your actions.

- If you do someone a favour then your fondness for that person is likely to increase, whereas if you're unkind to someone there's every chance that you'll start to like that person less.

- But to my mind, the most compelling support for the "outside-in" approach comes from studies of people who've had Botox injections.[14] It's been found, for example, that people who'd had injections to reduce the appearance of lines on their forehead were slower to experience feelings of fear and anger—both emotions that involve the muscles in the forehead—but not their experience of happiness, which of course has nothing to do with the muscles in the forehead. But there's more to this story, because it's been found that, in addition to reducing people's sensitivity to certain of their own emotions, Botox also reduces their ability to recognize those same emotions in others. This supports the so-called "facial feedback hypothesis," which suggests that when we process other people's emotional expressions, we actually enlist our own, corresponding facial muscles in that process. In other words, when empathizing with someone we automatically simulate their expression with our own facial muscles.

All of this goes to show that our actions can influence our thoughts and feelings—it doesn't matter whether it's about owning something, placing bets, relating to other people or expressing our emotions—how we appear on the outside can affect what's going on inside us. While our tells offer a window into our inner world, it's also true that our personal tells can shape what we're thinking and feeling.

2. Dominant Tells

When we meet people for the first time we instantly judge them in terms of whether they're dominant, friendly and sexually attractive.[1] Although we sometimes think that we're more interested in other issues, these three factors play a major role in the impressions that we form of other people. We share these concerns with our nearest relatives, the chimpanzees, who spend a lot of time sorting out their relative positions in the hierarchy.

In a chimpanzee troop the distribution of dominance displays, submissive displays and grooming creates a pecking order, which invisibly ranks individuals according to their rights to territory, food and sex. Individuals assert their dominance by adopting a posture which creates an impression of size and which signals a readiness to attack. This may take the form of a facing orientation, fixed gaze and heightening of the body. When there's a confrontation it may also involve stiffening of the limbs and erection of the ears and the hair on the back. A submissive chimpanzee, on the other hand, will turn away, avert its eyes, flatten its ears and hair, and create an overall impression of smallness. In most chimpanzee troops submissive individuals will even turn around completely, presenting their rear to the dominant individual, who will then go through the motions of mounting the submissive individual and producing a few non-copulatory thrusts. Through this ritual, individuals acknowledge their relationship to each other and the pecking order in the troop is affirmed.

We humans have inherited many of the postural signals used by our non-human relatives. Although we don't have especially mobile ears or erectile hair, we do use orientation, gaze, apparent size and posture as signals of dominance and submission in our dealings with each other.[1]

Tall Tells

In most animal societies there is a strong connection between height and social status. In the case of humans the relationship is overwhelming. Statistics show that taller people are more successful than short people. They're also healthier, more intelligent, and they tend to live longer.[2] This is not a modern phenomenon: recent excavations of an old graveyard in Norfolk, England, have revealed that taller people were enjoying longer lives as far back as the ninth century.[3] In fact, the symbolic association between height and power is very primitive. It goes back to the time when armies on the high ground had a strategic advantage over those below, and settlements on the hill were able to defend themselves better than those in the valleys. The association now forms part of our language—we speak of the "head" of the organization being "superior" to "those below," and of the need to "rise above" or get "on top of" our problems.

Women say that they prefer a man to be taller than them. It's also been found that tall men have greater reproductive success than short men, and that there's a strong but not overwhelming tendency in advanced societies for women to choose male partners who are taller, and for men to select women who are shorter than them. This, however, is not the case across the globe.[4]

Over the years, tallness has become an established ideal in men, and it's now rapidly becoming one in women. Tallness in men is linked to higher levels of the male hormone, testosterone, and to a more dominant personality.[5] In the history of the United States only three presidents have been shorter than the national average, and some, like Abraham Lincoln, towered over their contemporaries. Height is also supposedly linked to how much people earn—what's known as the "height premium." Cross-national comparisons show that this is more evident in some countries than in others—for example, the premium is much stronger in Latin America and Asia than it is in the United States and Australia. Moreover, the height premium is a lot more pronounced with men than women. Interestingly, the impact of height may occur where it's least expected. Even in universities, where the staff are supposed to be appointed on the basis of academic excellence alone, we find that assistant professors are 1.24 inches taller than the national average, associate professors are 1.5 inches, and full professors are 1.94 inches taller than the average person for their age and sex.[7]

One way to appear more dominant is to increase our apparent height by positioning ourselves above other people. Another is to sit straight or to stand erect. Psychologists have found that people who adopt an erect standing posture tend to be seen as more dominant than those who adopt a slouched posture, and that those who are trained to stand erect feel more confident and optimistic than those who continue to stand in their customary fashion.[8] It has also been found that when people succeed at a task they tend to respond by sitting up straight, whereas those who fail at a task are more likely to respond by slumping forward.

But an erect posture isn't a cure for everything. It is widely assumed that people who feel depressed or defeated can improve their state of mind by sitting up straight. In fact it's often quite the reverse. Research has shown that people who are given tasks involving failure show quicker recovery when they are allowed to adopt a slumped posture than when they are encouraged to sit up straight. Contrary to what you might expect, a slumped posture is actually an adaptive response to defeat—it enables people who feel dejected to gather their thoughts and to recover their confidence in their own time.[9]

Territorial Tells

Power is frequently linked to territory in the animal world. Among baboons, the dominant or "alpha" individual usually occupies the highest branches in a tree, defending its position from the subordinates below and taking on the role of leader and protector. It also lays claim to more territory, both in the way it physically occupies the space around it and the way it keeps other individuals at bay. It's exactly the same with humans. High-status individuals occupy more space—they have bigger houses, cars and offices. They also use up more of the space around them, and other people usually acknowledge their claims by allowing them extra space. High-status people seem to create an invisible boundary around themselves—not unlike a military exclusion zone—that other people approach with caution. Indeed, it's often the other people's hesitancy in approaching the invisible boundary that provides the most telling clues about how important the dominant individual is, and serves to reinforce that person's feelings of superiority.

Dominance is also revealed and reinforced by seating arrangements around a table.[10] For example, at a board meeting the chief executive officer usually sits at the head of the table, with those who are next in importance sitting closest to him or her. People who sit at the head of the table attract more attention than anyone else. They also do most of the talking and get deferred to more often. This is not simply because people who occupy this position happen to be dominant, because when people are randomly assigned to different seats around a rectangular table, the person who's been placed at the head of the table often attracts the most attention and does most of the talking. If you have a friend who's shy and retiring it's worth doing a little experiment: next time you have a dinner party, put them at the head of the table. It's likely that within minutes they'll be joining in, after half an hour they'll be interrupting other people, and within the hour they'll be dominating the conversation!

The importance that's attached to different positions is less evident with circular or square tables than it is with rectangular or oval tables. Rectangular and oval tables are fine for bilateral negotiations, where the two parties can occupy opposite and equivalent sides of the table. While this solution may not give rise to disputes about preferential treatment, it is likely to encourage conflict between the parties because of the opposing nature of the seating arrangement. Rectangular and oval tables are notoriously ill-suited for multi-party negotiations—one or more parties may threaten to walk out because they don't feel that the seats they're being offered reflect their importance in the negotiations.

Seating positions also influence relationships in other ways. Individuals sitting around a table are more likely to address their remarks to people sitting opposite them than to those sitting beside or at right angles to them, for example. This may explain why, when they're seated with strangers, people usually choose to sit furthest from high-status and low-status individuals, and closest to those who have the same status as them.

Where people choose to sit in restaurants, pubs and bars also exposes issues of status and control. In pubs and bars courting couples tend to sit beside each other so that both of them can see what's happening. In a restaurant, where food is the focus, they are more likely to sit opposite each other so that each of them can keep the other in view. When a couple is offered a restaurant table beside the wall, the man usually tries to sit with his back to the wall. This way he can keep a watchful eye on what's happening around him—rather like a dominant male chimpanzee surveys the scene from the top of a tree.

Standing Tells

The way people stand is another good guide to their status or the status they are trying to claim. Dominant individuals frequently adopt a "straddle stance," with their legs straight and their feet wide apart. Subordinate individuals, on the other hand, are more likely to adopt the "parallel stance," where the legs are straight and the feet are close together. The straddle stance offers more stability than the parallel stance, and this appears to explain why men, who have a higher centre of gravity, are more likely to use the straddle stance than women. However, this is not the only explanation for this choice, because men use this posture much more frequently when they're with other people—in other words, in situations where they're using posture for the purposes of communication.

Two basic messages are conveyed by the straddle stance. One is a macho message, the other a threat signal. The macho message comes from the resolute immovability of the posture—when a man plants his feet apart he is literally and figuratively telling everyone that he intends to stand his ground, and that he won't be moved. The threatening aspect of the straddle stance comes from the fact that it is a loosely veiled phallic display—by standing with his legs apart a man is actually putting his penis on display. Phallic displays are widely associated with dominance. A dominant male baboon, for example, will frequently display its erect penis to remind other baboons of his elevated social position. Of course, dominant men seldom expose themselves in this way, but they do try to draw attention to their penis and to inform others how big it is through the clothes they wear or the way they arrange their limbs. In the fifteenth and sixteenth centuries it was common for high-status men to wear a codpiece, a padded pouch on the outside of the breeches. Codpieces were frequently decorated and fashioned from eye-catching material; and the higher the man's status, the larger his codpiece.[11] The same principle applies in some traditional societies. In New Guinea, for example, men announce their position in the community by the size and decorative features of their penis sheath.

Although codpieces disappeared a long time ago, we can still find remnants of them in the shape of stonewashed jeans. Back in the 1970s, it was quite common to find young men wearing jeans where the crotch was almost entirely devoid of colour—a spectacle that was conveniently designed to draw the eye toward the crotch and remind everyone what lies beneath. In Italy, young men would go even further. Having bought a new pair of jeans, they would wear them in the shower, furiously scrubbing the material over their crotch with a hard brush until it almost looked bleached. Sporting their new jeans with a faded crotch, they would then parade themselves in public, drawing attention to their manhood.

Not being content with their faded jeans, young Italian men have also developed another phallic display—"the scrotch." If you watch them in public, you'll notice that they are constantly readjusting their crotch and scratching their testicles, often when they are alone but typically when they are with other men. Although it is largely unintentional, this is clearly a phallic display that plays a significant part in competition between men. In terms of its function, it is very similar to what the alpha male baboon does when he displays his erect penis to his fellow baboons. When a young man performs the scrotch he is unconsciously trying to persuade other males that he is dominant because he's well endowed. The implication is that a large penis and testicles need special attention, and that without constantly adjusting himself he would soon become very uncomfortable.

The scrotch isn't confined to Italy—it's found in most societies where macho attitudes are encouraged—and it's certainly not the only form of phallic display. There's also the "crotch-yank," where the hand is placed over the penis and testicles, and then yanked upward. The purpose of this gesture is to publicize one's masculinity, which probably explains why it became a favourite of various boy-bands and singers like Michael Jackson, who needed to remind the public about their endowments. It's noticeable that the more feminine Michael Jackson's face became, the more frequently the crotch-yank featured as part of his dance routine.

Sitting Tells

Sitting postures can also convey messages about dominance. Sitting postures are essentially about comfort, convention and communication. When somebody sits down they usually arrange their legs so they feel comfortable, so they don't violate any social norms, and so their posture conveys a certain message. The message that a sitting posture conveys need not be intentional. It's actually more likely to be motivated by unconscious desires. However, the fact that you aren't always aware of the messages you're sending via your sitting postures doesn't mean that other people are impervious to those messages. Although they may not react consciously, it's often evident from their responses that they are affected by how you sit.

Three basic sitting postures can be identified on the basis of where people place their feet: "straight-leg" postures, where the legs are extended; "step" postures, where the feet are placed directly under the knees; and "tucked" postures, where the feet are pulled back under the chair. When they get the opportunity, dominant people prefer to adopt straight-leg sitting postures. By stretching out their legs, they symbolically place more of the public space under their personal jurisdiction, thereby reducing what's available to others and creating the impression that their own needs matter more than those of other people.

On their own, step sitting postures don't necessarily offer any clues about dominance. However, the way that people position their knees does convey reliable information about whether they're feeling dominant or submissive. People who sit with their knees apart send clear, although usually unintended, signals that they are feeling dominant. This is most noticeable in the case of straight-leg sitting postures, where the legs are splayed and fully extended. A feeling of dominance is also conveyed by postures like the "anvil," where the legs are bent, the thighs are splayed and both feet are planted firmly on the ground, as well as by the "figure four" posture, where the ankle of one leg rests on the thigh of the other, so that the limbs look like the number 4. Both of these postures involve phallic displays. They are therefore used more frequently by men in parts of the world where there's a lot of emphasis on macho values, like the Latin American countries and the southern United States. Women don't like to perform these postures, largely because they can create an impression of sexual availability. A fair amount of suppleness and stamina is required to perform the figure four, which is why the posture is associated with youthfulness. When someone adopts the figure four, they are more likely to be seen as youthful, relaxed and dominant. Another thing worth noting is that occasionally someone will use the figure four as a defensive signal—in other words, they'll position their top leg so that it provides a protective barrier between them and other people.

Some sitting postures convey mixed messages, especially when the two legs are positioned differently. Because they convey a strong impression of relaxation, asymmetrical sitting postures tend to be more dominant than symmetrical postures. But there are exceptions. For example, when someone extends their legs and crosses their ankles, their extended legs show that they want to be seen as dominant. However, their crossed legs give the game away—they show that they're really quite reticent.

Relaxation is a key part of any dominance display because it suggests that the individual isn't concerned about being attacked and could easily respond if necessary. Relaxation is signalled by postural and movement cues—postural cues consist of low muscle tone, an absence of tension and asymmetric arrangements of the arms and legs, while movement cues consist of less movement and slower movements of the body. As Honoré de Balzac observed, "slow movement is essentially majestic." Submissive individuals display the opposite behaviour—they tend to adopt more symmetrical poses, to rearrange their arms and legs more often, to show more tension in their posture and to move their body quickly and more often. Through their posture dominant individuals show that they are unconcerned about being attacked and don't expect it to happen. Submissive individuals give the impression that they expect to be attacked—they're tense and defensive.

Elbow Tells

To appear dominant, people need to create an impression of physical strength, to look calm, and to appear unconcerned about any threats from others. One way to achieve this is by placing the hands on the hips. There are two main versions of this posture: the one-handed "arm akimbo" and the two-handed "arms akimbo." The two-handed version is more spectacular, but the one-handed version can be pointed at other people in a way that the two-handed version cannot. There are three components that make hand-on-hip postures dominant:

1. **The Expansion Component.** When someone places a hand on their hip they appear to be larger and potentially more threatening. When both hands are used, the effect is doubled. Hand-on-hip postures also expand the territory that someone occupies—rather like straight-leg sitting postures.

2. **The Threat Component.** Anyone who has ever tried to push through a large crowd knows how effective the elbows can be at clearing a path. Elbows are bony and sharp. They can be used to nudge, lever or prod people out of the way without causing the kind of offence that might arise if you were to use your hands. In this respect the elbows are a "second-grade weapon," but a weapon nevertheless. This makes it possible for the elbows to be used in an under-

stated, almost subliminal, way. With the arms akimbo the message is subtler—the elbows threaten people without them being fully aware of what's happening.

3. **The Preparatory Component.** The arms-akimbo posture is halfway between having your hands down by your side and having them raised and ready for attack. The posture is therefore a partial preparation for attack—one where the intentions of the person are disguised by the fact that the hands have conveniently come to rest at the hips. In the case of people who are armed with a sword or a pistol, placing the hand on the hip often brings the hand closer to the weapon. This allows the hand to be at rest while it is preparing for attack.

During the sixteenth and seventeenth centuries the arm akimbo posture was an accepted part of upper-class male deportment. People in high office were frequently depicted in portraits with an elbow fully extended—Hans Holbein's famous painting of Henry VIII is a good example—and sometimes with their elbow pointing menacingly at the viewer. At the time the arm akimbo posture was intimately connected with the profession of arms—so much so that those who wanted to pass themselves off as having a military background would do so by adopting the posture.[12] In 1532 Desiderius Erasmus, the great Dutch philosopher, complained about those who "stand or sit and set the one hand on the side, which manner to some seemeth comely like a warrior, but it is not forthwith honest."[13]

There have also been times when the arms-akimbo posture has caused offence. For example, after accepting the surrender of the Japanese at the end of the Second World War, General Douglas MacArthur was photographed standing beside the Japanese Emperor. While the Emperor stood to attention with his hands discreetly by his side, General MacArthur had his hands on his hips. The Japanese saw this casual attitude as a sign of great disrespect. In Japan it is impolite to stand with one's hands on one's hips; to do so in the presence of the Emperor, regarded by many Japanese as a deity, was unforgivable.

The straddle stance. This is Hans Holbein's famous portrait of Henry VIII, legs apart and elbows firmly pushed out—a strong, vibrant-looking monarch who is very much in charge of his destiny and that of his people.

Superficially all hand-on-hip postures look the same. On closer inspection, however, we find that there are actually four main variants, each involving a different position of the hand or hands.

1. **The Fingers Variant.** Here the fingers face forward, the thumb faces back, and the palm faces down. Men favour the "fingers variant" because they feel better prepared for attack with their fingers facing forward. Men tend to adopt this posture in order to assert themselves—either when they are feeling dominant, or when they feel that their dominance is being threatened. For example, when a goal is scored in a soccer match, members of the losing side

often assume the arms-akimbo posture, partly to threaten their opponents but also to reassure themselves. The posture can also be used as a gesture of defiance. When Mick Jagger was strutting his stuff in the 1960s, he frequently adopted an arm akimbo posture as part of his routine. This can be seen very clearly on recordings of the *Gimme Shelter* concert, when the defiant "Jagger Swagger" was at its peak.

2. **The Thumb Variant.** In this version the thumb faces forward, the fingers face back, and the palm faces up. Women show a stronger preference for the thumb variant than do men. The main reason for this is that women have a wider "carrying angle" than men. This means that they can bend their arms further back at the elbow, which makes it easier for them to place their hands on the hips with their thumbs facing forward.

3. **The Palm Variant.** The palm variant is the most affected of all the hand-on-hip postures. This is the rather unnatural, flexed posture of the hand, where the back of the hand is in contact with the hip and the palm faces away from the body. It's the hand position that is commonly found in sixteenth- and seventeenth-century portraits of kings, Cavaliers and generals—in other words, individuals who needed to distinguish themselves from the rest of society by adopting artificial poses.

4. **The Fist Variant.** Here the fist is in contact with the hip. This is potentially the most threatening version of the hand-on-hip posture. Because men recognize the disruptive potential of this version, they tend not to use it. Women, however, do use it—occasionally to show their defiance, and sometimes as a gesture of self-mockery. There's a famous photograph of Bonnie Parker (of Bonnie and Clyde fame) where she has a foot on the front fender of their car, a cigar in her mouth and a revolver in her right hand. Her left elbow leans on the lamp of the car, while her

right hand, holding the revolver, rests on her hip. When we look at the photograph, we see immediately that it's a picture of total defiance—not just because she's clutching a gun, but because she's showing her elbows!

Orientation Tells

How people orient their bodies toward others can also convey messages about dominance. When someone is talking to their boss they usually show their respect by orienting their body toward the boss. The boss, on the other hand, is much more likely to orient his or her body away from the subordinate. In their separate ways, the subordinate shows that they are totally focused on the boss, while the boss shows that they're dominant and keeping their options open.

There is, however, an entirely different set of messages conveyed by body orientation. For example, you'll have noticed that when two strange dogs approach each other for the first time, they often circle each other. Making sure that they don't approach each other head-on, the dogs present their flanks to each other instead. The reason for this is that in order to attack, dogs need to be face-on. By presenting their flanks they expose a vulnerable part of their body, and this shows that they don't intend to attack each other. This process is called "ritualization," and it's found throughout the animal kingdom, as well as among humans. It's nature's way of settling disputes through displays of dominance and submission, rather than through fighting, which can easily lead to injury and death. Like dogs, we humans also present vulnerable parts of our body, including our flanks, when we want to show that we don't have aggressive intentions toward someone else. So when an aggressive-looking stranger approaches you in a bar, you're much more likely to present the side of your body than to face the stranger directly. Standing face-on might suggest that you're ready for a fight, whereas exposing your flank shows that you're vulnerable and undefended, and that you don't present a threat.

These two scenarios show that the same orientation can convey very different meanings in different situations. That's because the meaning of orientation depends on whether or not people know each other. When two people aren't acquainted and there's a lot of uncertainty, direct orientation is more likely to be interpreted as a prelude to attack. But when they do know each other, it's more likely to be seen as a sign of respect, or even affection.

Face Tells

All five sensory modalities—sight, smell, hearing, taste and touch—are found on or near the face, and of these touch is the only modality also to be found elsewhere on the body. But the face isn't simply a location for housing all the sensory modalities—it's also the most important source of outgoing signals in the form of speech and features of the voice like accent and intonation, as well as myriads of expressions involving the eyes and muscles of the head and face. Some facial expressions, like the startle reflex, are entirely involuntary; others, like the smile, may be a genuine expression of pleasure or a deliberate attempt to create an impression of genuine pleasure. Because the face is partly under conscious control, it's a major weapon in our daily attempts to mislead and deceive each other. In spite of this, the face remains the prime source of information about our emotional states—it's by observing our faces that other people can tell whether we are feeling happy, sad, angry, surprised or frightened. By looking at our face, they can also tell whether we're feeling dominant or submissive.

The face conveys dominance signals in two ways. The first way is through "facial attributes"—for example, whether the face is wide or narrow, the eyebrows are large or small, the chin is square or round, or the eyes are close together or set wide apart. The second way is through "facial actions"—for example, how the eyes are widened or narrowed, the eyebrows raised or lowered, or the chin is pushed forward or pulled back. A person's facial attributes tend to last for decades, sometimes for most of their life. Facial actions, on the other hand, may change from one second to the next.

Several facial attributes are associated with dominance. People with square jaws are judged to be more dominant than those who have weak, receding jawlines. People who have prominent ridges above their eyes are also regarded as more dominant, and so are people with thin lips. Physiognomic attributes play a major role in how people are treated. Men who have a "dominant face" are likely to have sex earlier in life and to have more sex. Research has also shown that men who have more dominant faces are more likely to attain high rank in the army.[14]

Non-human primates and humans share many signals of dominance. Several species of apes and monkeys, for example, lower their eyebrows as a dominance threat signal. It's the same with humans. People whose brows are set low, or who lower them, are seen as dominant, while those who have raised brows, or who elevate them temporarily, are seen as submissive.[15] This is one of the reasons why women pluck their eyebrows — by making them thinner and raising them, women create a semi-permanent submission display, which men are supposed to find attractive. The language of raised and lowered eyebrows is widely understood. However, there are parts of the world, including Africa and Asia, where raised eyebrows are not interpreted as a sign of submission.[16]

One of the major features associated with dominance is "facial-width-to-height-ratio," sometimes abbreviated to fWHR. It's been found that people with relatively wide faces are much more aggressive, and this effect is especially noticeable in men. People with wider faces are also perceived to be more dominant.

Jaw size is another facial feature that signals dominance. There are two reasons for this. Firstly, the teeth are a very primitive and effective weapon, and secondly the development of a large jaw is promoted by testosterone, which in turn is linked to dominance and aggression. People who have large jaws are usually assumed to be dominant, while those with small jaws are assumed to be submissive. It therefore helps to have a large jaw if you want to get ahead in business, or if you want to have a successful career in the armed forces. If your jaw isn't prominent enough, you can always resort to plastic surgery and get it augmented. Alternatively you can make a habit of sticking out your jaw. The "jaw jut," which involves raising the head slightly or pushing the bottom teeth out beyond the top teeth, is a common gesture of defiance, and it's widely used in confrontations by children. But the people who're most attached to the jaw jut are politicians. When Italian dictator Benito Mussolini appeared in public he frequently jutted out his jaw to make himself look resolute. More recently we've seen other national leaders like Obama and Trump doing much the same thing.

If jutting out the jaw is intended as a sign of strength and defiance, then pulling it back is the opposite. When people are feeling threatened, either literally or figuratively, they often experience a strong impulse to pull their chin back toward their neck. This is the "chin-tuck." It's designed to protect the neck from real or imagined attack, while at the same time informing everyone that one is *not* being defiant. Politicians who are being harangued close-up by a member of the public will often try to show that they won't be intimidated by standing their ground, staring at the person and trying to look calm, cool and collected. If you watch them closely, however, you'll sometimes notice that their chin is pulled back—consciously they know that the person who's criticizing them isn't going to attack them, but their brain isn't taking any chances, so it draws the chin back.

People who have narrow eyes, or who narrow their eyes, are also seen as dominant. When the eyes are narrowed as a dominance signal, they take on the appearance of a visor—it looks as if the person is peering through a slit in their helmet. There are good examples of this in movies like *The Good, the Bad and the Ugly*, where Clint Eastwood and Lee Van Cleef narrow their eyes and adopt a "visor eyes" pose to make themselves look tough. They also produce other revealing signs of dominance. One is the lowering of the eyebrows; the other is the narrow, resolute set of the mouth and the absence of smiling. Lowered eyebrows convey an impression of dominance because they create a more confrontational stare. Because facial expressions of anger include lowered eyebrows, someone who makes a point of lowering their eyebrows is likely to appear angrier. Research conducted by Larissa Tiedens at Stanford University in California shows that displays of anger are frequently interpreted as a sign of strength.[17] This explains why so many people in positions of power affect an air of perpetual grumpiness—it makes them look dominant!

There are good examples of this "macho face" in movies like *The Good, the Bad and the Ugly*, where Clint Eastwood lowers his eyebrows, narrows his eyes and eliminates smiling altogether.

A good example of affected grumpiness can be seen when people look quizzically over the top of their spectacles, because it draws attention to the eyes—it says, in effect, "Look at me, I'm lowering my glasses so that I can get a clear, unobstructed view of you. There's nothing you can hide from me!" The *overlook tell* is therefore a gesture of confrontation; it's a prelude to what zoologists call an "agonistic stare." The effect of the gesture is even stronger when it's accompanied by a slight dip of the head because this makes the stare more threatening.

Thin lips are another sign of dominance because they show that someone is determined. As we shall see later on, smiling is a highly affiliative gesture—it's a sign of openness and acceptance, and that's why it doesn't feature in the roles played by Clint Eastwood and Lee Van Cleef. Researchers have found that men who are judged to be dominant, and who have high levels of testosterone, actually produce much smaller smiles, but that the same relationship doesn't hold for women.[18] That's partly because women who occupy powerful positions don't reduce their smiling in order to appear more dominant—in fact, they're more likely to use other techniques to show that they're in charge. There are, of course, some dominant individuals who never seem to smile at all. President Vladimir Putin of Russia is a good example of a national leader who's very sparing with his smiles. Although he's athletic, Putin isn't very tall, and he has a small chin. Not smiling gives him a way of making up for these deficits.

Of course there are times when dominant individuals need to smile. In these situations they often concede by producing a "closed-mouth smile," where the lips remain together, instead of an "open-mouth smile," where the lips are parted and the teeth are exposed. Dominant individuals typically favour two types of closed-mouth smiles:

1. **Sealed or Zipped Smiles.** Here the lips are kept together while the corners of the mouth are stretched apart. The result is an elongated line across the face, and a strong impression that everyone is being excluded from knowing what's inside the person whose lips are sealed. Sealed smiles are a favourite of high-ranking businessmen and politicians—you'll often find them on the photographed faces of directors in corporate brochures.

2. **Clamped Smiles.** Here the muscles around the mouth are tensed to show that the smile is being restrained. The actor Charlton Heston was a major exponent of the clamped smile—it was one of his trademark tells. The clamped smile offers a way of smiling without actually smiling. In this respect it's a masked smile, where the intention is not to conceal the smile but to draw attention to the failed attempt at concealment. The clamped smile suggests that the person has a strong impulse to smile but that they have managed to bring it under control. Quite often the aspect of control forms the main message of this smile.

Yawning Tells

Everyone knows two things about yawning: its purpose is to increase oxygen intake, and it's very contagious. The first is wrong—there's no evidence that yawning actually increases our intake of oxygen—but the second is true. Why yawning is so contagious remains something of a mystery, although it's known that people yawn when they see someone else yawn, when they hear them yawn, when they read about yawning, and even when they just think about it. Why we actually yawn is also a mystery. Various explanations have been put forward, the most recent being the suggestion that yawning "cleans the brain" by flushing out the cerebrospinal fluid. It's been discovered that yawning is controlled by very deep parts of the brain because there are some brain-damaged people who cannot move their mouth intentionally but who open their mouth automatically when they yawn.[19]

Most of us think yawning is a boredom signal. In fact there are four types of yawn, and they fall under the four Ts: tedium, transition, tension and threat.

1. **Tedium Yawns.** These are triggered by monotonous tasks, inactivity, tiredness and boredom. If you watch someone who's engaged in a repetitive task, or who's waiting in a long line to be served, you'll notice that they often yawn. Tedium yawns are the most common type of all.

2. **Transition Yawns.** These occur when people move from one kind of activity to another—for example, climbing out of bed and getting ready in the morning, or preparing to go to bed in the evening. Yawns also occur at social junctures—for example, immediately after someone has said goodbye to a close friend. Yawning can be used as an *activity tell*—in other words, when you see someone alone, reading a book, and they start to yawn, you know there's a good chance that they're about to do something different.

3. **Tension Yawns.** Tension yawns occur when people are uptight—usually when a dominant person is close and they feel awkward or embarrassed. Whenever people are

anxious they are liable to yawn—it's even been reported in Olympic athletes who are waiting in their starting blocks, and paratroopers who are about to jump out of the plane. These yawns are responses to stress. They are examples of "displacement activity" because they help to displace anxiety to some other activity.

4. **Threat Yawns.** In human as well as animal societies, dominant individuals produce threat yawns. Yawning is found in a broad range of species, including fish, birds, reptiles, monkeys and apes. If there were a Yawning Olympics, baboons would be the outright winners. While other primates yawn about ten times a day, male baboons produce ten to twelve yawns per hour, and sometimes as many as twenty-four per hour! This is not because baboons are tired or bored; it's because life in baboon society is so threatening. A large proportion of baboons' yawns are designed to assert dominance and to threaten potential rivals. As with other non-human primates, more yawning is produced by adult males than by adult females or by youngsters of either sex. Individuals with higher levels of testosterone also produce more yawning. The main weapon of baboons is their teeth. Male baboons have larger canines than females, and dominant males tend to have larger canines than other males. So it's usually the alpha male who produces most of the yawns, putting his large canine teeth on display. As his status increases, so does his yawning; when he loses his status, his yawning starts to decline.

Humans also use yawning as a dominance signal, although the basis is not exactly the same as it is for baboons. For one thing, men and women hardly differ in the size of their canines, which probably explains why there isn't a big difference in how often men and women yawn. However, when men do yawn they're much more likely to expose their teeth; women tend to cover their mouth with their hand.[20] This could be because women have better manners than men, but it might be a throwback to a time when there was a difference between the dental equipment of the sexes. Although our teeth are no longer our primary weapons, they are still used as a threat. If you observe dominant people you'll find that they often yawn at those moments when they need to assert themselves—for example, when they're feeling threatened and it looks as if someone else might try to usurp their position. This suggests that, for humans, the threat yawn is a *relic tell*—in other words, a tell that is left over from a time in our evolutionary past when our ancestors had larger canines and used them to intimidate each other.

Talk Tells

When people of different status are together, the most important person usually does most of the talking. This enables them to remind everyone else of their position. It also gives them a chance to hear the sound of their own voice, and to listen to their own opinions rather than those of other people. Dominant people are quicker off the mark when it comes to speaking. It's been found that when groups of people meet for the first time, the order in which they speak provides a fairly good guide to who will dominate the proceedings afterward. The first person to offer his or her opinion invariably assumes the role of leader; the last person to contribute tends to be the person who ends up taking orders.[21]

Dominant people interrupt others more, and they are more successful at seeing off people who try to take the floor from them. They do this by continuing to talk over the other person, by raising their voice, and by using non-verbal signals to discourage the other person. As a result, interruptions initiated by the dominant person tend to show shorter bouts of overlapping speech than those initiated by the subordinate person. Dominant people are more confident in their speech, with the result that they use fewer hesitations and speech disfluencies like *um* and *er*. They often make a habit of talking loudly. This is especially noticeable in Britain, where old class divisions come into play and members of the upper class sometimes drown out the conversations of other people.

Dominance is also evident in other aspects of speech. One of these

41

is what psychologists call "accommodation"—that is, the tendency of individuals to modify their speech style in order to align it with someone else's style. This can be done through shifts in accent, speech speed, formality or pitch. Accommodation usually takes place between people who like each other, but it also occurs when there are differences in status. In these circumstances the subordinate person tends to accommodate his or her speech to that of the dominant person. A few years ago, a team of sociologists analyzed a selection of interviews that had taken place on *Piers Morgan Live*. Each guest was rated separately for dominance and prestige, and the voices of Piers Morgan and his guests were analyzed in terms of their underlying variability. The researchers discovered that relative dominance determined whether Piers Morgan adapted his voice to that of his guest, or vice versa, and that in each case, it was the least dominant person who accommodated to the most dominant. Relative prestige, on the other hand, had no noticeable affect at all.[22] This illustrates yet again how sensitive we are to matters of dominance, and how readily we adapt to people whom we consider to be more powerful than us. Also, we invariably accommodate others without the slightest inkling that that's what we're doing.

Voice Tells

Vocal characteristics like pitch are often assumed to be a good guide to dominance and submission. It has been found that deep sounds are associated with dominance and threat, while high-pitched sounds are associated with submission and appeasement. This association is found throughout the animal world, from whales to shrews—a good example is the deep aggressive growl of a guard dog, as opposed to the high-pitched yelp of a submissive puppy.[23]

In the animal world, individuals with long vocal tracts produce much deeper sounds. Because large individuals tend to have longer vocal tracts, the depth of the sound they make provides a very good indication of how big they are, and how threatening they're likely to be. However, with humans there isn't a clear-cut relationship between body size and the depth of people's voices, so pitch doesn't provide a genuine tell of someone's size. Nevertheless, when people are presented with recordings of deep and high-pitched vocalizations, they consistently express the opinion that the deep voices belong to dominant individuals and the high-pitched voices to submissive individuals. Why pitch should provide a genuine tell of size among animals but not among humans is something of a mystery. It may be due to an evolutionary lag—in other words, the association between body size and pitch, which was present in our evolutionary ancestors, may have installed a set of assumptions in our minds that are still at work even though the association has long disappeared.[24] If vocal pitch doesn't provide evidence about body size in humans, it does offer significant clues about dominance. And it does this in several ways. Firstly, it's been discovered that men who have naturally deep voices have high levels of testosterone—for example, male bass and baritone singers, who have deeper voices, tend to have higher levels of testosterone than tenors. Secondly, it's known that testosterone is linked to dominance in men. Thirdly, vocal pitch often shows whether people are in a dominant or submissive state of mind. Individuals who are attempting to be dominant usually lower the pitch of their voice—that's why John Wayne advised men to "talk low, talk slow, and don't say too much." On the other hand, people who are trying to appear submissive usually raise their pitch. When mothers are talking to their babies they instinctively adopt a higher pitch than normal.[25] This has the effect of calming the baby. Of course mothers may not know it, but the reason why they raise their pitch is that babies are most sensitive to higher vocal frequencies.

The vocal pitch that individuals adopt often reflects their social standing. Members of subordinate groups often speak with a higher pitch than those who belong to more powerful groups in that society. We can see this very clearly in the United States during the heyday of Motown, when African-American singers like The Stylistics sang in a high-pitched, falsetto register that is normally reserved for women. The same kind of self-emasculation could be seen at work among the so-called "Coloureds" of South Africa during the apartheid era. The Coloureds are people of mixed race. Some are the descendants of

Malay slaves, others the progeny of relationships between Blacks and Whites. Under apartheid they lived in a political no man's land between the Blacks and the Whites, and of all the racial groups in South Africa they were the most insecure. Their marginal position was very evident in the high-pitched speech style they used. It became their badge of oppression, a way of showing that they didn't represent a threat to the White establishment.

Rising and falling intonation also carry important messages. Falling pitch is associated with statements, certainty and dominance, whereas rising pitch is a characteristic of questions, uncertainty and submissiveness. However, that's not always the case. When you talk to Australians, for example, you'll notice that they frequently make their declarative statements sound like questions by ending with a rising intonation. This has the effect of making their opinions appear less certain and less contentious, which in turn reduces the chances of conflict. However, in other respects Australians are becoming more assertive—or rather, Australian women are. For example, a study conducted around the turn of the century found that over the previous five decades the pitch of women's voices in Australia has gotten deeper. The voices of Australian men and women have been converging, and it's all because women are abandoning their submissive tones and starting to speak more like men.[26]

Touching Tells

If you watch people at an office drinks party, you'll notice that their position within the organization is often reflected in whom they touch and who touches them. Most of the touching that you'll see is between people who are at roughly the same level in the organization. One person pats their friend on the back, another rubs their colleague on the arm, and yet another plants a playful punch on someone's shoulder. All of these are *horizontal touches* because they're between notional equals. They're about friendship, camaraderie or light-hearted provocation, and they can be mutual or reciprocal—in other words, it's quite acceptable for people of similar status to have their arms around each other's shoulders, or for one of them to pat the other on the back and for that person to respond with a similar gesture.

Looking around the party you'll also notice *vertical touches;* that is, touches between people of different status. You'll see that, as the boss circulates among the staff, they place their hand on the shoulder of the young person who's just joined the company, or they'll squeeze the arm of the assistant who walks past looking for a drink. These touches are one-sided—neither the novice nor the assistant responds by touching the boss. In fact it's the nonreciprocal nature of each touch, rather than where the hand makes contact, that identifies it as a vertical touch—one that allows the boss to exercise their symbolic right to impose themselves, however affectionately, on their staff by using touch as a "status reminder.[27]

Status reminder. In relationships of unequal status, the more important person reserves the right to engage in non-reciprocal touch. Here US President Joe Biden pats UK Prime Minister Boris Johnson on the back to remind him who's really in charge.

Most vertical touches consist of a dominant person touching a subordinate person, but the reverse does happen. If the young person who'd just been touched responded by putting their hand on their boss's shoulder, it would suggest that they are more equal than they really are, and this could threaten the boss's authority. There are some situations, like walkabouts, where high-status people don't mind being touched by other people, but there may be instances where they dislike it, especially if they think it reduces their authority. There are also situations where touching can cause offence. For example, it's generally understood that it's the prerogative of members of the British royal family to initiate handshakes, and that—apart from shaking hands—touching the monarch is strictly out of bounds. When Barack and Michelle Obama were on a state visit to Britain in 2018, Michelle contravened royal protocol during a reception in Buckingham Palace by placing her hand affectionately on the Queen's back. The Queen appeared not to mind, but that didn't prevent some of her subjects from thinking that Michelle had overstepped the mark. In any other circumstances a pat like this would have gone unnoticed, but where the monarchy is concerned, any unsolicited physical contact may be seen as a challenge to its inviolability. It's evident that for certain members of the British public, touching still remains a touchy subject!

Looking Tells

The dominance hierarchy in a chimpanzee troop is reflected in the attention structure of the troop, so that subordinate individuals spend more time watching their superiors than vice versa, and all the attention is on the alpha member of the troop.[28] Business firms operate on the same principle. Here again, subordinate individuals spend more time watching their superiors than vice versa, and everyone's attention is focused on the boss.

The similarity between chimpanzee troops and business firms goes even further. When a dominant chimpanzee meets a subordinate chimpanzee, the subordinate individual goes through an appeasement display by lowering its body, averting its eyes and sometimes presenting its backside. Subordinate chimpanzees avert their gaze because staring is likely to invite an attack from the dominant individual. The greeting rituals in business organizations are often similar to those in a chimpanzee troop. Although employees don't present their backsides to their boss—at least, not literally—they frequently try to make themselves appear smaller and less threatening by lowering their head and keeping their hands and feet close to their body.

Patterns of gaze are regulated in a similar way. When two people are involved in mutual gaze, they are visually "locked" together. When they are of unequal status, the person who averts gaze, or "unlocks" first, tends to be the subordinate. The issue of who "out-looks" whom can have far-reaching consequences. It has been found, for example, that when two people meet for the first time, the person who out-looks the other is likely to be more talkative and influential when they go on to work together in a group.[29] In a business firm, if the boss and a subordinate happen to look at each other at the same time, it's usually the subordinate who breaks off first. Veiled challenges to the boss can, however, be delivered through the eyes. For example, instead of openly disagreeing with the boss, a subordinate can simply engage the boss in a subtle bout of ocular "arm-wrestling," holding their gaze for slightly longer than they would normally. If carefully timed, this can have the desired effect, without appearing to be disrespectful.

In conversations between people of unequal status, dominant individuals usually show visual dominance—that is, they spend proportionately more time looking at the other person while they are talking than they do while they are listening.[30] There are several reasons for this. First of all, because talking is a more controlling activity than listening, dominant individuals like to hang on to the speaker role. To manage this while they're talking, they usually watch the other person closely, making sure that they're listening and that they're not about to try to take over. The opposite happens when dominant people find themselves in the listening role. Now, by reducing the amount of time they spend looking, they can show that they're not prepared to flatter the other person and that they don't expect to remain in the listening role for much longer. It also enables them to play hard-to-get.

Subordinate people, on the other hand, spend proportionately more time looking while listening than looking while talking. By being more attentive while they're in the listening role they manage to reinforce the dominant person's feelings of self-importance, which may of course only encourage the dominant person to talk even more. The reason why subordinate individuals look less while talking is probably due to their sense of insecurity. The listener is always judging the speaker. Dominant people don't mind this aspect of the speaker role—

it doesn't upset them to know that a subordinate person is judging them. Subordinate people, however, are understandably anxious about how they appear when they are talking to dominant people. To reduce this anxiety they simply look at the dominant person less.

Relaxation is an essential feature of dominance.[31] It's displayed by sinuous and slow movements of the body. That's because the actions of dominant people are governed by what's called the "principle of economy," whereas those of subordinate individuals are governed by the "principle of effort." Subordinate people tend to be unsure of themselves when they're in the presence of dominant people. Like low-ranking chimpanzees, they're constantly on the lookout for trouble. This shows itself in their general demeanour and in rapid, jerky movements of the eyes. Dominant people are much more sure of themselves, so their eye movements tend to be smooth and unhurried.

Many years ago, when I was in the West African state of Burkina Faso, I was fortunate enough to have an audience with the Emperor of the Mossi. I was ushered into a reception room, where the Emperor sat, surrounded by his courtiers. The Emperor was a large man, with a very imposing presence. What struck me was how little the Emperor actually did for himself—actions that most people would normally do for themselves, like pouring a glass of water, were performed by the courtiers and servants who fussed around him. When he shifted his body or spoke, it was with enormous economy of movement. At times the only things that appeared to move were his eyes. When someone addressed him, he didn't switch his attention immediately, as most people would do. Instead, after a suitable delay, he would allow his head and eyes to drift toward the person, almost as though he'd been filmed in slow motion. The Emperor's actions were executed without the slightest hint of urgency. Every glance, every gesture, was performed at an imperial pace, in his own time. It reminded me of what Nietzsche, the German philosopher, said when someone asked him "What is aristocratic?" "The slow gesture and the slow glance," he replied.

3. Submissive Tells

In many ways, submission is the flip side of dominance. In his famous book *The Expression of the Emotions in Man and Animals*, Charles Darwin described how the relationship between dominance and submission is governed by what he called the "principle of antithesis."[1] Darwin pointed out that when a dog is in a dominant and hostile state of mind it walks upright and stiffly, and its head is raised. The tail is erect, the hair on its head and back begins to bristle, the ears are pricked and pointed forward, and the eyes assume a fixed stare. As the dog prepares to attack it bares its teeth and the ears are pressed back. When the same dog is in a submissive frame of mind its appearance is almost exactly the opposite. Now, instead of walking upright, it lowers its body and crouches. The rigidity of the back and legs gives way to a more flexible posture. The tail, instead of being stiff and held upright, is lowered and wagged from side to side. The hair becomes smooth, the ears are depressed and relaxed, the teeth are no longer exposed and the lips hang loosely. With the drawing back of the ears the eyelids become elongated and the eyes no longer appear round and staring.

Shrugging Tells

When Darwin came to apply the principle of antithesis to humans he selected the shrug. "With mankind," he wrote, "the best instance of a gesture standing in direct opposition to other movements, naturally assumed under the opposite frame of mind, is that of shrugging the shoulders." According to Darwin, the natural contrast to the feelings of helplessness associated with the shrug is the frame of mind associated with displays of indignation. In the case of the shrug, he tells us, the shoulders are raised, the elbows are pulled inward, the hands are raised and the fingers are extended. In contrast, displays of indignation are characterized by a squaring of the shoulders. The chest is expanded, the limbs are held rigid and the fists are clenched.

This all seems very convincing, but it is in fact mistaken, because displays of indignation are not the opposite of the shrug. Indignation, as Darwin calls it, involves a raised head, with the shoulders thrown back, whereas in the shrug the shoulders are raised and the head is typically placed to one side. The opposite of raising the head is lowering the head, and the opposite of throwing the shoulders back is curling them forward. What Darwin saw as the act of indignation was really a display of dominance. In humans, raising the head and drawing the shoulders back signals dominance, while lowering the head and drawing the shoulders forward signals submission. In the shrug, however, the head is placed to one side and the shoulders are raised. Neither of these actions has an opposite—it's not possible to lower our shoulders or to do the opposite of placing our head to the side. In this respect the shrug is a "wallflower action"—it doesn't have a partner and it's destined to remain on its own. In contrast, displays of dominance and submission are like ballroom dancers—neither can perform on their own. Each, by definition, takes its shape and movement from the other.

Although the shrug is forced, as it were, to sit on the side, watching the action, it is much closer to submission than it is to dominance. There are several reasons for this:

Shoulders. Raising the shoulders is an integral feature of the shrug, which owes its origins to the innate startle response. When we're exposed to a loud, unexpected noise we instinctively raise our shoulders and pull our head down. This enables us to protect our head and neck from injury. Raising the shoulders as part of the shrug is also self-protective, but in this context it's more symbolic. Because self-protection is such an integral part of submission, it means that the shrug has more in common with submission than with dominance.

Head. When people shrug they frequently place their head to one side. As we shall see later, canting the head is a submissive gesture. By adding this action to the shrug, the shrug is made more submissive.

Eyebrows. Another feature that is often added to the shrug is raised eyebrows. When this is done without the eyes being opened as well, the message is one of appeasement. Consequently, shrugs that are performed with raised eyebrows are much more submissive than those produced without this addition.

Messages. The message of the shrug is one of helplessness. Someone who shrugs is saying "I can't do anything about it," "I don't know" or "I'm not responsible." These messages of impotence are obviously much closer to submission than they are to dominance.

The shrug is the gestural cop-out *par excellence*. It's hardly surprising, therefore, that it's so popular in close-knit communities where people are constantly making demands on each other for favours or information, and where they need to find ways to refuse these demands without causing offence. The shrug can be performed in several ways, depending on how the various components of raised shoulders, raised arms, exposed palms, raised eyebrows and canted head are combined. The way people combine these components has a lot to do with their cultural background. In his famous study of Italians and Jews in New York City before the Second World War, anthropologist David Efron noted that while Italians tend to gesticulate with a wide circumference of movement, Eastern European Jews have a habit of keeping their elbows tucked in.[2] These differences are also discernible in the way they shrug: Italians tend to shrug with raised shoulders as well as raised arms, whereas Eastern European Jews tend to raise their shoulders while keeping their shoulders tucked in. The Italian shrug is much more expansive, relying on the self-protection provided by the raised shoulders.

The Eastern European Jewish shrug is doubly defensive because it relies on the protection provided by the raised shoulders as well as the elbows being tucked in close. The fact that the elbows are not on display also reduces the likelihood of the shrug appearing dominant.

French shrugs, on the other hand, tend to be economical. They often consist of nothing more than a mouth-shrug, where the mouth is forced into an inverted U by dropping the jaw, keeping the lips together and simultaneously drawing the corners of the mouth down. The classic French mouth-shrug is accompanied by the expression *boff!*, a vocalization that neatly summarizes the bored, disdainful tone that the French have added to the basic message of the shrug.[3] In fact, French shrugs frequently have a dismissive tone, almost as if the shrugger were saying "I'm helpless to comment, I'm bored and uninterested, and anyway it's irrelevant!" This contrasts with the messages conveyed by other ethnic variants of the shrug—while the Italians, for example, seem to be saying "What's it got to do with me, I'm innocent!", the message conveyed by the Eastern European Jewish shrug is something like "What can I do, I'm powerless?"

Although the core message of the shrug is one of helplessness, raising the shoulders can also be used to deny responsibility. The shrug is like a Swiss Army knife, because, aside from its prime function, it can also perform a whole host of other activities. As we'll see later on, the shrug can be recruited to indicate that we are finished speaking. In addition it can be used as a coquettish gesture or as a means of dismissing someone else's point of view, and it frequently features when people are feeling threatened. It's even been linked to lying and deception.

Defensive Tells

If strength and threat form the basis of dominance displays, then weakness and defensiveness form the basis of submission displays. Individuals who want to signal submission need to show that they aren't a threat and that their main concern is self-protection rather than attack. This can be done in three ways: by being inactive, by appearing smaller and by looking vulnerable. Inactivity reduces the threat to others because it's linked to the fear response. When individuals are in danger they frequently freeze.[4] This reduces their chances of being seen, but it also sends a very clear message that the individual is not preparing to attack—especially when it's combined with postural adjustments that are designed to make the person appear smaller. There are several ways that people try to look smaller than they actually are. One is by slouching; another is by squatting or sitting down. Wearing dull colours and avoiding hats and padded shoulders also helps.

The most potent messages of submission are those associated with vulnerability, especially in the way that people arrange their arms and legs. Standing and sitting postures are full of tells because dominant people tend to adopt "open" postures, while submissive people tend to adopt "closed" postures. There are several submissive standing postures. One is the "parallel stance," where the legs are straight and parallel. Schoolchildren adopt this posture when they're talking to their teacher, soldiers use it when they're addressing a superior officer, and employees assume it when they're talking to their boss. In less formal settings, subordinate people sometimes stand with their legs crossed, adopting a "scissors stance," where the legs are straight and one is crossed over the other, or the "bent blade stance," where all the weight is on one leg and the other is bent, with the foot positioned either in front or behind, with just the toes touching the ground. People who are shy or lacking in confidence also adopt these postures.

Submission is revealed in two aspects of sitting posture. One involves drawing back the feet and even concealing them so that they don't invade the public space and impose themselves on other people. The other feature involves keeping the knees together and/or crossing the legs, either at the thigh or at the ankles. These postures are the antithesis of open-legged postures, where the genitals are symbolically put on display. With the knees together and the legs crossed, the genitals are placed out of sight and out of bounds, and other people are prevented, again symbolically, from getting between the person's legs. The other important function of crossing the legs and keeping them close together is that this increases the amount of "auto-contact"—that is, where the body is in contact with itself. When people feel threatened, as they tend to do when they're being submissive, they often feel the need to reassure themselves by increasing auto-contact. Again, this is not something that people consciously decide to do. Most of the time it happens without them being aware of what they're doing and why they're doing it.

Self-comforting Tells

When we're talking to someone in a position of authority we tend to assume that our own actions, rather than those of the other person, are being judged, and this makes us feel self-conscious and insecure. We cope with these feelings in several ways. One is by engaging in auto-contact actions where we touch, hold or stroke ourselves. These self-comforting gestures serve to reassure us—just as they do when someone else touches, holds or strokes us. In this sense auto-contact actions are really *substitution tells*—they're comforting and reassuring things that we do to ourselves when there isn't anybody else around to do them to us.

The potency of auto-contact actions lies in the fact that physical touch is the best way to comfort someone. It's the most primitive and it's also the most effective. The importance of touch is reflected in the composition of our skin, which has millions of receptor cells that are sensitive to the slightest change in pressure, and in the structure of our brain, where it's been discovered that the area in the prefrontal cortex that's devoted to touch is much larger than the areas devoted to any of the other senses. Touch forms the basis of the initial contact between mother and child; it's touch that comforts the baby and makes it feel secure. That's why touch is so reassuring throughout our lives—it recreates those feelings of love and security that we once experienced as a baby. The sad part of this is that if you watch people who feel dejected, lonely or vulnerable—people lining up for benefits, people waiting in emergency, people appearing in court—they frequently touch themselves in a way that is reminiscent of how their mother comforted them. The same applies to people who are being submissive.

When people are feeling submissive they frequently stroke their hair, especially the hair at the back of their head. These actions can be traced back to the time when their mothers caressed their hair to comfort them, and when they supported them by cradling the back of their head. When people feel submissive they also touch their face, frequently placing their fingers on their lips. These self-comforting gestures also owe their origins to the way that mothers touch their infants: caressing their baby's face, playing with their baby's mouth and kissing their baby on the lips. Mothers also hug their children when they're distressed. Consequently, when adults are feeling insecure or submissive they often try to recover these reassuring feelings by performing actions that enable them to hug themselves. One example of this is the "arm grip," where the hand stretches over the chest to grab the bicep of the opposite arm; another is the "bandoleer," where the arm is extended over the chest to grip the opposite shoulder. In the "double bandoleer" both arms are crossed on the chest and each grips the opposite shoulder. These actions recreate the experience of being embraced. Other self-comforting actions recreate the sensation of being held by the hand. One is the "palm press," where the palm of one hand faces upward, holding the palm of the other hand. Another is the "dovetail," where the fingers of the two hands are intertwined. In both these actions the palms of the hands are either pressed together or kept loosely apart, creating a sensation that is very similar to holding hands, or having one's hand reassuringly held by someone else.

These submissive hand postures are in marked contrast to dominant hand gestures like "steepling," where the arms usually rest on the elbows, with the palms facing each other and the tip of each finger lightly touching its opposite number, making the whole arrangement look like the roof beams of a church. The steeple gesture is used by people who want to put their hands on display but who don't need to use them to comfort themselves. While submissive hand gestures like the palm press attempt to maximize auto-contact, the steeple gesture tries to keep it to the bare minimum. The fact that this gesture eschews self-comfort, along with circumstantial evidence about its use, has led to the conclusion that the steeple gesture is a manual expression of superiority. The gesture can either be performed with the tips of the fingers facing up or with them pointing down. Political figures like Donald Trump and Angela Merkel have used the second version extensively. In fact, when Merkel was German chancellor, she resorted to the steeple gesture so often that it became known in Germany as "der Merkel Raute" (or the *Merkel rhomboid*, a reference to its geometric shape), and when Madame Tussauds in London produced a life-sized model of Merkel, she was depicted with her characteristic steeple pose.

Head Tells

Charles Darwin noticed that when people feel submissive they have a natural tendency to lower their head, making themselves look smaller and less threatening. Darwin also suggested that the habit of nodding to signal "yes" was linked to submissive lowering of the head. Unfortunately for this theory, not every society signals affirmation by nodding or dipping the head. In India, for example, people roll their head from side to side to signal "yes" or to show agreement. This movement is quite different from the headshake, because in the head-roll the head is rocked from side to side in the same plane as the front of the body. The head can either be rocked repeatedly from side to side or the head-roll can be performed with a short, sharp movement of the head toward one of the shoulders. Although there are cultural differences in the head movements that people use to signal "yes" and "no," the habit of lowering the head as a sign of submission appears to be universal.[5] In fact, the head is used to signal submission in several ways:

> **Head-dip Tells.** When individuals walk between people who are having a conversation, you'll notice that they frequently duck their head down in order to make sure that they don't get in the way and to apologize for any inconvenience they may have caused. Some people produce an involuntary dip of the head when they approach someone who's important, especially when that person is unfamiliar to them or is involved in a conversation with someone else. By watching people's heads

when they approach high-status individuals, it's possible to identify how they feel; those who are relaxed about status distinctions don't usually produce any submissive tells at all, whereas those who feel that they are meeting or intruding upon an important person are likely to reveal their discomfort by dipping their head very slightly.

Head-nod Tells. Repetitive nodding is also an integral part of conversation. You often see people who are in the listener role nodding slowly while the other person is speaking. They do this both to show that they are listening and to demonstrate that they don't want to take over the speaker's role. Fast nodding also shows that the listener understands the speaker, but because it contains a sense of urgency, it shows either that the listener supports the speaker wholeheartedly or that the listener wants to the speaker's role for themselves. So while slow nodding sends the message "I understand what you're saying and I want to continue listening," fast nodding sends one of two messages: "I totally agree with you" or "I understand you, but hurry up, I want to say something now!" The distinction between these last two messages usually depends on where the listener is looking—at the speaker when they're being supportive, and away from the listener when they want the floor.

Head-cant Tells. As we've seen, submissive people frequently lower their head or cant it to one side. Head-canting serves as an appeasement display because it exposes the neck, which is a vulnerable part of the body, and because it makes the person look shorter and therefore less threatening. It also makes the person look helpless, rather like a baby with its head to one side. It's very likely, in fact, that head-canting owes its origins to the innocent feelings of helplessness that we experienced as a baby, tilting our head to one side and resting it on our parent's shoulder. We also find remnants of these early experiences in the shrug, which is often performed with the head tilted to one side. Head-canting tends to be used by people who want to appear submissive or sexually attractive, or both. There are several reports suggesting that women use head-canting more than men, but this has not been consistently supported by research.[6] A research project in Italy, conducted by Marco Costa, Marzia Menzani and Pio Ricci Bitti, looked at examples of head-canting in paintings from the thirteenth to the nineteenth century.[7] It was discovered that commissioned portraits of powerful men seldom include head-canting, but that depictions of religious or pious figures frequently do. In this study the researchers also found that head-canting is more pronounced among female figures than among male figures. Whether this is a case of art mimicking life or vice versa remains to be seen.

Head-canting. By tilting her head to one side, Jerry Hall, in the centre, sends a clear message of appeasement to the then Prince Charles.

Eye Tells

For territorial and solitary species, flight is the natural solution to a conflict where it looks as if one's going to lose. For these species it's better to run away and live to fight another day than to risk being injured. In a social species like ours, flight isn't really an option because our lives are so intertwined. This means that we can't simply run away when there's a confrontation—we need to find ways of living together. One way to do this is through the ritualistic medium of submissive displays. These enable us to resolve conflicts without damage or loss of life, and they allow us to continue working together.

When we look more closely at submission displays we discover that they contain symbolic elements of flight. This is noticeable in the way that members of social species use their eyes. When they meet a dominant individual, they engage in what the zoologist Michael Chance called "cut-off"—that is, they avert their gaze so as to visually remove the dominant individual from view.[8] This can of course also be done by covering the eyes. Cut-off offers several benefits for submissive people. Firstly, by removing the dominant person from view, the subordinate person is better able to reduce their sense of fear. Cut-off is like a psychological form of flight—it enables individuals to remove potential attackers from their mind. Secondly, cut-off shows that the subordinate person has no intention of attacking the dominant person. That's because looking at the other person could be a way of preparing to attack, whereas looking away is the opposite. Thirdly, the act of looking away and demeaning oneself actually serves to "cut off" any aggression from the dominant person. That's because submission displays are hard-wired. When we are confronted with someone who's trying to look small, defenceless and weak, there's a tendency for our aggressive impulses to switch off.

It's worth noting that cut-offs don't only appear in the presence of dominant individuals—they can occur in almost any situation where someone feels uncomfortable. In fact, the act of covering our eyes when confronted with an upsetting, aversive stimulus appears to be ingrained. Studies of the "startle reflex" show that when people are alarmed—for example, by a loud noise—they instantly and instinctively close their eyes. One reason for this is to protect their eyes; another is to remove the sight of something that would only deepen their sense of unease.[9]

Several ocular tells are associated with submission:

The Eye-dip. People frequently avert their gaze downward in order to appear submissive. This is usually a deliberate action, and it is designed to placate someone who's more dominant. The eye-dip is also used as a coy, flirtatious signal.

The Eye-shuttle. Submissive people frequently flick their eyes from side to side, often without moving their head. This is designed not only to try to take in everything that's happening around them, but also, instinctively, to search for possible escape routes.

The Eye Puff. Here the eyelids are pulled back to make the eyes look bigger. This conveys an image of innocent attentiveness, and when the other person doesn't recognize what's happening it can be very disarming. The eye-puff relies on the fact that babies have disproportionately large eyes, relative to the rest of their face.[10] Large eyes act as an innate releaser: we feel protective and nurturing whenever we encounter someone who has large eyes, or who has enlarged them to look more appealing.

It's worth noticing that all of these submissive ocular gestures are symmetrical—in other words, both eyes do the same thing. Asymmetrical movements of the eyes tend to be associated with more informal types of exchange, like friendship. There are, however, ways that these submissive ocular gestures differ from each other. Both the eye-dip and the eye-shuttle are motivated by negative feelings, like fear or shame, whereas the eye-puff gesture is designed to be disarming and solicitous.

Another way that people try to appear disarming is by wearing their spectacles or their sunglasses on the top of their head. Elevating the glasses in this way is rather like lifting the visor on a helmet—it shows that no threat is intended. When the glasses are placed on the forehead they create a "four-eyed" spectacle, with the simulated "eyes" of the glasses above and the real eyes below. Because the eyes of the glasses are larger, they take on the signalling role normally performed by the eyes. They become "supernormal stimuli," creating the impression that the person has extra-large eyes—in other words is like a baby. All along the French Riviera—in fact anywhere where people are carefree and on display—you'll see people strolling along, looking confident, well dressed and with their sunglasses perched on their head. If you were to ask them why they are wearing their glasses on their head they'd probably say it's a convenient place to put them. However, the real reason is that it makes them look youthful, unthreatening and attractive.

Eyebrow Tells

In adults, eyebrow position can convey several messages, depending on what's happening with the eyes. There are four basic postures involving the eyebrows and the eyes: 1) eyebrows in repose and eyes in repose—this is the expression of the face at rest; 2) eyebrows in repose and eyes widened—this is the threatening facial expression of anger, sometimes involving lowering of the brow; 3) eyebrows raised and eyes widened—this is the facial expression associated with the prototypical fear response; and 4) eyebrows raised and eyes in repose—the facial expression of submission.

The ancient Romans used the term *super cilium*, literally "raised eyebrows" to refer to the facial expression where the eyebrows are raised and the eyes are slightly closed. This is, of course, not the gesture of submission—it's the exact opposite, an expression of haughtiness or, to borrow from the Latin, superciliousness. The fact that this gesture and the facial gesture for submission are distinguished on the basis of whether the eyes are in repose or slightly closed shows how very complex facial expressions can be. Although the difference between the two gestures is a matter of millimetres, nobody confuses an expression of superciliousness with one of submission.

When people want to demonstrate that they are not a threat, they frequently raise their eyebrows. This makes them look attentive and impressed. When the eyebrows are pinched together at the centre they create an impression of concern. Of course the eyebrows can be raised with or without being pinched. When they are raised and pinched the result is a hybrid gesture that conveys submission and concern.

Several movie stars have performed successful double-acts with their eyebrows. In the Eyebrow Hall of Fame, Groucho Marx's eyebrows are king. We all remember Groucho for his enormous grease-paint moustache, his cigar and his rolling eyes. But what really carried the performance was his signature tell: the Groucho Marx "eyebrow flutter." Having delivered a punch line, Groucho would flutter his eyebrows up and down to show that he'd completed what he was saying. Here the eyebrows acted as a pair of full stops, or rather exclamation marks, allowing Groucho a moment of triumph and giving the audience the opportunity to be appreciative.

A few British actors have also used their eyebrows to good effect. The pre-war actor Basil Rathbone's eyebrows were virtually typecast for the role of superciliousness. Roger Moore's trademark tell is the single raised eyebrow—actually his left eyebrow—which he regularly enlisted in order to appear quizzical, seductive or all-knowing in his roles as the Saint and James Bond. Whenever a villain needed to be put down or a pretty lady needed to be impressed, his eyebrow would spring into action, sometimes even upstaging Roger Moore himself.

Smiling Tells

How people smile at each other can provide useful clues to their power relationship.[11] Darwin noticed that smiling and laughter often occur together. He concluded therefore that they have the same origins, and that smiling is just a weak form of laughter. This idea seems very convincing, especially when you consider how easy it is to shift between smiling and laughter, and how close happiness is to amusement. In many languages the words for smiling and laughter even have the same root.

However, this theory has been challenged by the discovery that chimpanzees have two quite distinct facial expressions that correspond to human smiling and laughter: a "submission face," where the lips are retracted and the teeth are exposed, and a "play face," where the lower jaw is dropped and the corners of the mouth are pulled back.[12] The chimpanzee's play face is very similar to human laughter because the mouth is opened wide and it's accompanied by rhythmic vocalization. At the same time the chimpanzee's submission face is very similar to the human smile because both are silent and the teeth are fully exposed. These two chimpanzee expressions serve very different functions. Yet human laughter and smiling often appear together and seem to serve the same purpose. This suggests that, during their evolution, human laughter and smiling have converged. For our distant ancestors they were quite different, but for us they are very similar.

If the chimpanzee submission face is designed to appease dominant individuals, does smiling serve the same function for humans? The answer is "yes," but it depends on how friendly the situation is and what kinds of smiles people produce. Take the case where two people are together and one has higher status than the other. When the situation is not very friendly, the subordinate person is likely to smile much more than the dominant person. Here, smiling performs the role of appeasement. However, when the situation is friendly, the dominant person may actually smile more than the subordinate person. The difference between these two situations, it turns out, is not that the subordinate person smiles less, but that the dominant person smiles more in the friendly situation. In other words, subordinate individuals produce similar amounts of smiling, regardless of whether the situation is friendly or unfriendly, but dominant people smile far less in unfriendly situations and much more in friendly situations. Marvin Hecht and Marianne LaFrance, who have studied this phenomenon, point out that while a subordinate person needs to smile to appease a dominant person, the dominant person is "licensed" to smile when he or she likes.[13] The clue to why the dominant person smiles more in a friendly situation becomes clear when we look at the different ways that people marshal their facial features into a smile.

We all know that some smiles are genuine and others are false. That's because we see people pretending to be happy, and we know what it feels like to smile when we're feeling miserable. Although we're constantly exposed to fake smiles, and spend a great deal of our time producing them for the benefit of other people, it's only since facial expressions have been studied in detail that we have come to understand what distinguishes genuine smiles from false smiles.

One of the first scientists to tackle this issue was the French anatomist, Guillaume Duchenne de Boulogne, who published his *Mécanisme de la Physionomie Humaine* in 1862, ten years before Darwin's book on the face appeared. Duchenne was fascinated by the musculature of the face—an interest he reputedly developed while examining heads chopped off by the guillotine. He was also the first person to apply electrical currents to the face to see how the muscles worked.[14]

Duchenne discovered that genuine smiles involve two sets of muscles. The first is the *zygomatic major* muscles, which run down the side of the face and attach to the corners of the mouth. When these are contracted the corners of the mouth are pulled up, the cheeks are puffed up and the teeth are sometimes exposed. The second set of muscles, the *orbicularis oculi*, surround the eyes. When these are contracted the eyes become narrow and crow's feet appear beside the eyes. Duchenne recognized that the critical clue to a genuine smile was to be found in the region of the eyes, because while the *zygomatic major* muscles are under conscious control, the *orbicularis oculi* are not. As he put it,

> *The emotion of frank joy is expressed on the face by the combined contraction of the* zygomaticus major *muscle and the orbicularis oculi. The first obeys the will but the second is only put in play by the sweet emotions of the soul . . . The muscle around the eye does not obey the will; it is only brought into play by a true feeling, by an agreeable emotion. Its inertia, in smiling, unmasks a false friend.*

The Duchenne smile. This is the genuine article: a real, heartfelt smile indicated by exposure of the teeth, raised cheeks, and tell-tale wrinkles at the corners of the eyes.

If you watch how subordinate people behave toward dominant people, you'll notice that most of their smiles involve the muscles above the mouth instead of those around the eyes—in other words, they're "mouth smiles" rather than "mouth and eye smiles" or what are known as "Duchenne smiles." Strictly speaking, mouth smiles are false smiles because they pretend to show enjoyment but they're really only motivated by the desire to appear sociable and unthreatening. But if you watch how dominant people behave toward their subordinates, you'll notice that they smile far less but that their smiles are more likely to be "mouth and eye smiles." This difference arises because subordinates use smiling for the purpose of appeasement, whereas dominant people have the licence to smile when and how they wish. Smiles that are designed to appease may differ from genuine smiles in other ways. They may, for example, involve the corners of the mouth being pulled sideways rather than up, so that the resulting expression looks more like a grimace than a smile. In more extreme situations the corners of the mouth may momentarily be drawn down, thereby incorporating fleeting evidence of the fear-face into the smile. In these and other ways, the smile may reveal what lies behind its façade, and therefore what someone is really feeling.

It has been found that women smile much more than men.[15] This may have something to do with the subordinate position that women occupy in society, although it doesn't explain why baby girls smile more than baby boys as early as two months. Investigations of the portrait photographs in school yearbooks show that as they get older, girls continue to smile more than boys, and that the difference is most pronounced after puberty. When women occupy positions of power they don't automatically abandon their smiling habits in favour of men's. It's been discovered that women who are in high-power roles don't smile any less than women in low-power roles, but that men who are in high-power roles do smile far less than those in low-power roles. Testosterone plays a part here, because men with high levels of testosterone tend to produce smaller smiles, with less activity around the mouth and eyes, whereas men with low levels of testosterone smile more frequently and produce larger smiles.[16]

These differences are reflected in the inferences that people draw on the basis of smiling. When men and women smile, they are both seen as happy, contented and relaxed. Unsmiling men, on the other hand, are seen as dominant, whereas unsmiling women are simply seen as being unhappy —or, in extreme situations, as adopting what's unkindly referred to as a "resting bitch face." These inferences may have something to do with the fact that women smile much more than men, so that while an unsmiling man appears to be fairly normal, an unsmiling woman can look quite unusual. Consequently, to appear normal a woman needs to smile much more than a man. A man, on the other hand, doesn't need to smile a lot because other men aren't smiling that much.

When people are asked to look at a smiling face and to decide whether the smile is genuine, they automatically look at the crow's feet areas on the outside of the eyes. They seem to know, instinctively, that genuine smiles wrinkle up this part of the face, and so that's where to look. However, although people clearly know where to look when they're deciding about the authenticity of a smile, they are quite happy to accept fake smiles instead. For example, when someone has committed a misdemeanour, other people are more likely to treat that person leniently if they offer an apology in the form of a smile. What's interesting is that it doesn't matter very much whether the smile that the person produces is genuine or false—provided it's some sort of smile, people are prepared to be lenient. This suggests that although we are capable of distinguishing a genuine smile from a false smile, we don't always exercise this ability—there are even times when we actively seem to suppress it. What's important to us is that other people smile at the right time. The fact that their smiling is a pretense hardly seems to bother us.

Blushing Tells

For Charles Darwin, it was the blush, not laughter, that distinguished man from the other animals.[17] Darwin's opinions about blushing were very much in line with attitudes that had developed during the previous century and were still in circulation in Victorian times. In the eighteenth century the English developed the idea that embarrassment and blushing are the outward signs of sensitivity to others. They reasoned that it was only possible for someone to become embarrassed if they were capable of feeling shame but incapable of concealing it. The English realized, of course, that this could not be said of foreigners. As Christopher Ricks has pointed out, it was "part of the Englishman's objection to foreigners that they are 'brazen-faced,' unembarrassable, and therefore untrustworthy. Especially the French . . . How can you trust a people whose very language does its best to conceal the existence of the blush?"[18]

The Victorians had an ambivalent attitude to blushing—they regarded it as a sign of sensitivity, but they also felt that it was inappropriate for men to show their feelings by blushing in company. Women, on the other hand, were actually expected to blush when something embarrassing happened. For example, if a young lady happened to be present when a gentleman mentioned the subject of sex, she was expected to show how shocked and innocent she was by blushing. Here blushing carried a double message, because in addition to declaring the lady's innocence it also showed that she was sufficiently informed about sex to be shocked. This double message of the blush—the fact that it admitted what it tried to conceal—fascinated the Victorians. So did the fact that blushing could not be brought under conscious control. The principles of order and self-control were central to Victorian society. Blushing represented a complete negation of those principles and therefore challenged the things that society stood for. That is why people found blushing so intriguing—it showed that genuine feelings could not be disguised, and that the emotions could triumph over reason.

Victorian scientists were fascinated and perplexed by blushing. Darwin himself recognized that certain animals redden when they become impassioned, but that there were no animal species that became embarrassed. Darwin concluded that only humans are capable of embarrassment because only they possess the sort of self-consciousness that gives rise to blushing. This, as he pointed out, represents much more than the capacity to think about oneself: "it is not the simple act of reflecting on our own appearance, but the thinking what others think of us, which excites a blush."

Self-consciousness and a concern with other people's opinions seem to be central to blushing. We often blush when we know that we've done something wrong or when we've violated other people's expectations of us, but we also blush when we've attracted the attention of other people by doing something positive. That's why we're as likely to blush when we've been caught out as when someone offers us a compliment. However, it's not just the recognition of our own failures and achievements that make us blush; we also blush when we see other people getting embarrassed, especially when we identify with them closely.[19]

Blushing involves the autonomic nervous system and it takes the form of increased blood flow to the cheeks of the face, and sometimes to the neck and chest. How blushing actually works is still something of a mystery, although there's lots of evidence to show that it's associated with unexpected and unwelcome attention from others. The individuals who are most prone to blushing are those who are most concerned about how other people see them, and who are most eager to behave properly and not do the wrong thing. When individuals do make a social gaffe or say something embarrassing, traitorous blushing often exposes them. Paradoxically, they can usually rely on blushing to get them off the hook, because blushing functions like an apology, showing that they adhere to the norms of the group. This can be seen in the responses that blushing evokes in others—it has been found, for example, that people who do something wrong and who then blush are treated much more leniently than those who make the same error but who don't blush.[20]

Blushing is an integral part of embarrassment, and it's often accompanied by other signs of embarrassment, like speech disturbances and half-hearted smiles, as well as looking down at the ground, touching the face or flicking out the tongue. In this respect blushing operates like a form of appeasement, showing other people our discomfort and regret. However, unlike other forms of appeasement, blushing is entirely outside our control—we can't redden our face deliberately and we can't switch off a blush once it's started. That's what makes it such a painful experience for the person who's blushing, and a significant tell for everyone else.

Tongue Tells

When children or adults are involved in a task they often push their tongue out between their lips. The "tongue show," as it's called, is associated with effort and concentration. It has been proposed that it also functions as an unconsciously motivated signal of rejection—in other words, people stick out the tip of their tongue to show others that they don't want to be approached.[21] There is in fact some experimental support for this theory because it has been found that individuals are more hesitant about approaching someone who is busy and showing the tip of their tongue than they are about approaching someone who is equally busy but whose tongue is concealed.[22] There may of course be nothing mysterious about all of this; it may simply be that we are slow to approach individuals who have their tongues out because we don't like disturbing people who are clearly preoccupied.

However, there is evidence that the tongue show is used in other situations to keep people at arm's length. In a detailed analysis of some film of a young couple kissing on a park bench, Adam Kendon found that the girl controlled the intimacy of the encounter by occasionally withdrawing, and that as she did so she would occasionally expose the tip of her tongue.[23] Presenting her tongue was a way of showing her boyfriend that she was temporarily inaccessible. In most cases of the tongue show people aren't aware that the tongue is sending a signal. The young girl on the park bench probably didn't know that she exposed her tongue, let alone that she was using it to control her boyfriend's enthusiasm. Although he responded to her tongue shows, it's very unlikely that he was fully aware of what was happening.

People also resort to the tongue show when they find themselves in situations where they need to conceal their strong dislike of someone, something or the situation in which they find themselves, but also feel the need to figuratively push the aversive stimulus away. Politicians like Gordon Brown, Boris Johnson and George W. Bush have all been recorded doing the tongue show in challenging situations—either by pressing the tip of their tongue discreetly out between their lips or by producing a covert version, where the tip of the tongue is pressed against the inside of their cheek. In principle, exposed versions of the tongue show are there for everyone to see, whereas the covert versions are intended to be hidden. Both types can be seen as having an infantile origin, which derives from the baby's habit of ejecting the mother's breast from its mouth by pressing on it with the lip of its tongue. In later life we occasionally fall back on the same action—but this time symbolically, as a way of ejecting someone or something from our presence, hopefully without other people knowing.

When people are embarrassed, they often produce a brief "tongue flick." This is quite different from the tongue show, because while the tongue show can be sustained for several minutes, a tongue flick usually lasts no longer than a second—the tongue simply darts out of the mouth and then flicks back again. While the tongue show is associated with mental concentration and with inaccessibility, the tongue flick is a tell of embarrassment. When someone is being teased or they feel that they've been caught out, it's not uncommon to see them flick out their tongue, sometimes while they're smiling. It appears that this brief exposure of the tongue is designed to acknowledge what's just happened, to mark the fact that it's ended, and to share this with others.

Grooming Tells

In the world of apes and monkeys, individuals who occupy similar positions in the social hierarchy normally take turns to groom each other by removing insects, lice and dead skin from each other's hair. This type of grooming is reciprocal: it's an expression of friendship and solidarity between equals. As such, it's quite different from what takes place when a subordinate individual grooms a dominant individual. In this situation the grooming is about the ratification of power. That's why it's all one way, directed from the subordinate toward the superior, never the other way around.

When we compare this with human touching, we find that it's the same between friends, but quite different between people of unequal status. Friends, for example, frequently reassure and show their affection by touching each other. However, where power differences are concerned, human patterns of touch are the opposite of apes and monkeys—because while dominant people reserve the right to touch their subordinates, subordinates need to ensure that they don't touch their superiors. With humans, therefore, status grooming has largely been shifted to speech, so that when we want to curry favour with our boss, we resort to "grooming talk." In other words, instead of using our hands to stroke their body, we use our words to stroke their ego.

Grooming talk is designed to help people appear likeable and unthreatening to others. The desire to be liked by other people is very deep-seated—in fact it's essential to a social species like ours—and it's especially important when the people we're hoping to impress happen to be more powerful than us. There are two basic strategies that individuals can use in this kind of situation: The first is "self-deprecation"—saying seemingly negative things about oneself. The second is "other-promotion"—saying positive things about someone else. Self-deprecation can be achieved by minimizing one's own achievements, concealing one's talents, or denying any responsibility for one's own achievements or those of other people. Submissive people often use these techniques when they're talking to dominant individuals. This makes them appear unthreatening, and it makes the dominant person feel more self-important.

Powerful people sometimes use self-deprecation strategies with their subordinates, but their intention then is usually to invite contradiction. When the boss turns to a subordinate after making a presentation to a client and says, "You know, I don't think I did very well," the boss isn't inviting the subordinate to agree; they're laying a "flattery trap" by discreetly inviting the subordinate to say something complimentary like "That's not true, boss. You were brilliant!" Flattery traps are also used by subordinates and by equals. For example, when a couple is returning from a dinner party and one of them says, "The other people at dinner tonight were gorgeous," they are not encouraging their partner to agree with them. They are hoping that their partner will say something like, "Nonsense, darling. They couldn't hold a candle to you."

The attraction of the flattery trap is that it enables us to receive a compliment without having to say it ourselves. By luring people into making compliments we can get them to say things that they cannot disown later on, and that are likely to influence how they think about us in the future. Years ago, psychologists discovered that if people can be persuaded to publicly endorse opinions that aren't their own, they are far more likely to agree with those opinions later on.[24] The same applies with the flattery trap. If you can entice someone to say positive things about you, they're more likely to be impressed by you in the future.

People can ingratiate themselves to others in several ways. One is by agreeing with everything another person says; another is by doing a person favours. The third, and by far the most popular strategy, is by complimenting and flattering someone.[25] When we compliment someone we're aware of what we're doing but are very seldom aware of our motives or the way that they unconsciously shape what we're trying to achieve. Most of us would be horrified to discover just how much we alter our behaviour in the presence of powerful and attractive people, in the hope that they'll like us and find us interesting. And yet we're constantly doing it—agreeing with what they say, concealing our real opinions, telling them how clever they are, and generally behaving in a way that makes us more acceptable.

Ingratiation is a pervasive part of our social lives; it's also the essential lubricant in business. It oils the wheels of the organization, reducing the friction between people at different levels and smoothing their ascent up the corporate ladder. Research reveals the sad truth that individuals who make a business of ingratiating themselves with their superiors enjoy more career success than those who concentrate on getting the job done properly.[26]

Ingratiation has obvious benefits for corporate employees because it allows them to curry favour with their boss, at very little cost to themselves. However, it always carries the risk that it will be recognized for what it is, and that the motives of the ingratiator will be called into question. When the ingratiator is of lower status than their target, there's a much greater danger that the target will decide that the ingratiator is not being sincere, simply because they have so much to gain. People use several tricks to make their ingratiation less transparent:

Downgrading. To disguise their motives people often choose a less potent version of ingratiation; for example, complimenting someone rather than doing them a favour. Because favours involve more time and effort than compliments, they're much more likely to get noticed and to raise suspicions. Also, favours can sometimes imply reciprocation, whereas compliments don't.

Diluting. Another trick is using a "diluted" rather than a "concentrated" form of ingratiation; for example, complimenting the boss on a particular phrase in his speech rather than on the whole speech.

Simplifying. Strategies that combine different types of ingratiation are much more obvious than those that consist of just one kind. That's why the most effective forms of ingratiation are those that consist of a single type.

Camoflaging. To work properly, ingratiation needs to be conducted in the right context and it should be consistent with the relationship that the ingratiator has with the target. No suspicion is raised, for example, when a junior member of the board compliments the CEO on their speech to the investors. However, when the same person makes a flattering remark about the CEO's new hairstyle it's likely to set alarm bells ringing. The CEO's personal assistant, on the other hand, could comfortably comment on their boss's new hairstyle because it's part of their role to make sure that the CEO looks smart.

Selecting. Research shows that people who have high self-esteem like to be flattered but those with low self-esteem don't. It also reveals that people regard compliments that are consistent with how they see themselves as being genuine, and those that are at odds with how they see themselves as being phony.[27] For example, a chess master who considers themselves brilliant but unattractive would regard a compliment about their intelligence to be genuine, but a compliment about their looks to be false. To be successful, an ingratiator needs to know not only who to flatter but what to flatter them about.

Covering. We are much more likely to take a compliment at face value when it's directed at us than when we hear it being targeted at someone else. Maybe that's because our critical faculties become weaker when we're being flattered, or because we're more objective or suspicious when someone else is being flattered. Either way, the people who are least impressed by flattery are those who observe it happening to others. They're also the ones who are most likely to undermine the efforts of ingratiators by calling their motives into question. Seasoned ingratiators who know this try to ensure that other people aren't present to witness their attempts at ingratiation, or if they are that they feel obliged to support the ingratiator's opinions.

People use these strategies to enhance their ingratiation and to reduce the chances of being found out. It may not be necessary, however, to go to all these lengths, because most people are suckers for flattery. As the Earl of Chesterfield remarked in a letter to his son in 1752: "Every woman is infallibly to be gained by every sort of flattery, and every man by one sort or another."

4. Conversation Tells

The most obvious thing about conversations is that people take turns. It's unusual for more than one person to be speaking at a time, and when it does happen for any length of time it's because the conversation has temporarily broken down. The reason why we take turns is because of the limitations of our brains: we cannot talk and listen to someone else at the same time. Psychologists who study conversation have found that people are remarkably skilled at taking turns. They've discovered that the time that elapses between one person completing their turn and the next person starting to talk can be so brief as to be almost non-existent—in some instances it's less than fifty thousandths of a second! These are called "smooth transitions" because the switch between one speaker and the next is so seamless.[1]

The universal rule of conversations is "one person at a time," and although most conversations follow this rule, there are times when people speak at the same time and don't listen to each other. Some cases of "overlap talk" arise because the listener is trying to interrupt in order to take over the speaker role. However, as we shall see later on, other cases of overlap talk arise, not through competition, but purely because the listener wants to encourage the speaker.

In order to take turns in a conversation it's necessary for the speaker and the listener to show each other whether or not they want the floor. In principle this could be achieved by each person declaring what he or she wants, but this method would be very clumsy and inefficient. Instead, turn-taking is organized through a set of conventionalized signals that people produce while they are talking or listening.[2] Any conversation therefore operates at two levels: an "official" dialogue, where people exchange ideas and opinions, and an "unofficial" dialogue where they exchange signals about turn-taking and demonstrate

76

how committed they are to the conversation. By using turn-taking signals the listener can indicate whether they want to "avoid" the speaker role or to "take" it, and the speaker can signal whether they want to "hold" the floor or "yield" the floor to the listener. In other words, conversationalists can find themselves in four basic positions.

Turn-avoiding Tells

A listener can demonstrate that they don't want to take over the role of speaker and they're happy to remain in the listener role in several ways. One is by producing "back-channel" signals.[3] These consist of verbal responses like *uh-huh, yes* and *yeah,* repetition of the speaker's words, nods and brief smiles, which are designed to show that the listener agrees with the speaker or understands what the speaker is saying.

As we saw in the last chapter, the meaning of nodding depends on its tempo, with slow nodding conveying agreement, and rapid nodding signalling either enthusiastic agreement or impatience and a desire to take over the role of speaker. Headshaking also conveys different messages, depending on how rapidly the head is moved from side to side. When the head is shaken rapidly it shows that the listener disagrees with the speaker and would like to take over the speaker role. When the head is shaken slowly it can convey an entirely different meaning. If, for example, the speaker has just told an incredible story and the listener responds by shaking their head slowly, it demonstrates that the listener shares the speaker's incredulity, and implies that the listener doesn't want to assume the speaker role.

There are three other ways the listener can show that they don't want the floor. The first is by producing an "attentiveness display." By remaining silent, orienting toward the speaker, and gazing intently at the speaker, the listener can show that they're interested in what the speaker has to say and therefore has no desire to take over the speaker role.

The second is by producing an "unintention display." Unintention displays are the opposite of "intention displays." For example, if you're listening to someone and you want to say something, you can usually request the floor by producing an intention display, like lean-ing forward, lifting a finger or opening your mouth slightly. These movements get the message across because they are preparatory to speaking. Unintention displays, on the other hand, consist of actions that hinder your ability to speak, like folding your arms, pressing your lips together or placing a hand or a finger over your mouth—in other words performing actions that are the opposite of preparatory movements to speak.

The third way listeners demonstrate that they don't want the floor is by asking questions. These can take the form of queries that stand on their own, like "Do you come here often?", or they can take the form of tag questions like "Isn't it?" or "Don't you think?", which are tagged on the end of statements. Asking questions invites the other person to assume the speaker role or to continue occupying it. Women often use this ploy when they meet a man for the first time; they produce lots of back-channel signals and ask lots of questions, which make them look attentive. A man who is treated in this way by a woman tends to assume that she is genuinely interested in what he has to say, and this encourages him to keep talking—sometimes to the point of taking up permanent residence in the speaker role. Because the man is so caught up in what he's saying, he often forgets to ask the woman about herself. Women often start out facilitating men's conversations, and then end up regretting it.

Turn-taking Tells

When you're in the listener role you can show the speaker you want the floor in several ways. One is by producing "alerting signals"—for example, raising your hand or widening your eyes slightly to show the other person you want to speak. Another way is by opening your mouth and breathing in audibly—in other words, producing slightly exagger-ated versions of the preparatory movements that you would normally perform just before you start speaking. The third way is by produ-cing "negative back-channel." Instead of supporting the speaker with back-channel signals, you can try to persuade the speaker to give up the floor by sighing, looking away, appearing unimpressed or impatiently nodding your head—in other words, doing things that are designed to discourage the speaker from continuing. Finally, you can always try to take the floor by interrupting the speaker. Interruptions occur when two people are talking at the same time, but not all cases of simultaneous talk count as interruptions. There are three kinds of overlap talk:

Supporting. This occurs when the listener makes a positive remark while the other person is talking. For example, while the other person is talking the listener might say "Completely agree." Although this interjection overlaps with the speaker's talk it doesn't count as an interruption because it's not designed to transfer the speaker role to the listener—it's intended to keep the speaker and the listener in their present roles.

Sniping. This occurs when one person is talking and the listener says something like "Rubbish!" or "I don't agree." Again, although there is overlap talk, these interjections are not necessarily cases of interruption because the listener may have no intention of usurping the speaker's role—the listener may simply want to express a point of view, and possibly unsettle the speaker in the process.

Interrupting. Interruptions occur when the overlap talk is a product of competing desires for the floor—for example, when one person is speaking and the other person talks across that person in an attempt to secure the floor for themselves. Successful interruptions occur when the speaker relinquishes the floor to the interrupter, and unsuccessful interruptions occur when the speaker manages to see off the challenge and hold on to the floor.

Interrupters use several tricks to ensure success. One is to raise their volume—it's been discovered that interrupters who talk louder than the other person are more likely to acquire the floor.[4] Another trick is to appear resolute. Interrupters who talk without hesitation, and who remain unaffected by the fact that the other person is also talking, are more likely to succeed. So are interrupters who continue to talk beyond the point where most interrupters give up the challenge.

There are two critical points in overlap talk. One is the "accident point" and the other is the "challenge point." For example, when the listener thinks the speaker is about to give up the floor and starts to talk, both of them are likely to end up talking at the same time. Because the interrupter has no intention of grabbing the floor from the speaker, they are likely to stop talking at the accident point, which is about one second into the overlap talk. By stopping at this point, rather than later, the interrupter shows the speaker that the overlapping talk was accidental. They can also get this message across by stopping the interruption in mid-sentence rather than at the end of the utterance. The other critical point in overlap talk is the "challenge point." This is the point where interrupters normally give up the challenge, and it occurs about two to three seconds after the beginning of overlap talk. Interrupters who are serious about taking the floor may need to go beyond this point, and in the process they lay themselves open to the accusation that they are interrupting. Half-hearted attempts at interruption tend to peter out before they get to this stage.

Interruptions are affected by a variety of factors, including status, gender, familiarity and culture. When there's a status difference, the high-status person is more likely to interrupt the low-status person.[5] On balance men are more likely to interrupt women than vice versa. In this context interruption is often used as a means of exercising control over the conversation and therefore over the other person. That's why men are more likely to interrupt women during the early stages of acquaintance—when they're treating them as women rather than individuals and trying to assert themselves. People have very different attitudes to interruption, and so do different cultures. In Mediterranean societies interruption between close friends is often the norm, so it's not unusual to find situations where several people are speaking at once. This is also true of some Jewish families, where interruption is used as a way of showing solidarity and enthusiasm.[6] To categorize these interruptions as battles for control of the floor is to misunderstand them—they're just a way of getting involved and voicing one's opinions.

Turn-yielding Tells

So far we've looked at what happens when the listener wants to continue in his or her role, as well as the various strategies listeners can use in order to usurp the speaker's role. But what about the speaker? How do speakers hold on to the floor, and which signals do they use when they want to relinquish the floor?

When speakers want to give up the floor they send "turn-yielding signals" to the listener. As we've already seen, some of these signals are transmitted before the end of the turn, making it possible for listeners to make a "smooth transition," where the beginning of their turn coincides with the end of the previous speaker's turn. One of the ways speakers signal the end of their turn is by altering their pattern of gaze—if the speaker is looking elsewhere, they may signal that the turn is coming to an end by looking at the listener.[7] This is crucial when there's a group of people—in this situation the person whom the speaker looks at last has an increased chance of becoming the next speaker.[8]

The end of an utterance usually marks the "completion point" of a turn, but because each turn contains so many completed utterances this in itself is not enough to show when the speaker is about to end their turn. Additional signals are required. One of these is a drop in vocal pitch. Hand gestures can also serve as signals that the turn is coming to an end. Occasionally the end of a turn is marked by a particular phrase; for example, habitually completing a turn with the expression "I don't know" or "I don't know, really." Some people shrug their shoulders, which conveys a very similar message at the end of their turn. Starkey Duncan, who's made a detailed study of turn-taking signals, has pointed out that people sometimes produce turn-holding signals at the same time as turn-yielding signals, and that when this happens the presence of a single holding signal is enough to eliminate the effects of any number of yielding signals.[9]

81

Turn-holding Tells

In order to hold on to the floor the speaker needs to give the impression that they have more to say. This can be done in several ways, often involving the eyes. In a two-person conversation the listener usually looks more intently at the speaker than the speaker does at the listener. One reason why speakers are less visually attentive than listeners is because they need to marshal their thoughts while they're talking, and they find it more difficult to do this when they're faced with the distracting sight of the listener. The other reason is that looking serves as a turn-yielding cue. So for the speaker who wants to continue talking it's better not to look at the listener too much—it might give the false impression that the speaker is about to give up the floor.

Visual dominance. In conversations between people of unequal status, the person of higher status (in this case, US Vice-president Mike Pence, on the right) tends to look proportionately less when listening to the person of lower status (Senator Dan Sullivan, on the left).

From the speaker's point of view, the end of each utterance represents a potential completion point that the listener may construe as the end of their turn. To continue talking, the speaker needs to produce additional signals to show that the end of the utterance doesn't mean the end of the turn. The Dutch psychologist, Johanneke Caspers, has discovered that speakers use speech melody to indicate that they want to continue talking. To signal this intention the speaker raises the pitch on the final stressed syllable and maintains the pitch at this level until the next pause.[10]

Speakers can reinforce the impression that they intend to continue talking by producing narratives in the form of stories or jokes. Another way is by enumerating a series of points. For example, in a discussion about religion the speaker is less likely to be interrupted if they inform their companion that there are five proofs for the existence of God, and then start to go through them one at a time. They are unlikely to be interrupted while talking about, say, the third proof of God, because the listener knows there are still two more proofs to come. A similar floor-holding technique is found in the use of expressions like *and, also, moreover* and *in addition*—all these speech "connectives" inform the listener that the speaker has more to say.

The hands are sometimes used for the same purpose. As we'll see in the chapter on foreign tells, it's not unusual for Italians to hold the floor by counting with their fingers. Having indicated that they're going to produce a list of points, the speaker either raises or clasps each finger in turn to show where they are in the list of things they're talking about, and therefore how many points they still intend to cover. The advantage of this manual method of enumeration is that the number of issues to be covered is not left behind in something the speaker said earlier—it's crystallized in what the speaker is doing with their hands at that very moment, so it's difficult to ignore. Using the hands in this way also gives the speaker an excuse to keep their hands moving, which is a sure sign that they intend to keep talking.

Speakers can also hold the floor by discouraging interruptions and by not succumbing to them if they do occur. They can discourage interruptions by being emphatic, by looking away from the listener, by keeping the hands in motion, by producing lists, and by talking in a way that minimizes the opportunities for listeners to start talking. Speakers who hold strong opinions use a range of attempt-suppressing strategies to prevent listeners taking over from them.

When speakers are interrupted, they can do several things to hold or retrieve the floor. Talking louder is one option. Another strategy is to use what Albert Scheflen called a "transfix."[12] If you watch people in conversation you'll notice that when speakers are interrupted they sometimes continue to hold the posture they were in when they were interrupted. A speaker who had their hand raised at the time will freeze it in mid-air, just as if they were playing a game of "statues," and they'll continue to hold that position until they're able to regain the floor. By keeping their hand in this fixed position, they show that they've not completed their turn and that they intend to remain that way until the speaking role returns. When they realize that they're not going to get the turn back immediately, they're likely to lower their hand. In this way they're able to signal that they're abandoning their claim to the speaker role.

Alternatively, speakers can hold the floor by relegating the other person to the listener role and making sure they stay there. As we have already seen, one of the things listeners do spontaneously is produce back-channel. This can take the form of supportive nods, *uh-huhs* and various remarks intended to encourage the speaker while demonstrating that they have no desire to take over the role. People who like to hold on to the speaker role instinctively know that the best way to keep the other person in the listener role is to encourage them to produce back-channel. This can be done in two ways. One is by using expressions like *You see?*, *Don't you think?*, *Right?*, *Okay?* and *Know what I mean?*[13] These expressions are examples of "back-calling" because they call on the listener to provide back-channel and therefore push the other person deeper into the role of listener. The other way to elicit back-channel is by rewarding the listener whenever they produce back-channel. If the speaker smiles or looks affectionately at the listener every time they say *uh-huh*, it shouldn't be long before the listener is producing more back-channel, and in the process excluding themselves from taking over the role of speaker.

An expression like *You know what I mean?* can serve as an instance of back-calling, especially when it has a rising, interrogative contour. But the same expression can also serve as a "comprehension marker"

84

or an "agreement marker"—in other words, as a declarative statement that summarizes the presumed understanding or agreement between the speaker and listener. When the speaker says *You know what I mean?*, they aren't necessarily asking the listener to provide back-channel; they may simply be trying to get the listener to accept their point of view.

Some speakers try to do all the talking to ensure that they have the listener's undivided attention. When speakers defend their role aggressively, listeners are inclined to respond by orienting their body away, averting their gaze and generally looking for an opportunity to escape. This is an inversion of the normal state of affairs, where the listener pays more attention to the speaker than the speaker does to the listener. A listener who's retreating in this way does not represent a threat to the talkative speaker because they're not after the speaker role. However, in order to secure their occupancy of the speaker role, the speaker may need to make sure that the listener remains in theirs. Sometimes this can be done physically. For example, during the nineteenth century, the conversational convention of "button-holding" (or "button-holing") was practised—the speaker would grab hold of a button on the listener's coat in order to get his attention and stop him getting away. The English essayist Charles Lamb provides a slightly exaggerated description of the practice:

> *I was going from my house in Enfield to the India-house one morning, and was hurrying, for I was late, when I met Coleridge, on his way to pay me a visit; he was brimful of some new idea and, in spite of my assuring him that time was precious, he drew me within the door of an unoccupied garden by the road-side, and there, sheltered from observation by a hedge of evergreens, he took me by the button of my coat, and closing his eyes commenced an eloquent discourse, waving his right hand gently, as the musical words flowed in an unbroken stream from his lips. I listened entranced; but the striking of the church recalled me to a sense of duty. I saw it was of no use to attempt to break away so, taking advantage of his absorbtion in his subject, I, with my penknife, quietly severed the button from my coat and*

decamped. Five hours afterward, in passing the same garden, on my way home, I heard Coleridge's voice, and on looking in, there he was, with eyes closed—the button in his fingers—and his right hand gracefully waving, just as when I left him. He had never missed me.[14]

Talk Tells

When we're talking to people, we tend to focus on what they say, rather than how they say it or the precise expressions they use. Careful attention to the actual words that people use can often provide a unique insight into what they are thinking.[15]

PRONOUNS

People who frequently use the word *I* tend to be concerned with themselves, although it does depend on the context in which the word is used. Those who prefer to use *we* are often trying to avoid making any reference to themselves as individuals. Use of *we* can also denote an inclusive frame of mind—for example, a person might go on holiday with their partner and then talk about the experience using *I*, while another might use *we* to give the impression that they'd been on holiday with their partner, even though they hadn't. The pronoun *we* is capable of performing a range of differing tasks. When people use *we* they often mean *I*, while on other occasions it may be intended to signify *you*. For example, when your doctor asks "How are we feeling today?", they're not including themselves—they're asking about you. Likewise, when someone says to their partner "We need to fix that fence," they're not including themselves or volunteering to help—they're simply giving their partner an instruction.

ATTRACTORS

People differ widely in terms of how comfortable they are with being the centre of attention. Individuals who like to be in the limelight tend to talk about themselves. They also show a preference for "dropping," which can take the form of "name-dropping," "place-dropping" or "experience-dropping." Of these three, name-dropping is the most effective means of increasing one's social status because it exploits the need that all of us have to keep our opinions consistent. For example, if you like person A and you know that person A likes person B, then you are more likely to like B, because it keeps your opinions in line with each other. If you were to decide that you didn't like B your opinions would be unbalanced. The same balancing principle applies with name-dropping. When your work colleague comes over to you and tells you about a famous person whom they've just met, they're not simply passing on a bit of news—they're actually encouraging you to admire them more because someone whom you admire has been prepared to spend time with them.

DEFLECTORS

People who are shy or who want to avoid the attention of others often resort to linguistic "deflectors." In conversation they frequently ask the other person questions about themselves, or they steer the conversation toward topics that are closer to the other person's interests. This automatically shifts the spotlight away from them and reduces the chances that they will have to reveal something about themselves. The other deflecting strategy that shy or insecure people use is to talk about impersonal matters. This deflects attention from themselves and the other person, and shifts it toward less threatening topics like the weather.

CONTRASTORS

Words like *but, however* and *nevertheless* are used to set up a contrast. These are favoured by people who like to point out that things aren't always what they seem, or who want to put forward another point of view. People often set up contrasts by describing one set of affairs, only to negate part of it later on. For example, your friend might tell you that their partner is very loving but doesn't like public displays of affection. By setting up this contrast, your friend is doing several things: they're showing you that they don't have a one-dimensional view of their partner, and that they don't fully approve of their partner's desire for privacy.

SOFTENERS

People often say things that are designed to soften the impact of what they are going to say next. If you're going to criticize someone, you might say something like "I don't want you to take this the wrong way" before you tell them what you think about their table manners, the company they keep or their inability to arrive on time. Softeners like "I hope you don't think I'm being rude" and "I don't want to be critical" are usually two-faced because they provide a cloak under which people can be rude and critical while denying that it's their intention to do so. The sociologist Eugene Weinstein called these linguistic devices "pre-interpretations," or "printerps" for short.[16] The potency of the printerp lies in its ability to defuse other people's negative reactions— by telling someone that you don't want them to take your next remark the wrong way, you are in effect ruling out their normal response. You're also providing yourself with a linguistic bunker—somewhere you can hide if the other person does take offence and brings out the big guns. Of course it doesn't follow that the person who is offered a printerp automatically accepts it. For example, you might say to your friend "I don't want you to take this the wrong way." Before you've had a chance to say anything else, your friend might jump in and say "But!" This is your friend's way of rejecting the softener, showing that your efforts to prepare the ground for what follows simply haven't worked. Weinstein pointed out that interpretations can also be offered after-ward. A remark like "That's not what I meant" is a "post-interpreta-tion," or what he calls a "posterp"—it's designed to rule out certain interpretations retrospectively.

The "pre-apology," or "prepalog," also tries to mitigate the effects of what's about to follow. When people say things like "I hate to tell you this, but . . ." or "I've never done this before," they are trying to get the other person to lower the standard against which their next remark or next action is likely to be judged. Prepalogs play an important role in requests because they protect the "face" of everyone concerned. Saying something like "I don't want to be a nuisance, but . . ." warns the other person that a request is about to be made and that it's not based on any presumption. Because it's polite and submissive, it puts the other person in an awkward position where a refusal is likely to make them appear unreasonable or churlish.

HEDGES

Everyday speech is full of expressions like *well, sort of, kind of, like* and *you know.* These conversational fillers are sometimes called "hedges."[17] There has been a lot of debate about why people use hedges, and about who uses them most. People often use hedges like *kind of* (or *kinda*) and *sort of* (or *sorta*); for example, when they say things such as "It's kind of cold today." These hedges indicate imprecision; they show that the speaker should not be held to account for the inaccuracy of the statement, and they suggest that there's something peculiar about whatever they're describing. In the United States most educated people prefer *kind of* and *sort of* to *rather,* although *rather* is often favoured by upper-class people in the northeastern states—presumably because of its exclusive, English associations. *Kind of* is generally preferred to *sort of,* but *sort of* enjoys a lot of popularity in the southern states.[18]

For a long time the expression *you know* was considered a sign of powerlessness, and that is why women use it more often than men. There is now some doubt whether women do use the expression more frequently. It's also becoming clear that *you know* performs several different functions, depending on where it appears in an utterance, whether it's preceded by a pause, and whether it's spoken with a rising, falling or level intonation. Janet Holmes, who has made a special study of *you know* in everyday speech, has discovered that women don't use the expression more frequently, but that men and women often use it for quite different purposes. While women use *you know* to underline their confidence in what they're saying, men use it to express uncertainty and to show that they're being imprecise.[19] *You know* can be used as a form of "back-calling"—in other words, as a means of eliciting back-channel and support from the listener, and enabling the speaker to continue in their role. When it's used as a "verbal filler" it can perform the same task as expressions like *sort of, you see* and *I mean,* which speakers use to keep speaking and to discourage other people from trying to take the floor. When it appears at the end of an utterance, *you know* can be used to show that the speaker is prepared to relinquish the floor. Equally, the expression can take on a "search function," helping the speaker to remember the next word or phrase. This is often what's happening when *you know* is preceded by a pause.

Posture Tells

The way people use their bodies often provides clues to their commitment to a conversation. When two people are talking to each other, they usually spend some of the time looking at each other and the rest looking elsewhere. People who spend a lot of time looking away give the impression that they are not interested in the other person. Knowing this to be the case, even when we find someone extremely boring we try not to look away too much, for fear that we'll reveal our feelings. Instead, we watch the other person politely, creating the false impression that we find them interesting.

The three main sources of information provided by the body are the eyes, the torso and the legs. People are generally aware of what they're doing with their eyes, so gaze doesn't always prove to be a very reliable source of information about individuals' feelings toward each other. Because people are far less aware of where their torso is facing, it's often a much better indicator of their feelings. However, when it comes to gauging someone's commitment to a conversation, the best place to look is at their legs and feet.

There are two reasons for this. One is that people are often quite unaware of these parts of the body. In fact, if we were to produce a scale of body awareness, we'd probably find that people are more aware of their front than their back, and most aware of their head and face, followed by their arms, hands and torso, and least aware of their legs and feet. The second reason why the legs are especially informative is that they are associated with primitive impulses of flight. When people feel threatened they react either by defending themselves or by trying to escape. In the process of preparing to escape they often produce intention movements that give rise to various movements and postures.[20]

Because these are outside conscious control they reveal people's true feelings about the person with whom they're interacting.

THE PARALLEL STANCE

Here the legs are straight and parallel, so that the feet are planted close together and the weight of the body is evenly distributed between them. People who adopt the parallel stance are usually being non-committal—they're neither showing that they intend to go nor that they wish to stay.

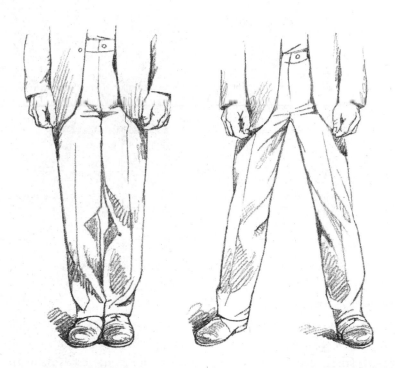

THE STRADDLE STANCE

Again the legs are straight, but this time the feet are spread apart. As we saw earlier, the straddle stance is typically a posture of dominance because it widens the body, takes up more space and surreptitiously draws attention to the genitals. But because the feet are set apart, the straddle stance is also a posture of immovability—it shows that the person can't be dislodged and doesn't intend to go. If you watch a group of young men standing in a circle—say, in a sports club after a match—you'll often find them adopting the straddle stance. This posture is an expression of their solidarity. By standing with their legs apart they're showing that they're macho *and* that they have no intention of leaving.

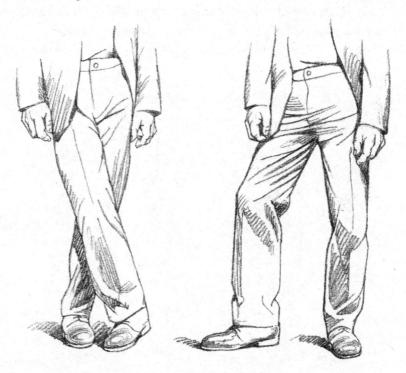

THE SCISSORS STANCE

In the scissors stance the legs are crossed, just as if they were the blades of a pair of scissors. This posture can be performed with both legs straight (the "scissors stance") or with one leg bent across or behind the other (the "bent blade stance"). The scissors stance is the classic posture of immobility. It's a perfect example of an "unintention display" because it shows that the person is committed to the conversation and has no intention of leaving. Because it is completely devoid of any suggestion of impatience, the scissor stance also comes across as a gesture of submissiveness.

THE BUTTRESS STANCE

In the buttress stance most of the body's weight is on the "support" leg, while the other leg acts as a buttress—rather like a flying buttress on a cathedral. In this posture the support leg is straight and the buttress leg is either straight or bent—typically it's bent at the knee and the foot is positioned so that it's pointing away. This standing posture enjoyed enormous popularity as a form of male display from the Middle Ages until the middle of the nineteenth century—in fact from the appearance of men's hose until the disappearance of tight breeches. It enabled gentlemen to "show the leg" and to assume a posture that distinguished them from the common classes.[21] Nowadays the buttress stance pretends to be a convenient way of resting one leg while the other supports the body. What it really suggests, however, is that the person might want to leave. That's because of its close similarity to the act of walking. When someone starts to walk away they automatically transfer the weight of their body onto one leg so that the other leg is free to take a step. That's very similar to what happens in the buttress stance, where most of the body weight is supported by one leg. Although the other leg doesn't actually take a step, the fact that it could do so shows that the buttress stance is potentially a disguised intention movement to depart. This is especially the case when someone repeatedly shifts their weight from one foot to the other. When you see someone with the buttress stance it's worth looking at where the toe of their buttress foot is pointing because it often shows what they're thinking. Sometimes the foot is pointing at someone whom the person is secretly thinking about; on other occasions you might find that it's pointing in the direction where they're hoping to make their escape.

One of the lessons we learn from watching conversations is how skilled people are at synchronizing their turns and timing their interjections and interruptions down to a few milliseconds. In spite of our remarkable talent for co-ordinating conversations and knowing what to say to each other, we have very little conscious awareness of the principles on which our expertise is based. Next time you get a chance, ask someone whose conversation you've just witnessed what they've been doing, and see what they say. You might find that they offer you a fairly detailed account of who said what to whom. But they won't be able to tell you how they oriented toward the other person, how they used their hands and eyes to hold the floor, or how they managed to ward off several attempted interruptions. Most of us are like this. In spite of our immense talent as conversationalists, we're remarkably ignorant of the tells that we produce and those to which we respond. Listening to other people's conversations and watching them more closely won't necessarily make us more interesting conversationalists. But it will give us a much better understanding of the way that people try to control the floor and attempt to influence each other.

5. Greeting Tells

Greetings perform several important tasks. They provide people with an opportunity to acknowledge each other and to enter into conversation. They also give people a chance to demonstrate that they can be relied upon to abide by the wider conventions of society. Finally, they allow people to reaffirm or work out what kind of relationship they have or are going to have with each other. Greeting rituals differ enormously from one culture to the next. However, within a community they tend to follow a fairly stereotyped pattern—that way the participants know what's expected of them and what the other person is likely to do next. In spite of this, there is always enough variation between greetings to allow inferences to be drawn about the participants. In fact, by watching how people greet each other it's often possible to see what kind of people they are, what they're trying to achieve, and what their attitudes are to each other.

Transition Tells

Most greetings consist of three phases: 1) a "recognition phase," where the participants notice each other and signal their mutual recognition; 2) an "approach phase," where they move toward each other; and 3) a "meeting phase," where they shake hands, embrace, etc.[1] When a large distance separates people to begin with, and there are others around, it can take quite a while for them to get through all these phases. On the other hand, when people start off close to one another, there's a tendency for the approach phase to disappear and for the other phases to be compressed into one.

The way that people behave during each phase can be very revealing. In Western society, the recognition phase can take several forms, depending on how well the participants know each other and the level of intimacy they are trying to achieve. Basically there are two clusters of distance signals. One consists of "polite" signals, like raising the eyebrows, smiling with the lips together, presenting the palm of the hand and nodding or dipping the head. The other cluster consists of "enthusiastic" signals, like waving one or both arms, open-mouthed smiles, laughter and loud calls to the other person. In order to underline their feelings of exhilaration, people often widen their eyes and drop their jaw, simulating the facial expression of surprise. As a rule, people who are acquainted tend to exchange polite recognition signals, whereas people who know each other well are more likely to exchange enthusiastic recognition signals, especially when they haven't seen each other for some time. However, because recognition signals imply equality, they are seldom used between people of different status.

Similar distinctions are noticeable during the approach phase. Polite distance signals, for example, are often followed by a detached approach, with one or both parties walking slowly toward the other. This detachment can often be seen in the way that people avert their gaze, cross their arms over their body or engage in forms of displacement activity, like touching their hair or rearranging their clothes, as they walk toward each other. Enthusiastic distance displays, on the other hand, are usually followed by a hurried approach, where the attention of each party remains fixed on the other person, and where there are preparatory signals that indicate whether the parties are lining up to embrace or kiss each other or shake hands.

Normally there's no doubt about what's going to happen when two people reach each other, simply because of the situation, precedence, the nature of their relationship, or the amount of time they've been apart. But there are occasions when it's not entirely clear how people are going to greet each other. If there's any doubt, however, people often use the approach phase to show whether they intend to hug, kiss or shake hands. You only need to stand in the arrivals lounge of an international airport to see how differently people behave, depending on how they're about to greet each other—the approach phase that precedes a hug or a kiss is usually quite different from one that occurs before a handshake. When people do have a problem deciding what to do, it's usually about whether they should shake hands or greet the other person verbally.

Greeting rituals can be divided into two types: greetings of respect, which are designed to emphasize differences in power, and greetings of solidarity, which convey messages of friendship and equality. In medieval Europe, men and women would pay homage to their over-lord by kneeling on one knee. Later on the bow was introduced for men. This was done by drawing back the right leg so that both knees were bent, and by leaning forward. Removing or doffing the hat was also part of the greeting ritual, and this was done either before or during the act of bowing. The corresponding salutation for women at the time was the curtsy, which involved genuflecting both knees and lowering the body.[2] All these greetings of respect involved body lowering. They were also distinguished by asymmetry, which meant that the subordinate person greeted the superior while the superior effectively did nothing.

Greetings of solidarity, on the other hand, were symmetrical—they consisted of a mutual kiss, and sometimes an embrace. Kissing was used as a gesture of affection as well as a sign of goodwill between men and women, and between members of the same sex. Although the handshake was around at the time it was not used as a greeting. Instead it was employed to seal agreements. Writing during the seventeenth century, John Bulwer described how the handshake in England was used to secure financial agreements and how the language of the hand-shake differed from one London market to another. The "fish dialect of Billingsgate," he tells us, was very different from the "Horse Rhetorique of Smithfield."[3] It was only much later, toward the end of the Victorian era, that the handshake was recruited as a greeting of solidarity.

Handshake Tells

Several theories have been proposed to account for the evolution of the handshake as a method of greeting. It's been suggested, for example, that the mutual handclasp offers people an open-handed chance to physically connect with each other, while demonstrating that they aren't carrying anything that could harm the other person. Recently it's been proposed that handshaking gives people an opportunity to exchange chemosignals contained in palmar sweat, because people frequently sniff their own hand after they've shaken hands with someone else.[4] The latter theory is supported by the fact that in some parts of the world, like the Middle East, the hands are drawn toward each participant's face during the handshake.

The big question is, do handshakes make a difference to people's relationships with each other? The answer is yes, they do. This is illustrated by a rather clever experiment conducted by Allen Konopacki in the United States, where a 25-cent coin was left in a public telephone booth.[5] Most of the strangers who used the booth immediately afterward picked up the coin and put it in their pocket. As they were emerging from the booth a student would approach these people and ask them whether they had seen his quarter. Over 50 percent lied and said that they hadn't seen the coin. In the second half of the experiment the student greeted each person emerging from the booth, introduced himself, shook their hand, and then asked whether they had seen the quarter. Now, only 24 percent of the people who had pocketed the coin lied. In this situation shaking people's hands clearly made a difference because it created a bond of solidarity that made it much more difficult for people to lie.

One of the things that recommends the handshake as a greeting of solidarity is its symmetry—the fact that both people perform the same action. However, when we look more closely at how people actually shake hands, we find that they often perform slightly different actions, and that these serve as an important source of information about the kinds of people they are and how they feel about each other.[6] These *handshake tells* aren't always apparent to people who aren't involved in the handshake. In some cases they're not even noticed by the other person who's involved in the handshake.

Handshakes can vary according to who initiates them, how the hand is presented, how many pumps they include, who controls the handshake, whether they are accompanied by a smile, what people say when they greet each other, and so on. The grip itself can vary according to how tightly or limply the hand is held, the temperature of the hand, how dry or damp it feels, its position in relation to the other person's hand, and what the rest of the body is doing. Basically, there are eight types of handshake:

1. **The Bonecrusher.** One of the cardinal rules of handshaking is that the grip should be neither too tight nor too limp, and that each person should adjust the pressure of their grip to that of the other person. There are people who violate these requirements by squeezing the other person's hand. Sometimes this is done unwittingly. Most of the time, however, it's done as a show of strength or a way of putting the other person in their place. People who want to show others that they are not as weak and ineffectual as they look often use the bonecrusher as a form of compensation.

2. **The Limp Handshake.** A limp handshake occurs when someone offers a hand that is totally relaxed. It doesn't exert any pressure on the other person's hand, and it doesn't contribute to the mutual production of the handshake. A person who offers a limp handshake is someone who, in more senses than one, doesn't connect with the other person. Like their hand, they remain passive and detached—they're simply not focused on the person they're greeting. This often happens with people who are self-important or who have to shake hands with lots of people. Chairman Mao, for example, is reputed to have had a very limp, non-committal handshake. Sometimes a weak handshake is a cultural convention—in West Africa, for example, handshakes tend to be very soft.[7] However, other motives are sometimes at work. Women who want to cultivate an impression of languid femininity often present a rather limp hand to the person they're greeting. Strong people often do the same, but in their case it's to emphasize their

strength. It's said that ex-heavyweight champion Mike Tyson offers a relaxed, almost tender hand when he greets people outside the boxing ring—the complete opposite to what used to happen inside the ring.

3. **The Firm Handshake.** A firm handshake occurs when the fingers are wrapped around the other person's hand and the grip is neither too tight nor too loose. William Chaplin and his students at the University of Alabama conducted a detailed investigation of the relationship between handshake style and personality.[8] They discovered that people who are extroverted and emotionally expressive tend to use a firm handshake, whereas people who are neurotic and shy don't. They also found that people who have an open attitude to new experiences use a firm handshake but that this only applies to women. Men who have an open attitude to new experiences are no more likely to use a firm handshake than a limp handshake.

4. **The Limpet Handshake.** There are some people who won't let go when they get hold of someone's hand—instead, they hang on like a limpet. There are several motives behind the limpet handshake, but they all come down to the issue of control. By holding on to someone's hand after a handshake someone can set the agenda and engage the other person for much longer than they would otherwise have wished. We have all encountered people like this, or else we've seen them in action. They are so desperate to make sure someone doesn't leave, or that they don't take over the conversation or change the subject, that they grab their hand and won't let go. It's interesting that people who are trapped in this way seldom have the nerve to pull their hand away. They usually remain stuck to the person until they can think of an excuse to extricate themselves, or until someone else comes to their rescue.

5. **The Clammy Handshake.** People who have sweaty hands often try to disguise this fact by wiping their hand on their

clothes before they shake hands with someone. A quick wipe may remove the surface sweat, but it doesn't always remove the clammy signs of anxiety. Another trick that people with sweaty hands use is to cup their palm slightly so as to reduce the surface area of their hand that comes into contact with the other person's during the handshake. Not every clammy hand, however, is a sign of nervousness. It is estimated that 5 percent of the population has hyperhidrosis, a chronic sweating condition, which is due to genetic factors rather than to anxiety.

6. **The Reinforced Handshake.** When people want to make their handshake more enthusiastic or intimate they sometimes clasp the other person's right hand in both their hands. This is just one of several versions of the reinforced handshake—in other versions the left hand may be placed on the other person's shoulder, upper arm or forearm. People who produce reinforced handshakes automatically put themselves in control of the greeting by increasing the amount of physical contact, and therefore their commitment to the other person. Single-handed handshakes can sometimes be indifferent, but a reinforced handshake cannot.

7. **The Relocated Handshake.** In a symmetrical handshake the participants' hands should meet midway between them— in other words in the middle of no man's land. There are two ways that the handclasp can be relocated so that it takes place in one person's space. The first is the "huddled handshake," where one person pulls the other person into their personal space, thereby creating a handshake that's on their own terms. The second is the "invasion handshake," where someone fully extends their arm so that the handclasp is forced to take place in the other person's space rather than in their own. To the outside observer the culmination of these two types of handshake may look rather similar; participants, however, are fully aware of the difference, as they can feel who is pushing or pulling whom,

and who ends up deciding where the handshake is going to take place.

8. **The Dive-bomber Handshake.** Some people have a habit of lifting their hand, and then diving it down into the handshake. For a long time, this was one of Vladimir Putin's tricks—as he approached someone he was about to greet, his hand would go up and then swoop down to meet the other person's. This technique not only made him seem taller but also created the sensation that he was on top and the other person beneath him. Putin isn't the only politician who does this—Justin Trudeau also occasionally resorts to the dive-bomber handshake, even though there's no need for him to try to look taller.

9. **The Upper Handshake.** Another way that people can make a handshake asymmetrical and impose themselves on the other person is by rotating their forearm so that their own hand ends up on top, and the other person's below. Even though they may not be consciously aware of what's happening, the person who manages to get their hand on top—in the prone position—automatically gains an advantage over the person whose hand is below, in the supine position. That's because prone positions are usually associated with dominance and control, while supine positions are linked to submission and passivity. Even if they are completely unaware of the position of their hands, the person whose hand is on top will feel more dominant, and the person whose hand is below will feel more submissive.

Although we tend to think of handshakes as unimportant, they can reveal a great deal about the way people resolve issues of dominance. For a handshake to work it's essential that the participants co-operate so that their hands actually meet. By watching how people position their hands it's possible to see if both parties have their hands in the same position, or if one person is literally trying to gain the upper hand. What one person stands to gain by having their hand on top, the other stands to lose, not only by having their hand below but also by having to accept that position in order to make the handshake work.

POWER TELLS

The way politicians shake hands tells us a lot about the silent expression of power. Like most men who occupy positions of power, President Harry Truman was used to having his own way, and this showed in the way he shook people's hands. When he met General Douglas MacArthur at Wake Island in 1950, the two of them were photographed shaking hands, with Truman's hand above and MacArthur's hand below. Consistent with this, Truman is talking and smiling, while MacArthur is looking disappointed. The two men were not seeing eye to eye at the time, and it wasn't long afterward that Truman took the drastic measure of relieving MacArthur of his command of the UN forces in Korea. There is also a photograph of President Harry Truman in 1953, just before he stepped down, greeting President-elect Dwight Eisenhower. Once again Truman has his hand on top and Eisenhower has his below—exactly what you'd expect from the imperious president and the much more easygoing president-elect.

When John F. Kennedy met Richard Nixon for their famous televised debate in 1960, the two men were photographed shaking hands. There's no indication in the face of either of them as to who was feeling more confident at the time—both are smiling and looking very composed. However, their handshake does contain a crucial *tell*—Kennedy has his hand on top, while Nixon has his below. This is a perfect example of a *foretell* because it appears to prophesy Kennedy's victory over Nixon. Of course foretells aren't really prophetic. They just look that way because both the *tell* and the event are caused by other factors—in this case, possibly Kennedy's popularity and Nixon's unconscious realization that he wasn't going to win the election.

The upper handshake. A dominance display is often revealed by literally taking the upper hand when shaking hands. Following their televised debate, JFK, who not only won the debate but went on to win the 1960 US presidential election, has his hand on top, while Nixon, the loser, has his underneath.

When heads of state meet in front of the cameras, it's essential that they both appear in a positive light and that neither overshadows the other. When two statesmen are standing side by side, there's often nothing to favour one over the other. However, when they're shaking hands, the person on the left of the picture has a natural advantage because their arm is showing, while that of the other leader frequently remains hidden. This is the "left-side advantage." In the days when George W. Bush and Tony Blair were meeting up, Bush usually appeared on the left of the picture and Blair on the right. When viewers looked at these images they simply saw two heads of state greeting each other. They seldom noticed the asymmetry of the picture, and the way it affected their perception of these two leaders. Because more of Bush's arm was in view, he appeared, subliminally, to be more in control and therefore the more powerful of the two. This effect was more pronounced when the two leaders were standing close to each other, engaged in a "huddled handshake," because in these circumstances one hardly saw the arm of the person on the right at all. Some politicians seem to know this instinctively, and they sometimes take steps to try to minimize the disadvantages of appearing on the right of a picture. There are two ways of doing this:

1. **Relocating the Handshake.** By extending their arm early and forcing the handshake to take place in the other person's space, a politician can ensure that more of their right arm appears in the photograph. This is exactly what Nikita Khrushchev did when he met President Kennedy in Vienna in 1961. At the time Kennedy was feeling distracted because his back was giving him a lot of trouble. Khrushchev, on the other hand, felt that he could run rings around Kennedy, whom he regarded as a political lightweight. This is apparent in the way that he took the initiative during the handshake. As they approached each other, Khrushchev, who was on the right, reached forward so that the handshake took place in Kennedy's body zone rather than his own. With his arm extended, Khrushchev looked confident and friendly. Kennedy, whose arm was bent, looked cautious and tense. With this simple ruse, Khrushchev had managed to turn the meeting to his own advantage. A very similar event took place when President Nixon met Chairman Mao in Peking in 1972. In the famous photograph of their meeting, Nixon appears on the left, but Mao appears to dominate the encounter because he has his arm fully extended and it looks as if he is shaking Nixon's hand, rather than the reverse.

2. **Opening the Handshake.** When two politicians are shaking hands and facing each other directly, the politician on the left has the "left-side advantage." However, when the two politicians are oriented more toward the camera,

the left-side advantage starts to disappear because the arm of the person on the right comes into view. There is a famous photograph of Richard Nixon shaking hands with Elvis Presley, in which Presley appears on the right of the picture. Because both men are oriented toward the camera, Presley's entire right arm is visible, and he therefore appears to be just as important as the president.

Politicians who discover that they are about to end up on the right side of the picture don't need to resign themselves to looking passive when they shake hands with someone. By extending their arm toward the other person or by angling their body toward the camera they can effectively eliminate the disadvantages of appearing on the right.

The symbolic importance of handshakes cannot be overestimated, especially in the political sphere. The relationship between the United States and Cuba, for example, has been very tense ever since Castro overthrew a US-backed government over sixty years ago. Although there have been high-level contacts, they have not been made public for fear of upsetting the exiled Cuban community in the States. However, when Bill Clinton attended a meeting of world leaders at the United Nations in 2000, he happened to bump into Fidel Castro. On the spur of the moment the two leaders shook hands, exchanged a few pleasantries and then went their separate ways. When a White House spokesman was asked if Clinton had shaken hands with Castro, he denied that anything of the sort had happened. Later on, when the White House realized that too many people had witnessed the handshake to allow a cover-up, it relented and admitted that a brief, impromptu exchange had indeed taken place and that the two men had shaken hands. The fact that it was considered necessary to deny that a handshake had taken place illustrates how powerful the handshake can be as a symbol of acceptance. In politics a handshake is never neutral.

Nowhere was the power of the handshake more evident than in the historic meeting that took place between the Israeli Prime Minister Yitzhak Rabin and the PLO Chairman Yasser Arafat on the White House lawn in 1993, orchestrated and overseen by Bill Clinton. Before the meeting took place there was a lot of tension because nobody knew how Rabin and Arafat would behave when the moment came for them to shake hands. The White House Press Secretary at the time, George Stephanopoulos, remembered the preparations in great detail:

On Saturday morning we practised the handshake. This was just a dry run; four guys in jeans around my desk, trying to figure out how to make this diplomatic tango flow. First came the signatures, with multiple copies of the treaty, all needing multiple signatures. Then the President would turn to his left, shake Arafat's hand; turn to his right, shake Rabin's hand; take a half-step back, with his arms slightly lifted from his sides, and hope that Arafat and Rabin would reach across his belt for the picture of the decade . . . The last thing I said to Clinton was "think about your face." He knew enough not to have a big grin at the big moment; but if he overcompensated, it might look glum . . . We practised a closed mouth smile.

When the big day came, everything worked according to plan:

The ceremony floated past like a dream. Rabin still looked fretful; Arafat was ecstatic; and at the climactic moment Clinton seemed more presidential than ever—calm, confident and fully in control as he took his half-step back with his half-smile in place, and gently cleared a path. The crowd took a collective breath. Then Arafat and Rabin grasped each other's hands, pumped them up and down, and the entire lawn exploded.[9]

The famous photograph of Rabin and Arafat shaking hands is full of fascinating tells. Clinton completely dominates the occasion—not only is he in the centre of the picture, unobstructed by the others, but he stands a good head and shoulders above Rabin and Arafat, reinforcing the message that the United States is bigger, stronger and more benevolent than any other country. The most interesting feature of the photograph is the way that Clinton's arms are stretched out, with the hands open, extending beyond and including the other two protagonists. With this posture Clinton takes on a quasi-religious role. Not only does he seem to be solely responsible for the *rapprochement* between Israel and the Palestinians, but he also appears, rather like the famous statue of Christ the Redeemer above Rio de Janeiro, to be offering a benediction on the newly formed relationship.

Trump Shakes

When Donald Trump became US president and entered the White House, he found a wealth of opportunities to lord it over other people. One way he managed to achieve this was by transforming the humble handshake. As we've seen, the underlying logic of the handshake is its symmetry—by performing the same greeting activities, the two people involved show each other, and the world at large, that they're notional equals. This didn't appear to suit Trump, because during his time in office, he succeeded in defiling the sacred symmetry of the handshake in a number of ways.

THE YANK-SHAKE

In our society, the handshake typically involves two people approaching each other, extending their right arms, clasping hands, pumping them up and down a few times, possibly continuing to hold on for a short while, and then disengaging. Trump introduced his own version of the ritual where, once he'd clasped someone's hand, he'd pull them toward him with a jerking motion. This was the "yank-shake." Trump sometimes performed it so violently that the other person briefly lost their balance and looked like they might even fall down.

There are a few reasons why Trump might have considered it appropriate to give people a massive yank while shaking their hand. Maybe he thought he was conveying his enthusiasm—showing that he was so pleased to see them that he felt the need to draw them closer to him. The more likely explanation is that this was Trump's way of imposing himself and unsettling the other person—in effect, doing something that the other person didn't anticipate, catching them off guard and, quite literally, throwing them off balance. For someone like Trump the attraction of being unpredictable is that it undermines the other person's ability to figure out what he is going to do next, while at the same time ensuring that he remains the centre of attention. In this regard Trump's yank-shake had a lot in common with his political pronouncements, many of which were impulsive, unheralded and, of course, self-aggrandizing.

Soon after Trump became president, Canadian Prime Minister Justin Trudeau made a visit to the White House. Trudeau obviously had advance knowledge of the infamous yank-shake, and he arrived at the White House fully prepared. When he alighted from the official limousine, Trudeau approached Trump, who was waiting to greet him, and he promptly stepped right into Trump's personal space, bracing himself by grabbing the top of Trump's right arm with his left hand. With this simple, pre-emptive manoeuvre, Trudeau prevented Trump from pulling his arm back, and in the process succeeded in neutralizing Trump's yank-shake. As a result, Trudeau was able to avoid the ignominy of being physically and symbolically buffeted around by Trump in front to the cameras.

Neutralizing the yank-shake. Justin Trudeau braces himself by grabbing Donald Trump's shoulder in order to prevent Trump from performing his favourite yank-shake, where he dominates the handshake by tugging the other person towards him. Notice too Trudeau's attempt to assert himself by jutting out his chin.

THE CLENCH-SHAKE

When two people shake hands there's a shared understanding about how long it's appropriate for them to hold hands. Close friends may of course continue to hold on to each other for some time after the handshake is over, but this mutual expression of affection is definitely out of place when heads of state greet each other. When Japanese Prime Minister Shinzo Abe visited the White House in 2017, he and Trump sat down beside each other for the traditional photoshoot. Two unusual things happened during the ensuing handshake. Firstly, while continuing to hold on to Abe's hand, Trump patted the top of his guest's hand no less than six times. Pats like these pretend to be a gesture of inclusion and affection, but their true purpose is to remind the other person—and the millions of people watching on TV—who's really in charge. Trump was able to get away with this, knowing that Abe was extremely unlikely to reciprocate by patting him back. Secondly, Trump actually gripped Abe's hand for an unprecedented 19 seconds—way beyond what anyone would normally expect of a handshake. Abe was clearly mystified by Trump's persistent pretense of approval, because when Trump eventually decided to release his grip, Abe turned his head to the side, with an enormous look of undisguised relief on his face.

THE PALM-UP PLOY

Yanking, clutching and patting people's hands were by no means the only weapons in Trump's handshake armoury. He also devised a means of concealing his overbearing intentions in what appeared to be a friendly and solicitous gesture. During photoshoots in the White House, when Trump and a visiting head of state were seated beside each other, facing the cameras, Trump typically positioned himself on the left of his guest. Whether this was by choice or for some other reason isn't clear. What we do know, however, is that the person with the "left-side advantage"—in other words, the visiting head of state—usually finds it very easier to get their hand on top during the handshake, whereas the person seated on their left—in these cases, Trump—finds it almost impossible to perform a dominant, upper handshake. Faced with this situation, Trump routinely did what was least expected of him—he extended his arm toward his guest, with the palm of his hand emphatically facing upward. This, as we've already noted, is the hand position that's normally assumed by someone who's submissive, or who's been forced by a dominant person to adopt that position.

The palm-up ploy. Seated on his guest's left, Trump can't conveniently get his hand on top during the handshake, so he makes a show of offering his hand palm-up instead. This means that Trump doesn't have to extend his arm across his body, and he's able to tense his biceps to exert control over the handshake.

On one occasion, Justin Trudeau actually found himself in this very situation during a White House photoshoot. When Trump presented his hand, palm-up, performing what in other circumstances would be an appeasement gesture, Trudeau paused, stared at Trump's open palm, and gave a wry look of bewilderment and disbelief before shaking Trump's outstretched hand. We'll never know what was going through Trudeau's mind, but he showed all the signs of being surprised and suspicious, knowing, as he did, that it was completely out of character for Trump to put himself in a subordinate position. A very similar incident occurred when Vladimir Putin visited the White House. He too, he found himself being offered Trump's hand, palm-up, and like Trudeau, showed signs of genuine surprise before taking Trump's hand and posing with him for the cameras.

The real reason why Trump routinely adopted this ploy is that, being positioned on his guest's left, he wasn't able to perform an upper handshake without twisting his body into absurd contortions. Instead, Trump concocted a sham version of a conciliatory gesture, making it look like he was amicably offering his guests a chance to get their hand on top. Actually, the deception went further, because, what his guests failed to appreciate is that by presenting his hand palm-up, Trump was now in a position to flex his bicep and thereby to completely dominate the handshake. In other words, what Trump lost in terms of palm position, he surreptitiously gained through a superior opportunity for control.

We've seen that handshakes perform a number of functions, the most important of which is probably to exchange reciprocal messages about equality. During his occupancy of the White House, Trump managed to subvert the inherent egalitarianism of the handshake, not only by yanking people but also by hanging onto their hand, repeatedly patting their hand and conspicuously presenting his own hand palm-up. Whether or not he realized it, Trump's techniques were designed to transform a symmetrical greeting of solidarity into an asymmetrical greeting of respect, where he became the deserving recipient. Each of his customized handshakes was built on a strategy of stealth—with Trump concealing his self-serving agenda while ostensibly doing nothing more than innocently, even generously, shaking someone's hand.

Hugging Tells

Before the Berlin Wall came down, hugs were an integral part of politics in Eastern Europe. In those days a manly bear hug was the standard greeting between communist leaders, with possibly a kiss or two on the cheek thrown in for good measure. Nowadays the political bear hug has all but disappeared, largely because of its association with a defunct political ideology. Today's politicians in Eastern Europe are much more likely to shake hands.

Outside the political arena, the embrace serves as a greeting ritual for people who are very close, who haven't seen each other for a long time, or who feel the need to express their affection or to comfort or console each other.[10] There are several types of hug, and each contains important tells.

Full-frontal Hugs. These are the real thing—hugs where the bodies of two people completely overlap or almost overlap entirely. The intensity of a full-frontal hug is usually dependent on a number of factors: how long the hug lasts, where people position their arms and hands, and how forcefully they hold on to each other. Not surprisingly, it's been found that people who're emotionally attached to each other tend to engage in longer hugs, and that longer hugs convey stronger feelings of affection and attachment. When two people take part in a full-frontal hug, each person can reach the other person's back with their hands, either by extending one arm over their shoulder and the other around their arm or waist—what we might call a "high hug"—or by extending both arms around the other person's arms or waist—in other words, a "central hug." Given these options, a social embrace may involve, say, both parties producing a high hug, one person doing a high hug while the other does a central hug, or both doing a central hug. In the last two cases, one person will automatically wrap their arms over the other person's arms, and who does that is usually determined by the participants' relative heights. Because about four out of five people are right-handed, most people who perform a high hug tend to extend their right hand over the other person's left shoulder, while positioning their head beside the other person's left shoulder (i.e., with their right cheeks facing each other). However, it has been suggested that other factors—for example, people's feelings toward each other—might also play a part in determining whether people lead with their left or right arm. In a majority of full-frontal hugs—but especially in high hugs—both parties end up with their head to the side of the other person's, which means that some coordination is required to make sure that there isn't a clash of heads. While focussing on the intricacies of the high hug, let's not forget that it's also possible for someone to wrap their arms around the other person's neck (and in very rare instances, their head). Because of mechanical constraints, this "neck hug" can only be performed by one of the two people. Comparing high, central and neck hugs, we notice two things: First, there's also a hug where one or both parties place their hands not around the other person's back but on their bottom. A "bottom hug" is of course a sexualized hug, and it therefore has no place in polite, social encounters. The second, more general point to note is that, bottom hugs notwithstanding, the higher up the other person's body people position their arms and hands, the greater the intensity of hugs and the amount of enthusiasm and affection they convey.

Half-moon Hugs. A half-moon hug is produced when two people face each other while they hug, but their bodies only partially overlap. It's often used by people who are worried about the sexual inferences that might be drawn if they were to opt for a full-frontal hug.

Side-on Hugs. A side-on hug occurs when two people are standing side by side and one or both of them puts an arm around the other person and gives them a squeeze. This type of hug is often used by people who happen to be standing beside each other, possibly facing others, or who are worried that their intentions might be misconstrued if they were to hug the other person head-on.

Straight Up Hugs. How comfortable people are with a hug can often be seen in what they do with their pelvis and where they place their feet. Those who are committed to a hug, and who are not trying to exploit it for other purposes, usually stand up straight, so that their body doesn't make contact, or almost makes contact, with that of the other person.

Concave Hugs. People who are reluctant to hug someone tend to reveal their feelings by placing their feet further away. This reduces the chances of their body coming into contact with that of the other person. Pelvis position is another critical tell, because people who are uncomfortable about hugging tend to pull their bottom away from the other person.

Convex Hugs. When someone wants to show that they are attracted to the person they are hugging they sometimes position their feet close, and push their pelvis toward the other person. Because most of the "official business" of social interaction takes place above the waist, what individuals do with their feet and hips during a hug may be noticed by the person who's being hugged, but it's seldom spotted by the other people who happen to be nearby. For the student of tells, however, they are a rich source of information about what is happening between people "unofficially."

Patted Hugs. Watching people hugging each other it's noticeable how many hugs include multiple pats on the back—usually by one person rather than both people. Patting is very revealing because it looks like a form of reassurance, and that's how we all tend to think of it. However, the real purpose of patting during a hug is to act as a release signal—it's a "release pat." Watch two people who are about to embrace each other and you'll soon spot the critical role that patting plays in bringing the hug to a close. You'll see a man walk over to a woman he knows and wrap his arms around her. She responds by placing her arms around him. A few seconds later she pats him on the back. The man immediately releases his hold and they both disengage. What the man doesn't realize is that he's unconsciously acting on instructions from the woman—by patting him on the back she's telling him that the hug is over. The woman is equally oblivious to what's happening—she may know that she's patting the man on the back, but she doesn't realize that she's using the pat as a "termination signal." Release pats typically occur after a hug has started, but there are occasions when both appear to happen simultaneously—when one person is worried about another's intentions, they might pat them on the back at the onset of the hug, if not before it actually begins. In the context of the embrace, patting therefore serves as a *stealth tell*—it pretends to be something it's not. It may look like a gesture of affection, but its real purpose is to draw the hug to a close, and to do so without causing any offence.

Kissing Tells

Some societies have strict rules about how individuals should greet each other based on their gender, age and social rank. There are also unwritten rules in our society, but these tend to be more fluid and ill defined. There are situations, for example, where it's not entirely clear whether we should kiss someone on the cheek or shake their hand, even though the choice that we make could have far-reaching consequences.

Broadly speaking, there are two types of kiss:

1. **Cheek Kisses.** These tend to be social kisses, and they're used for greetings and farewells.
2. **Mouth Kisses** There are essentially two types of mouth kisses: those where the lips are closed, and those where the lips are parted and the tongues become involved. Open-mouth kisses are part of romance and sex, whereas closed-mouth kisses tend to function as signs of affection—for example, when a parent kisses their child on the lips. Lip-kisses will often feature in greetings and partings between lovers and partners, but in our society they're extremely uncommon in social greetings between friends, acquaintances and even relatives. Historically, however, that wasn't always the case.

The English are widely regarded as rather cold and undemonstrative. It therefore comes as something of a surprise to discover that there was a time when the English were the undisputed kissing champions of Europe. During the fifteenth century it was common practice for men and women to exchange kisses of friendship, even when they were strangers.[11] When the Dutch scholar, Desiderius Erasmus, visited England in 1499 the custom had reached epidemic proportions. He wrote a letter to a friend, telling him: "Whenever you come you are received with a kiss by all; when you take your leave, you are dismissed with kisses; you return, kisses are repeated. They come to visit you, kisses again; they leave you, you kiss them all around. Should you meet anywhere, kisses in abundance, wherever you move, there is nothing but kisses."[12] These kisses were not the customary pecks on the cheek that one finds today—they were kisses on the lips! Most Europeans at the time considered this practice highly improper, and even the French (whom we now regard as a nation of great kissers) were scandalized by the English social habit of kissing on the lips.

The English kissing custom started to decline during the sixteenth century, but it lasted up to the Restoration in 1660, when it was abandoned. At that point the English joined the league of non-kissing nations. However, over the past few decades things have started to change and social kissing is now making a serious comeback.

The way that people kiss each other socially tells us a lot about what kind of people they are, their attitudes to each other and how they feel about kissing.

Hand Kisses. Up until the last world war it was common for men in Europe to greet women by kissing their hand. This practice has disappeared among young people, but there are still some elderly men who have retained the custom of kissing women's hands when they meet them.

Head Kisses. Kissing someone on the forehead or the top of the head is another one-sided way of kissing people—it's how parents kiss their young children and it's also used as a form of benediction. If someone kisses you on the head it shows that they have a protective attitude toward you.

Cheek Kisses. Social kisses typically consist of kisses on the cheek. In countries where the convention is established, everybody knows which side to start and how many kisses to exchange. In countries like the United States, United Kingdom and Canada, where kissing customs are still evolving, people are often unsure about which cheek to kiss first, and how many times they should kiss the other person.

Vacuum Kisses. When people ostensibly kiss each other on the cheek they sometimes miss the target altogether and end up kissing the air instead. These "vacuum kisses" fall into two types: "missed kisses," where the parties' cheeks touch but their lips don't connect with the other person's cheek, and "air kisses," where they go through the motions without making any physical contact at all. Air kisses appear when people are uncomfortable about physical contact, and both types of vacuum kiss are common among women who don't want to disturb their make-up or leave traces of lipstick on the other person.

Feigned Kisses. If you watch people kissing socially, you'll notice that there are some people who press their cheek against the other person's without even pursing their lips, let alone kissing the air. These "feigned kisses" pretend to be real kisses but they don't offer anything more than the cheek. They tend to be produced by people who are passive by nature, and who would rather be kissed by somebody than have to kiss them. The interesting thing about a feigned kiss is that the other person doesn't usually notice it—it's only people nearby who see what's really happening.

Vocalized Kisses. Some kisses on the cheek are silent, while others include an audible smack of the lips. Other kisses are accompanied by loud vocalizations like *Mwah!* Sometimes these sound like signs of appreciation, and on other occasions they come across as something of a joke. In spite of the exaggeration and the laughter that accompanies them, these sounds are actually signs of discomfort being made by people who want to distance themselves from the kiss by mocking it. People who are totally at ease with social kissing—like the Italians or the French—don't accompany their kisses with vocalizations. It's only those who are self-conscious about social kissing—like the British—who find it necessary to exaggerate and accompany their kisses with loud noises. It's their way of drawing attention to the kiss so that they can disown it.

Lateral Kisses. It's feasible for two people to kiss each other on the lips while holding their heads erect, but most people prefer to incline their head to one side when they perform a lip-kiss, just as they do when kissing someone on the cheek. Observation of people in public places like airport lounges and railway stations reveals that when two people kiss each other on the lips or cheek, the majority lean their head to the right. This suggests that hugging and kissing share a rightward bias—with people wrapping their right arm over the other person's left shoulder when they perform a high hug, or leaning their head to the right when kissing someone. The evidence shows, however, that lateral preferences for kissing are not as ingrained as one might expect. It's been found, for example, that lovers show a strong tendency to incline their head to the right, whereas when parents kiss their children, they're more likely to lean their head to the left. Further evidence for the variability of lateral preferences was borne out by a detailed investigation of cheek-kissing practices in ten French cities, where it was discovered that while some cities exhibited a rightward kissing bias, others showed a leftward kissing bias. Because kissing requires careful timing and coordination, it's obviously important that the members of a community share the same expectations, regardless of whether they place their head on the left or right. The fact that kissing practices can vary so dramatically within the same country reminds us of the power of social conventions and their ability to override and replace the natural inclinations of our brains and bodies.[13]

Sandwich Kisses. In most cases of social kissing the hands don't play a role, other than to clasp the other person politely by, say, the arm or shoulder, if at all. However, in lip-kisses between partners or lovers, you might occasionally notice one person—usually the male if it's a heterosexual encounter—grasping the other person's head and sandwiching it between their hands before and during the kiss. Typically, actions like these pretend to be a gesture of enthusiasm, but in most cases they serve to guide and control the kiss, making sure that the other person can't get away. There was a famous example of a sandwich kiss after the final soccer match of the 2023 Women's World Cup. As the victorious members of the Spanish team were filing past to collect their winners' medals, Luis Rubiales, the president of the Royal Spanish Federation, kissed one of the players, Jenni Hermoso, on the lips. Mind you, this wasn't an instance where both parties eagerly steered their lips toward each other, but one where Rubiales clasped his hands on the sides of Hermoso's face and planted a seemingly uninvited kiss on her lips. Rubiales' actions caused an immediate uproar—Hermoso said that she felt assaulted, her team-mates demanded Rubiales' resignation, and he insisted that the kiss was consensual. At the time the incident completely overshadowed the Spanish team's victory, as well as the celebrations that would normally follow, and since then there have been resignations and legal proceedings against Rubiales. Looking back, it seems that the critical feature of this kiss—but by no means the only one—was its one-sidedness and the way that Rubiales framed Hermoso's face between his hands. Had they both performed this action, or had Rubiales not used his hands at all, this might have turned out very differently.

Naming Tells

When people meet for the first time they usually introduce themselves or someone else introduces them. Self-introductions are fairly straightforward—they can occur at the beginning of an encounter or some time after people have struck up a conversation. An introduction performed by someone else tends to be a bit more complicated because the introducer has to orchestrate the meeting, name the people being introduced (the introducees), and possibly say something about them.

When introducers describe or "package" introducees, they need to perform three tasks: 1) they need to legitimize the introduction; 2) they need to say something favourable about one or both people; and 3) they need to provide a basis on which the introducees can construct a conversation. The ideal package does all three of these things. However, some introducers are so eager to legitimize the introduction that they end up exaggerating the achievements of the introducees ("This is Susan—she's the most brilliant pianist in the country!"), while others are so concerned about offering an authentic description that they fail to offer the introducees anything to talk about ("Can I introduce you to Charles—he's working on a revision of Fermat's theorem!").

The essential part of an introducer's role is to name the introducees ("Susan, I'd like you to meet Charles. Charles, this is Susan."). While this requirement seems simple enough, it is fraught with all kinds of problems, not least being the prospect that the introducer will forget someone's name. Because introducers are under a lot of pressure to perform, it's very easy for them to botch this crucial part of the introduction. It's often quite difficult to introduce people whom one doesn't know well. But knowing somebody well doesn't necessarily make things any easier, because it's quite common for the introducer to draw a blank when he or she tries to remember the name of a close friend. Fortunately introducers can use several strategies to save their own face, and that of the person whose name they are struggling to remember.

One strategy is for the introducer to ask the person what their name is at the start of the introduction. "I'm sorry," the introducer might say to one of the introducees, "but I can't remember your name." When the introducee says "Margaret Smith," the introducer comes back with "Yes, I know it's Margaret; I just wasn't sure about your surname!" Another strategy is for the introducer to create an audible space where the name is normally offered, in the hope that the person will quickly provide his or her own name. In this situation introducees are usually very obliging. When the introducer, for example, says "And this is. . ." and leaves enough space to indicate that they are about to offer the name, the introducee will usually come to the rescue. "Margaret Smith," she'll say, before anyone notices that the introducer has forgotten her name. Another strategy is to package each person so that the omission of their name isn't obvious. Yet another is to hurriedly excuse oneself at the critical point where names are normally provided—for example, "May I introduce you to each other . . . Oh no! My mother-in-law has just arrived! I have to go! . . . Could you please introduce yourselves to each other?"

Some people make a point of remembering someone's name when they're introduced to them. For example, when he's introducing Bill to Tom, the host says, "Bill, may I introduce you to Tom?" As they are shaking hands, Bill says "Hello, Tom," and Tom says "Hi, Bill." Repeating someone's name in this fashion provides a very convenient way of remembering their name, as well as showing the other person that you've taken the trouble to remember it. In the United States and Canada, where this practice is fairly widespread, it is judged very favourably. People who repeat names are liked more than those who don't, unless the person who's doing it has something to gain by being pleasant, in which case name repetition is seen as a form of ingratiation.

There are several reasons why someone might forget the names of people whom they've just met: they're not paying attention; there are too many distractions; there are too many names to remember; and they're so anxious that they can't file the information away. The people who are best at remembering names are highly motivated. Many use a mnemonic to help them. The British Prime Minister Benjamin Disraeli is reputed to have had a remarkable memory for names, but it wasn't infallible. Asked what he did when he couldn't remember someone's name, he confessed that he always resorted to the same strategy—he'd turn to the person and say, "How is the old complaint?" Disraeli claimed that it always worked.

Parting Tells

Memory is governed by "primacy" and "recency"—the things we remember best are those that we heard first or heard last. It's the same with social encounters. What shapes our opinions more than anything else is what happens when we first meet someone, and what happens when we leave that person. That's why we invest so much effort in greeting and parting rituals—we instinctively know that the way we appear to others depends on how we say hello and goodbye.

In some respects parting rituals are rather similar to greeting rituals. Like greeting rituals, they are concerned with transition.[14] They also have a rather similar, but reversed, temporal structure to greetings—while greetings consist of a "recognition phase," an "approach phase" and a "meeting phase," partings are made up of a "separation phase," a "withdrawal phase" and a "farewell phase."

Imagine that two young people, a man and a woman, are having a drink in a bar after work. At some point the woman realizes that it's time for her to leave, so she quickly steals a glance at her watch. This is the first "advance cue" that she intends to leave, and it marks the beginning of the "separation phase." This phase provides the young man and woman with an opportunity to coordinate their expectations so that they are both on the same "departure schedule," and nobody gets left behind in the unfolding sequence. This is achieved through a complicated exchange of signals. For example, after the woman has glanced at her watch, the man might absentmindedly touch his briefcase. They continue talking for a while. She then orients her body toward the door, unconsciously signalling where she's aiming, and he immediately responds by finishing his drink. At each stage in this choreographed sequence, each person is signalling their intention to leave and the other is providing clearance—one person's actions are effectively saying "I'm planning to leave; what do you think?" and the other person's responses are saying "That's fine by me. I'm quite happy to draw this to a close."

The signals exchanged by people who don't know each other very well are usually very tentative. The signals exchanged by close friends are also quite subtle. But even when the signals between friends are bold and explicit, they're usually accompanied by mitigating assurances that are designed to make sure that the other person doesn't feel abandoned. If, for example, the young woman in the bar had suddenly got to her feet and announced "I'm off now," she would probably have tried to reassure the man that it wasn't her choice and that her imminent departure had no bearing on their friendship whatsoever.

When people part company they need to do two things: bring the encounter to a successful close, and show that the relationship they enjoy with the other person won't be affected by their departure. To get the first part of this message across, the participants need to send out "closure signals"; to convey the second part of the message they need to provide each other with "relationship signals."

People can use an enormous range of closure signals. Some are linguistic, others non-verbal. One of the ways that people draw a conversation to a close is by reducing the amount of time they spend looking at the other person, and the amount of "back-channel signals" they produce while the other person is speaking. As we've seen, back-channel signals consist of nods and *uh-huh* sounds that are designed to encourage the other person and to show that we don't want to take over the speaker role. Reducing these signals usually sends a clear message to the other person that the conversation is starting to wind down. The head, arms and legs are also used to get this message across. Rapid nodding of the head, shifting the weight from one leg to another, placing the hands on the armrest of the chair—all these "intention displays" are used to show that we are preparing to leave. Some closure signals are bold and clear. Most, however, are very subtle. But even when they are barely visible, most closure signals manage to reach their target.

Relationship signals are designed to reassure the other person that the end of the encounter does not signal the end of the relationship. This message is conveyed by several kinds of talk:

Justification Talk. People who are about to leave often announce that they're going because they have to, not because they want to leave. At a dinner party, for example, a guest might turn to the hostess and say "I'm sorry we have to leave so early, but we promised the babysitter we'd be home by eleven o'clock."

Continuity Talk. People try to reassure each other by projecting their relationship into the future. When they say goodbye to someone they say things like "See you soon," "Let's keep in touch" or "I'll call you next week."

Evaluation Talk. People try to protect their relationship by expressing their gratitude to the person they're leaving. When they leave a social gathering, for example, they tell the host and hostess how much they enjoyed the evening. Similarly, when they bump into an old school friend and are saying goodbye, they often express their pleasure with remarks like "It's good to see you again."

There's often a lot of pressure on departing guests to exaggerate their appreciation, especially when they've heard other guests telling the host and hostess how much they enjoyed the evening. They feel a) that they should not be outdone by the previous guests, and b) that they should say something original. This can very rapidly give rise to a form of "gratitude escalation," where each departing guest feels compelled to produce a more florid expression of thanks than their predecessor. Mark Knapp captures the situation thus:

Take, for example, the final moments of a cocktail party. Several guests are lined up ahead of you saying goodbye to the hostess;

you hear each guest preceding you say something like: "Cynthia, we've had a great time. It was so much fun. Thanks a lot . . ." Now it's your turn. Because of the attending farewells preceding you, you may be forced to add emphasis which you may not feel, but which is demanded lest you be seen as unoriginal and unappreciative. Hence you boom out with: "Cynthia . . . just fantastic! I can't remember when I had a better time. You and Zeke must come over to our house sometime." Later, as your wife questions the wisdom of your spontaneous invitation, you discover that you yourself aren't sure why you extended the invitation in the first place.[15]

During a parting ritual people often move away from each other and then back again. If you watch people saying goodbye, you'll notice how one of them takes a step back, or several paces away from the other person, and then returns to their former position, sometimes repeating this process a number of times. This is the "yo-yo phenomenon." It's very common in spaces that encourage this kind of movement, and where the participants aren't under any pressure to leave in a hurry. If you watch people chatting on the street you'll often see one or both of them moving away and then back again as a prelude to leaving altogether.

Some years ago, when I was watching people in the centre of Oxford, I recorded one couple that made a total of seventeen moves away from each other before they finally separated! On the surface the yo-yo phenomenon looks like a bad case of indecision—or a theatrical *fausse sortie*, where an actor pretends to exit and then returns immediately to the stage. But it's neither; it's the consequence of closure signals and relationship signals competing with each other. When people start to close a conversation, one of the things they do is move away. Similarly, to show that the relationship is still important, they move toward the other person. In order to signal that they want to bring the encounter to a close *and* that their relationship is still intact, people frequently end up moving back and forth. It's the alternation of these two types of signal that gives rise to the yo-yo phenomenon.

Before people physically separate, they may hug, kiss or shake hands—the decision often depends on what they did when they greeted each other. However, this doesn't necessarily mean the end of the separation phase because they will often recycle some of the earlier elements of the ritual, sometimes repeating the entire sequence before they actually move away from each other. The "withdrawal phase" of the parting is often fairly straightforward—one or both people simply turn on their heel and walk away. But even at this late stage in the proceedings there are tells that reveal what people are thinking.

When people are approaching each other they usually focus on the front of their body—adjusting their tie, buttoning up their jacket or rearranging the front of their hair. However, when people move away from each other they usually focus their attention on the back of their body because they know that this is most likely to be noticed by the other person. The way that people adjust the back of their body is often a giveaway. For example, when someone smooths the back of their hair just as they are about to withdraw, it shows that they recognize—even unconsciously—that they may be observed from behind as they walk away.

The habit of attending to the back of the body prior to leaving is very much the prerogative of women, simply because women are more likely to be judged or admired from behind than men. Women will sometimes put their hand behind them and pull their jersey down over their bottom as they're about to walk away. This is the *hind-hide tell*, and it shows that the woman in question is concerned about her backside being scrutinized, either critically or appreciatively. Women who are proud of their backside, or who wish to draw attention to it, are more likely to flatten out their dress before they walk away.

While people are moving away, they sometimes enter a "farewell phase," where they throw a glance over their shoulder, or turn around and wave, before continuing on their way. When the parting is inconsequential people don't turn around. But when the parting has an emotional significance they often experience a strong temptation to turn around and have a final look at the other person before going on their way. One of the reasons why people turn around is that they regret the parting and don't want the separation to take place, or they want the other person to think that's the case. Another motive is to check whether the other person is still watching them—when you've just left someone it's always reassuring to discover that they haven't broken off yet, and that they're watching you until you finally disappear from view. Partings, like greetings, are all about ratifying relationships and providing the other person with reassurances. The fact that these goals are regularly achieved by the exchange of brief utterances and fleeting gestures shows what a crucial role tells play in our lives.

6. Political Tells

Politics is all about appearances—it's as important for politicians to convince other people that they have certain principles as it is to conceal the fact that they are prepared to abandon these principles in favour of power, money or fame. In public polls about the integrity of different professions, politicians regularly appear near the bottom of the league table, usually just above second-hand car salesmen. This reflects the widespread public distrust of politicians, and the recognition that what they pretend to do and what they actually do are very different things. Politicians have long recognized this two-faced feature of politics. In many cases it seems to be what attracted them to the profession in the first place.

Health Tells

Although politicians come in all shapes and sizes, some aspects of appearance are more conducive to success than others. Height seems to be a significant factor—especially when you consider that only three of the past US presidents were shorter than the national average for their period. Abraham Lincoln, for example, was a big person in more ways than one, measuring in at 6 feet 4 inches. Of course there have been more diminutive, and no less effective, heads of state—like Mussolini and Haile Selassie—but they made up for their lack of height in other ways, and where possible concealed it. Mussolini made himself look taller by standing on a box when he addressed the crowds from his balcony. We're told that whenever Haile Selassie sat on the imperial throne a pile of cushions would be placed under his feet so he could avoid the indignity of having his feet dangling in mid-air. It's widely assumed that Napoleon was also short—we sometimes refer to some-

one who's short and overbearing as having a "Napoleon complex" —
but there's no evidence to support this notion. In fact Napoleon was
about 5 feet 6 inches, which was the average height of a Frenchman in
his day. It's possible that he simply looked short beside the grenadiers
of his Imperial Guard, who were specially selected for their height, and
that's why we still think of him as unusually short.

It's essential for political leaders to look fit because people unconsciously associate the health of the body politic with the health of
their head of state. That's why President Franklin D. Roosevelt, who'd
had polio, tried to hide both his physical disability and the fact that
he spent so much time in a wheelchair. It's why presidents since have
publicized their physical health—why Barack Obama wanted everyone to know that he was a talented basketball player, why George
W. Bush went jogging in public, why Bill Clinton did the same, why
George Bush Sr. played tennis, why Ronald Reagan pressed weights,
and why Richard Nixon squeezed all the publicity he could out of
his early days as a football player. There are even photographs of the
young Nixon playing American football without a helmet—a practice that, his critics reckoned, explained some of his peculiar political
decisions in later life. There's also an early photograph of George W.
Bush playing rugby for Yale, where he's tackling a Harvard player and
has his left arm around the poor guy's neck while appearing to punch
him in the face with his right hand—both actions being against the
rules and the spirit of the game, even in his day. John F. Kennedy and
Bobby Kennedy were brought up in a family that believed in the virtues of team games, although JFK found it difficult to take part after
he'd injured his back during the Second World War. Once, when he
was addressing a group of sports coaches, Bobby Kennedy announced
that "Except for war, there is nothing in American life—nothing—
which trains a boy better for life than football." While in the White
House, neither Donald Trump nor Joe Biden was seen engaging in
any strenuous sporting activity, unless you include riding around in
a golf buggy or sauntering across the green. Instead, both of them got
their physician to issue glowing reports on the state of their health.
One of Trump's reports claimed that "his strength and stamina are

extraordinary," which, given Trump's penchant for hyperbole, made it sound like he'd dictated the words himself. Trump's efforts to impress everyone with his physical prowess certainly aren't new. Back in 2007, there was a bogus, stage-managed interlude during WrestleMania23, when Trump overpowered WWE's Vince McMahon, wrestled him to the ground and then went around, punching his fist triumphantly in the air and soaking up the adulation of the crowd. No wonder his followers thought he was a tough guy.

Symbolically, the fitness of the US president is very important. One need only think of the time when President Jimmy Carter went jogging with his aides and collapsed from exhaustion. The famous photograph of Carter, with his legs buckled underneath him and a vacant look on his face, sent a reverberating shudder around the country. It was this revelation of his vulnerability, coupled with the failed attempt to rescue the US hostages in Iran, that led to the freefall in Carter's popularity and to his eventual defeat by Ronald Reagan. Photographs, and their ability to engrave an image on people's minds, play a critical role in the public image of politicians. For example, when George W. Bush nearly choked on a pretzel it was fairly easy to dismiss the incident as a joke. However, had a photographer been present to record the event, we might have been exposed to a very undignified spectacle (definitely not what one expects from the leader of the Western world!) and Bush's reputation could have been irreparably damaged.

Over the years, Canadian prime ministers have also publicized their sporting accomplishments. In 2012, Justin Trudeau dusted off his pugilistic credentials and stepped into the ring for a charity boxing match against Senator Patrick Brazeau, pummelling his opponent, taking several hits himself, but winning on a TKO in the third and final round. His father Pierre Trudeau was also no slouch, having captained his school ice hockey team and, in later life, being awarded a second-dan black belt in judo. Stephen Harper was a keen hockey player, and ended up writing a popular book on the subject. Prime Ministers Jean Chrétien and Lester Pearson were also very competent sportsmen, and they made sure that their enthusiasm, and sometimes their sporting skills, were widely known.

But the politician who's expended more effort than any other in projecting an image of manly vigour is of course Vladimir Putin. For years the Russian public has been treated to news about his achievements on the ice rink and judo mat. If that wasn't enough, they, and the world at large, have now been spoiled with images of a bare-chested Putin riding bare-back through the countryside, or churning up the water as he swims butterfly across a lake. It always pays for national leaders to look strong and healthy, even in an autocracy, because if you aren't fit, people might think that you're not fit for office either.

Hair Tells

One feature that helps to create an impression of youthful vigour in a politician is a full head of hair. Several years ago, Neil Kinnock, the former leader of the Labour Party in Britain, who had hardly any hair himself, wrote a teasing letter to William Hague, then leader of the Conservative Party, to warn him that his lack of hair was likely to disqualify him from ever becoming prime minister. Several months later the Conservative Party was defeated at the polls and Hague was forced to resign, only to be replaced by Iain Duncan Smith, a man with even less hair than Hague.

Because babies often don't have any hair on their head and people lose their hair as they get older, baldness can be a sign of extreme youth as well as age. In Hague's case the lack of hair, coupled with his baby-like features, made him look too young. It gave the impression that he was unprepared for a life in politics. All things being equal—which of course they never are in politics—it's an advantage for politicians to have a full head of hair and to look youthful and dynamic. This has definitely been the case with Justin Trudeau, who's benefited enormously from his boyish head of hair, not to mention his boyish good looks. But the politician who's tried, probably more than any other, to capitalize on their hair is Boris Johnson, the former British prime minister. For many years, the blond, disarrayed, hirsute thatch on top of his head has been his trademark—not one that he carefully combed into place, but rather a mop that he deliberately ruffled, thereby creating a devil-may-care impression of someone who's just got out of bed. Instead of leaving his hair alone when in public, as most people do, Boris Johnson has a peculiar habit of constantly touching his hair, rearranging and running his fingers through it. There are two basic reasons why people constantly touch their hair: one is because they're anxious and need to comfort themselves, and the other is to draw attention to themselves. Inspection of the settings where Boris Johnson touches his hair shows that it's not when he has reason to be worried but rather when he stands to gain something by drawing attention to himself. Fluffing his hair is therefore Boris' way of getting other people to focus on him.

Beards are a different matter altogether. Because they are associated with age and maturity, beards don't offer male politicians any special advantage, unless—as in the case of Fidel Castro—the beard is being used to support an image of the politician as a revolutionary. When the CIA was thinking of ways of removing Castro during the 1960s, they concocted a plan to insert thallium salts in his shoes, which would cause his iconic beard to fall out and expose the unknown face beneath. Although they never pursued the idea, they realized, quite correctly, that without his beard Castro would have been unrecognizable.

Walking Tells

Politicians also try to create an impression of youthful vigour through their postures and movements. Interestingly, posture provides less opportunity to convey an image of strength, largely because it's easier to fake. That's why politicians put so much effort into the way they move their head, arms and hands, and the way they walk.

The way an animal moves provides a very clear picture of its strength, agility and determination, and it's the same with politicians. John F. Kennedy was the first president of the television age, and he used it to full advantage. During the famous Kennedy–Nixon debates in 1960, those members of the public who had listened to the first debate on radio put Nixon ahead. However, those who'd watched the debate on television put Kennedy ahead of Nixon, and as things worked out, actually offered a more accurate prediction of the final result. It's television's capacity to capture those rather primitive aspects of demeanour—to put appearances on a par with substance—that helped Kennedy to get elected, and that has made or broken politicians ever since.

How politicians walk sends very strong messages about what they're like—or rather, how they want others to see them. These messages are sometimes conveyed by walking speed. It's reputed, for example, that Canadian Prime Minister Jean Chrétien had a habit of bounding up flights of stairs to show how lively he was, especially when journalists were present to witness the spectacle. Likewise, whenever British Prime Minister Harold Wilson was boarding an airplane he made a habit of running up the stairs so that everyone thought he was fit. But it was Ronald Reagan who managed to transform walking into a form of art. If you ever watched him closely you'll have noticed that he moved in a way that conveyed an impression of weighty momentum—and, by suggestion, of political substance as well. This was partly achieved by his resolute stride—making it look as though his aides were struggling to keep up with him—and partly by the energetic way he moved his arms.

When people walk, they swing their arms through an arc in the sagittal plane (the plane that's in line with the movement of their body through space). The full extent of the arc, forward and back, provides an index of vigour, because young people tend to swing their arms higher at the front and further up at the back, partly because they move faster than older people. Swinging the arms *across* the body also helps to create an impression of masculine strength.

There are two factors at work here: one being the difference between men and women, and the other being the exaggerated effect of body-building on gait style. When men and women stand upright, there's a tendency for men's arms to rotate slightly inward (what physiologists call "pronation") and for women's arms to rotate slightly outward (what physiologists call "supination"). This sex difference is partly due to the fact that women can bend their arms further back at the elbow than men. This is called the "carrying angle," and it's been explained as a consequence of women having wider hips than men and spending more time carrying babies.

Because women have a greater carrying angle than men, their arms swing further on the back-swing than men's. In order to distinguish themselves from women, and to emphasize their masculinity, men use more upswing than back-swing. The other reason why men show more pronation in their arms is that the *latissimus dorsi* muscles under their arms are more developed. This has the effect of moving their shoulders forward and rotating the arms inward. This effect is very noticeable in body-builders. Because body-builders have over-developed *latissimus dorsi* and deltoid muscles, their arms are pronated more than most, and the gap between their arms and chest is accentuated, giving them a more simian, ape-like appearance. Also, because their thighs are over-developed, body-builders tend to have a more rolling gait, swinging their legs outward as they move forward.

It's often said that a picture is worth a thousand words. It's also true that, in politics, a moving image is worth a thousand pictures—especially when it comes to walking style. News footage of Barack Obama striding through the White House or across the lawn gave the impression of a happy, energetic young man who was totally in control. Obama managed to create this impression by subtly incorporating features of an athlete's gait into his walking style, by swinging his arms across his body and by rotating his hands so that they faced backward. At the same time, by keeping his hands open and relaxed he eliminated any suggestion of latent anxiety, and created a subliminal image of someone who was completely comfortable in his role.

During his presidency Bill Clinton also adopted a macho walking style, and George W. Bush dutifully followed in his footsteps. Indeed, George W. Bush was probably the fittest US president there's ever been. When he was in office he could easily run a seven-minute mile, which put him in the first or second percentile in the fitness rankings for men of his age. It was obvious that Bush was fit, both from his build and the way he walked, although there was a strong suggestion of artifice in his gait because he didn't have the muscles to warrant the exaggerated "power walk" that he was carefully cultivating at the time. Nevertheless, Bush's walking style sent a very clear signal of fitness to the electorate. It also had the potential to unnerve people who met him. This happened when Prime Minister Tony Blair met President Bush at Camp David in 2002. The television news footage showed the two leaders walking together, Bush casually dressed in a leather bomber jacket, and Blair in an open-necked shirt. Bush is striding out, doing his presidential power walk, with his arms pronated and extended away from his body, and his hands relaxed and facing backward—just like a bodybuilder. Not to be outdone, but not wanting to mimic his host, Blair strolls along with his hands casually tucked into his front trouser pockets—something he never does in public. Here Bush has clearly upped the ante in the masculinity stakes and Blair has tried to match him. By tucking his hands into his pockets Blair is trying to show that he's also cool and relaxed, but that he's not prepared to play Tonto to Bush's Lone Ranger.

Speaking of the Wild West, we shouldn't overlook Vladimir Putin's "gunslinger's gait"—his peculiar, lopsided way of walking, where he swings his left arm through an enormous arc, while keeping his right hand tucked in, close to his body. The asymmetric reduction of arm swing seen here is often an early sign of Parkinson's disease, but that doesn't appear to be the explanation in this case, because there have been several prominent figures in Putin's circle who've also adopted the gunslinger's gait.[1] These include men with military connections, some of whom were trained by the KGB, as well as Dmitry Medvedev, who wasn't in the KGB but who never seems to pass up an opportunity to ape his master. We're informed, in fact, that KGB agents were trained to walk with their dominant hand close to their body so that they could quickly reach for their gun or control it if it was already in hand. This may account for why Putin and his coterie decided to keep their right hand close by, but it doesn't explain why they also made a point of swinging their left arm so dramatically. Maybe it's because they wanted to borrow at least one feature of the "power walk" or because they needed to remind each other, through their walking style, of their continuing loyalty to the values of the old KGB.

Defensive Tells

In *The Prince* (1532), his famous treatise on politics, Machiavelli observed that "men rise from one ambition to another; first they secure themselves from attack, and then they attack others." The threat to politicians can come from other political parties, the electorate or the media. It can also come from their own party, in which case politicians may find it necessary to attack their allies more vigorously than their foes. In order to survive, politicians need to be constantly on their guard against attack. If you watch politicians making political speeches you'll notice that they often gesticulate with their hands while they're talking. Careful inspection of their hand movements shows that when politicians are feeling insecure they often produce hand postures that are symbolically defensive—their hands may, for example, cross their body or the palms of their hands may be pushed forward as if they are about to parry an imaginary blow.

The facial expressions of politicians can also be revealing. One of Bill Clinton's trademark tells was the "oxbow mouth," where the lower lip is pushed upward, shaping the mouth into an inverted U. Bill Clinton used this expression when he wanted to show that he was determined. Other politicians, both at the time and since, have used this facial gesture for the same purpose. While the oxbow mouth provides a display of resolution, the fact that it also involves a tensing of the muscles of the chin shows that it is essentially a defensive gesture—it's how people react when they think someone is, metaphorically, about to punch them on the chin, and it's how politicians give themselves away when they're feeling vulnerable. That's why Richard Nixon was photographed so often with an oxbow mouth during the Watergate scandal, and why Bill Clinton frequently produced the same facial expression during the Monica Lewinsky affair.

Politicians can defend themselves against attack in five other ways: 1) by adopting a friendly demeanour; 2) by modulating their voice so that they sound more attractive and less threatening; 3) by producing appeasing signals; 4) by kissing babies; and 5) by creating the impression that they're popular and adorable.

Friendly Tells

Politicians often attempt to ward off aggression by presenting themselves as amiable individuals—in other words, as the kind of people whom nobody would ever have any reason to attack. Ronald Reagan had this down to a T. His smiles, for example, were typically broad and generous. Unlike those of many other politicians, which are restricted to the mouth region, Reagan's smiles frequently extended to the eyes, showing that his feelings of friendship and enjoyment were genuine. The key thing about a genuine smile is that it's much more likely to elicit reciprocated smiling from other people, and this in turn is likely to make them feel more positively disposed to the person who smiled in the first place. Genuine smiles are like magnets—they act at a distance, realigning people's feelings and making them point in the same direction. That's what makes them so effective as a defensive weapon in politics.

Reagan frequently employed an upgraded version of the smile—the "drop-jaw smile." It's no accident that Bill Clinton, who was equally preoccupied with outward appearances, also made a habit of using the drop-jaw smile—possibly even more than Reagan—and that, when she was campaigning for the presidency, Hillary Clinton made extensive use of it too. But what distinguishes the drop-jaw smile from other smiles and makes it so special?

Smiles can include various degrees of mouth opening. At one extreme are cases of "sealed" or "zipped" smiles, where the corners of the mouth are pulled sideways and the mouth isn't opened at all. Then there are instances where the lips are parted, producing either a "top-teeth smile," where just the upper teeth are seen, or a "full-teeth smile," where both the top and bottom teeth are exposed. Beyond this, there's the "drop-jaw smile," where the mouth is opened wide and either the top teeth or both sets of teeth are exposed. The distinctive feature of the drop-jaw smile is that it looks almost exactly like the chimpanzee "play face," which is the evolutionary precursor of human laughter. Because they are more dramatic, drop-jaw smiles can be seen at a greater distance. But what really sets drop-jaw smiles apart from other smiles, and recommends them to politicians, is the fact that they *look* like laughter. This affects other people in three ways. Firstly drop-jaw smiles convey a primitive message of playfulness. Secondly, they don't contain any suggestion of appeasement, like other smiles do. Thirdly, because laughter is much more contagious than smiling, drop-jaw smiles are likely to induce the same feelings in other people. A drop-jaw smile therefore makes a politician look playful and unthreatening, and makes other people feel playful and unthreatened too.

The politician who, in recent times, has probably made most use of the zipped smile is Donald Trump. There are occasions when Trump produces a genuine Duchenne smile, as well as times when he offers a full-blown fake smile, but when he's on show he often resorts to a zipped smile, where his mouth is closed, his teeth remain hidden, and his facial expression is largely controlled by the risorius muscles, which pull the corners of his mouth sideways. The advantages of using a zipped smile are threefold: it signals his pleasure; it gives the impression that he's slightly circumspect; and it makes his face look proportionately wider, thereby making him look dominant. On occasion Trump will combine his zipped smile with a puckered chin, producing what psychologists call a "blended" facial expression. It's very unlikely that Trump is ever aware that he's doing this, but his puckered chin is an important giveaway, because it shows that he's unconsciously worried about being punched—metaphorically, of course—and that's why he feels compelled to defend himself by tensing the muscles in his chin. In terms of its underlying motivation, this blended facial expression is therefore very similar to the oxbow mouth. It's evidence that, despite his never-ending attempts to appear tough and macho, there are times when Trump actually feels vulnerable and defensive.

Vocal Tells

In his day, Ronald Reagan had a number of endearing tricks up his sleeve. One was his deep voice; another was his breathy way of speaking. Deep voices are associated with dominance, masculinity and concern—all qualities that Reagan managed to project with his voice. "Breathy" voices are often contrasted with "tense" voices. In a breathy voice there's a high rate of airflow over the vocal cords, while in a tense voice the rate of airflow is low. As a result, tense voices tend to sound metallic, whereas breathy voices sound relaxed and airy—in fact it's often said that a breathy voice sounds like "voice mixed with air." People with breathy voices sound warm, while those with tense voices tend to sound cold.[2] However, breathy voices are acoustically inefficient because they require a lot of effort and because they're more difficult to understand. On the whole, women tend to have more breathy voices than men, which is one of the reasons why they sound more warm and sexy. Women with particularly breathy voices include the Hollywood actress Audrey Hepburn and the British actress Joanna Lumley.

Male politicians who speak with a breathy register don't necessarily sound more feminine—they just sound warmer. In Reagan's case, however, the story doesn't end there, because he often spoke in a whisper, especially when he was on television. In recent years whispered voices have become very popular, particularly among male movie stars. Whispered speech is, by definition, breathy speech at a lower volume. The attraction of quiet, low-volume speech is that it creates an illusion of physical closeness and psychological intimacy. When Reagan used to deliver his cozy, fireside chats on television all these vocal qualities were combined—the depth of his voice making him sound masculine, his breathiness making him sound warm, and the whispered delivery making him appear intimate and friendly.

Politicians with deeper voices are generally thought to be more dominant and authoritative, and they're therefore more likely to attract votes from the electorate. As a rule, both men and women show a preference for male and female politicians who speak with a lower pitch, but it depends on which candidates they're up against. During the 2012 US House elections, for example, it was found that, when they were competing against a male opponent, the candidate with the lower voice tended to win; but when they were up against a female opponent, the candidate with the higher pitch tended to come out on top, especially when the opposing candidates were male. This suggests that while voters show a preference for candidates with deep voices, this preference can be overridden when female candidates, with higher voices, are in the frame. It also begs the question as to whether deeper voices are a true reflection of more effective leadership, and here there doesn't seem to be any supportive evidence. In other words, voters may prefer politicians with deeper voices, but they'd be mistaken if they thought that their preferred candidates were actually more competent.[3]

Appeasement Tells

One way for politicians to avoid being attacked is to signal that they have no intention of attacking others.[4] Another way is to produce an appeasement display that "cuts off" other people's aggression. The first strategy can sometimes be seen during Question Time in the UK House of Commons, when the government of the day and the opposition face each other across the large table on which are situated the two dispatch boxes. In the front rows, right in the middle of their party, but on opposite sides of the house, sit the Prime Minister and the Leader of the Opposition—looking for all the world like oriental potentates at the head of their armies, ready to do battle. At Question Time the standard practice is for the Leader of the Opposition to rise to his or her feet, to approach the dispatch box, ask a question and then sit down. Next, the Prime Minister rises and approaches the dispatch box. He or she then answers the question (or, more typically, doesn't answer the question) and sits down. The rules of the house entitle the Leader of the Opposition to ask three questions altogether.

The way that the Prime Minister and the Leader of the Opposition position themselves at the dispatch boxes reflects the temperature of their political exchange. When the exchange is reassuringly polite, each tends to face the other directly while standing at their dispatch box. However, when the debate gets heated, there's a marked tendency for the Prime Minister and the Leader of the Opposition to orient their bodies away from each other. This is "flanking," and it's found throughout the animal world. As we've seen, when dogs meet in the park for the first time, they usually approach each other side-on, presenting their vulnerable flanks to each other in order to signal that they don't intend to attack. It's exactly the same in the House of Commons. By orienting their bodies away from each other, the Prime Minister and the Leader of the Opposition may appear to be directing their remarks toward their supporters who are seated behind them. In fact they are instinctively exposing the undefended sides of their body in order to show that they have no intention of getting into a physical fight—just like dogs behave when they meet in the park.

Baby-kissing Tells

Elections are a time for politicians to run around kissing babies. Sometimes it seems like "open season"—wherever you look politicians are lifting babies up, hugging them and planting their lips on their poor unsuspecting cheeks. It's generally assumed that politicians kiss babies because they want people to think that they're healthy, nurturing, loving individuals. In fact, baby-kissing is nothing of the sort—it's merely a way for politicians to defend themselves against attack. For example, when a dominant baboon is chasing a subordinate baboon it's not uncommon for the retreating baboon to pick up an infant baboon and to use it as a shield. This has the immediate effect of "cutting off" the dominant baboon's aggression. It works because baboons, like humans, are programmed not to hurt babies. So when a politician picks up a baby and holds it aloft, they're not showing how much they love babies—they're actually using the baby to "cut off" the aggression that they unconsciously feel the electorate harbours toward them.[5] In other words, the politician isn't saying "Look how much I love babies. Aren't I a caring person?" Instead they're effectively saying "Look, I'm holding a baby. Don't attack me! You might accidentally injure the baby!"

In 2023, George Santos, the disgraced former member of the US House of Representatives, who at the time had been indicted on twenty-three Federal charges, appeared in the halls of Congress, mysteriously clutching a two-month-old baby. This caused something of a stir because, as far as most people knew, Santos hadn't fathered or adopted a baby. As he was walking through the corridors, Santos was approached by an activist, and he got into a heated exchange, shouting "And the next time you try to accost me with a child in my hand … I want him out of here!" This outburst provides a further clue to what was actually happening here. Santos was using the baby as a protective shield, a means of deflecting the mounting aggression toward him, and he had no hesitation in pointing out that this meant he was now off limits.

Some politicians don't carry or kiss babies, presumably because they don't feel threatened or because they don't feel the need to enlist the kind of protection that a baby affords. The British Prime Minister Margaret Thatcher was one of these—in fact it's very difficult to find a photograph of her kissing, let alone holding, a baby. There was a famous occasion, however, when she was visiting a farm and chose to lift up a baby cow. History does not recall whether she actually kissed the calf, or if she did, where she planted the kiss. President Lyndon B. Johnson, it seems, also preferred to pick up animals rather than babies. He once grabbed his pet beagle by the ears and lifted the unfortunate dog off the ground. The dog didn't seem terribly concerned, but animal lovers everywhere were incensed. Instead of making LBJ look endearing, it had the opposite effect, and it wasn't long after this event that his popularity went into decline.

Adulation Tells

Another way politicians can deflect aggression is by making themselves appear popular and adorable. This works on the simple psychological principle that we are more likely to feel positively disposed toward someone if they're popular. Their true qualities aren't that important—what actually shapes our feelings and makes us want to associate with someone is the fact that other people like or admire that person. It's exactly the same with politicians—the more we see them being applauded or adored, the higher they rise in our estimation. Politicians understand this process, and that's one of the reasons why they go to such lengths to surround themselves with admirers.

Basically politicians have three categories of admirers: the general public, the party faithful and their adoring spouse. The most convincing demonstrations of public adulation occur when a politician moves through a crowd of the party faithful who are clamouring to touch them. The more eagerly people reach out, the faster the politician moves through the crowd and the more they appear to enjoy the experience, the more irresistible, even god-like, the politician appears to be. This kind of adulation is essential to politicians and it can be achieved in several ways. As the sociologist Max Atkinson points out in *Our Masters' Voices*, politicians use a fascinating range of strategies to elicit applause from an audience.[6] One trick is to use "contrasting pairs," where an undesirable option, for example, is compared to a highly favourable outcome. Another is the "three-part list," which conveniently provides the audience with clues about when to start applauding. The way that politicians control applause is also critical. For example, a politician who tags a remark onto the end of a punch line once the applause has begun is likely to kill off the applause. On the other hand, politicians who choose their moment carefully, and who use their hands to dampen the applause, are likely to give the impression that they're both modest *and* in control. Ideally, of course, a politician should only attempt to discourage applause when it already shows signs of ending.

In the United States it's traditionally been assumed that the task of the First Lady is to stand by her man. For example, Bess Truman, the wife of President Truman, believed that her role in life was to "sit beside her husband, be silent, and be sure that his hat is straight." In fact the main responsibility of the First Lady is to elevate the President in the eyes of other people by appearing attentive and impressed. Nancy Reagan played the "adoring wife" role to perfection. Michelle Obama also did a fine job of elevating her husband, while at the same time creating the impression that she and Obama were a winning team. During his time in the White House, Trump was less fortunate. Watching him and his wife, one got the distinct impression that Melania was doing her level best but that she was struggling to come across as a fully supportive wife. There were times, in fact, when she avoided holding Trump's hand in public, and on one occasion, when he reached out to her, she actually swatted his hand away.

There are also instances when the tables are turned, and presidents or prime ministers show how much they adore their wives. However, these occasions are rare, and they're often ironic. When John F. Kennedy and the First Lady made a state visit to France in 1961, Jackie was at the height of her popularity. At a state banquet JFK jokingly remarked that he would be remembered as the man who accompanied Jackie Kennedy to Paris. Psychologists have found that men who are associated with attractive women gain an enormous amount of admiration from other men. By drawing attention to Jackie, and being ironic, JFK was only doing himself a favour.

Most of the adulation aimed at politicians comes from people who can be seen or heard. There are, however, cases where adoring members of the public remain out of sight. If you'd watched Ronald Reagan or Bill Clinton when they were in office, you'd have noticed that they often identified individuals in the crowd. Reagan, for example, would sometimes nudge Nancy, point to someone out of view, wave and give them a huge smile. Some of these people, one suspects, did not actually exist—they were "phantom friends" whom Reagan would pretend to wave at in order to make himself look amiable and popular. This suspicion is reinforced by the fact that Reagan had very bad eyesight, which made it difficult for him to pick out individuals at a distance. Other politicians since have also used variants of this technique. While she was running for president, Hillary Clinton seemed to take great pleasure in singling out certain supporters in the audience, pointing at them, waving and giving them a big, beaming smile. Donald Trump too has frequently addressed specific members of his audience during his rallies. By picking out individuals in the crowd, whether real or fictitious, politicians are trying to show that they're not remote or standoffish, and that making personal connections is really important to them.

Transferred Tells

When a politician is addressing a crowd of supporters, and they're accompanied by their spouse, it's always worth taking a careful look at the spouse rather than the politician for clues as to how the politician is faring. When a politician is riding high, they invariably look confident and upbeat, and their spouse tends to look buoyant too, with both of them appearing to be on the same emotional page, as it were. However, even when a politician is doing badly—for example, their poll ratings have slumped—they're likely to mask any concerns they may have about their political future and put on a brave face. In fact, some politicians are so good at acting the part, that it can be quite difficult to figure out whether they're genuinely upbeat or merely putting on a show. The pressure on politicians to pretend arises from the fact that they're so often "on stage," being constantly scrutinized for signs of doubt, indecision or dejection by their friends, enemies and the public. Although a politician's spouse may also be a focus of interest, they frequently feel, quite understandably, that the spotlight isn't really on them and that they don't therefore need to put on a show of confidence if they don't feel that way. Public events where a politician is accompanied by their spouse often provide revealing illustrations of the way that tells can be "transferred" from one person to another. When the politician is, say, feeling depressed about their future prospects but managing to mask their emotions, it's quite common for their spouse, who has less pressure on them to perform, to come across looking depressed themselves. Here, without any awareness of what they're doing, the spouse will actually be channelling and exposing the feelings that that the politician is going to such lengths to conceal.

Offensive Tells

When politicians are not defending themselves against attack, they're usually attacking other people. Their aggressive motives are sometimes concealed in their iconic hand gestures or made explicit in their verbal insults. There are five aggressive actions that politicians mimic when they're feeling aggressive, and each is associated with a different group of hand postures:

1. **Punching**. When politicians want to make an emphatic point they frequently form their hand into a fist and use it like a club to beat time to what they're saying. Sometimes the closed fist is raised in the air as a salute, at

other times it may be slammed down on the lectern as a way of emphasizing a key point, or out of anger or frustration. In its role as a club, the aggressive implications of the fist are obvious—it is being used, symbolically, to crush whatever the speaker feels needs to be destroyed. There are occasions when the hands are used to grab an object that could serve as a symbolic weapon. For example, when Nikita Khrushchev addressed the United Nations in 1960, he got so cross that he took off his shoe and banged it on the lectern!

2. **Prodding**. Politicians often use an extended forefinger to make their point or to issue a warning. Sometimes the finger is raised in the air, didactically. At other times it may be used like a dagger or a sword, thrusting downward or in the direction of the audience or an imaginary adversary.

3. **Gripping**. In order to harm someone it's sometimes necessary to grab hold of them first. When they are making political speeches, politicians often reveal their aggressive feelings toward others by grabbing hold of imaginary people or issues and then shaking or squeezing them.

4. **Scratching**. The fingernails provide a primitive means of tearing into other people's flesh. Women sometimes threaten other people, either seriously or playfully, by baring their fingernails. There's a very fine divide between grabbing an imaginary friend and threatening them with one's fingernails—it all comes down to a slight inward curl of the fingers that lines the fingernails up for attack.

5. **Threatening**. When politicians are speaking, they sometimes present the backs of their hands to the people they're addressing. This may look like a self-protective gesture, but it's actually a *knuckles display*—a means of showing the hard, potentially offensive parts of their hands, rather than the soft and kindly palms.

The knuckles display. At first glance it looks like Barack Obama is shielding himself with his hands, but this is actually a dominance and potentially threatening display because he's showing other people his knuckles—the hard, manly features of his hands.

6. **Chopping.** As the martial arts demonstrate, the outer edge of the hand can be used to chop and injure other people. Politicians who want to cut through an issue often use a downward chopping motion of the hand. The British Labour politician Tony Benn did this. John Major also used this gesture when he was British prime minister: when talking about a sensitive issue he would bring his hand down and to the side in a cutting motion to show that he wished to sweep issues and problems away. Major had been a keen cricketer—it's possible therefore that what appeared to be a dismissive, sweeping action of the hand was really a symbolic cricketing stroke that he used to knock other people's ideas all the way to the boundary.

Although Major was a consummate politician, he disliked the rough-and-tumble of parliamentary Question Time, especially when he was prime minister. This was evident from the "flight response" that he exhibited at the dispatch box. Whenever he rose to answer a question, he would place his notebook on the dispatch box, and then address the house. But a fraction of a second before he'd completed his statement, he would begin to make tiny preparatory movements, like moving his feet or rearranging his notebook. Sometimes, as he was finishing his statement, he would give the dispatch box a tiny push to propel himself backward. His barely concealed eagerness to return to his seat showed that he was never entirely comfortable with the cut-and-thrust of Question Time.

Insulting Tells

Party politics is very much like primitive warfare. A set-piece battle between two tribes in New Guinea, for example, often begins with the two warring parties taking up positions on nearby hills, making sure that they're far enough apart to avoid each other's missiles but close enough to be heard by the other side. From their secure vantage points the warriors then shout boasts and insults at each other. After a while, they descend into the valley, a skirmish takes place, someone is wounded, and the two armies return to their villages to lick their wounds and to talk endlessly about their courageous exploits during the campaign.

Talk, it turns out, is an important part of primitive warfare. The same is true of politics. In both cases the opposing factions spend a lot of time boasting about themselves and their glorious achievements, and slagging off the other side. Boasts and insults are essential to politics because they provide parties and politicians with a means of enhancing their own reputation and self-esteem, while dismantling that of the opposition. Apart from undermining people, insults also serve other valuable psychological functions. One is to enrage the person who's under attack to the point where they engage in a hasty and ill-considered response that makes them look even more ridiculous. Another function is to increase one's own reputation as the originator of well-aimed, amusing and destructive portrayals of other people.

Political insults fall into several categories:

Party Insults. This category of insults is aimed at the opposing party, rather than at individual politicians in that party. Typically they draw attention to the incompetence of the other party, like Winston Churchill's famous remark about the British Labour Party: "They are not fit to manage a whelk stall." Harold Macmillan's damning dismissal of the Liberal Party also falls into this category: "As usual the Liberals offer a mixture of sound and original ideas. Unfortunately none of the sound ideas are original and none of the original ideas are sound."

Cold Insults. The purpose of these insults is to make someone appear cold and unemotional. Referring to Robert Peel, Benjamin Disraeli said: "The Right Honourable gentleman is reminiscent of a poker. The only difference is that a poker gives off the occasional signs of warmth."

Emasculating Insults. These are designed to undermine someone's masculinity. Prime Minister Lloyd George, for example, once said of Herbert Samuel, the Liberal politician, "When they circumcised Herbert Samuel they threw away the wrong bit."

Unqualified Insults. These insults create the impression that the person does not have the necessary qualifications to do the job. Winston Churchill, for example, once described Clement Attlee as "a modest man who has much to be modest about."

Anthropomorphic Insults. Here the person being insulted is compared to an animal so as to make him or her appear beastly or ineffectual. Picking on him once again, Churchill described Clement Attlee as "a sheep in sheep's clothing." On the same ovine theme, Denis Healey once said of Sir Geoffrey

Howe: "Being attacked by him is like being savaged by a dead sheep."

Unprincipled Insults. Here the target of the insult is represented as someone who pretends to have principles but in fact doesn't have any at all. Adlai Stevenson, for example, described Richard Nixon as "the kind of politician who would cut down a redwood tree and then mount the stump to make a speech for conservation."

Phony Insults. These insults draw attention to the deceitful and phony aspects of someone's character. Gerald Ford, for example, once said "Ronald Reagan doesn't dye his hair; he's just prematurely orange."

Stupidity Insults. Here the person is represented as unintelligent. Lyndon Baines Johnson's famous remark about Gerald Ford is a good example: "He is so dumb he can't fart and chew gum at the same time."

Insults are the cruise missiles of political weaponry. If the target is right and they're carefully aimed, they can have a devastating effect on how a politician is perceived. In some cases the damage can be permanent. The British now find it extremely difficult to talk about Geoffrey Howe without referring to dead sheep, while in America it's almost impossible to have a conversation about Gerald Ford without someone mentioning chewing gum or farting.

Interview Tells

Political interviews are supposed to differ from ordinary conversations in several ways: Typically the interviewer should make the first move, set the agenda, ask the questions, and have the last word. The politician, on the other hand, is expected to follow the interviewer's lead, to answer the questions without waffling, and not to ask the interviewer

questions unless clarification is needed. This is the way political interviews are supposed to be conducted. In practice, however, they often
turn out to be disturbingly different.

Interviewers ask politicians two types of question: "closed questions," which require a "yes" or "no" answer, and "open questions,"
which allow the politician to give an answer without saying "yes" or "no."
Regardless of which type of question they pose, interviewers are always
trying to get politicians to give "direct" answers—that is, responses that
address the question, rather than "indirect" answers that don't address
the question at all. In the early 1990s, Sandra Harris studied political
interviews in Britain and discovered that "direct" answers featured in
only 40 percent of politicians' responses.[7] In other words, 60 percent of
their responses failed to address the interviewers' questions.

This tendency to dodge the question was most marked with closed
questions, which are by far the most common type of question that
interviewers put to politicians. Here Harris found that only 20 percent of closed questions elicited either a "yes" or "no" answer. When
she compared political interviews with other types of interview she
found that the percentages of indirect answers were much lower in
other types of interview, ranging from 4 percent for medical interviews
to 15 percent for magistrates' interviews—compared with 60 percent
for politicians! The fact that politicians don't provide straight answers
to straight questions is a major reason why the public regards them as
evasive. It's also why they're seen as underhanded and slimy. Research
by Peter Bull and his colleagues at York University shows that politicians dodge questions in several ways, including the following:[8]

Making a Political Point. In the vast majority of cases where
politicians fail to answer the question, it's because they're
using the opportunity to make a political point that's not directly relevant to the question. This suggests that politicians
and interviewers see political interviews quite differently—
while the interviewer is trying to get the politician to answer
the question, the politician is using the question as a soapbox
from which to make their views known to the public. It also

shows how politicians work to their own agenda, deciding in advance what they're going to say in an interview, regardless of what questions they're asked.

Going On the Attack. This is the next most common response. Politicians often dislike the questions they're asked. Sometimes it's because they feel the question is biased or intended to make them look silly; at other times it's because they think the question is factually incorrect or just plain objectionable. Faced with an annoying question, politicians can either play by the rules and offer something that sounds like an answer, or else they can attack the question and say what they dislike about it. Attacking the question is actually a fairly common response and it offers two clear advantages: it puts the spotlight back on the interviewer, and it helps to unnerve the interviewer and discourage them from asking difficult questions later on. It's even more intimidating when the politician attacks the interviewer by suggesting that they're uninformed, biased or unreasonable. Politicians differ in their preferences for these two strategies, with some preferring to attack the interviewer and others preferring to attack the question. While he was in office, Donald Trump perfected the art of doing both. When he wasn't berating journalists who'd asked awkward questions for being "disgraceful," "sleazy," "fake," "rude" and "terrible" or for talking too loudly, he was attacking the question itself, either for being "nasty," "racist," "snarky" or "stupid." During the COVID-19 crisis, Peter Alexander, the NBC correspondent, asked Trump, "What do you say to Americans who are watching right now, who are scared?" Trump shot back, "I say that you're a terrible reporter, that's what I say. I think it's a very nasty question and I think it's a very bad signal that you're putting out to the American people." In one fell swoop, and without addressing the question, Trump assailed both the questioner and the question.

Giving Half an Answer. The next most common way of dodging a question is to offer an incomplete answer. This happens when a politician responds to a question that has several parts, or deals with only part of a question, or starts to answer the question but gets distracted and fails to provide a full answer.

Refusing to Answer. Politicians often refuse to answer questions when it's clearly legitimate for them not to give an answer—for example, when they're asked to divulge confidential information or to make predictions. In these cases they can get away by appealing to a higher principle, such as the need to keep a secret or to be discreet.

Ignoring the Question. This often happens when the interviewer interrupts the politician to ask another question. Instead of answering the new question, the politician simply continues to answer the original question, behaving as if the new question had never been asked.

Repeating the Answer. Politicians may refuse to answer a question, insisting that they have already answered it. This also conveys other messages—it suggests, for example, that the politician is fully aware of what's happening, and that he or she is not prepared to play along with the interviewer. There are, however, cases where the politician will use the same form of words in response to apparently different questions. This is intended to make the politician look confident, and the interviewer incompetent.

There are several reasons why politicians' answers are equivocal and vague. For a start, using imprecise language allows politicians to give answers that don't offend anybody. When the electorate is divided on a controversial issue it's obviously not in the politician's interests to give an answer that's likely to alienate large numbers of people—it's far better to say nothing on the subject, while appearing to voice an opinion, or to answer a different question altogether.

Another reason why politicians equivocate so much is that they don't like being constrained or bossed about by interviewers. When she was British prime minister, Margaret Thatcher was extremely evasive in her answers during political interviews, partly, one suspects, because she wanted to show that she was her own person, and that she was quite capable of setting the agenda for the interview. However, when it came to closed questions—that is, questions that require a "yes" or "no" answer—she was often prepared to give direct answers. This highlights how Margaret Thatcher liked to play the dominant role—on open questions she would equivocate in order to show who was boss, while on closed questions she would give direct answers to show that she was supremely confident and wasn't worried about alienating people who disagreed with her.[9]

In TV interviews the spotlight is very much on the politician. After all, it's the politician who does most of the talking and who's on the screen most of the time. Because interviewers play a supporting role, it's natural to assume that they have less responsibility for what happens during the interview, or that the interplay between interviewer and politician isn't important. However, this interplay *is* extremely important. It was very evident in the interviews that took place when Margaret Thatcher was in power. It was not unusual, for example, for interviewers to interrupt Margaret Thatcher—in fact she was interrupted more often than any of the other political leaders at the time. At first it was assumed that this might have had something to do with the fact that she was a woman, while all the interviewers and other political leaders were men. This would have been consistent with the general finding that men interrupt women more often than they do other men, and more often than women interrupt men or other women. It was even suggested that Margaret Thatcher was being interrupted more often because she was inadvertently giving off more "turn-yielding" signals, which misled interviewers into thinking that she was about to stop talking.[10]

The fact that Margaret Thatcher tended to give long, rambling answers may also explain why she was interrupted so often; as she began to drift away from the question, interviewers would ask another question in order to try to bring her back to their agenda. What's interesting about these cases of interruption is that Margaret Thatcher hardly ever gave up the floor—when she was interrupted by the interviewer she simply kept on talking as though nothing had happened. This reinforced her image as a tough politician and exasperated the interviewers who had to deal with her.

In the early days of television, political interviews were modelled on the affable exchanges that took place in gentlemen's clubs. In 1951, for example, when Leslie Mitchell interviewed British Prime Minister Anthony Eden, he began by saying, "Well now, Mr. Eden, with your very considerable experience in foreign affairs, it's quite obvious that I should start by asking you something about the international situation today—or perhaps you would prefer to talk about home? Which is it to be?" On that occasion Eden chose to talk about home affairs.

Political interviews in Britain remained obsequious until the arrival of Reginald Bosanquet, who is credited with producing the first aggressive interruption of a British politician, although by today's standards it was a model of reticence. It happened in 1957 when Bosanquet interviewed Harold Macmillan. "Sir," he interjected, "as time is short could we question you on a domestic matter which I think is uppermost in our minds at the moment?" "If you must," replied Macmillan.

Gone are the days when interviewers apologize for interrupting or allow politicians to set the agenda for the interview. Nowadays interviewers have much more power, and they're quite prepared to be combative. Politicians are now understandably nervous about interviewers, especially when, like the BBC's Jeremy Paxman, they're reputed to eat politicians for breakfast. Paxman is best remembered for a television interview in which he asked Michael Howard, then Home Secretary, whether he had threatened to overrule the director of the Prison Service. The Home Secretary gave an evasive answer, so Paxman kept repeating the same question until he eventually got a satisfactory answer—having, by that stage, posed the same question a total of fourteen times!

A remarkably similar event took place in the Canadian Parliament in 2017, when Justin Trudeau was repeatedly asked how many times he had been in communication with the Ethics Commissioner, following concerns about a holiday he'd spent in the Bahamas as a guest of the Aga Khan. During the parliamentary session, opposition MPs posed the same question to him no fewer than eighteen times, but each time Trudeau managed to politely dodge the question by not answering it. Trudeau's determination to evade the question might very well have been inspired by watching recordings of his father, Prime Minster Pierre Trudeau, being waylaid and grilled by two journalists, back in 1970. This particular exchange (sometimes referred to as "the scrum") is very revealing, not only because of the journalists' persistence but also because, at several points, Trudeau *père* succeeded in turning the tables, forcing the journalists to answer *his* equally awkward questions. Ever the consummate politician, Pierre Trudeau came across as confident and unfazed, but every now and then he showed signs of being unsettled, particularly in his mouth movements. He also resorted to his famous shrug, which on this particular occasion seemed intended to shrug off the difficult questions he was being asked. Pierre Trudeau was in fact known as a shrugger—so much so that when Walter Stewart penned a book about him, he titled it *The Shrug*.

For a combative interview to take place it's necessary for both parties to play by the rules. There are occasions when both parties get hot under the collar—the altercation in 1988 between Vice President George Bush and Dan Rather, the CBS anchor, over the Iran–Contra affair is one example—and there are times when the interviewee decides that enough is enough and leaves.[11] Henry Kissinger, for example, walked out on Jeremy Paxman when Paxman asked him, quite rightly, whether he felt like a fraud accepting the Nobel Peace Prize.

Because interviewers now potentially wield more power than politicians, politicians need to find ways of ensuring that interviewers don't give them a tough time. One way to do this is for politicians to stamp their authority on the interview by showing that they are not prepared to be interrupted. Another is to be emphatic about their opinions. George W. Bush, for example, frequently uses the expression "make no mistake about it" to press home his point of view. One of his signature tells was a "micro-nod," a barely perceptible dip of the head, which he tagged onto the end of a statement, like a corporeal full stop—as if to say, "There you are, I've told you now. There's nothing more to be said on the subject!"

Another option available to politicians is to intimidate the interviewer. This can be done by undermining the interviewer, attacking the question, and suggesting that the interviewer is misinformed or biased—in short, by breaking the interviewer's rhythm and undermining their confidence. One way to do this is by producing lots of "negative back-channel signals." These are the discouraging signals that people use when they're in the listener role—things like puzzled expressions, displays of disbelief, gaze aversion and preparatory speech movements. Listeners use these signals to indicate that the speaker isn't making sense, that they don't agree, and that they'd like to take over the speaker role as soon as possible. They are the opposite of "back-channel signals." Back-channel signals are the encouraging signals—such as nods and *uh-huh* sounds—that listeners produce when they want to show the speaker that they understand and agree with what they're saying, and that they have no intention of taking over the speaker role in the conversation. When George W. Bush was being asked awkward questions, he often resorted to negative back-channel signals in order to throw the interviewer off balance. He did this by looking around, by smiling artificially, and by giving the impression that he was about to start speaking. Negative back-channel can certainly help politicians to keep difficult interviewers at bay. After all, it's what interviewers use when they want to give politicians a difficult time.

Because politics relies so heavily on appearances, subterfuge and pretense, it's a source of endless fascination to those who're interested in understanding human behaviour. Since politicians spend so much time pretending to be something they're not, there's a much greater chance that they will inadvertently reveal their true feelings, or their real intentions, in what they do. The high drama of politics, the way that politicians abandon their colleagues, cut secret deals, switch allegiances, create smokescreens, cover their backsides, deflect blame and take credit where it isn't due—all these things make the appearance of tells all the more likely.

7. Royal Tells

On a state visit to Brazil, the Duke of Edinburgh is reputed to have asked a Brazilian admiral whether the glittering display of medals on his chest was won on the artificial lake outside the capital, Brasilia. "Yes, sir," replied the admiral, "not by marriage." Royalty is of course not based on achievement—it's based on parentage and marriage. Like celebrities, the royals are constantly in the limelight, but while celebrities need to work hard to stay there, the royals—as we're constantly being reminded—remain famous regardless of what they do.

People who want to retain a position of dominance often need to remind others how important they are—they need to adopt an imposing demeanour, insist on their point of view, and see off anyone who might try to challenge their position. That's not the case with royalty. Because their position derives from who they are rather than what they do, they don't need to behave assertively. Because they're secure in their position, and because people are always deferring to them, they can actually afford to send out affiliative and friendly signals. In some cases they may even try to endear themselves to other people by behaving submissively.

Friendly Tells

People often feel awkward and self-conscious when they meet royalty—they get flustered, tongue-tied and don't know what to say. Even powerful individuals who run large corporations can be reduced to gibbering, inarticulate idiots when they meet members of the royal family. To counter this effect, and to put people at ease, the royals make a habit of producing friendly signals—they smile, make jokes and are attentive to what people have to say. This is the modern face of royalty. However, if you watch some of the early film footage of the British royal family you won't find much smiling. Although George V, for example, is reputed to have had a good sense of humour, he didn't show it in public. Most of the images we have of him are rather severe. When this was pointed out to him he replied, "We sailors never smile on duty." His first son, Edward, Prince of Wales, was renowned as a practical joker, although this side of his character became less evident after he succeeded to the throne as Edward VIII, and it seemed to disappear altogether after his abdication. George VI, who succeeded his brother Edward, projected an image of someone who was serious and unfunny. He seldom smiled in public, preferring to adopt the dutiful demeanour of his father, George V.

The person largely responsible for the shift to a more engaging style of royal behaviour was Queen Elizabeth, the Queen Mother. During the blitz in late 1940 she made several visits to the East End of London, where she met people and talked to them about the hardships they were experiencing. Those who met her were struck by her friendly informality, and by the way she focused on what they were saying. In his diaries, Harold Nicolson describes the effect she had on people at the time:

> ... when the car stops, the Queen nips out into the snow and goes straight into the middle of the crowd and starts talking to them. For a moment or two they just gaze and gape in amazement. But then they all start talking at once. "Hi! Your Majesty! Look here!" She has that quality of making everybody feel that they and they alone are being spoken to. It is, I think, because she has very large eyes which she opens very wide and turns straight upon one.[1]

The accessibility of the monarchy was given a further boost in 1970 when Queen Elizabeth II, who was on an official visit to Australia, performed the first royal "walkabout" by strolling along a cordoned crowd and meeting people who had come to wave at her as she drove by. In those days the walkabout offered people an opportunity to shake hands with the Queen and, very occasionally, a chance to exchange a few words with her. Over the last forty years or so, the royal walkabout has become even more informal, with the late Queen and the Duke of Edinburgh making a point of engaging people in conversation. Whenever Charles, Anne, William, Harry and their spouses moved down a line of well-wishers, there was often even more joking, smiling and laughter.

Humour plays a major role, both in the public's perception of the monarchy and the monarchy's perception of itself. Robert Lacey relates an incident when the late Queen and Prince Philip were driving down a muddy lane near Sandringham, and the vehicle splashed mud all over a woman walking down the lane.[2] The woman shouted something, and the Queen called back to her, "I quite agree with you, madam." "Hmmm," said Philip, "what did she say, darling?" The Queen replied, "She said, 'Bastards!'" When he was a young man, the Duke of Edinburgh was known for his pranks, and the late Queen, like her mother before her, had a reputation for being a gifted mimic. Anne has a bluff, irreverent sense of humour, while Charles does a good line in wry self-effacement—or at least he did, before he ascended to the throne. Humour also lubricates the royal family's relationship with the public. For example, even today, if you watch Charles shaking hands with members of the public you'll notice that the exchanges are often interspersed with laughter, some of it provoked by his amusing remarks, some of it in response to what other people are saying.

These good-humoured exchanges carry important messages because they show that Charles doesn't always stand on ceremony, and that he possesses the quality that the British value more than any other—a sense of humour. Robert Provine from the University of Maryland has discovered that laughter often functions as a submissive signal—in other words, that subordinate individuals use laughter to appease dominant individuals, while dominant individuals try to get people to laugh so that they can retain the upper hand.[3] This was very evident before Charles became king—he would move through a crowd, cracking the occasional joke, ostensibly to make everyone feel relaxed but really so that he could elicit appeasing peals of laughter. Sometimes one of the crowd would make a wisecrack that got Charles laughing. The fact that this happened didn't undermine the idea that laughter is about appeasement—it just showed that, every now and then, Charles was happy to briefly play the role of being submissive.

One of Charles's signature tells is his habit of raising his eyebrows. He uses this gesture in conversation, usually when he's talking to someone he doesn't know well, and when he wants to show that he's being attentive. Charles's eyebrow-lift is invariably accompanied by a very slight widening of the eyes, which shows that he's interested in what the other person is saying. The degree of eye-widening is critical, because if he raised his eyebrows without opening his eyes, or slightly narrowing them, it would suggest that he was being haughty. Equally, if he were to open them wide it would give the impression that he didn't believe what the other person was saying. As a rule dominant individuals don't raise their eyebrows; if anything, they lower them in order to appear more threatening. By raising his eyebrows, Charles is therefore producing a submissive display. He's trying to appear attentive, but in the process he's unintentionally producing an appeasement signal. This doesn't necessarily mean that Charles comes across as being submissive—because his identity depends on his royal status he can afford to produce the occasional appeasement display without appearing submissive.

Distance Tells

The pomp and circumstance surrounding the monarchy is designed to give it a sense of mystery and detachment, and to underline the fact that members of the royal family are very different from the rest of us. Gravity and formality are essential features of royalty because they separate the monarchy from its subjects. The problem, of course, is that formality comes into conflict with accessibility, making it difficult for a sovereign to inspire both respect and affection. The competing demands on monarchs have been recognized for a long time. In *The Book of the Courtier*, published in 1528, Baldassare Castiglione wrote about the difficulty that the ruler encounters when he tries to combine mildness and fierceness.[4] Writing in 1641, Sir Robert Naunton described how Queen Elizabeth I had "the stile to winne the hearts of the people." She did this by "coupling mildnesse with majesty"—the first she had inherited from her mother, the second from her father.[5] Nowadays royalty still has to contend with the competing demands of appearing regal and affable. One without the other doesn't work. It's essential that royals appear elevated but not out of reach, and that they come across as friendly without being overly familiar.

One way that the monarchy retains its distance is through its demeanour. Members of the royal family usually remain physically inaccessible and contact with them tends therefore to be on their own terms. During walkabouts it's the members of the royal family who decide whom they're going to greet. They're also the ones who initiate the greetings by extending their hand and who bring the exchange to an end, often again with a handshake. Symbolic distance is also reflected by physical distance, with the monarch standing within arm's range but not too close to the other person.

Symbolic distance is sometimes conveyed by language—for example, the way that members of the royal family might refer to *we* or *one* when they mean *I* or *me*. The use of *we* by monarchs has a long tradition—it derives from the notion of the ruler as more than a single individual, which is said to go back to the time when the Roman Empire was split in two, with one Emperor in Rome and another in Constantinople. Queen Victoria is reputed to have said "We are not amused" to show that she, herself, was not impressed. This is misleading on two counts. Firstly, there is no record that she ever used this expression. Secondly, there is lots of evidence that Queen Victoria was frequently amused—her journals repeatedly include the phrase "I was very much amused," and it's known that she was given to uncontrollable attacks of the giggles.[7] But royal use of the term *we* isn't always straightforward. Edward VIII, for example, often used the term in correspondence with his beloved Wallis Simpson. In one letter he wrote, "not anybody or anything can separate WE . . . God bless WE." [8] The reference here was not to himself, but to both of them, where "WE" was obtained by combining the first letters of Wallis and Edward.

Members of the royal family are more likely to use the pronoun *one* when referring to themselves. Years ago, when he was asked about the prospect of becoming King, Charles replied, "I didn't wake up in my pram one day and say 'Yippee . . .' you know. But I think it just dawns on you, slowly, that people are interested in one." The use of *one* often replaces the first person with the third person singular, making it sound as if the speaker is talking about someone else instead of themselves. This draws attention away from the speaker and shifts it toward their role. When someone refers to themselves as *one* it reduces their individuality. But most crucial of all, it creates a distance between the speaker and the person who's being addressed because it treats the speaker as if he or she isn't actually present.

Hand Tells

Symbolic distance is also conveyed by posture and gesture. If you watch members of the royal family, you'll notice that they have distinctive ways of holding their hands:

The Handclasp. The late Queen had several hand postures, but her favourite seemed to be the "handclasp," where the palm of one hand was placed in the palm of the other—in her case the left hand usually resting on top of the right. The Queen also employed a related posture, where several of the fingers of one hand clasped one of the fingers of the other hand. In both of these postures the hands were linked in front of the body, and in most cases they were positioned demurely on the lap. Both these postures were essentially defensive; because the hands were occupied, they also appeared to be unthreatening.

The Handbag. Like many women of her generation, the late Queen often walked around with her handbag suspended from her arm. But unlike that of other women, hers was largely decorative. It wasn't stuffed full of make-up, parking tickets and money, because someone else carried things for her. The

Queen did occasionally use her handbag to send cryptic signals—it was known, for example, that when she reached for her handbag, it was a signal to her assistants that she was about to move on to something else.

The Crane Posture. The Duke of Edinburgh, the late Queen's husband, had a habit of walking around with his hands clasped behind his back. This is the "crane posture," and it was widely recognized as one of the Duke's trademark tells. He also performed the "half crane" by placing his left hand behind his back when he was shaking hands. The act of placing the hands behind one's back is a dominant gesture because it exposes the body and leaves it unprotected from frontal attack. It's the body's way of saying "Look at me. I'm so confident that nobody will attack me that I'm prepared to keep my hands behind my back, where they're not in a position to defend me." As far as we can tell, the Duke of Edinburgh only adopted the crane posture after the Queen's coronation; prior to that he preferred to clasp his hands in front of him. One of the things that attracted the Duke to this posture was the fact that it made him look confident. The other is that it made him look very different from the Queen—because while her hands were neatly folded on her lap, his were tucked away behind him. So strong was the Duke of Edinburgh's need to distinguish himself, that if the crane posture hadn't existed, he would have needed to invent it.

The Pouch Posture. In order to ensure that he wasn't confused with his parents while they were alive, Charles initially avoided both the handclasp and the crane. Instead of clasping his hands in front or behind him, he developed a habit of slipping his left hand into his jacket pocket. This is the "pouch posture," and in Charles's case it consists of several discrete elements. First there's the act of turning up the flap, so that the hand can be placed in the jacket pocket; then there's the business of placing the hand in the pocket and leaving it there for a while; alternatively, there's the abbreviated sequence where he fiddles with the flap without placing his hand in the pocket. The pouch posture is clearly motivated by an unconscious desire to conceal the hand—not both hands, mind you, just his left, less dominant hand. When people conceal one or both of their hands it shows that they either want to hide their feelings or that they need to restrain their impulses. When Charles puts his hand in his pocket he sometimes uses his thumb as a "stop," so that while his fingers remain hidden his thumb is still exposed. This, in itself, is interesting because actions that give prominence to the thumbs are "macho" gestures—it's what tough guys do when they tuck their thumbs into their belt or push their hands into their trouser pockets and leave their thumbs outside.

Touching Tells

Touch is often used as a marker of status. The social psychologist Nancy Henley has pointed out that while high-status individuals reserve the right to touch their subordinates, they in turn aren't entitled to touch their superiors. Touch, she suggests, acts as a "status reminder"—the idea being that by observing patterns of touching in a group of people it's possible to work out who has control over whom.[9] We can see this very clearly with royalty. When members of the royal family are doing a walkabout, it's they who initiate the handshake and who therefore grant people permission to touch them. Because of the association between power and touch, there are strict rules against people unilaterally touching the monarch. Apart from shaking hands, nobody is allowed to touch the person of the monarch. When this rule is violated, as it was when the Australian prime minister put his arm around Queen Elizabeth in 1992, it almost caused an international incident.

This tactile attitude of Australians toward royalty goes back a long way. When Edward, the Prince of Wales, visited Australia in 1920, it seemed as though everyone was trying to make contact with him. He recorded the spectacle in his journal:

> The "touching mania," one of the most remarkable phenomena connected with my travels, took the form of a mass impulse to prod some part of the Prince of Wales. Whenever I entered a crowd, it closed around me like an octopus. I can still hear the shrill, excited cry, "I touched him!" If I were out of reach, then a blow on my head with a folded newspaper appeared to satisfy the impulse.[10]

There was a time, during the Middle Ages, when it was widely believed that people who suffered from scrofula, a glandular disease that was called "the King's evil," could be cured by being touched by their monarch. This belief in the "royal touch," as it was called, lasted from the time of Edward the Confessor right up to 1714, when Queen Anne performed the last royal touch by an English monarch.[11] Although people no longer believe in the curative power of the royal touch, there is something very primitive about the desire to touch and be touched by royalty. That's why so many people reach out to shake their hand. In these situations, touch becomes a medium of assimilation—by touching a member of the royal family people feel that they are incorporating some of the royal magic into themselves and connecting themselves to something that's timeless.

The way people touch each other sometimes exposes things about their relationship that they would rather keep hidden. A dramatic case of this occurred in 1953. At the time Princess Margaret was having a secret love affair with Group Captain Peter Townsend, who had been equerry to her father, the King. The secrecy was necessitated by the fact that Margaret was only twenty-two, while Townsend was thirty-eight. To complicate matters further, he was divorced, which meant that a relationship with him was out of bounds. The romance became public knowledge during the coronation. Before the ceremony began, Princess Margaret was waiting in Westminster Great Hall. Townsend was standing nearby. She turned toward him and absentmindedly brushed a piece of fluff from his lapel. It was this tiny gesture—this tell of intimacy—that revealed to the world that Princess Margaret was in love with Peter Townsend.

One of the things that made Princess Margaret's gesture so noticeable was the fact that she belonged to a family that was not given to public displays of affection. Even to this day, the royal family rarely touch other people, except to shake hands, and there's far less physical contact between the family members in public. In fact, if it were a foreign country, psychologists would probably refer to the royal family as a "non-contact culture"—that is, a society where touch is reduced to the bare minimum. For example, back in 1953, when the Queen and the Duke of Edinburgh went on a round-the-world tour of the Commonwealth, they left Charles, who was five years old at the time, in the care of his nanny. When they returned six months later, Charles was taken to the airport to greet his parents. When his parents appeared, they didn't lift Charles up and give him a big hug or a kiss; instead they greeted him with a handshake—in other words, they resorted to a greeting that most people at the time reserved for strangers and acquaintances, but not for children, and certainly not for their own child whom they hadn't seen for half a year!

The low frequency of touch within the royal family is partly due to the fact that its members need to project an image of inaccessibility, even among themselves. It also arises from the heavy schedule of duties that the Queen and the Duke of Edinburgh had to fulfill, and the reduced opportunities they had to be with their children. When Charles was young he would usually only see his mother twice a day—for half an hour in the morning and half an hour in the early evening. The rest of the time he was cared for by nannies.[12]

If there were a scale for measuring royal touch, the late Queen and Prince Philip would probably have been at one end, and Princess Diana at the other. The tactile side of Diana's personality was evident, both in the way that she brought up her children—she was constantly cuddling and touching William and Harry—and the way she related to members of the public. While the established members of the royal family were busy cultivating an image of regal detachment, Diana's instinct was to make contact with individuals. When people were waiting to meet her she would often rush over to greet them. Instead of keeping her distance, she would move into their physical space, creating the impression that she was meeting them on their terms rather than hers. Diana's style in public was one of "immediacy."[13] By getting close to people, being open and receptive, and giving them her undivided attention, she created an atmosphere of informality and warmth that made an indelible impression on those who met her— one that, in many respects, was similar to the feelings that the Queen Mother had aroused during the Second World War.

People who met Diana felt touched by her—all of them figuratively, and some of them literally. When Diana opened a purpose-built AIDS clinic at the Middlesex Hospital in 1987, she was photographed holding hands with a young man who was suffering from AIDS. This image had an enormous impact on people's perceptions of the disease. At the time there was a great deal of prejudice toward AIDS sufferers. By sitting down beside an AIDS patient and holding his hand, Diana completely rejected such prejudice. With no more than a touch, she demonstrated that people with AIDS are no different from any other patients suffering from life-threatening diseases.

It's often said that Diana was adored because of her charity work, because she was vulnerable and because she was so beautiful. All these factors undoubtedly played a part, but the thing that endeared her to the public more than any other was the way she physically touched people. Touch is the most primitive expression of love and friendship. By reaching out to individuals, Diana touched a very deep chord in people.[14] She also showed her feelings—something that the royal family seldom did at the time. While Diana was alive, Charles seemed content to accept the restrictions on outward displays of emotion dictated by royal convention. Diana, on the other hand, vaulted over these restrictions to get to people, and they loved her for it. After Diana's death, Charles became much more tactile in his relationship with William and Harry. He was seen hugging and even kissing them—doing things that Diana did with the boys, but which he himself was seldom exposed to when he was a child.

Charles Tells

When they were together it was always assumed that Diana was the shy one and that Charles was rather composed. It's true that Diana was a shy person. But it's also the case that Charles is given to spells of self-consciousness. This is evident from the range of "displacement activities" that he produces when he's in the public eye. In addition to those elements of the "pouch posture" that we discussed earlier, these include the following:

The cuff-link fiddle. When he appears in public, Charles has a habit of fiddling with his cufflinks, as well as with his tie, lapels and jacket pocket. These displacement activities are designed to give him greater peace of mind.

The Cuff-link Fiddle. Several of Charles's habits consist of *threshold or transition tells*—that is, they occur as he's crossing an invisible boundary from one situation to another. Watch him emerge from a chauffeured car at a gala performance and you'll see how he characteristically draws his hand across his body and reaches for the opposite cuff. This is Charles's "cuff-link fiddle," which he resorts to whenever he's on display and in transition. Although Charles has made the cuff-link fiddle his own, it's very similar to the *anxiety tells* that other people display when they're approaching someone—like crossing their arms over their body, rearranging their clothes or touching their hair. Most people have access to a range of anxiety tells, dropping one in favour of another. But Charles has remained faithful to the cuff-link fiddle since he first discovered it as a young man. His cuff-links have become emotional lightning conductors, a means of dispelling his anxieties and providing him with a sense of security—very similar, in fact, to what psychoanalysts call a "transitional object."

The Tie Tuck. Charles's habit of straightening out his tie is another one of his threshold tells. He usually does this by tucking his tie into his jacket. In fact the action is now so ingrained in him that he will straighten out his tie even when it doesn't need straightening, or when it isn't even there! When he's wearing black tie he sometimes slips his hand under the lapel of his jacket, just as if he were wearing a tie and wanted to straighten it out.

The Finger Clasp. When he's in public, Charles has long had a habit of either holding one hand in the other—usually the left in the right – or, more typically, briefly clasping the finger or thumb of one hand with the fingers of the other hand. These actions seem to be both defensive and self-comforting, momentarily creating a barrier between himself and others, while clasping his hands reassuringly together.

The Finger Point. When Charles' father was in conversation with members of the public, he would frequently intersperse his remarks by pointing things out with his index finger— often directing people's attention to what he was talking about or wished to discuss. Charles appears to have adopted the same habit since he too discovered that manual pointing provides a convenient means of orchestrating conversations.

The Earlobe-rub. Another of Charles's tells is the "earlobe rub," which involves grabbing his earlobe and surreptitiously giving it a quick rub. He does this when he's feeling mildly self-conscious.

The Aside. Charles has a very distinctive way of talking out of the side of his mouth, which he does when he wants to put brackets around what he's saying—it's his way of showing that he's changing, for example, to a more jocular mood. Actors sometimes produce an "aside" as a way of showing that they're dealing with a parenthetical issue or that they're colluding with the audience. That is what Charles is essentially doing when he talks out of the side of his mouth—he's stepping out of his normal role and into a more intimate role that he hopes to share with his audience.

The fact that he exhibits any displacement activity at all is quite revealing. After decades of royal duties we would expect Charles to be fairly immune to the unsettling presence of large crowds. Evidently, he isn't, because whenever he's confronted by lots of people his hand reaches for the security of his tie, his cuff-links or his pocket. Although Charles is very much a man of the world, these little forms of displacement reveal a sensitive and potentially vulnerable side of his character.

Diana Tells

Diana had several quite distinctive mannerisms, most of them associated with shyness. She had a habit, for example, of looking down at the ground when she was talking to people, and she was also given to bouts of blushing. These outward signs began to disappear with age, but her feeling of awkwardness was never far from the surface. There were six facial expressions that Diana made her own:

The Eye-puff. Diana had very large eyes, which she accentuated by adopting an "open-eyes" expression. One of the things that people find irresistible about very young babies is the size of their eyes relative to the rest of their face—their huge eyes serve as "innate releasers," making people feel protective and nurturant. Grown women can appear more vulnerable and elicit similar responses by expanding their eyes. This is what Diana did—she widened her eyes and made people feel that they needed to look after her.

The Spencer Smile. Diana was renowned for her radiant smile. This wasn't an artificial smile—it was the genuine article, the heartfelt smile with all the features of authenticity, like symmetry and activation of the muscles around the eyes.

The Pursed Smile. Diana had an unusual habit of pursing her lips and pulling them to one side while she was smiling. This was in fact a restrained smile, and she used it when she was feeling shy or embarrassed. By restraining her smile in this way she showed that she was amused, but that she felt the need to contain her amusement.

The Dipped Smile. The dipped smile is performed by smiling while the head is lowered and the eyes are looking up. This reproduces the look that the young child gives to grown-ups, where the eyes are looking up at the adult. When Diana adopted this expression it made her appear younger and more vulnerable. As we shall see in the discussion of *sexual tells*, the dipped smile is also a "come-on," and that's why Diana appeared so seductive when she used this smile.

The Head-cant Smile. Occasionally Diana would tilt her head to one side while she was smiling. As we saw earlier, head-canting also gives the impression of vulnerability and submissiveness. By tilting her head to one side Diana made herself appear completely unthreatening.

The Turn-away Smile. This occurred when Diana's head was turned away from the other person while looking at them and smiling. This produces what Charles Darwin called a "hybrid expression," made up of actions that convey two opposing messages: smiling, which signals approach, and turning away, which signals avoidance.[15] The tension between these two messages gives the hybrid expression its irresistible appeal—like a metal alloy, it's stronger than its constituent elements.

When people talk about Diana's smile it's the turn-away smile they usually remember. In many ways this was Diana's signature tell because it encapsulated both her openness and her shyness, and it highlighted her indecision. The turn-away smile is neither one thing nor the other—it's neither an attempt to turn away nor a wholehearted smile. In this respect it's rather like Diana herself—someone who was like everyone else and who shared their sentiments, but someone who also happened to be a member of the royal family.

Wedding Tells

Sadly, when Prince Charles and Lady Diana appeared in front of the cameras to announce their engagement, the signs weren't promising. When they walked across the lawn together, Charles was ahead of Diana and the two of them didn't appear to be in synch. What's more, Charles wasn't modifying his behaviour to synchronize it with Diana's. In fact, if we were to get hold of a still photograph of the two of them walking together on that occasion, and we applied the "cut-out principle" by imagining what it would look like if we removed Diana from the scene, leaving Charles on his own, it wouldn't seem as if anyone was missing!

During their interview with the press, instead of standing beside or reassuringly behind Diana, Charles positioned himself slightly in front of his fiancée. When they were asked if they were in love, Diana responded appropriately, although rather shyly, by saying "Of course." Instead, Charles offered his rash, roundabout and flippant answer: "Whatever love means." What happened next was equally revealing, because when the interviewer came back and said, "Obviously it means they're deeply in love," Charles lowered his eyes and surreptitiously bit his bottom lip. This is a gesture of self-restraint, suggesting that even as he uttered those famous words, Charles knew that he'd said the wrong thing.

During the wedding ceremony, there were other signs of foreboding. For example, as Diana was proceeding down the central aisle of Westminster Abbey on the arm of her father, she turned her head and smiled at people on either side. At one point, however, her expression changed, and it became obvious that she was searching for someone in the congregation. Much later it emerged that the person she was looking for was Charles's former girlfriend, Camilla.

When Diana drew up beside Charles at the altar, he turned, smiled at her and graciously told her how lovely she was looking. But from that point on, he paid Diana very little attention. In fact, it seemed as if Charles's mind was elsewhere, because while he was reciting his vows, Diana watched him intently, but when she was reciting her vows, Charles's eyes were all over the place—down at the ground, up at the ceiling, everywhere except at his bride. Then, while the Archbishop of Canterbury was speaking, Charles discreetly ran his finger under his eyelids, as if he were wiping away imaginary tears. As we've already seen, this eye-wipe gesture is an unconscious distress signal—it's what people do when they're feeling sad, nostalgic or regretful. There's no way of knowing what Charles was thinking at that moment, but we can be fairly sure that something serious was bothering him.

Fast forward a generation to William and Catherine's engagement interview, which couldn't have been more different from that of William's parents. During their interview William and Catherine spent a lot of time looking at each other, checking and involving each other and generally showing that they care. For example, when they were asked a question, Catherine would glance at William, thereby transferring the question to him. William would look at Catherine, start to speak and then look away. While William was speaking, Catherine kept her eyes on him, and moments later he'd steal another glance at her. This constant shuttle of the eyes back and forth was an important clue to their relationship—it showed that they were thinking about each other.

There was also synchrony in their patterns of gaze. Catherine would look at William, and then moments later—right on cue—he'd look at her, and this sort of thing happened repeatedly, with each of them initiating the sequence. When taking turns to answer a question, William and Catherine frequently produced "smooth transitions"—in other words, seamless transfers of the speaker role from one person to the next. For example, Catherine would be answering a question, while William was primed. Then, at the precise moment that she stopped speaking, William would take over, and he'd do so without even glancing at her. In order to produce smooth transitions two people have to know each other really well, and they need to be able to anticipate what the other person is going to do next.

Instances of attentiveness and coordination were also repeatedly in evidence during William and Catherine's wedding ceremony, as well as in the split-second timing of their mandatory wedding kiss on the Buckingham Palace balcony. Their wedding tells were encouraging—thankfully, Catherine didn't need to go searching for rivals in the congregation, and William didn't produce any giveaway tells to suggest that he was feeling sad, nostalgic or regretful.

During their wedding, William and Catherine's marriage looked promising because their actions showed them to be attentive, supportive and in synch with each other. Of course, this didn't automatically guarantee them a blissful marriage. But it did mean that they were starting from the right place, and that they'd therefore be better equipped to deal with any problems they encountered in the years ahead.

William Tells

One of the things that William, Prince of Wales, has inherited from his mother is his height. At 6 feet 3 inches he's very tall for a member of the royal family—in fact, when he ascends to the throne he'll be the tallest British monarch ever, taller even than Henry VIII. For a long time William had a habit of stooping. It was an adolescent way of making himself look less conspicuous. In his case it was also a way of hiding from the unwanted attention of the press and people who treated him as if he was somebody special. The stooping habit has now largely disappeared, but William can still be socially withdrawn—just like Diana was on occasions. In fact, several of William's tells can be traced to his mother, although there are also a few tells that he owes to his father:

The Head-dip. Like his mother, William is naturally reticent. That's one of the reasons he rode around on his motorbike with his helmet on—it allowed him to travel incognito. William doesn't like to be treated differently and he has a strong dislike of the press, because of the paparazzi, whom he sees as responsible for his mother's death. When he's on display or feeling pursued, his natural instinct is to lower his head and look down. It's his camouflage, his way of pretending that the people who are bothering him aren't there. Like Diana, William also had a habit of lowering his eyes when talking to people. This wasn't another escape attempt—it was simply an expression of his shyness. William's maternal grandfather, Lord Spencer, was a rather shy person too. In his youth he was also very good-looking. As a teenager, William was unusually handsome for a member of the royal family, and that's partly why so many young girls found him irresistible. The other thing they liked about him was his reserve—it allowed them to imagine that they were doing the chasing. This is borne out by the fact that, in 1998, he received more than a thousand Valentine cards. It was illustrated even more dramatically that year when William travelled with Charles and Harry to Canada. There he was repeatedly mobbed by hundreds of screaming girls—just as if he were a pop star!

The Spencer Smile. Like Diana, William has an infectious smile, which we're seeing more and more since he became a father. The smile is broad and generous, and it usually shows signs of genuine pleasure. This is particularly noticeable when his guard is down and he's feeling unthreatened. When William is under pressure to appear jovial his smiles are usually more artificial—they're briefer, his gaze is averted, and they don't enlist the muscles around the eyes. William also uses the pursed smile that was so characteristic of his mother. Like her, he compresses his lips and pulls them to one side.

The Lean-in Shake. Something else that William has inherited from his mother is the habit of leaning into a handshake. Most people, when they greet someone for the first time, will retain a fairly upright posture—it's their non-committal way of appearing neither to hold back nor to appear overly eager. William, however, frequently dispenses with convention and leans forward into his handshakes with other people. Like his mother did before him, he's showing the other person that he wants fully to engage with them.

The Tie Tidy. One of William's *threshold tells* is the "tie tidy." For example, when he gets out of a car wearing a tie and jacket and he walks toward a building, he often straightens out his tie. Like other threshold tells this action occurs when he's in transition—it's a way of marking the change, preparing for what's about to happen, and displacing anxiety. Although William's "tie tidy" and Charles's "tie tuck" both involve ties, they're guided by quite different motivations. When Charles tucks the end of his tie away he's making sure—functionally and metaphorically—that there aren't any loose ends around and that what's superfluous is put out of view. When William tidies his tie he's not trying to conceal anything—he's just smartening up what's already visible.

Some of William's tells have clearly changed since he became married and started a family. Gone, for example, is his habit of touching the top of his head, which he used to do when he was feeling anxious or exposed. There are, in fact, recordings of him doing this from a very early age, all the way through to his early adulthood, but he now seems to have abandoned the habit altogether, at least when he's in public. One possible explanation for this change is that, as his hair began to thin, there was less comfort to be gained by touching the top of his head. However, there are other tells to which William continues to be devoted. One of these is the handclasp. Whenever we see him standing still in public, it's very likely that that he'll have his hands respectfully clasped in front of him. If he's accompanied by his wife, Catherine, she'll be doing a handclasp too—with the slight exception that while William usually holds one hand with the other, Catherine is inclined to use a few fingers of one hand to hold a few fingers of the other. This tendency on the part of the Prince and Princess of Wales to copy each other and to perform the same action also extends to other aspects of their behaviour. It's not unusual, for example, to see the two of them adopting the same posture, or to find them mirroring each other by walking in step. Also, as we've already noticed, their actions are often highly synchronized, with one of them picking up where the other leaves off. The fact that William and Catherine are so naturally sensitive to each other, and that their actions are so intertwined, shows that they're very much on the same page, both physically and psychologically.

In spite of their evident closeness, William and Catherine aren't very demonstrative when it comes to displaying their mutual feelings in public. This contrasts with Harry and Meghan, who, in similar circumstances, seem to need no encouragement when it comes to demonstrating their affection for each other. From the very beginning of their relationship, there's been lots of evidence to show how deeply Harry and Meghan feel for each other—during their wedding, for example, Harry became so overwhelmed that he bit his lower lip as a means of keeping his powerful emotions in check, and he's constantly on the lookout for ways that he can support and protect Meghan. Having spent so many years as a TV star before she met Harry, it's hardly surprising to find Meghan falling back on her acting skills when she and Harry find themselves in front of the cameras. When she's close to and facing Harry, for example, one of her theatrical tricks is to let her eyes roam, almost as if she's visually caressing every part of his face. Her smile is often spontaneous. But she also employs a celluloid version where, instead of appearing suddenly, it's slowly unveiled, as if she's exposing one alluring feature of her smile at a time. These displays of

Meghan can be highly effective at communicating positive emotions, but that's partly because they're a legacy of her theatrical training.

The royal family is definitely an unusual species and, as we've seen, it's one that's constantly evolving, not only in its pageantry and spectacle, but also in terms of its tells. It's very easy to forget that before the late Queen ascended to the throne, the royals were largely inaccessible—there were some exceptions, but as a rule they didn't engage with members of the public. With the arrival of the royal walkabout, all that changed. Even the regal wave has evolved. Like her parents before her, the late Queen had an unusual habit of waving by rotating her wrist, rather than by moving her hand from side to side, as most people do. That archaic style of waving has now disappeared, and it has been replaced by a much more colloquial version. Consequently, when royals like William and Catherine wave at the public, the actions they perform with their hands are essentially the same as those produced by the people who're waving back at them.

8. Anxiety Tells

People become anxious when they feel threatened. This is a normal, self-protective response to a perceived danger, and it often precedes actions that are designed to deal with the threat. How anxious someone feels is likely to depend on their personality and how threatened and helpless they feel. Most people only feel threatened and anxious occasionally. Some people, however, don't appear to experience any anxiety at all, while at the opposite extreme there are people who seem to be in a permanent state of apprehension.

Psychologists distinguish between two types of anxiety: "trait anxiety" and "state anxiety." As the term implies, trait anxiety refers to anxiety that is a trait; in other words, part of someone's personality. A person with trait anxiety tends to feel anxious, regardless of the situation. State anxiety, on the other hand, is a response to a particular situation. This is the adaptive way to respond—to feel anxious when circumstances are threatening, and to feel relaxed when the situation isn't threatening. Of course the whole notion of threat is highly subjective—people who have high levels of trait anxiety, for example, tend to see most situations as threatening.

When humans or animals are under attack they have several strategies at their disposal: fight, flight or freeze.[1] Each of these responses involves very different actions—attacking or defending oneself against the assailant, running away or keeping perfectly still. Although they differ superficially, these strategies are all associated with heightened physiological arousal, which involves increased heart rate, breathing and palmar sweating. These processes are automatic and involuntary—in other words, people don't have any control over them—so they provide a very reliable indication of emotions. One of the distinguishing features of heart rate is that people don't always notice small increases but they do notice when their heart starts pounding. In the case of sweating, people are often painfully aware that their anxiety is evident to other people, and that is why they go to such lengths to cover it up. Heart rate and sweating are united by the fact that they're almost impossible to fake; breathing is different because people can pretend to breathe faster or slower than normal.

As a rule, we don't want others to notice our symptoms of anxiety, because it shows that we aren't fully in control. It also undermines our confidence, exposes our weakness and puts other people at a potential advantage. Although we can't always control our anxiety, we can take steps to ensure that other people don't notice it. In fact it's often in our attempts to conceal our anxiety that we reveal what we're really feeling.

Sweating Tells

Sweating is central to thermoregulation—when we get hot our sweat glands produce more sweat, which evaporates and cools the surface of the skin. But sweating also occurs in response to highly charged emotional events, like giving a speech in front of a crowd of strangers, sitting in the dentist's chair, or preparing to jump out of a plane with a parachute. Research on sweating shows that while thermoregulatory sweating occurs all over the body, but less noticeably on the palms, emotional sweating is concentrated on the face and the palms of the hands, where the sweat glands are most densely packed.

Emotional sweating often catches people unawares, especially when they're inclined to be self-conscious. I've often watched people who appear to be completely composed stand up to give a speech, only to see perspiration pouring down their forehead a few minutes later (it's also happened to me on several occasions). One minute you're feeling confident and in control, and the next you're sweating profusely. Sometimes all it takes is a stray idea, a moment of self-doubt, to initiate the sweating. Once you start to perspire it's very difficult to stop. That's partly because sweating, like blushing, is very labile, but it's also because sweating feeds on itself—when you realize that other people can see you sweating this makes you even more anxious, which in turn encourages you to continue sweating, and so the vicious cycle continues. But sweating need not disqualify people from being an effective public speaker. British Prime Minister Tony Blair was a good example of someone who would often sweat profusely when speaking in public but who didn't allow it to hinder him in any way.

People can detect increases in their heart rate and sweating. They recognize, however, that while an increase in their heart rate isn't evident to others, an increase in their perspiration is. The way people react to their own sweating is often very revealing, and so are the little tricks that they use to cover it up. If you watch people who are about to shake hands with someone important, you'll see that they sometimes wipe their right hand discreetly before extending it for the handshake. This is usually done on the pretext of performing a completely different task, like putting their hand in their pocket or straightening out their jacket. For good measure, it's usually done when other people's attention is elsewhere. One way to reduce the chances of sweating is to remove some of one's clothing. You often see male politicians take their jacket off when they walk on to the stage to make a speech. This is partly done to create an impression of informality and resolve— to show the audience that the politician is prepared to get his hands dirty—but it's also done to help the politician keep cool, calm and collected.

Breathing Tells

When people are breathing normally they breathe about once every five seconds, each time taking in about 600 cubic centimetres of air. Breathing is largely performed by two sets of muscles: the muscles of the chest, and the muscles of the abdomen. In normal breathing the abdominal muscles do more work than the chest muscles. The chest muscles, however, are more involved in deep breathing, and there's a tendency for women in the West to use their chest muscles more than men.[2] The reason for this difference between the sexes is not entirely clear, but it may have something to do with the cultural premium that is placed on women having a flat stomach and large breasts. When someone feels threatened and anxious their breathing rate increases, they breathe more with their chest, and their breathing becomes shallower. As the psychologist William James put it, "When a fearful object is before us we pant and cannot deeply inspire." [3] This is a natural defensive reaction, and it serves the purpose of preparing the individual for "fight or flight." However, there are cases where people continually hyperventilate in the absence of any immediate threat by breathing too fast and by taking in too much air. Someone who's hyperventilating is likely to increase their breathing rate from once every five seconds to once every three seconds, and to increase their air intake by 50 percent. Although hyperventilation draws more oxygen into the lungs, it has the adverse effect of reducing the amount of carbon dioxide in the body, which in turn makes the person feel disoriented, dizzy and anxious.

People who breathe normally—that is, slowly and with large tidal volume—tend to be confident and emotionally stable. In contrast, people who breathe fast and with shallow breaths tend to be worried, shy and unsure of themselves. Habitual hyperventilators pay a high price, because they're prone to chronic anxiety, panic attacks and even heart problems.[4] It is still not known what causes what—whether unusual breathing patterns are responsible for disabling psychological effects, or whether people develop unusual breathing patterns because they feel anxious and despondent. However, it is possible to alleviate people's feelings of anxiety by getting them to breathe properly. This supports the idea that our moods are influenced by the way we breathe, rather than vice versa.

Breathing is one of those things that we do without thinking—although we can deliberately alter our breathing pattern, we never have to think about breathing because our autonomic nervous system does the job for us. Maybe it's because we don't think about breathing, or because we take it for granted, that we pay so little attention to it. When we're with other people we're seldom aware of how fast they're breathing, or whether they're breathing more with their chest than their stomach. If we were more attentive to how people breathe we'd know a lot more about what they are feeling.

Posture Tells

The three options available to an animal under attack—fight, flight or freeze—are reflected in the way that anxious people use their bodies to defend themselves, to escape symbolically, and to appear inert and unthreatening.

The "fight" response is reflected in the rigid postures that anxious people adopt, where the muscles are tense and the body creates a defence against the outside world. Wilhelm Reich referred to this as "body armour," and Alexander Lowen called it "psychosomatic armoury."[5] Lowen noticed that people who are anxious and who therefore feel the need to protect themselves from others often show hypertonicity of the chest wall—the region that is most likely to be subjected to a frontal attack. He also made the point that the arms and hands are potential weapons, which can be used for attack or for counter-attack. When people rely on their hands and arms, there's no need for any other form of defence. However, when aggression isn't an option they often transform their body into a protective shield. Lowen suggested that "psychologically the armour is the expression of the attitude of stiffening to meet an attack rather than striking back. Dynamically the tension in the front is produced by pulling back the shoulders and pelvis, thus putting all the frontal muscles on the stretch at the same time that they are contracted. When the front and the back of the body are thus encased in a rigid sheath of tight muscles, we can say that the organism is armoured."[6]

The "flight" response is found in the way that anxious people move their bodies. While the movements of confident people tend to be smooth, those of anxious people are often jerky and uneven. This can be seen in their breathing pattern, which sometimes consists of a series of "stepped" inhalations rather than a single, smooth inhalation of air. Anxious people are often restless, producing lots of sudden hand movements close to the body, as opposed to infrequent movements that are smooth and away from the body. The constant shifts of posture produced by anxious people look like an overflow of excess energy, which in one sense they are. But these agitated movements are best understood as disguised and regressive attempts to escape from what is perceived as a threatening situation. When an anxious person taps their foot impatiently it means that they're preparing their feet for a getaway, and when they play with their hands or fiddle with their keys it shows that they want to get down on their hands and knees and crawl away as fast as possible. Most of the time they don't notice what they're doing, let alone recognize the significance of their actions. Other people are often oblivious too—even if they do notice the person's agitated movements, they don't necessarily recognize them as an expression of their desire to escape.

The freeze response is revealed in people's postures. Anxious people tend to adopt rigid postures and to sit or stand in ways that maximize auto-contact. When they're standing, they're inclined to select postures like the "scissors stance," where the legs are straight and crossed, either at the knee or at the calf. When anxious people are sitting they often cross their legs, usually at the thigh, but sometimes at the calf or the ankle. When their legs aren't crossed, they tend to be close together, often with the feet tucked under the chair. As we saw earlier, these are essentially submissive postures, but they also help people to feel less anxious. Crossing the legs, for example, gives people the feeling that their genital region is protected, and this makes them feel more secure.

Postures that bring the thighs together also increase the amount of contact that people have with themselves, and therefore the degree of comfort that they feel. Ideally, most people prefer to be comforted by others. But if others aren't available or willing, people often resort to comforting themselves. One way they achieve this is by pressing their thighs together. An extreme version of a self-comforting posture is "the pretzel." Here the legs are crossed at the thigh and the foot that belongs to the leg on top is curled around the ankle of the other leg, making the person look as if they've been tied up by a mad contortionist. As we saw earlier, leg-cross postures often serve as "unintention displays" — they show other people that the person has no intention of moving. In this respect they're examples of the freeze response—it's what animals do when they're in danger of being spotted by a predator.

Anxiety also produces other forms of inactivity. For example, when people feel anxious they often feel the need to urinate, although when other people are nearby the impulse is usually reduced. Even when they're not feeling anxious, men find it difficult to urinate with someone standing beside them. This extended "micturition latency," as psychologists have labelled it, is most evident in public toilets, where men are often flanked by complete strangers.[7]

Hand Tells

Anxiety is often evident in the way that people use their hands. When people are feeling anxious they often manipulate objects—you'll see them playing with their keys, twisting the ring on their finger or tugging at their clothes. Anxious people also touch themselves as a means of gaining comfort. They may rub their hands together—this was one of George Bernard Shaw's trademark tells—or they may tug their earlobe, stroke their chin or run their fingers through their hair. Where people touch themselves is often very revealing. For example, there's a good chance that a man who tugs at the skin under his chin is either worried about his looks and/or the fact that he's putting on weight.

Zoologists have discovered that when animals have conflicting motives they often engage in "displacement activities" that are quite unrelated to their immediate goals.[8] This also happens with humans. When people experience conflicting motives—as they do when they feel anxious—they often produce "self-directed behaviours" that draw off some of the excess energy and give them a temporary feeling of composure. These actions are sometimes called "adaptors" because they help people to adapt to their internal conflicts. The main focus of self-directed behaviours like adaptors is the head and the face.[9] If you go into a hospital waiting room or an area where people are lining up to receive benefits or charity handouts, you'll notice that people frequently touch themselves on the face—one person might support their chin in their hands, while another is scratching the side of their face or smoothing down their hair. These self-comforting gestures are often unconscious; they're designed to alleviate the anxiety that people feel when they find themselves in awkward situations.

It's noticeable that when individuals perform self-directed actions, they don't make contact with just any part of their body—instead they touch themselves where other people might caress or stroke them if they were available to do so.[10] Anxious people spend so much time stroking their hair because this is how their mothers comforted them when they were babies. Self-comforting adaptors are therefore "substitution tells" as well as "regressive tells"—they take people back to a time when their parents alleviated their distress by touching and caressing them. As adults we don't usually have our parents around to provide us with a sense of security. So instead, we do to ourselves what our parents once did to us.

When people feel anxious they often externalize their anxiety by fidgeting or by manipulating objects that are close at hand. One thing they do is play with their glasses. How they manipulate them can be very revealing. For example, people who chew or suck the ends of their glasses are actually engaging in a form of oral fixation. They're like the baby who sucks its thumb or chews its blanket—they're taking comfort from having something in their mouth. Then there are people who hold their glasses in their hands, opening and closing them but making sure that they look symmetrical. These people tend to be neat and compulsive, and they have a strong need to be in control. People who are constantly removing their glasses tend to be indecisive and evasive—they can never decide whether they should have their glasses on or off. In some cases it's done to confound other people, so that they don't know what's going to happen next. Then there are people who constantly breathe on their glasses and polish the lenses. They too need to be in control and to know what's happening—they need a clear view of the world.

The purpose of some adaptors is to offer protection rather than comfort. There are five main "protective" adaptors. These include the "eye-cover," where a hand is placed over the eyes, the "mouth-cover," where a hand is placed over the mouth, and the "face-cover," where the palms of both hands are used to cover the whole face. People often use these covering gestures when they've received bad news or when they've just witnessed something distressing. All three actions can be seen after the results of a political election have been announced—victor-ious candidates can usually be seen smiling, laughing and raising their hands, while the defeated candidates are covering their eyes or mouth, or even their whole face. By covering their eyes, people are preventing themselves from seeing the thing that is distressing them, and by cov-ering their mouth they are simultaneously concealing their distress and preventing themselves from saying something they might later regret. These covering gestures are essentially symbolic. For example, when you hear about a plane crash on the radio, you are as likely to cover your eyes as your ears—by covering your eyes you are behaving as if you had actually seen the accident, not just heard about it.

The other two "protective" adaptors are the "head-clasp" and the "cradle." The best place to see these gestures is at a sporting event like a football match, especially when there's a lot at stake for both sides. When a player shoots at goal and narrowly misses, you often see the supporters clasp their head in despair—the hands rise up and cover the top of the head, creating a manual crash helmet. This is a nat-ural, unlearned response, and it's found all around the world. It works metaphorically because it's designed to shield the head, not against physical blows, but from the psychological damage of witnessing some terrible spectacle.

In 1996 the England football team played Germany in the semi-finals of the European Championship in Turin. At the end of the full period the score was 1–1, so the match had to be decided by a penalty shootout, where selected players from each side take turns at getting the ball past the other team's goalkeeper. The teams were level at five points apiece, when Gareth Southgate, the England midfielder, stepped up to the line to take his shot at goal. This was a crucial point: if he missed and the next German player got the ball in the net, Germany would win and go on to the final, and England would be out of the competition. When Southgate placed the ball, walked back and started his run he knew how important it was to get the ball into the net. Maybe it was the weight of responsibility resting on his shoulders, or maybe he had a momentary loss of concentration—but, instead of striking the ball cleanly, he tapped it softly, and the German goalkeeper had no problem stopping it before it got near the goal mouth. As Southgate turned and began his lonely walk back across the pitch, he realized the grave consequences of his missed penalty. While he was walking back toward his team-mates, with his eyes downcast, Southgate did what so many football players do when they're in the depths of despair—he "cradled" the back of his head in his hands.

There isn't much that a football player can do to console themselves in this kind of situation—they can't talk to themselves or pat themselves on the back or give themselves a hug. However they can comfort themselves by performing the "cradle." Although they don't realize it, by placing their hands around the back of their head they're repeating the action that their parents used to support their head when they were a helpless baby. The sense of security that they felt then is intimately connected in their mind with the sensation of having the back of their head supported. By clasping the back of their own head, the player is therefore substituting themselves for their parent.

The eye-cover, cradle and head-clasp. Clear demonstrations of disbelief and disappointment are evident in these gestures when the Liverpool football team narrowly fails to score against Manchester United.

The "cradle posture" isn't only seen on the football pitch—it can be found wherever people feel insecure and need to protect themselves from threats, either real or imagined. If you watch a heated boardroom meeting you're likely to witness examples of the "cradle." In fact there are two postures you're likely to see, which look very similar, but their functions are quite different. One is the "cradle"; the other is the "catapult." In both gestures the hands are clasped around the back of the neck, but while the elbows are pulled back and the chest is expanded in the case of the catapult, the emphasis in the cradle is on supporting the head. The catapult is in fact a disguised gesture of aggression. By pulling the elbows back and expanding the chest, someone increases their apparent width and makes themselves look threatening. While the hands appear to be taking refuge behind the head, they are actually cocked and ready to ambush anyone who strays too close. As we've seen, the purpose of the cradle is completely different. Here the hands perform a purely supportive role—there is no sense in which they are being pulled back in preparation for attack. Both the catapult and the cradle can be seen in business settings when people feel threatened. The catapult is likely to be used when one person wants to intimidate another; the cradle when individuals feel the need to comfort themselves. The first is a disguised form of counter-attack, while the second is a surreptitious form of self-assurance.

Neck Tells

When someone performs the "cradle," they can either clasp the back of their head or their neck, or else they can position their hand or hands somewhere in between. Touching one's neck is in fact a common sign of anxiety, and it can take several forms. When people become alarmed or distressed, they often clasp the front of their neck with the palm of their hand or, more discreetly, they lightly touch the front, back or side of their neck with a finger. Like the "chin-tuck," which was mentioned earlier, covering the neck with a "neck-clasp" is an instinctive means of shielding one of the most vulnerable parts of the body. On the other hand, more modest "neck-touch" gestures reflect a less urgent, or possibly a more secret, need for self-protection. A person who's feeling anxious, and who covers or touches their neck, isn't necessarily worried about being physically attacked; they may do so because they're feeling psychologically threatened or because they've seen something that distresses them. When he was watching his football team, Philipe Scolari, the former manager of Chelsea, would often grimace and clasp his neck when things weren't going his way—it was his method of shielding himself from the distressing scene he was witnessing.

But the hands aren't the only means of protecting the neck—another, occasionally more subtle technique is to raise the shoulders instead. As we've already seen, raised shoulders are an integral part of the "startle reflex," where someone, for example, reacts to a loud noise or a shocking event. Whenever you notice someone hoisting their shoulders and keeping them raised, there's every chance that they're doing so because they're feeling vulnerable. Again, it doesn't mean that they're worried about being physically attacked; they could simply be doing so because they feel the need to protect themselves psychologically. This self-protective gesture is the "shoulder hoist," and it differs from two other gestures where the shoulders are raised deliberately, namely the "shoulder flick" and the "shoulder hop." In both of these gestures, the shoulders are raised suddenly and then immediately lowered. The shoulder flick is often deployed when someone wants to reject an accusation or another person's opinion by literally flicking it away with a sudden movement of their shoulders. This gesture isn't usually accompanied by a qualifying facial expression. The shoulder hop, on the other hand, is a coquettish gesture—you'll often see it used by young women, both as a flirtatious signal and as a way of disarming whoever they're talking to. In these instances, the shoulder hop is frequently accompanied by a colluding smile and raised eyebrows, or a quizzical facial expression, which is intended to show that the person in question is being friendly and companionable. During conversations, people will sometimes tag a shoulder hop onto the end of their turn, using it to suggest that what they've just said should be taken lightly.

Face Tells

Anxiety often shows on the face. An anxious smile is quite different from a genuine smile because it lacks the contraction of the *orbicularis oculi* muscles around the eyes and the wrinkled crow's feet that appear beside the eyes, which are the hallmarks of a genuine smile. Like other false smiles, anxious smiles tend to appear rather suddenly, to last longer than you'd normally expect, and then to disappear quite swiftly. Anxious smiles are also given away by unusual muscular activity around the mouth. In a genuine smile the corners of the mouth are pulled upward by the *zygomatic major* muscles, whereas in an anxious smile the corners of the mouth may be pulled sideways or even downward. Jinni Harrigan and Dennis O'Connell at California State University at Fullerton found that when people are anxious their faces show more signs of the fear expression, and that as anxiety increases women smile less than men.[11]

We tend to think of laughter as an expression of happiness and amusement, but it can also be a sign of anxiety. A good example of this may be found in the famous experiments on obedience conducted by Stanley Milgram during the 1960s.[12] Milgram set up a bogus lab at Yale University, complete with a phony "experimenter" in a white coat, and an equally phony "learner," whose task it was to remember lists of words. People who volunteered to take part in the experiments were invited to train the learner by giving him electric shocks. The volunteers didn't realize it, but the learner was in league with the experimenter and never actually received any shocks.

The surprising finding was that when they were urged to do so, quite ordinary people were prepared to administer powerful electric shocks to the learner, especially when he was sitting in an adjacent room where it was possible to hear but not see him writhing about in agony. Although the volunteer subjects were prepared to administer these electric shocks, many of them were clearly uncomfortable about performing the task they'd been given. This often resulted in bouts of inappropriate laughter—in fact a third of the volunteers who took part in the experiment produced nervous laughter and smiling. When the learner made a mistake, the experimenter would instruct the subject to give the learner an electric shock, each time increasing the voltage. When the subject complied and flicked a switch, the learner would scream in pain, cry out for help, complain that he had a weak heart, or go completely silent. These cries of pain and pleas for help caused the subjects a lot of distress, but that didn't stop them giving the learner an even bigger shock a few moments later, and then laughing when they heard him screaming. When they were interviewed afterward, the subjects could not explain why they'd burst out laughing. Initially it appeared that they were amused by the pain they were inflicting. But that wasn't the case—their laughter was simply a nervous reaction to the punishing regime that they had created with the help of the experimenter.

When people are feeling anxious they tend to reduce the amount of time they spend looking at others. They also spend more time searching for "bolt holes" and "escape hatches"—ways of escaping from their current discomfort. Indeed, the gaze of anxious people often focuses on how they can get out of a situation, rather than how they can make a positive contribution to what is happening. Anxious people are more likely to look away when they're in a conversation. This is largely because they're worried about the negative consequences of disagreement. In fact anxious people don't necessarily differ from confident people in terms of how much time they spend looking at the other person during a conversation—so long as there are no disagreements. However, as soon as there's any sign of disagreement, anxious people start to reduce the amount of time they spend looking at the other person.[13] For an anxious person the eyes are like a double-barrelled shotgun. Provided the safety catch is on and things are going smoothly, there's nothing much to worry about. But as soon as the atmosphere turns tense the eyes become a primed weapon—that's why it's best to keep them hidden.

Another ocular tell of anxiety is blinking. The primary purpose of blinking is to lubricate the surface of the eyes, to spread the tear film evenly over the cornea, and to keep it clean and healthy. Blink rate is affected by a variety of factors. These include features of the environment, like temperature, humidity and lighting, but they also include attentional factors, such as whether someone is reading or watching something closely. The average blink rate is about fifteen blinks per minute (with women showing a higher rate than men), but this drops dramatically when people are reading. John Stern from Washington University in St Louis has studied blinking extensively. He has discovered that there is a strong link between someone's blinking rate and their emotional state—the more tired or anxious they are, the more frequent their blinking.[14] Stern points out that President Nixon was a great blinker. During the Watergate hearing, when asked questions he didn't want to answer, Nixon's blinking rate rose enormously.

The face also becomes involved in anxiety tells through face-touching. Whatever their mood, people are constantly touching their nose, mouth, cheeks or eyes. The mouth is apparently touched more frequently than the nose or eyes, and we're told that the chin is touched more often than the cheeks, mouth or hair. It's also been found that people have a marked tendency to touch their face, nose and eyes with their non-dominant hand rather than their dominant hand. It seems like the reason for this is that the dominant hand comes into contact with more potentially infectious surfaces, as well as other people, and that touching one's face and mucous membrane with the non-dominant hand therefore reduces the chances of infection. The explanation as to why the hand and face are so intimately involved in anxiety tells is that they're closely connected in our neurophysiology.[15] There are several reasons why people are inclined to spontaneously touch their face. Sometimes they do it to comfort themselves or to alleviate feelings of uncertainty or awkwardness. Covering the mouth with the hand, for example, is a classic sign of embarrassment—it's designed to conceal one's feelings by obscuring a revealing part of the face, but of course it often has the opposite effect of publicizing those feelings. A similar logic often informs people's attempts to conceal their lies—even if they're not aware of what they're doing, by covering, say, their mouth with their hand, they're attempting to hide the source of their deception. People may also cover parts of their face on the superstitious assumption that if someone can't see their whole face, then they won't be able to figure out what they're thinking. You'll often see chess players, for example, with their hands covering part of their face or clasping their head— ostensibly to steady themselves, but in reality, to reduce the amount of personal information they're making available to their opponent. On other occasions people may touch their face for entirely different reasons—for example, to draw attention to themselves or to show that they have no desire to take over the speaker role in a conversation.

Another reason for touching the face is to protect it from attack, either literally or figuratively. As we've already noted, you often see people cover their face when they've witnessed or been told something shocking. Watching the audience during a horror movie provides lots of examples. However, there are also instances where people touch their face pre-emptively, in order to defend it from being attacked. If you've watched the TV cooking series *Hell's Kitchen*, you'll be well aware of the format, the colourful language and Gordon Ramsay's often belligerent approach to the participants. On at least two occasions, I've noticed that when Ramsay was about to provoke or insult a participant, he would nonchalantly place his hand on the side of his face beforehand, giving the impression that he was simply being thoughtful. On one occasion, Ramsay's real reason for touching his face soon became apparent, because after he'd indirectly accused a female participant of showing off, she became enraged, lurched at him and tried to slap him. Fortunately for Ramsay, his hand was poised no more than a few inches away from where it needed to be in order to intercept the woman's hand as it hurtled toward his face. Clearly, Ramsay's brain was fully primed, because the moment he decided to be provocative, it instructed his hand to move into a position where it could be used defensively. Had Ramsay not taken the precaution of strategically positioning his hand beside his face beforehand, it's very likely that he'd have ended up with a very red face, not to mention the indignity of being thumped on his own TV program.

Mouth Tells

The most telling signs of anxiety are associated with the lips, mouth, throat, esophagus and stomach—in fact the entire gastrointestinal tract from lips to anus. If you think of yourself as a tube through which your food passes, it's not surprising that your emotions affect the essential parts of you. The real reason why your moods are so intimately connected with your digestive system is that it has a completely integrated system of nerves called the enteric nervous system. The enteric nervous system, which is almost a brain in its own right, responds to the same neurotransmitters as the central nervous system, and that's why changes in one system so often cause changes in the other. When people feel anxious, several reflexes associated with the digestive system come into play:

Dry Mouth. One of the early signs that someone is feeling anxious is a dry mouth. This is produced by a temporary shutdown of the saliva glands. There are visual as well as auditory cues that indicate when someone has a dry mouth—not only does the person look like they're chewing sawdust, but their voice also sounds dry and mechanical too.

Coughing. When people become anxious they often get a tickling sensation in their throat, which makes them cough, sometimes uncontrollably. The feeling that there is an excess of saliva at the back of the throat also causes coughing.

Swallowing. After President Clinton had uttered those famous words "I did not have sexual relations with that woman, Miss Lewinsky," he looked down and then swallowed hard. Most people, when they feel anxious, have an overwhelming desire to clear their throat by swallowing. Women can usually achieve this without being noticed, but because men have a larger Adam's apple, they tend to have more difficulty concealing this kind of nervous swallowing.

Biting Lips. According to Charles Bell, the Victorian anatomist, the lips are, of all the features, "the most susceptible of
action, and the most direct indices of the feelings."[16] This can
be seen both in the movement of the lips and how they come
into contact with the teeth. Several lip-biting gestures are associated with anxiety. First there's the "lip-bite," where either the
top or, more typically, the bottom lip is held between the teeth.
As we saw earlier, this is a gesture of self-restraint, a symbolic
way of preventing ourselves from saying something that we
might regret later on. But it can also be a gesture of anxiety
or embarrassment—in other words, a way of holding on to
ourselves with our teeth. Then there's the "lip-lip-bite" gesture, where both the top lip and the bottom lip are pulled
inward and held tight between the teeth. This gesture, which is
sometimes referred to as the "disappearing lips," was a trademark tell of the great American athlete Carl Lewis when he
was picking up medals. When Lewis was interviewed on TV
he would frequently reveal his discomfort by pulling his lips
in and securing them between his teeth. In every other respect
Lewis always came across as confident and articulate—it was
only his "lip-lip-bite" that gave him away.

Nail-biting. People who habitually bite their nails tend to
score low on psychological tests of self-esteem, and high on
measures of anxiety. It has also been suggested that nail-biting
is a sign of inhibited hostility, with nail-biters turning their
aggression inward upon themselves, rather than outward
toward other people.

Mouthing Objects. When people feel anxious they often have
a desire to put something in their mouth. This is a throwback
to the comforting experience of sucking the breast and, following that, sucking the thumb. The most common forms of
oral comfort behaviour found in our society are chewing gum,
smoking cigarettes and vaping. Smoking is often portrayed as

a sign of coolness, and smokers as people who are in control. In fact, smokers often use cigarettes to calm their nerves and control their anxiety. The oral comfort provided by chewing gum is evident from the amount of gum that coaches and team managers get through while they're watching a soccer game. For example, if you watched Alex Ferguson when he was the manager of Manchester United, you'd have noticed that his gum-chewing reflected the temporary fortunes of his team. When Manchester United was ahead and playing well, Ferguson's chewing was slow and cogitative. However, when the team was behind or playing badly, the speed and pressure of his gum-chewing increased dramatically.

Talk Tells

Anxiety is also revealed by the voice. When people are feeling anxious there's an overall increase in muscle tension, and this leads to an increase in pitch, or what linguists call "fundamental frequency." Perturbations in pitch—what linguists call "jitter" and "shimmer"— are also evidence of anxiety.[17] Loudness is another indicator—it's the opposite of slow and soft speech, which is usually a symptom of sadness or depression.[18]

When people feel anxious they tend to talk faster and to talk less. That's because they don't want to cast other people in the role of listener for any longer than necessary, and thereby draw attention to themselves. The best way to achieve these goals is to reduce what one has to say and to increase the speed at which one says it. Although anxious people speak faster, they are often quite slow when it comes to answering questions—that's because they spend more time thinking about what kind of answer they're going to give.[19]

The relationship between anxiety and pausing isn't straightforward because it depends on whether people have trait or state anxiety—in other words whether they are chronically anxious or simply anxious in certain situations. It's been found that when chronically anxious people are talking they tend to pause less—they're agitated and they want to hurry through what they're saying. On the other hand, when acutely anxious people are talking, they tend to pause more than normal. That's because they have to deal with their immediate feelings of anxiety at the same time as deciding what they're going to say next. The pauses that are a feature of acute anxiety are often filled with speech disfluencies, like *um* and *er*, which enable speakers to show that they have more to say, and that they want to retain the floor. Both chronically and acutely anxious people are inclined to stutter. Stutterers tend to stutter more when they're anxious, and so do non-stutterers; even people who hardly ever stutter are more likely to do so when they're feeling threatened and insecure.[20]

One of the things that people dread is public speaking. Most people experience some degree of "speech phobia," but there are some people who are completely disabled by their fear of public speaking. It's often said that the more experience one has at public speaking, the easier it becomes. This may be true for lots of people, but for some it remains a source of deep anxiety. Regardless of how often they do it, and how accomplished they've become, they continue to worry about being the centre of attention, forgetting their lines, and looking ridiculous in front of so many people.

Because anxiety is a negative emotional state it's difficult to control, and the tells associated with anxiety are therefore difficult to conceal. This works both ways—it makes it easy for us to detect the anxiety of other people, but it also makes it easy for them to identify our feelings of anxiety too. People try to conceal their anxiety in different ways. One is by working on their state of mind so that they no longer feel anxious; another is by trying to cover up their anxiety tells. The only problem with this strategy is that it frequently produces a *tell-suppressing tell*, which gives the lie to the person's attempt at concealment. People who surreptitiously take a drink of water when their throat is feeling dry or who wipe their hand on their clothes before shaking hands often reveal more about their internal state than they would have done had they not tried to cover up their anxiety in the first place. In other words, tell-suppressing tells are often more revealing than the tells they're designed to cover up—that's because they point to the person's anxiety as well as to their desire to conceal it. So if you don't want other people to know how anxious you feel, make sure they don't notice your anxiety tells. And whatever you do, don't let them catch you trying to conceal them.

9. Sports Tells

If you're a keen fan of track and field, and especially the short sprints like the 100-metre dash or the 110-metre hurdles, you'll have noticed that when the athletes are lining up in front of their blocks just before the race, every now and then one or two of them will start jumping high into the air, often tucking their feet under them. When you see this happening, you probably assume that these leaping antics are merely designed to keep the athlete's muscles warm and to prepare their body for the explosive effort that's about to take place. Be that as it may, there's actually another explanation for these high jinks, one that's inspired by what happens in the wild. When a herd of gazelles, for example, become aware of the presence of a stalking lion, they'll usually start to move away, often leaping high into the air as they do so. This is called "stotting," and it's generally accepted that it's the gazelles' way of publicizing their physical fitness, and therefore discouraging the lion from pursuing them individually. When athletes leap in the air before a race, it's not because they're worried about predation, but rather it's their way of showing the other contestants how physically fit they are and how difficult it's going to be to catch them. Couched in these terms, we might even regard this leaping routine as athletes' subtle attempts to intimidate their competition—to suggest that since their own victory is inevitable, there's no point in anyone else making any effort.

Sportsmen and women attempt to get inside the heads of their opponents and to mess with their thinking in countless ways, not only before the contest has begun but also while it's taking place. Watch what happens during a major tennis tournament, for example, particularly before service takes place, and you'll often see players briefly running on the spot or swaying from side to side as they crouch down to receive the serve. These energetic actions are not unlike stotting;

they send a very clear message about the player's fitness, suggesting that they've got lots of fuel in their tank. Swaying from side also offers additional benefits, because it makes players look and feel more like a moving, rather than a static, target, and it reduces the chances of them being caught flat-footed when the ball appears over the net.

One way that tennis players can try to disconcert and throw their opponent off balance is by making a rowdy, verbal assault on the umpire. That's what the *enfant terrible* of tennis, John McEnroe, did repeatedly during the 1980s, on one occasion shouting at the umpire "You cannot be serious! You are an incompetent fool, an offense against the world!" Since then, McEnroe has tried to excuse himself by claiming that his youthful outbursts were due to the professional and personal pressures he was under. It's quite possible, however, that in addition to providing an emotional release, McEnroe's diatribes were also a disguised means of disrupting the flow, noisily altering the mood of the game and putting his opponent at a psychological disadvantage. Some commentators have suggested that McEnroe's game actually improved after he'd vented his anger. An alternative explanation is that it only seemed that way, and that because McEnroe's tantrums seriously disturbed his opponents' routine and concentration, it was their performance that actually got worse! But McEnroe didn't restrict his invective to umpires—he was also prepared to insult and belittle his opponents, on one occasion claiming that he had more talent in his pinkie finger than his rival, Ivan Lendl, had in his whole body.

Chess has also had its share of mavericks and obsessive competitors, like Wilhelm Steinitz, the nineteenth-century World Chess champion, who ended up in a mental hospital, and who allegedly challenged God to a chess match, while graciously offering the Almighty a one-pawn advantage. But by far the most disruptive chess world champion of modern times was Bobby Fischer. During the 1972 "Chess Match of the Century," which took place in Reykjavik between the American and the reigning Soviet world champion, Boris Spassky, Fischer arrived late, repeatedly complained about the arrangements and made outlandish demands. He insisted, for example, that the cameras be switched off and that the first seven rows of seats for spectators be removed, and he complained about distracting noises only he could hear. Even if Fischer's demands were dismissed as a symptom of his paranoia, they nevertheless created the sort of self-centred, disorderly environment in which he thrived and which had the effect of unsettling Spassky. Eventually the Soviet delegation became so annoyed by the unruly spectacle that they too started to make accusations and demands. But by then the psychological damage had been done. Fischer beat Spassky and became world champion.

Trashing Tells

When it comes to getting under an opponent's skin and messing with their head, very few strategies are as effective as "trash talking." Here, players deliberately set out to undermine and disorient their opponents through the use of insults, threats, jibes or joshing. Trash talking appears in a variety of guises, ranging from good-humoured banter, which is simply designed to amuse, all the way through to high-octane belittling, where the intention is to injure an opponent's pride in order to gain the upper hand.[1] Light-hearted trash talking is typically motivated by a desire to entertain and amuse team-mates, possibly even the spectators, to get other people on-side, and to demonstrate a gift for verbal dexterity, which is evidently lacking in one's opponent—unless, of course, they manage to come back with an effective piece of repartee. On the other hand, the main goal of serious trash talkers, even if they're not entirely aware of it, is to wind up and emotionally disturb their opponent to the point where they become so befuddled that they're incapable of exercising their natural sporting skills. Here, trash talking may consist of mockery, rudeness or insults, but to be properly effective it's got to be personal, drawing attention to some negative characteristic, real or imagined, of the person being targeted. People who are the butt of trash talking may be justifiably annoyed by what's said about them. But what often upsets and angers them even more is the trash talker's presumption—the fact that they've had the impertinence to be disrespectful and to ignore the consequences of their own actions.

Trash talking can occur at any stage of a sporting contest. When he first got started, Muhammad Ali was known as "The Louisville Lip." Long before he stepped into the ring with his opponents, Ali would start to soften them up, taunting, insulting and mocking them. He announced that Sonny Liston was "too ugly to be world champion," and he called Floyd Patterson "the rabbit." But his biggest verbal blows were reserved for Joe Frazier, whom he repeatedly referred to as "ugly," "a gorilla" or "Uncle Tom"—in other words, a Black person who tries to please White people. But Ali didn't just wind up his opponents before the match; he continued to do so during the fight itself and after it was over. He even goaded his opponents after he'd knocked them down and they were lying flat on the canvass—just when they were least likely to respond. In contrast, Ali reserved more flattering descriptions for himself, calling himself "the prettiest thing that ever lived" and as "the greatest." Looking back, we can see that some of Ali's bombastic and cutting remarks were meant to be tongue-in-cheek, while others were designed as much to amuse his fans as to wound his opponents.

Trash talking features in a wide range of sports, where there's often more than one major exponent. In basketball, for example, Larry Bird and Michael Jordan were long considered to be legendary trash talkers, putting down their rivals while entertaining everyone else. But there are certain sports, like ice hockey and cricket, where trash talking appears to have put down roots and become an integral part of the game. In ice hockey, bad-mouthing and challenging the other side is known as "chirping," whereas in cricket it's referred to as "sledging."[2] For example, back in the eighties, Steve Thomas, the ice hockey star who played for the Maple Leafs and Islanders, delivered a memorable "chirp," when he shouted at one of his opponents, "You look like you did a 100-yard dash in a 50-yard gym!" Then there was the occasion when Brendan Shanahan of the New York Rangers hollered at Kings player Sean Avery, "Lose my number! Don't ever call me again, because I'm tired of listening to you criticize your teammates all the time!"

Cricket boasts a number of memorable "sledges"—like the time legendary England cricketer Fred Trueman was fielding near the gate onto the pitch and a new batsman, who'd just walked through the gate, turned to close it after him. "Don't worry," said Trueman, "you won't be out there long enough." Another case involved Shane Warne, the Australian fast bowler, who was just about to bowl to Daryll Cullinan, a South African. "I've been waiting two years for another chance at you," announced Warne, no doubt with a touch of menace; to which Cullinan casually replied, "Looks like you spent it eating!" The backlist of chirps and sledges shows that they're frequently met with repartee, which suggests that in the process of putting someone down, they often provide an opening for the person to come back with an even better wisecrack.

Some sports are virtually devoid of trash talking, whereas it's practically endemic in other sports. The high frequency of chirping in ice hockey is probably due to the inherent physicality of the sport and what appears to be its more relaxed attitude to fisticuffs, at least in the United States and Canada. On the other hand, the presence of sledging might have something to do with the close proximity of several members of the fielding side to the batter, coupled with the relative silence of the game and therefore the opportunity to hear what the players are saying. However, the big puzzle about trash talking is whether or not it actually works—does it have the desired effect of upsetting someone and throwing them off balance, even when they're simply the butt of an idle joke? Here the experimental evidence is somewhat mixed, suggesting in some cases that it doesn't impair the performance of people at whom it's directed, while on other occasions it does.[3] We might decide that whether trash talking actually works across the board is not really the issue, and that what really sustains the practice and keeps it going, certainly in its more playful forms, is the widespread belief that it helps to soften up the opposition. At the same time, it gives individual players a chance to display their quick wit and wordplay, while giving everyone else an opportunity to appreciate the colourful language and good-humoured banter.

If good-humoured banter constitutes a mild, playful version of trash talking, then wind-ups represent the other extreme. Wind-ups are most likely to affect someone adversely when what's said to them is especially hurtful, and when they have a particularly short fuse. Wind-ups certainly don't pull any punches. Their sole purpose is to make someone angry and therefore to put that person at a psychological disadvantage. The basic reason why they work is that anger prepares us to attack. It's linked to heightened activity in the left frontal hemisphere of the brain, an area that's involved in physical approach. When someone makes you angry this part of your brain experiences unusual activity, and your natural impulse is to blame the person responsible and/or to punish them for their actions, as well as for making you angry. In your desire to seek retribution, however, you're prone to make risky as well as overly optimistic decisions—you're more likely to underestimate the danger of taking things into your own hands and to overestimate your chances of being successful if and when you do.

The Classic Wind-up

In the 2006 Football World Cup, France faced Italy in the final. The celebrated French footballer, Zinedine Zidane, had recently been awarded the "Golden Ball" as the best player of the tournament, and he represented a very real danger to the Italian team. This was borne out during the first half of the match, when Zidane put France ahead with a superb penalty. A few minutes later Italian defender Marco Materazzi racked up a goal and levelled the scores. Because the scores were still level at the end of the full period, the game was extended into extra time. Twenty minutes later an incident took place that was to completely change the course of the match and to leave an indelible mark on Zidane's career.

As Materazzi and Zidane brushed past each other, Materazzi briefly grabbed Zidane's jersey. Zidane responded sarcastically, telling Materazzi that if he wanted the jersey, he'd give it to him after the match was over. As Zidane was jogging back, we're told that Materazzi replied, "Preferisco quella puttana di tua sorella"—"I'd prefer the whore who's your sister." Zidane turned on his heel, walked calmly up to Materazzi and, in front of millions of viewers, head-butted him in the chest. Materazzi fell backward, making it look like he was in considerable pain. The referee ran over to Zidane and showed him the red card—from this point on Zidane would play no further part in the match. With Zidane off the field, the French team appeared completely disheartened. When the match went to a penalty shootout, Italy won 5–3 and became the world champions. Had Zidane managed to keep his cool and ignore Materazzi's taunt, there's every chance that France would have defeated them. By winding Zidane up, Materazzi ensured that didn't happen. France lost because Zidane succumbed to a classic wind-up.

Menacing Tells

Trash talking is by no means the only method available when it comes to disorienting your opponents—it's also possible to put them off their stride by menacing them. Superficially, these two techniques might appear to be quite similar, but they're actually very different, because while trash talking sets out to provoke anger, menacing is all about creating fear. Menacing tactics are found in both individual and team sports. In cricket, for example, the bowler may attempt to terrorize the batter by delivering a fast, short ball that bounces and rises near the batter's head, or one that, without bouncing, is delivered above the batter's waist level—"bouncers" or "beamers" in cricketing parlance. In baseball we occasionally see similar strategies at work, particularly when the pitcher produces a high-and-inside fastball, or one that's designed to gain back the plate. Like other sports, baseball is not without examples of verbal intimidation—like the time, in 2019, when Todd "the Todfather" Frazier responded to a complaint made by Philadelphia Phillies pitcher Jake Arrieta by threatening "to put a dent in his skull." Ice hockey, too, is no stranger to menacing tactics. These include body checking from behind, checking an opponent who's not in control of the puck, and "spearing" with the pointed end of the stick, even when it falls way short of actually making contact with an opponent's body.

By far the most theatrical form of sporting intimidation is the haka, which is performed before rugby union matches by the New Zealand All Blacks. Here the team appears in formation, chanting and executing various movements in unison. Similar pre-match rugby rituals are found in other Pacific islands, like Samoa, Tonga and Fiji. Although we're constantly being told that the All Blacks haka is *not* a war dance, but rather a ceremony for welcoming strangers, it certainly has all the trappings of a war dance: a lot of foot-stamping, thigh slapping, arm slapping, facial grimacing, tongue lolling and, rather ominously, gestures that look uncomfortably like throat-slitting, not to mention some of the chants, which include explicit threats like "We live!" and "You die!" There's also an unfortunate lop-sidedness with the haka because it's only performed by the All Blacks, while the opposing team is required to watch the spectacle from a suitable distance.

While many rugby spectators, as well as players from other nations, treasure the tradition of the New Zealand haka and would hate to see it disappear, some opposing teams have regarded the ritual performance as a form of intimidation and attempted to nullify its effects. Historically, there have been several instances where, faced with the haka, opposing teams have produced a "haka riposte"—a demonstration of their refusal to be cowed. This has taken various forms, like linking arms in solidarity, adopting their own formation, advancing right up to the haka, and staring down the All Black players. To show how unimpressed he was by the haka, Australian wing David Campese started doing warm-up exercises while it was in progress.

Intimidation is also a feature of solo sports where individuals compete with each other. For example, it's reported that in order to unsettle other players, golf maestro Tiger Woods would stand very close to them when they were putting or teeing off—thereby imposing himself and suggesting that these players couldn't even claim the personal space around them. At the London 2012 Olympic Games, South African swimmer Chad le Clos caused a big stir when he took gold in the men's 200-metre butterfly, beating the legendary and seemingly invincible American Michael Phelps into second place. Four years later, at the Rio 2016 Olympics, the two swimmers were preparing for a semi-final of the same event when le Clos started shadow boxing in front of Phelps. Afterward, le Clos tried to dismiss his performance as just fooling around, but it was obvious at the time that Phelps interpreted it very differently, because he pointedly averted his eyes from le Clos's antics while adopting an expression that later became known as the "PhelpsFace"—an unusual blend of annoyance, disdain and disgust.

A standard feature of sports like boxing and mixed martial arts is the so-called "staredown," which frequently takes place during official weigh-ins. The two fighters will face each other, often head-to-head and sometimes nose-to-nose, attempting to stare each other down without wavering or blinking. Being locked together in a primitive, agonistic stare enables them to demonstrate that they won't back down and that they mean serious business. Squaring off against each other, the fighters will usually try to look thoroughly menacing—standing tall, flexing their muscles, not breaking gaze and assuming a threatening, if somewhat enigmatic, facial expression with their jaws clamped tight. Apart from those unusual occasions when they end up shaking hands, physical contact between the fighters is generally discouraged. However, it's not uncommon for these restraints to be cast aside and for the situation to get spectacularly out of hand.

Utter mayhem erupted at the press conference that took place prior to the 2002 World Heavyweight Championship fight between Lennox Lewis and Mike Tyson. We're told that Tyson was waiting on stage for Lewis, staring in the direction where he was about to appear. When Lewis emerged, Tyson strode purposefully up to him, but he was blocked by one of Lewis's minders. Tyson threw a left hook, all hell broke loose, the two fighters ended up on the floor, and in the ensuing mêlée Tyson got his teeth into Lewis's leg. This wasn't the only time Tyson resorted to biting, because in 1997 during his WBA heavyweight match against Evander Holyfield he'd managed to remove a one-inch piece of cartilage from Holyfield's right ear, and soon afterward he bit Holyfield's left ear as well. As it happens, Tyson isn't the only person to have recruited his teeth as a weapon. In 2005 British Lions rugby player Danny Grewcock was sent home from New Zealand after biting the finger of All Blacks hooker Keven Mealumu during a test match. Soccer is also no stranger to biting, the most famous practitioner being Uruguayan footballer Luis Suarez, who reputedly sunk his teeth into opponents on no fewer than three separate occasions. This tendency of sportsmen to bare their fangs—sometimes even removing bits of flesh and then spitting them out—offers a rather extreme example of the lengths to which some sportsmen will go in an attempt to subdue and strike fear into their opponents. After all, biting someone is an extremely primitive practice—an atavistic action that, quite literally, sets out to treat one's adversary as a form of prey.

The stare-down. Mixed martial arts fighters at the weigh-in before their contest fix one another with an unbroken stare, each sizing up their opponent while signalling their determination to win.

In fact, the predator–prey relationship lies at the very heart of attempts to intimidate an opponent. Casting oneself in the role of predator—in other words, as someone who's bent on destruction—is designed to elicit a complementary response from one's adversary, ideally stripping them of any desire to counter-attack and transforming them into a hapless victim. Whenever animals and humans are faced with a serious threat, the fight-flight-freeze response is automatically activated. The goal of intimidation in the sporting arena is to produce a threatening display that induces sufficient fear to dissuade an adversary from fighting back and instead encourages them to freeze or flee. Animals that realize they're being preyed upon typically enter a chronic state of hyperarousal, where their entire being is focussed on evasion and where their normal functions are dramatically compromised. That's exactly what happens in the sporting world when individuals and teams that are being intimidated become distracted, losing their composure as well as their ability to compete effectively.

Of course, not all attempts at intimidation end with the other side capitulating. In nature documentaries, for example, we've seen how a lone wildebeest being chased by a lion may refuse to accept its role as prey, turn on its heels and attack the aggressor. Situations like these, where the nominal prey switches roles and becomes the predator, can be found across the entire gamut of sport. This was a fighting strategy repeatedly used by Muhammad Ali—where he would dance around the ring, often with his arms down by his side or performing his famous foot shuffle, doing his best to evade his attacker, only moments later to move forward, pummel his opponent with a volley of blows, and then retreat once more to dance around the ring. As we all know, Ali made a habit of menacing his opponents verbally. But what made his threatening invective so distinctive was its humour. For example, nobody thought that Ali meant it when he issued a warning to other fighters, saying that if they ever dreamt of beating him, they'd better wake up and apologize immediately.

The most primitive way for players to appear menacing is to draw attention to their superior height or size, or to give the impression that they're a lot taller or bigger than they really are. In sporting events where stature matters, competitors need to take account of relative size, largely because it tends to correlate positively with aggression, risk proneness and a history of winning. In men's ice hockey, for example, it's been found that taller and heavier players are more likely to be penalized for aggressive behaviour.[4] Aside from feeling that they're smaller, contestants can end up feeling intimidated in several other ways. An opponent's convincing display of calm confidence can often disorient players and lead them to doubt their ability to cope with the challenges ahead. Equally, a well-established reputation for being a natural-born winner, or for coming from behind or having surprises up one's sleeve, can do the trick. Players and teams can also feel threatened and unsure of themselves when their opponents have just enjoyed a successful phase of play or have added points to their tally, followed up by extravagant celebrations. Loud and vociferous supporters, especially when they surround the sporting arena in large numbers, can easily discourage individuals and teams. The same is true when players have to compete away from home, especially when the contest takes place in rival territory.

There are actually two opposing schools of thought regarding "home advantage": One is that playing on one's own patch gives individuals and teams a competitive edge because they feel protective about their territory. In addition, they're operating in familiar surroundings and are supported by more of their loyal fans. The counter-argument is that playing at home can raise expectations and therefore impose greater pressures on players to succeed, which causes them to "choke" and under-perform.

In addition to trash talking and intimidation, contestants can try to get inside their opponents' heads, erode their confidence and hamper their performance by resorting to the three Ds: "distraction," "demoralization" and "deception."

Distraction Tells

Players may become distracted whenever their attention is drawn away from their immediate sporting goals and toward extraneous concerns that may actually interfere with them. Broadly speaking, this can happen in two ways: through "internal distraction," where a player, for example, allows their mind to wander from the task at hand, or through "external distraction," where someone else, or other people, set out to interfere with the single-minded focus that a player is trying to sustain. Attempts to distract rival players don't always work—in fact, they may sometimes have the opposite effect of galvanizing a player's resolve and improving their performance.

We see this when footballers who are about to take a penalty are greeted by jeers and booing by the opposition's fans, which only strengthens the penalty-taker's determination to succeed. There are, however, instances on the playing field where distraction serves its intended purpose. A memorable example of this took place during the 1984 European Football Cup Final penalty shootout between Liverpool and Roma, when the Liverpool goalkeeper, Bruce Grobbelaar, walked over to the goal, smiling for the cameras, and promptly pretended to eat the net before taking up his position in the goal mouth. When the Roma player struck the ball, he missed the goal altogether. Grobbelaar repeated this routine with the next Roma kicker, but this time he added his famous "wobbly legs" routine, which looked like an exaggerated caricature of fear. This diversionary performance also ended with the Roma kicker missing the goal, and Liverpool went on to win the penalty shootout 4–2, becoming the European Champions. Of course, we'll never know if the Roma penalty-takers would have been on target had they not been confronted by Grobbelaar's antics, but there's every likelihood that his unnerving distractions helped to secure the victory for Liverpool. In recent years, new rules have been introduced in an attempt to curb the use of brazen distraction techniques by goalkeepers. While goalkeepers will no longer be allowed to clown around during penalty shootouts, they'll need to find more subtle ways to divert the attention of their opponents.

Demoralizing Tells

Demoralizing also plays an important part in sport, offering a shortcut to success by undermining an opponent's confidence and therefore their ability to play to the best of their ability. Like distraction, demoralizing may either be self-inflicted or instigated by players' opponents, and this can occur in individual as well as team sports. One way to demoralize an opponent is by giving the impression that you're finding the contest unusually easy—that it's "no sweat." A celebrated example of this occurred during the marathon at the 1952 Summer Olympics in Helsinki, when the Czech athlete Emil Zátopek, who'd already won gold in the 5,000- and 10,000-metre races but who'd never actually run a marathon before, decided to enter the event. Some miles into the race, Zátopek caught up with Jim Peters, the British runner who was favoured by everyone to win the marathon, and innocently enquired if he was going fast enough. After a brief conversation, Zátopek took off and disappeared into the distance. Zátopek won the race but Peters failed to finish—which shows that an effective way to undermine the competition is to give the impression that you've still got lots of fuel left in your tank, especially when it looks like the other contestants are running on empty.

If there's one thing that disheartens track athletes it's being overtaken at speed, especially on the final lap. What's even worse is being overtaken by someone who's so confident of winning that they begin to celebrate their victory long before they're anywhere near the finishing line. That's exactly what happened in the 5,000-metres final at the Helsinki World Championships in 1983. Going down the back-straight, Dimitri Demetriev was in the lead and Eamonn Coghlan was behind him. As the Irish athlete passed Demetriev at the top of the final bend, Coghlan looked around, grinned and pumped the air with his fist. Coghlan was so convinced that he had the race in the bag that he took time off to perform an advance victory celebration. The strategy worked because the Russian looked thoroughly dejected and made no attempt to respond. Being overtaken at speed, especially in the latter stages of a race, can be extremely disheartening because it gives the impression that one's rival has lots of energy to spare, and because it requires extra effort to catch up with them. Being overtaken by someone who's already celebrating their victory is even more demoralizing, because it suggests that they've got every reason to feel completely confident about winning.

Deception Tells

Whenever teams or individuals compete, it's important that they conceal certain thoughts or emotions, as well as their intentions and goals, so that their opponents find it more difficult to work out what they're thinking or feeling, and what they're likely to do next. This process gives rise to a peculiar symmetry, where both sides are simultaneously trying to read what's going on in their opponents' heads while trying to disguise what's happening in their own. As you might expect, athletes who have a special talent for deceiving others are also skilled at reading their opponents and spotting their attempts at deception. For most players, the best way to conceal their thoughts and feelings is to come across as emotionally neutral—in other words, to offer the other side as little information about themselves as possible. We often see this in the demeanour of players who are about to enter a contest, especially in their serious, enigmatic facial expressions, which are designed to mask any signs of anxiety and to create an impression of resolve and determination. Players often feel justifiably nervous before a competition, but they also recognize the importance of remaining opaque. That way, their opponents are less likely to capitalize on knowing what they're really feeling.

Players will also disguise their true intentions in an effort to both reduce their opponents' options as well as their ability to react quickly. In cricket, for example, bowlers frequently attempt to conceal whether they're about to deliver a ball with topspin or backspin. They achieve this by standardizing their body movements until the very last moment, when all is revealed by their wrist action. Because the cricket ball travels so fast, batters aren't able to track it throughout its flight, so instead they calculate the ball's speed and trajectory at two points: initially, when it leaves the bowler's hand, and again when it bounces on the pitch.[5]

But the strategy that's even more effective than disguise is that of deception—pretending to entertain certain thoughts or emotions, or planning a certain line of action, while convincing the opponent that we're about to do something completely different.[6] When players are feeling nervous before a competition, they'll often try to hoodwink their opponents by strutting their stuff, standing tall, puffing out their chest, and generally creating an image of unwavering confidence. When these performances are convincing, they can often undermine the opposition's confidence, while at the same time reinforcing the actor's beliefs in their own chances of success.

It's also possible to disorient an opponent by doing the exact opposite of puffing oneself up. "Sandbagging" is one technique; "self-handicapping" is another. Instead of drawing attention to their fitness, an athlete who's sandbagging does everything in their power to conceal it; for example, by appearing to limp before the event, wearing lots of bandages, or generally giving the impression that they're not in peak condition. It's an attempt to reduce the amount of effort that an opponent feels they need to invest in order to win. Self-handicapping is the verbal equivalent of sandbagging. Here the athlete finds a way to inform the other contestants that they aren't fully fit or to subtly refer to their own recent failures. As a sporting strategy, self-handicapping offers competitors a number of advantages: If they do badly, they can always excuse themselves with reference to their supposed handicap. If, on the other hand, they do well, they can let everyone know that they succeeded in spite of their ostensible handicap. The hidden danger with self-handicapping, however, is that while individuals are trying to lower their opponents' expectations, they may inadvertently weaken their own beliefs about their ability to succeed.

The natural world is full of compelling instances of both disguise and deception. Disguise is found, for example, wherever creatures resort to camouflage as a means of hiding from predators or potential prey, while instances of deception can be seen in the way that male cuttlefish masquerade as members of the opposite sex in order to gain access to receptive females, or how certain orchids mimic the odour and appearance of female insects so as to encourage males of the same species to copulate with the flower and in the process to disseminate its pollen. In the sporting world, deception is potentially much more effective than disguise. That's because while disguise simply keeps one's opponents guessing, deception endeavours to send them off in the wrong direction, which opens up opportunities for the person doing the deceiving. Since deception provides one's opponents with misleading information, whereas disguise merely reduces the amount of information that's available to them, it follows that deception is likely to be the superior strategy.

Zoologists have drawn a valuable distinction between what they call "honest signals" and "dishonest signals"—where honest signals publicize an animal's genuine qualities or intentions, and dishonest signals lay claims to qualities or intentions that an animal does not possess but would like others to think that it does.[7] Dishonest signals are an integral feature of deception in sport because they involve communications that are fake and intentionally misleading. They can be found across the full gamut of sporting activities, in many cases organized on recurring principles of deception.

Rugby Union, for example, is famous for it "dummy pass," where a player who's running with the ball gives every indication that they're on the verge of passing the ball to a team-mate, only to hold on to the ball and try to run with it. The success of a dummy pass will largely depend on contextual factors and whether the opposition players "buy" the dummy—in other words, are convinced that it's a real pass in the making rather than a pretend one. Successful dummies often involve slightly exaggerated movements, and they tend to occur in situations where it appears to be in the interests of the ball carrier to pass the ball. On the other hand, dummy passes are more likely to fail when the opposing player who's being "sold" the dummy has a high level of anticipation, spots the deception and tackles the person carrying the ball. What's instructive here is that a rugby player who's running with the ball, trying to avoid being tackled, may produce honest as well as dishonest signals within the same dynamic performance—where honest signals are those that the player is unaware of and/or unable to change, and dishonest signals are those that are consciously controlled and designed to deceive the opposition. In the case of the rugby side-step, dishonest signals tend to be located in the head, eyes and arms. The main reason seasoned rugby players are so much better than novices at anticipating side-steps is that they instinctively pay more attention to their opponents' trunk and thighs—in other words, those parts of the body that are more likely to produce honest signals.[8]

Similar examples of disguise are evident in tennis, where players are constantly trying to read the so-called "advance cues" of their opponent so they can work out what kind of shot they're about to play and where it's likely to land.[9] To reduce their opponents' ability to exploit these cues, tennis players will often try to disguise their shots, in some cases making misleading head, eye and body movements, as well as delaying their return shots to the very last moment, so that the other person has less information to go on and less time to respond.

Tennis offers other examples of disguise, one being the habit that some tennis players have of "grunting" whenever they hit the ball. Monica Seles was renowned for her guttural yelps and squeals, but there were also times when the Williams sisters, Serena and Venus, appeared to be making a serious bid to become Queen of the Grunters. There's still some debate about the advantages of grunting. Those in favour argue that it tenses the muscles in the abdomen, which in turn increases the power behind the shot. Back in the eighties, when Jimmy Connors dominated men's tennis, he was widely regarded as King of the Grunters, and it was even claimed that his serves were more accurate when accompanied by one of his loud grunts. In the opposing camp are those who dismiss grunting as rude, antisocial and distracting for the opponent. When Jennifer Capriati played Monica Seles in San Diego some years ago, she actually complained about Seles's ear-piercing grunts, only to be informed by the umpire that they were well within the normal range. However, it's now being suggested that the real purpose of grunting—even though it's not recognized by tennis players—is to mask the sound of the racket on the ball, so that information about its speed and spin becomes degraded, thereby putting the person who's receiving the serve at a disadvantage.[10] Auditory cues also play an important role in other sports. Footballers, for example, are able to determine the speed of a penalty kick from the sound of the boot striking the ball, and fencers are said to rely on the sound of their opponent's footwork for information about the direction and speed of their movement across the piste.

Deception is common in basketball, where it's frequently accompanied by misleading movements of the head and eyes. When producing a "head fake," basketball players will turn their head and eyes in one direction, giving the impression that's where they're focussed, only moments later to pass the ball in a completely different direction.[11] Here, as elsewhere, split-second timing is vital, because the time that elapses between turning one's head and eyes, and then passing the ball, needs to be long enough for opponents to be fooled but not so short that they don't have time to be duped into acting incorrectly. In these situations, players who focus on their opponents' head and eye movements, rather than on other, more informative parts of their body, are inevitably more susceptible to this type of deception. In addition to head fakes, basketball players also employ "ball fakes," where they pretend to be about to pass the ball but end up holding on to it, and "shot fakes," where they give the impression that they're about to make a shot but don't actually do so. Similar fakes can also be found in sports like team handball and beach volleyball.

Boxing too is famous for its deceptive ploys, and the same is true of other combative sports like karate, judo and fencing. Among other things, boxing is renowned for the "feint," where a boxer gives the impression of punching with, say, their left hand, only to stop short and deliver a blow with the right hand instead—the logic being that a feint should elicit a defensive response to one part of the body, leaving other parts of the body exposed to immediate attack. A rather similar technique in soccer is the "step-over," where a player who's dribbling the ball down the field tries to deceive the other side by stepping over the ball, as if they're about to change tack, but actually continues in the same direction. Cristiano Ronaldo is probably the best-known exponent of the step-over, a trick he's used to good effect on numerous occasions. Skilled performances like the step-over are an enduring feature of the theatrical side of football. Other famous instances where footballers have "showboated" their virtuosity might include Johan Cruyff's dramatic changes of direction while remaining in possession of the ball, and Alessia Russo's exquisite backheel nutmeg goal against Sweden during Euro 2022.

When it comes to deception, soccer has probably attracted more discussion than any other sport. This may have something to do with the alacrity with which football players fake injuries, as well as their penchant for "diving"—that is, pretending that they've been fouled or tripped by a member of the other side, and then writhing on the ground in a pantomime of pain. Psychologists have examined real-life cases of diving, and they've identified certain overblown features that are associated with dives. These include the tendency of faking players to throw their arms up in the air, with their hands open, and to arch their back as they're falling.[12] These actions are all designed to accentuate the spectacle and to draw the referee's attention to the supposed infraction. But the exaggerated nature of fake diving is what gives it away—this, after all, is not what happens when people are really tripped and fall down naturally.

The other iconic soccer arenas where deception occurs are the "free kick" and the "penalty shootout." When a free kick is awarded, the player taking the kick can either execute a conventional parabolic kick, which rises and falls in the same plane, or else they can apply spin to the ball at the point of contact so that it assumes a curved, lateral, accelerating trajectory—what's commonly referred to as "bending the ball." Curved free kicks place enormous demands on the goalkeepers, partly because the human visual system isn't very well equipped to deal with that type of acceleration. Moreover, if goalkeepers focus on the initial movement of the ball, there's every chance they'll miss it, whereas if they take account of the spin-induced curve of the ball they're much more likely to be in a position to intercept it.[13]

Penalty shootouts, on the other hand, take place when both teams have the same number of points after extra time. Their purpose is to decide which side is to win the game by securing more successful penalty kicks from five separate attempts (or more if the two teams continue to be tied, at which point they enter a phase called "sudden death").[14] The shootout takes place at one end of the football pitch, with the goalkeepers from both sides taking turns to defend the goal, while selected kickers from the two sides try to get the ball past the opposing goalkeeper. As anyone who's ever witnessed them knows, penalty shootouts are full of nail-biting tension—like a drama-laden combination of *High Noon*, *The Magnificent Seven* and *Gunfight at the OK Corral* all rolled into one.

Each phase of the penalty shootout conforms to the same basic choreography—the goalkeeper from one side positions him or herself in the centre of the goal, a kicker from the other side takes the ball, places it on the penalty spot (which is 12 yards away from the goal line), and then walks away, pauses, runs up and kicks the ball. Although there are limits on how long they may take, kickers are able to vary their timing, their angle of approach, how they connect with the ball and where they aim it. Kickers will frequently attempt to fool the goalkeeper by producing dishonest signals about their intentions. Goalkeepers may also be involved in the reciprocal process of trying to hoodwink the kicker about whether they're planning to move from the centre of the goal, and if so in which direction. Both the goalkeeper and the kicker are therefore bound together by similar concerns—trying to read each other's intentions while concealing their own, deciding how and when to proceed, and producing misleading signals about what they're going to do next.

During shootouts, goalkeepers are unfortunately disadvantaged on at least three counts. Firstly, it usually takes a mere 400 milliseconds from the moment the ball is kicked till the moment it crosses the goal line, and secondly the statistics are against them, because roughly 80 percent of shots at goal are successful. Thirdly, goalkeepers have to deal with time pressure, because if they're going to try and reach one of the goalposts in time to intercept the ball, they can't afford to wait until the kicker has kicked it. By then it's usually too late. This not only means that goalkeepers have to commit themselves earlier—typically no later than the point when the kicker's non-shooting foot hits the ground—but also that they're usually unable to respond to anything that the kicker does after they themselves have moved one way or the other. In some cases, the goalkeeper may have prior knowledge about a kicker's tactical preferences, but a lot of the time they simply have to decide in advance whether they're going to protect the centre of the goal mouth or make a move to cover the left or right side of the goal.[15]

All things being equal, it's advantageous for goalkeepers to try and cover the right side of the goal (looked at from their point of view) because in 60 percent of cases that's where penalty kickers aim the ball.

Since the majority of kickers are right-footed, it's easier for them to aim at the right, just as it's more convenient for left-footed kickers to go for the left side of the goal. As we've already seen, some goalkeepers may try to distract the kicker, in the hope that the kicker will become so confused that they miss the goal mouth altogether. Goalkeepers may also try to encourage kickers to aim for one side by giving the false impression that they're about to dive in a particular direction or by almost imperceptibly positioning themselves off-centre so as to encourage the kicker to aim for what appears to be the undefended side of the goal.[16] In principle, goalkeepers can improve their anticipation of a kicker's intentions; for example, by observing the position of the kicker's torso during the run-up and by noticing how they place their non-shooting foot on the ground, both of which can provide important, albeit rather late, clues to where the kicker is aiming the ball.[17]

Kickers can try to deceive the goalkeeper in a number of ways.[18] One is by looking at one side of the goal before booting the ball in the opposite direction. Another is to approach the ball at an angle, which misleads the goalkeeper into thinking that they should cover one side of the goal rather than the other. Kickers can also gain an advantage by timing their run-up so that the goalkeeper has already made a commitment to go one way or the other before they actually kick the ball. Research on high-stakes penalty shootouts suggests that there are fairly reliable indications as to whether a kicker is likely to succeed or fail. For example, kickers who are especially nervous, and therefore more prone to failure, will often try to get the task over as quickly as possible. This means they're more likely to place the ball on the mark impatiently, and to spend less time composing themselves before taking their shot at goal. For some kickers, the intimidating spectacle of a confident goalkeeper guarding the goal is enough to raise their anxiety levels—to make them even more worried about choking, missing the goal and letting their team down. Some kickers cope with this by averting their eyes from the goalkeeper and/or by keeping their back to the goalkeeper for as long as they can.[19] By behaving like this, kickers are abiding by the universal principle that one of the most tempting ways to cope with an aversive stimulus is to not look at it, or to reduce the amount of time that one is exposed to it. Even if they're not aware of it, that's effectively what worried kickers are doing. By studiously ignoring the goalkeeper, however, kickers automatically reduce the amount of information they can glean about the goalkeeper's disposition, which is one of the reasons why they tend to be less successful.

Giveaway Tells

To gain a psychological edge over their opponents, players need to project a particular image of themselves, while at the same time ensuring that their opponents aren't able to read them. In spite of their best efforts, most players reveal crucial things about themselves, which, if their opponents actually noticed and knew how to interpret, could give them an enormous strategic advantage. These "giveaways" may either be deliberate or unintended, often without the person even being aware of them. Either way, giveaways can provide an important source of information about players' thoughts and feelings, and what they're planning to do next.

As we've seen, players who are trying to delude their opponents will often inadvertently produce dishonest signals that give them away. Footballers performing a dive, for example, frequently overplay their hand, creating an exaggerated, cartoon version of what happens when a player is genuinely tripped and falls down naturally. However, it's not just the mechanics of the dive that expose its dishonesty; it's often what happens immediately afterward that can be just as revealing. After players have dived and are lying on the ground, they'll often do a rapid peek-a-boo—sometimes stealing a glance through their fingers—so they can check what's happening around them, see how the referee is responding, and find out if the dive has had the desired effect.

Close inspection of penalty shootouts shows that goalkeepers and kickers often produce giveaway tells too. Kickers, for example, will often expose their anxiety in their impetuous behaviour, avoidance tactics, facial expressions and overall demeanour. Because it's so difficult to control all the muscles in the face, players' facial expressions often provide vital clues to their current state of mind. For instance, if you watch what's happening when a team is losing, you'll often find that while several players are making a concerted effort to mask their feelings, others are unwittingly revealing their disappointment in their sad, pained, worried or detached facial expressions. Players who become disheartened tend to hang their head and look down at the ground, and they're also inclined to lick or bite their lips, or to bite the inside of their mouth. In extreme cases, other "distress signals" may appear. We've already seen, for example, how a footballer who's missed a shot at goal will often perform the "cradle" gesture by placing their hands behind the back of their head, and how supporters will frequently resort to the same gesture, along with other symbolically self-protective actions like the "head-clasp" and "eye-cover." Notice too what happens when a footballer who's committed a foul is summoned by the referee and issued with a yellow or red card that is going to exclude them temporarily or permanently from the game. In these situations, the player who's being carded will almost invariably produce an enormous shrug, lifting their shoulders, raising their elbows and presenting the palms of their hands—all as a means of denying guilt and insisting on their innocence.

Another common reaction is evident during rugby matches, when one of the teams scores a try. If you watch how the members of the other team behave while they're waiting behind their try-line for the conversion to take place, you'll notice that several of them are standing with their hands on their hips. Why this happens with such regularity is something of a mystery, because in most situations the act of placing one's hands on one's hips serves as a signal of assertiveness, whereas in this context it appears to reflect the players' dejection and feelings of despondency. We can only assume that, by adopting an arms-akimbo pose, these team members are unconsciously trying to reassert themselves—signalling that they won't be outdone, while at the same time using the posture to remind themselves that they haven't been defeated.

Among the rich variety of sports, singles tennis stands out as brimming with giveaways. In almost every round the players' behaviour provides revealing insights into their state of mind. There are several reasons why this is the case, including the fact that the reputational and financial stakes are so high in professional tennis. In addition, there are almost unlimited opportunities for the players to produce giveaways, and the game itself is so gladiatorial. Some of the tennis giveaways to watch out for include:

Distress Signals. When players find themselves in trouble, they're liable to try and curb their anxiety by touching themselves, by focussing on their equipment or by fiddling with their clothing. Players who've just experienced a run of bad play will often try to reassure themselves by stroking their hair, wiping their forehead or blowing on the palm of their hand to cool it down. During rest periods, they might wipe their racket down or check it out by gently tapping it on the ground. Players who are falling behind will frequently adjust their shirt or their skirt. Some players have their own distinctive methods for coping. Roger Federer, for example, likes to play with his headband. In his case the adjustment is usually subtle, but it's much more likely to appear when he's in trouble than when he's comfortably in the lead. Rafael Nadal, on the other hand, has a habit of fiddling with his shorts. During a match he'll repeatedly grab the seat of his pants and pull it away from his backside. Since this happens throughout the game, it's clearly a nervous tic rather than a means of keeping cool. It's Nadal's way of making himself feel comfortable—physically as well as mentally.

Racket Tuning. In between bouts of play, tennis players will occasionally focus their attention on their racket and start to adjust the strings, almost as if they're painstakingly tuning their racket. There appear to be practical as well as psychological reasons for this widespread habit. After repeated contact with the ball, racket strings will start to move slightly, so in order to maximize the efficiency of the racket it may occasionally be necessary to straighten out the strings. That's the practical side. On the psychological side, fiddling with the strings clearly provides the player with a welcome refuge, a distraction from the spectacle of their opponent and the spectators, and an opportunity to make minor adjustments that might improve the quality of their shots going forward. Players are actually much more likely to engage in racket tuning when they're on a losing streak, not so much when their game is going well. This suggests that racket tuning is essentially a "displacement activity" involving a stereotyped and repetitive sequence of actions that helps the player to deflect their anxiety but has very little practical value in itself.

Ball Selection. When players are about to serve, we frequently find them in possession of several balls, discarding the ones they don't want until they end up with just two. The reason for what looks like a strange ritual is that the players are trying to select two balls: a smooth one and a fluffy one. Newer balls are smoother, whereas older balls tend to be fluffy and have more grip. Because smooth balls have less resistance and travel faster, they're considered more suitable for the first serve. While fluffy balls are slower, they're much easier to control, which means that they're better for the second serve, where players place more emphasis on accuracy than on speed. So next time you see a player discarding some balls and keeping others, remember that they're not being superstitious or whimsical—there's method in their madness.

Chest Exposure. One way that male players try to intimidate their opponent is by taking off their top and exposing their muscled, tanned and hairy chests. This pretends to be a pragmatic exercise—an excuse to change clothes or a way of cooling down—but the amount of time some players remain exposed suggests that they're trying to remind their opponent that they're dealing with someone who's tough.

Routines. The little routines that players perform around the court and during the match give them a sense of familiarity and security, which in turn helps them to remain calm and focus their energies on the game. In the uncertain world of tennis, personal rituals offer the assurance that some things are predictable. For example, when Novak Djokovic serves, he has a habit of bouncing the ball with his racket on the ground several times. He then shifts the ball to his left hand and bounces it manually, sometimes more than a dozen times. This metronomic routine helps to frame his actions, giving him a chance to concentrate on his serve and to decide what he's going to do next. Rafael Nadal also has his own routines. When he sits down during a break, for example, he has two bottles of water, which he carefully lines up, so that their labels face forward. He's also very fussy about his socks—they both have to be 15 cm up his leg, and the sponsor's label has to be visible. But when he's serving, his routine is very different from Djokovic's, because while Djokovic varies how often he bounces the ball on the ground before serving, Nadal consistently bounces the ball on the ground five times—never more, never less.

Tummy Pats. Normally, tennis players relate to each other in a reasonably polite and friendly manner. There are tells, however, that reveal their true feelings toward each other. One of these is the "tummy pat," which usually occurs at the end of a game when one player—typically the winner—pats the other player on the stomach as they're leaving the court. On the face of it, this action looks innocuous, even affectionate, but it's actually a disguised gesture of rejection. In fact, when one player pats another player on the tummy, they're frequently performing an unconscious "intention movement" by positioning their hand so that they can push the other player away. When players like Federer and Nadal pat other players in this way at the end of a game, it's most unlikely that they, or the player whose tummy is being patted, recognizes the ill-disposed significance of this gesture.

Team Tells

The success or failure of sporting teams depends not only on the skills and determination of its members but also on how cohesive and closely bonded they are as a team. The leader or leaders play an important role in giving direction and bolstering the confidence of the team members, both before the match begins and while it's in progress. Team spirit is also heavily dependent on the relationships and interactions between the members of the team. One way they're able to offer mutual support is by saying encouraging things to each other; another is through physical contact, whether it takes the form of a pat on the back, a ruffle of someone's hair or a prolonged hug. Not surprisingly, a positive correlation has been found between how much the members of a team touch each other during competition and the team's chances of winning. Psychologist Dacher Keltner and his colleagues at Berkeley conducted a wide-ranging research project on the role that touch plays in National Basketball Association games, and they discovered a broad range of touching actions, including high-fives, fist-bumps, head pats and chest bumps.[20] They found that teams that engaged in greater touching early in the season were more likely to be successful later in the season, and that members who used touch to encourage, console or congratulate their team-mates helped to empower the team as a whole. Sex differences in touching have also been found in basketball teams, with female players engaging in more same-sex touch than male players.[21] This is particularly noticeable when women's teams are doing badly, as opposed to when they're doing well.

Informal observation of contact sports like American football and Rugby Union exposes a great deal of touching between players, including examples of head-patting and bum-patting. These forms of touch are largely restricted to male sports, their purpose being to offer someone encouragement while surreptitiously treating them as a relative novice. Touching a team-mate on the head or the bum is definitely an intimate action, and therefore one that presupposes a close, personal relationship. But because it also contains elements of presumption and condescension, these forms of touch may be seen as a way of redressing the imbalance between the parties concerned, as well as a means of making both the toucher and the person being touched feel good about themselves.

It's very likely that touching in sport operates on a feedback loop, so that the more individual team members support, encourage and congratulate each other with touch, the more successful the team is likely to be, and the more successes a team notches up, the more reasons the team members have to celebrate their achievements by making physical contact with each other. However, it's worth emphasizing that touch in sport isn't restricted to success. In doubles tennis, for example, the partners will regularly pat or fist-bump each other, regardless of whether they've just won or lost a point. Here, as elsewhere in sport, touch plays a vital role in bonding team players, and keeping them in close contact, physically as well as psychologically. It follows that the more they like and respect each other, the better team members will understand one another, and the sharper they'll be at predicting what their team-mates are going to do next. Anticipation is of course one of the keys to success in sport, and anything that enhances players' abilities to read and predict the game is only to be welcomed.

While those involved in team sports are naturally able to reassure and inspire each other, both with words and deeds, individual players are denied this luxury. In sports like tennis, squash, boxing, wrestling and judo—all of which are essentially duels—the contestants are singularly alone, apart from occasional contact with, say, their coach and/ or noisy exhortations from their supporters. The fact that singles tennis players don't have anyone present to support them may explain why they appear to spend so much time on court talking to themselves, congratulating, cajoling or even scolding themselves, and physically touching and reassuring themselves too—almost as if they're providing themselves with the companionship they would have enjoyed if they'd been involved in a team sport.

The solitary nature of the game may also provide clues to why singles tennis players spend so much time focussed on their racket— the tool on which they rely so heavily, and their only true companion. Maybe that's the reason why, every now and then, we find singles tennis players venting their anger on their racket and smashing it to pieces—

not because they feel they've personally made a mess of things, but because their disloyal racket has let them down. Over the years, several famous tennis players have lost their cool and ended up demolishing their racket. The list of men's players includes Andy Murray, Nick Kyrgios, Roger Federer and Novak Djokovic, while the women's list includes Aryna Sabalenka, Victoria Azarenka, Serena Williams and Coco Gauff. But the prize for the greatest racket-wrecker must surely go to Alexander Bublik from Kazakhstan, who managed to destroy three of his rackets during a match, and another two soon afterward.

Celebration Tells

It's now widely recognized, although not universally accepted, that sportsmen and women have a right to celebrate their victory, provided they aren't obscene and don't unnecessarily demean or insult their defeated opponents. In recent years, sporting celebrations have become ever more inventive, flamboyant and eye-catching. In searching for what makes them similar or different to each other, it appears that four main ingredients form the basis of most modern sporting celebrations, namely "spotlighting," "elation," "potency" and "amusement."[22] These four constituents of celebrations are not unlike the four "humours" of medieval medicine, except that in this case they combine in various ways to produce different types of celebrations.

Consider what happens on the running track: when a competitor crosses the line first, they frequently stretch out their arms, with the palms of their hands exposed, with a broad grin on their face. This fleeting spectacle has two important constituents: the outstretched arms drawing everyone's attention while symbolically inviting everyone to join in the celebration, and the smile, an expression of the athlete's unbounded pleasure. In this single act of celebration, we find the arms "spotlighting" the athlete, while the smile publicizes their "elation." But athletes also celebrate their victory in other ways—for example, by raising an arm and punching the air as they cross the finishing line. This celebratory performance conveys a very different message altogether, underlining the athlete's "potency." There may also be other occasions when athletes celebrate their achievements not by smiling, stretching out the arms or punching the air, but by dancing, performing hijinks or clowning around, purely for the purpose of "amusement." Let's take a closer look at each of these four celebratory ingredients.

SPOTLIGHTING

For a sporting celebration to work properly, it needs to draw everyone's attention to the person or team that's just won. Because winning confers status, people need to be reminded who the winners are. The main purpose of celebrations therefore is to shine a light on the victor, ensuring that they, rather than any of the other contestants, become the sole focus of attention. Immediately after a contest, there's often a stark contrast between the behaviour of winner and losers. For athletes who've spent years preparing for a competition, losing can be a heart-breaking experience. This is often evident in their body language. Athletes who've won often appear to be energized, while those who've been beaten look like they're on the verge of collapse. Similarly, winners' behaviour is often physically open and expansive, whereas the actions of losers— especially those who had hopes of being more successful—tend to be physically restrictive.

Not only do losers try to avoid the limelight, they also make themselves look smaller and inconspicuous. While winners often strut around with their head held high, losers tend to lower their head and eyes, to avert their gaze and become disengaged. Where winners are animated, losers are usually deadpan and expressionless. However, even when losers are trying to put on a brave face, their restrained emotions may occasionally come to the surface, momentarily exposing their feelings of sadness and disappointment. However, the differences between winners and losers aren't just behavioural—they're also intimately connected with their physiology. That's because the experience of winning often confers a welcome concoction of feel-good hormones like endorphins, testosterone and adrenalin, whereas losing simply offers a dose of cortisol, the anxiety hormone. Winners don't always take part in victory celebrations, and they're not the exclusive preserve of winners, because there are instances where losers behave almost exactly like winners. The best place to see this is at the end of a city marathon, where athletes, who're miles behind the leaders, still behave like winners as they cross the finishing line, waving their arms around and beaming with joy. For them, it's obviously not about winning—it's about completing the course and doing so in a sufficiently respectable time that warrants celebration.

ELATION

Smiling, as we know, is the quintessential way we humans share our happiness with others, and that's why it plays such a central role in the spontaneous displays of sporting winners. While smiles may be common among winners, they tend to be rare among losers—unless the losers in question have performed far better than they'd expected, in which case they're very likely to be joyful too. There are three other points worth reminding ourselves about winning and smiling.

The first is that there's clearly a time and place, even for smiling. Although winners display their happiness during their victory lap of the stadium, they're inclined to adopt a more sombre expression when they're standing on the podium, listening to their national anthem. At this point in their celebration, there's a good chance they'll actually start crying or make a valiant effort to suppress their tears.

The second point worth noting is that when an athlete wins an important event, not having assumed that victory was a certainty, it often shows in a facial expression of gleeful surprise—they raise their eyebrows, widen their eyes, and open their mouth wide. The result is a blended expression of shock and jubilation. In recent years there have been some famous examples of this, one being the look of intense surprise and joy on Kelly Holmes's face when she won the women's 800 metres at the Athens Olympics. Another was Mo Farah's look of sheer happiness and disbelief when, having already taken gold in the men's 10,000 metres at the London Olympics, he won the men's 5,000 metres too.

This brings us to the third point, which is that when athletes win, their reaction to victory is almost instantaneous. In some cases, they may start to celebrate their triumph beforehand, but if they do wait, they certainly don't leave much time between winning and smiling. The speed of this reaction is also present in other ways that people celebrate their triumphs.

POTENCY

When individuals win an important event, they sometimes celebrate their victory with "potency signals." This can be done in several ways: by performing "power gestures," by making loud and threatening noises, and by producing menacing facial expressions. Power gestures frequently involve a clenched fist, which is used to publicize the person's physical strength and what's sometimes referred to as their "formidability"—in other words, their ability to overcome their opponents. Power gestures can appear in various guises; for example, as an "air punch," where the winner straightens their arm and thrusts their clenched fist into the air above them, or a "fist pump," where the arm is bent at the elbow and the clenched fist is punched upward, rather like a boxer's uppercut. Given its animation and its undisguised phallic appearance, the fist pump contains strong overtones of male sexual assault and threatened emasculation—none of which, incidentally, seems to discourage professional women tennis players from using this gesture whenever they score an important point against an opponent. These and similar actions can also be temporarily frozen in a static pose, where, for example, someone produces a "strong man pose" with both fists clenched and the arms raised and bent at the elbow, or a one-armed version of that posture. Both static poses and dynamic representations of potency invariably involve flexing of the muscles, which further serves to accentuate an image of the person's strength.

Potency signals can also be vocal. When they've won an event, athletes will sometimes open their mouth wide and let out a deafening roar, and the same is true of victorious swimmers, boxers and exponents of the martial arts. These roars are intended to signal fighting quality, and to keep current and future competitors in their place, and that's why they often sound like the growl of a lion or tiger. As we've noted, roars aren't solely reserved for victory celebrations at the end of a contest—in tennis, they can often be seen and heard when a player wins a crucial point. Producing roars like this gives tennis players a chance to rub their opponent's nose in it, while showing their supporters how determined they are to continue playing well. What little empirical evidence there is about roars suggests that they might convey information about upper-body strength, and that they're linked to impressions of formidability but that they aren't associated with actual fighting success.[23] This raises the possibility that while roars provide information about fighting potential, factors other than fighting potential can determine the outcome of actual fights. In addition to gestures and roars, potency signals can also appear as facial expressions of anger, where the eyebrows are lowered, the gaze is intensely piercing, the mouth is open and the teeth are bared.

The roar and clenched fist. Rafael Nadal celebrates winning a crucial point in the match by clenching his fist and producing a loud roar. These triumphant actions are intended to reinforce his resolve, and to persuade both his opponent and the spectators that he's on a winning streak.

The enduring attraction of these potency displays is that they enable winners to celebrate their triumph over their opponents, to claim that their victory was fully deserved, to demonstrate how pleased they are with their achievement, and to discourage their defeated opponents from thinking that there could have been a different outcome, or that there might be one in the future. We can therefore think of potency displays as a special type of threat signal, one that enables victors to intimidate their rivals and, for the time being, to assume the position of top dog. In fact, some evidence shows that triumph displays can be helpful in certain situations. It's been found, for example, that if footballers celebrate after scoring a goal during a penalty shootout, then the chances of the next kicker doing likewise are significantly increased.[24] It's very possible therefore that by celebrating after a successful shot at goal, kickers actually enhance the confidence of the team-mates who follow them and/or that they manage to diminish the confidence of the other side's goalkeeper.

AMUSEMENT

It's very seldom that victory celebrations turn out to be private, solo affairs. They typically involve not only other players but also spectators, especially when the intention is to entertain and amuse them. We can see this with association football, which has probably spawned a broader range of triumph displays than any other sport.[25] After scoring a goal, football players will often perform the slide, running and slithering across the pitch on their knees, with their arms held aloft. Sometimes they'll kiss their wrist, their index finger, their tattoos or the team badge on their shirt, or they'll direct their gratitude upward toward the heavens. At other times, they'll raise their arm, with their index finger pointing upward, or they'll perform somersaults or backflips, or they'll run around the pitch with their arms outstretched, pretending to be an airplane. During these celebrations, goalscorers will sometimes be mobbed by their jubilant team-mates, while on other occasions they might get together in an impromptu dance routine. In football, however, there are limits to what's permitted during victory celebrations. For instance, players are no longer allowed to remove their top, although this didn't prevent the England Lioness, Chloe Kelly, from whipping off her shirt and running around in her bra after she'd scored a goal at Wembley during Euro 2022.

Whenever American football players score a touchdown, their natural instinct is to celebrate their achievement. However, the National Football League (NFL) has strict regulations about celebrations, banning any that are lewd or offensive, and backing this up with hefty fines for players who break the rules. In spite of these restrictions, certain touchdown celebrations are tolerated, including a range of highly individualized "touchdown dances," where players produce inspired gyrations and pirouettes for the benefit of their appreciative audience. Over the years, numerous touchdowns celebrations have evolved, most of them extremely inventive and original. Terrell Jones, who played for the 49ers, Eagles and Cowboys, created several memorable celebrations—like the time he danced with the cheerleaders, or when he grabbed a fan's bucket of popcorn and poured the contents all over his gaping mouth and face. Other famous players have also devised novel touchdown celebrations. Chad Johnson, for example, once paused his merriment to autograph a pile of jerseys; on another occasion he ran over and proposed to one of the cheerleaders.

The Canadian Football League is much more lenient than the NFL, and probably because of this, its touchdown celebrations are even more outlandish—like the Winnipeg Blue Bombers, whose players form a circle, throw the ball in the air, and then all fall backward as if the ball was an exploding hand grenade. And if this wasn't enough, several Canadian stadiums have devised special touchdown celebrations for their home team, supported in some cases by fluttering flags, a charging horse and even a buzzing airplane. Dazzling signature performances like these obviously draw attention to the players and the team as a whole, but their prime purpose is to create a sense of occasion and to entertain and amuse the people who're watching.

Whenever footballers celebrate by jumping onto and mobbing a successful team-mate, they're effectively engaging in an adult version of the children's practice of "rough-and-tumble play," thereby giving themselves licence to regress and experience the carefree emotions they once enjoyed as children. In their studies of American football fans, psychologists have isolated a process called "basking in reflected glory." They found that, by identifying with a successful team, fans were able to make some of the team's triumphs their own, while at the same time enhancing their personal social standing.[26] When soccer players congratulate or mob one of their team-mates, they're engaging in a similar process by taking some of the glory for themselves. What's equally interesting is how team players respond when the opposite occurs, when, say, a member of the team makes a mess of things. Here, instead of dissociating themselves—a natural, self-protective thing to do—team members will typically reassure and identify with their disappointed team-mate, and in that way help to redefine the failure as inconsequential. These repeated scenes underline the latent power of team membership, showing how individual members will automatically elevate the psychological needs of a downcast team-mate above any desire they may have had to distance themselves from failure.

As we've found, victory celebrations perform a host of different functions. In addition to offering an emotional release from all the tensions that build up before and during a competition, they also provide winners with a means of drawing attention to themselves, showboating their sporting skills, expressing their delight, intimidating their opponents, connecting with their team-mates, and involving and entertaining spectators. In some cases, several of these functions are performed at the same time. For example, in 2012 when Robert Harting, the German discus thrower, won gold at the London Olympics, ripping off his top, exposing his muscled torso, running around the stadium in a state of unbridled joy and whooping up the crowd, not a single function of sporting celebrations was omitted from his frenzied performance.

With sporting celebrations, however, timing is of the essence, because while it's fine to celebrate afterward, it's often ill-advised to do so before the event has been completed. There have been several disheartening, and sometimes quite comical, instances where contestants have celebrated their victory prematurely—like at the 2009 Chicago Marathon when the Romanian athlete, Adriana Pirtea, started waving triumphantly at the crowds as she came down the final straight where, in the last moments of the race, she was overtaken and beaten by another athlete on the line. There have also been cases where competitive cyclists, thinking that they were on the verge of winning a race, have let go of their handlebars, raised their hands in celebration and then crashed, only to be overtaken by other cyclists at the finishing line.

All things being equal, we'd naturally suppose that when Olympic athletes mount the podium to receive their medals, the degree of elation they display would be related to which medal they'd won—that gold medal winners, for example, would smile more than silver medal winners, who in turn would smile more than bronze medal winners. However, psychologists have discovered that this tends not to be the case, and that while gold medal winners produce the most smiles, silver medal winners actually smile appreciably less than bronze medal winners. The explanation that's been offered for this counter-intuitive finding is that silver medal winners are more likely to engage in what's called "counterfactual thinking."[27] Having missed out on the gold medal, they're inclined to wonder what would've happened if, for instance, they'd got a better start or timed their run differently, and it's this preoccupation with "what if?" that leaves them feeling relatively discontented. Bronze medal winners, on the other hand, tend to construe their situation quite differently. Instead of trying to imagine what might have happened, they're often just grateful to find themselves among the medals.

Contestants who make a habit of winning often gain a lot of admiration, but at the same time they may also attract a fair amount of envy, especially from those people whom they've beaten consistently. Seasoned athletes and players who recognize that this is happening are able to cope with other people's resentments in a number of ways. One is to be modest about their own achievements; another is to flatter and compliment their opponents in order to defuse their envy. This may explain why the winners of track-and-field events are often the first to congratulate the other competitors afterward, and why gold medal winners are so quick to invite the silver and bronze medal winners to join them at the top of the podium. Most medal ceremonies occur without incident. Unfortunately, that's not what happened at the 1980 Moscow Olympic Games, when Steve Ovett got gold in the men's 800 metres and Seb Coe, who was expected to win, was beaten into second place. At the end of the medal ceremony, Ovett smiled and extended his open hand to a grim-faced and somewhat reluctant Coe. Reporting on the event, journalist Clive James wrote that in hesitating to take Ovett's hand "it looked like he'd just handed him a turd."

Muted celebration. Jamie Anderson (left) won silver, while Anna Gasser (centre) and Zoi Sadowski-Synott (right) won gold and bronze, respectively, in the snowboard women's Big Air at the PyeongChang Winter Olympics. Silver medal winners often appear less joyful than their opponents—that's because they're inclined to wonder about what might have been, while the others have reason to be thrilled with what they've achieved.

Although there are national and cultural differences in the various ways sporting celebrations are performed, they're nevertheless to be found throughout the world and in most sports. This desire to celebrate triumph, and to involve others in the process, appears to be innate. So too is smiling, which plays such a significant role in sporting celebrations and is even found in the spontaneous reactions of congenitally blind athletes who've won sporting events. Interestingly, blind Paralympic athletes behave in much the same way as sighted athletes—raising their hands and punching the air when they're victorious, and lowering their head and slumping their shoulders after they've been defeated.[28] Being world champion does, however, confer some unusual privileges. One of these is the unwritten right to devise and use one's own unique triumph display. It was only because they were world beaters that Usain Bolt was entitled to strike his famous "lightning bolt" pose, and Mo Farah was able to perform his distinctive "Mobot" posture.

Winners' Tells

For many lovers of sport, the holy grail is being able to predict which individuals or teams are going to win important contests. After a sporting event is over, it's easy enough to see why a certain person claimed victory, or why one team beat its rival, but the big challenge is determining in advance who or which team is most likely to emerge as the winner. One source of evidence that people rely on is of course "form"—say, the known history of a contestant's victories and defeats. However, information about form isn't always available, and there may be new circumstances that render it unreliable. Another way to spot likely winners is size, particularly in sports where physical strength is crucial. Naturally, the premium that's placed on size is something that we humans share with other animals, where, across a vast range of species, it's usually the larger, stronger individuals that triumph in physical confrontations. But this isn't always the case. For instance, when male Magellanic penguins get into a fight before the eggs are laid, it's usually the larger individual that wins, but once the eggs are laid, it's often the smaller of the two, defending its mate and future offspring, who comes out on top. The fact that motivation plays a part in deciding such contests is also relevant to contests between humans, where individuals who're more confident or determined, or who're prepared to take greater risks, often end up as winners.

Some fascinating findings about winners and losers have emerged from recent research conducted by sports psychologists. It's been found, for example, that when people are presented with whole-body photographs of pairs of contestants who've competed with each other, they're able to able to identify which of them was the winner at levels

241

way above chance.[29] This isn't entirely surprising of course, because the people who're making these judgments are able to do so on the basis of relative size. What is astonishing, however, is that when people are presented with photographs of only the contestants' faces, even very briefly, they're able to spot the winners with similar accuracy. This shows that they're picking up on something in the contestants' faces that provides clues to how they're likely to behave in a contest. There's now evidence to show that this is precisely what they've been doing. Research on facial "width-to-height ratio"—otherwise known as fWHR—shows that individuals with proportionately wider faces are seen as more masculine, dominant and threatening, and that particularly in sports where physical strength is an issue, they're more likely to win contests.[30] It's been discovered that in mixed martial arts contests, the person with the wider face stands a better chance of becoming the winner.[31]

Having a wide face, however, is just one aspect of male formidability. Other facial features include heavy, low-set brows, a thick neck and a big, strong chin. What's important is that these characteristics of formidability are linked, not only to strength and therefore the ability to mete out physical punishment, but also to the capacity to withstand the physical punishment that's meted out by one's opponents. It's essential that boxers, kick-boxers and mixed martial arts fighters are able to go on the offensive, but if they don't have a "granite" or "iron" chin, their chances of success are seriously reduced. But formidability isn't simply confined to the head and neck—it's also crucial that contestants are able to absorb physical blows to the rest of their body as well.

Comparative physique is just one of the things that separates winners from losers—there's also the issue of how contestants behave, both before and during their confrontation with each other. We've seen, for example, how, in penalty shootouts, it's often the kickers who show signs of hesitancy and avoidance who end up failing to score goals, while it's those who act with confidence, taking their time and closely watching the goalkeeper, who tend to be successful. Regardless of which sport they're involved in, it's vital that contestants come across as confident, and possibly even dominant, but that they also make a special effort to avoid appearing submissive. One way to give an impression of submissiveness is to smile in situations that are poten-tially confrontational. Bearing this in mind, psychologists have found that professional fighters who smile before a match are more likely to lose to opponents who adopt a stony-faced expression.[32] There are two very good reasons why it's a bad idea for sportsmen and women to come across as submissive. One is that doing so may embolden their opponents, and the other is that it may have the unintended effect of weakening their own resolve. After all, it's not only other people who're able to see how we're behaving—we may also unwittingly be influ-enced by our own actions.

10. Sexual Tells

Tells are an essential part of courtship. In fact, without them there would be no such thing as courtship or love, and sex as we know it would cease to exist. The importance of tells lies in the simple fact that courtship, love and sex require people to exchange signals—signals about sexual orientation, inclination, availability, readiness and compatibility. Even though we may not intend to, we are constantly sending and receiving sexual messages. While other people are looking us over and deciding how sexy, attractive, enthusiastic or desperate we are, we're busy making the same decisions about them. In this regard *sexual tells* are like grains of pollen—they aren't always evident, but they're everywhere.

Body Tells

One of the bases on which people make sexual inferences about each other is their "secondary sexual characteristics." Psychologists use this term to distinguish the "primary sexual characteristics" of men and women—like the penis and testes of the male and the vagina, uterus and ovaries of the female—from their non-procreative character- istics. In men these include facial and chest hair, a deep voice and a bigger, more muscular body. In women they include breasts, a wider pelvic girdle and the deposit of more fat on the thighs and buttocks. Nature's intention, it appears, is that these secondary sexual character- istics should serve as sexual cues, enabling men and women to assess each other's fitness as a mate. To a large extent, Nature's intentions are fulfilled—in the absence of any other information, men do find women with large breasts and an hourglass figure more attractive.[1] And women, on the whole, express a preference for men with hairy chests, square shoulders and neat bottoms.[2]

The things that men and women look for in partners are, however, highly susceptible to the influence of culture, fashion and circumstance. The physical attributes that men in our society regard as attractive in a woman are often very different from those that get men's pulses racing in other parts of the world. Within our own society there have been marked historical variations in people's notions of beauty. Compare, for example, the delicious plump ladies painted by Rubens with the extremely thin catwalk models of today.

David Buss, from the University of Texas, has conducted a large, cross-cultural survey on what men and women look for in a partner.[3] He reports that men universally prefer a woman who is young and shapely with unblemished skin. Women, on the other hand, place greater store on the man's wealth and his ability to provide security. The divergent criteria employed by men and women reflect their differing motives in the mating game—the man needs a partner who can produce lots of healthy children and who's strong enough to care for them, while the woman, it seems, needs a man to provide for her, and to protect her and the children. Buss and his colleagues have shown how the heterosexual mate preferences of men and women depend to a large extent on whether they're pursuing short- or long-term relationships. When it comes to short-term liaisons, women—much like men—tend to go for good looks and youthfulness, as well as virility in a partner. They're frequently looking for novelty, sexual excitement and the thrill of seduction and doing something illicit. Searching for affirmation, and in some cases evidence that men find them attractive, may also be a powerful motivating factor. On the other hand, men who're pursuing short-term relationships will, like women in a similar situation, be interested in the thrill of the chase, sexual excitement, and possibly conquest too. Typically, their preferences are for nubile, younger women, with healthy skin, teeth and hair— in other words, the indicators of high reproductive value. Interestingly, when men are searching for a long-term partner, their criteria aren't all that different from those that they apply when they're looking for a short-term fling. In sharp contrast, women who're looking for a life partner often change gear completely—instead of opting for a charming hunk, they're more likely to search for slightly older men who're distinguished by their ability to provide material resources, who have social status and, in an ideal world, are also committed, loving and caring.

Whether they're looking for a fling or a permanent union, there are very good evolutionary reasons why men and women should apply quite different mate selection strategies. These strategies can, however, be shaped by external factors, including historical and cultural forces. The relative number of men and women in circulation—the so-called "sex ratio"—can have a profound effect on how the sexes relate to each other.[4] When there are disproportionately fewer women, for example, they're more in demand. As a result, men become more chivalrous and less dismissive, and, when they do secure a partner, they go to greater lengths to ensure that she doesn't get poached by other men. Sociocultural factors can also influence mating strategies, particularly where notions of female beauty are concerned, with men, for example, setting their sights on fuller-bodied women when foods supplies are unreliable. Economic conditions can also play a part. Terry Pettijohn and John Jungeberg found that the idealized female body shapes that men prefer during boom times differed from those that they found attractive during a recession. When they compared the photographs of women selected as Playboy's "Playmate of the Year" between 1960 and 2000, they discovered that men preferred more petite women with larger eyes during boom times, and more busty, full-figured women during recession—when they were presumably more in need of dis-traction, stimulation and encouragement.[5]

Women who possess the physical attributes that men desire are much more likely to be noticed by men. But it doesn't always follow that men are more likely to approach them or, if they do, that they're likely to hang around if they don't get any encouragement. In fact, men are much more likely to pursue a woman who isn't beautiful but who gives off the right signals than a woman who is gorgeous but doesn't appear to be available. In contests between courtship signals and looks, courtship signals usually win hands down.[6]

It follows from this that a woman who has all the right physical attributes, and who accompanies these with all the right signals, is likely to be more attractive to men than one who has the attributes but doesn't produce the signals, or vice versa. The Oxford philosopher Robert Burton reached this conclusion in his *Anatomy of Melancholy*, first published in 1621.[7] "It is true," he wrote, "that those fair sparkling eyes, white neck, coral lips, turgent paps [swelling breasts], rose-coloured cheeks, &c., of themselves are potent enticers; but when a comely, artificial, well-composed look, pleasing gesture, an affected carriage shall be added, it must needs be far more forcible than it was." Nowhere is this more evident in modern times than in the case of Marilyn Monroe—a woman who had what it takes and knew how to use it. If you've seen the movie *Some Like It Hot* you'll remember the remarkable scene where she walks down the railway platform, while Tony Curtis and Jack Lemmon stare at her undulating bottom—moving, as Jack Lemmon describes it, "like Jell-O on springs." The reason why Marilyn's wiggle is so effective here is that it draws attention to her feminine hips. This brings us to the observation that the prime purpose of seductive behaviour is to accentuate secondary sexual characteristics. This in fact is the clue to why certain seductive signals are used by women but not by men, and vice versa. When a woman pouts her lips, arches her back or leans forward so that her breasts are pressed together between her arms, she's accentuating the physical attributes of her sex. These actions are "illuminations"—they give prominence to a particular feature of a woman's appearance, just like the accentuated letters in a manuscript. A man who pulls himself up to his full height in the presence of a woman, and who expands his chest or lowers his voice, is essentially doing the same thing—he's illuminating the differences between himself and other men, and between himself and the woman, making his appearance more masculine and, by contrast, hers more feminine.

Action Tells

Not being content to look different, men and women have conspired to behave differently as well. These differences in behaviour—what Ray Birdwhistell neatly referred to as "tertiary sexual characteristics"—provide men and women with a way of emphasizing their gender and making themselves more attractive to members of the opposite sex.[8] When a man is trying to appear attractive to a woman he's more likely to engage in prototypical male behaviour—like sitting with his legs apart, extending his feet into the shared space, splaying his arms, and generally creating the impression that he needs lots of space to accommodate his masculine frame. He will also shift his body more frequently, changing postures, enlisting his hands to underline what he's saying, and gesticulating away from his body.

In contrast, the woman's gestures are likely to be toward her body. To appear feminine she's inclined to keep her movements slow, her gesticulation modest and her legs close together, and to cultivate the impression that she needs less physical space for her body, not more. When it comes to facial expression, however, the situation tends to be reversed, with the woman being lively and animated, while the man tries to give the impression that he's more controlled.

Despite increasing sexual equality, men and women try to appear attractive to the opposite sex by acting according to type—men behave in a more manly fashion, while women act in a more feminine way. One way that men try to be manlier is by being dominant. Many of the "illuminations" of men's behaviour—like standing tall, expanding the chest, and standing or sitting with the legs apart—are in fact dominance signals, while those of women—like sitting with the ankles crossed, canting the head to one side, and touching the face—happen also to be submissive behaviours. However, this doesn't mean that during courtship men only use dominance signals, or that women restrict themselves to submissive signals. There are numerous instances where the roles become reversed, as well as instances of the woman taking the role of mother and the man that of a child. These departures from socially prescribed roles, coupled with regressive excursions into the world of play, are an essential part of courtship. Laughing, tickling and generally playing the fool give the man and woman a chance to experiment with their roles and to show each other that they're harmless and unthreatening, just like children. Fooling around also enables them to introduce the nurturing, loving activities that form part of the relationship between parent and child into their own relationship.

Availability Tells

With most mammals it's the male who does the sexual advertising, showing females that he's strong, healthy and resourceful, and that he'll make a perfect mate. In heterosexual human relationships, however, it's usually the other way around, because most of the sexual advertising is done by the woman—it's the woman who is dressing up, styling her hair, and wearing make-up and perfume. But things weren't always this way. For example, in seventeenth-century England, during the age of the "dandy," it was the men of polite society who dressed like gaudy peacocks and their women who looked like plain peahens. It's equally true to say that while women today do most of the sexual advertising, men are taking on an increasing share of the burden by spending money on clothes, keeping up with hairstyle fashions, and wearing aftershave and cologne. Clothes, jewellery, make-up and perfume are all worn on the person. But other forms of sexual advertising don't appear on the person, like wealth and possessions. In this area of advertising it's usually men who do most of the work, investing in cars, apartments and gadgets to impress potential mates.

We advertise our sexual availability in a number of ways. These include the clothes we wear, how we wear them, which parts of our body we expose, the postures we assume, the facial expressions we adopt, how we move our eyes and what we say.

When young people enter a nightclub or a bar they usually begin by surveying the scene. Sometimes they do so innocently, to see if their friends are there, but most of the time they're making a quick assessment of the available talent. They do this in two main ways:

Scanning. People map out their social environment by scanning it visually. Monika Moore, who made an extensive study of courtship strategies, has identified what she calls "the room encompassing glance," where the head and eyes move together, rather like radar, tracing an arc through the room, and then returning to their original position.[9] The purpose of scanning is to perform an initial survey and not necessarily to focus on a specific person or group of people. That comes later.

Promenading. Instead of casting their eyes around, people sometimes check out the room by walking around. The advantage of promenading is that it enables individuals to be noticed by other people, and to examine them at close quarters. In this way, promenading is rather similar to the Spanish and South American *paseo*, when young men and women stroll back and forth, watching each other and being seen.

With hundreds of young people milling around and checking each other out, the spectacle in a nightclub is very similar to a "lek."[10] Leks are the "singles bars" of the animal world—patches of ground where males and females of the same species congregate so that the males can display to the females, and the females can decide which male to mate with. Lekking occurs in a wide range of species, including bats, antelopes, frogs, Canada geese and the greater prairie chicken. In all these species there is pronounced "sexual dimorphism"—in other words, the males look very different from the females, and males who display at a higher rate usually manage to mate with more of the females. This, of course, is often what happens in a human "lek" like a nightclub, where the more flamboyant and active males tend to be more successful.

If you watch people in a nightclub you'll notice that their behaviour is often extravagant. This is partly because they're competing with each other for attention. But it's also because of the low lighting, which makes it difficult to see what others are doing, and the ambient noise, which makes it difficult to hear what they're saying. People usually respond to this situation by increasing the amplitude of their signals—by raising their voice, exposing more of their body and dancing wildly. Some people simply keep repeating themselves to the same person. Interestingly, much the same thing happens with birds. It's been discovered that birds that nest in noisy habitats deal with the problem of noise by increasing the amplitude of their signals and by singing louder.[11] They also incorporate a lot more redundancy and repetition into their songs—just like those bores in nightclubs who can't stop repeating themselves!

In order to attract attention in a nightclub, people need to signal their sexual availability. They do this in one of two ways: by "broadcasting," so everyone present knows that they're sexually available, or by "narrowcasting" or "targeting" a specific individual. For example, a woman may broadcast her availability by wearing revealing clothes, exposing parts of her body or dancing provocatively. In doing so she wants everyone to know that while she might be available to *someone*, she is definitely not available to just *anyone*—a distinction that lots of men find difficult to understand. Women's broadcasting is often linked to their menstrual cycle—it's been found that when women are in the middle of their cycle and therefore most receptive, they are more likely to visit singles bars and nightclubs without their current partner and to wear clothes that reveal more of their body, and that they are more attracted to men with masculine features.[12] Not only are they more sexually available; they're also looking for men who are likely to be more sexually active.

Approach Tells

When it comes to heterosexual romance, men like to think that they're the ones who make the first move and who decide how fast the relationship should progress. All the research on human courtship shows that this is simply not the case, and that, as Darwin put it, courtship is almost always a matter of "female choice." In nightclubs, bars and at parties, it's the woman who invariably makes the first move. She does this by producing an *approach tell*—a signal that's not too explicit but that is sufficiently clear to show a man that he may approach her. It's her way of giving him "clearance."

When a man responds and walks across the room, he's doing so at the woman's behest. From his point of view things usually seem quite different—because he's made the effort to cross the room he's inclined to think that he's the one who's taken the initiative. Men are far less likely to engage a woman who hasn't shown that she's approachable, although there are obviously cases where men will advance on a woman who hasn't even noticed them, let alone given them clearance.

When the man takes the initiative in this way his chances of success are usually reduced, simply because he's denying the woman a chance to be in control. He might be able to get around this by appearing to be submissive or by giving the impression that his intentions are entirely non-sexual.

Women produce a variety of approach tells—some in "clusters," others individually. They include the following:

The Strobe Glance. A woman who's attracted to a man will sometimes stare across the room at him until she manages to catch his eye. When this happens, she can rely on either frequency or duration of eye contact to signal her clearance.[13] She can rely on frequency by holding his gaze for a second or two and then averting her head and eyes slightly, but not so far that she appears to be removing herself from the interaction altogether. Then, while the man continues to look at her, she turns her head and eyes back toward him and repeats the cycle all over again. Monika Moore claims that it usually takes three brief glances to get the message across to the man.[14]

The Eye-lock. Instead of using several brief glances, a woman can show a man that she's approachable by holding his gaze for slightly longer than she would in other circumstances. When we look across a crowded room and happen to catch a stranger's eye, we usually avert our gaze within a second or two. This allows us to disengage before there's any suggestion that we're staring or might wish to pursue the interaction. By fixating her eyes on a man and holding his gaze for longer than normal, a woman shows the man that she might be prepared to take things further.[15]

The Eye-flicker. When a woman catches the eye of an attractive man she can usually grab his attention by performing an "eye-flicker." Here the upper eyelids are raised very slightly and for a fraction of a second, so that the gesture remains almost imperceptible and only evident to the person at whom it's directed. The brief elevation of the upper eyelids may sometimes cause the eyebrows to rise as well, but it's the eyes rather than the eyebrows that carry the real signal. By opening the eyes in this way, a woman shows a man that he's the person she's looking at. The flick of the eyelids also transforms the signal into a question—it makes the man feel that the woman is saying to him, "What next?"

The Hair-Flick. Having caught a man's eye briefly, a woman will sometimes flick her hair to show him that she's approachable. She can do this either by running her hand through her hair or by tossing her head so that the hair bounces up and assumes a slightly different position. These actions also serve as a "youth display" because it's only young women who have soft, flexible hair that can convincingly be rearranged or flicked. As women get older their hair becomes less pliable and the hair-flick becomes less of an option. It's not unusual, however, to find women with lacquered or very short hair actually flicking their head when they come across a man they fancy.

The Pout. A woman can indicate that she's approachable by looking at a man and pouting her lips. She can convey the same message by subtly licking her lips. These gestures draw attention to a distinctive feature of female physiology—the fact that women have fuller lips than men. When boys enter puberty their body is flooded with testosterone. This encourages the growth of their jaw. Girls' faces remain fairly childlike over the same period. Increasing levels of estrogen, however, actually discourage the growth of facial bone, and lead instead to a thickening of the lips. After puberty, fuller lips become a feature of sexual dimorphism. Consequently, when a woman pouts or licks her lips, she automatically draws attention to one of her secondary sexual characteristics, and to the fact that as people become sexually aroused their lips become engorged with blood. The same effect is of course achieved with red lipstick. When these signals are targeted at a man they usually constitute an invitation. It's essential, however, that these gestures be subtle and brief, because although a woman might want a man to know that she's approachable, she wouldn't want him to think she's a pushover.

The Smile. When a woman wants to invite a strange man to approach her, the signal she's most likely to use is a smile— usually a brief smile that's confined to the mouth.[16] In these circumstances she's unlikely to perform a full smile, partly because full smiles tend to be reserved for friends and acquaintances. This conforms to the principle that, in order to be effective, approach tells should always be muted. This applies as much to smiles as it does to actions involving the head, eyes and lips. It's very unlikely that a broad smile between strangers will be regarded as an invitation; it's much more likely to be interpreted as a sign of recognition. The same applies to exaggerated stares, pouts and rearrangements of the hair—because they're not muted they're likely to be seen as a joke rather than as a sincere but tentative invitation.

Flirting Tells

Flirting tells fall into three broad categories: "come-ons," "put-offs" and "hang-ons." Come-ons consist of *approach tells,* which give the other person permission to make a move, and *promotion tells,* which are designed to promote sexual interest and move the relationship on to the next stage. Put-offs are the exact opposite of come-ons—they express a total lack of interest and are designed to reject the advances of the other person. Hang-ons, on the other hand, put the courtship process on hold—their purpose is to stall the relationship without discouraging the other person's interest.

In the mating game women use all three types of tells, while men tend to concentrate on come-ons. Men usually flatter themselves that they make most of the moves in courtship, and that they control the whole process, but as we've seen it's women who are really in charge.[17] In the early stages of an encounter women produce a lot of come-ons, even when they aren't actually attracted to the man and have no intention of taking things any further.[18] They also mix come-ons with hang-ons in order to increase ambiguity and to foster the illusion that the man is in charge of proceedings. In fact, men are notoriously bad decoders of women's tells, often assuming that a woman is interested in them when she isn't. "Sexual overperception bias," as it's called, is found in both sexes, but it is especially prevalent in men, particularly those who are confident about interacting with women, and who think they've got a lot to offer them.[19] A man who's suffering from this condition will automatically assume that an attractive woman is aiming her availability signals at him personally, when she's either broadcasting them to everyone or not producing any at all. Men also tend to inflate come-ons in their mind, and to assume that put-offs are only hang-ons. This tendency of men to misread women's signals is part of a more widespread insensitivity. Not only are men less observant, they are generally not as tuned in to other people's needs as women are.

Speed Dating

Some years ago I presented a TV program about the body language of love and attraction. At the time, speed dating was all the rage, so we decided to explore the subject in the program. The great advantage of speed dating is that it offers young people a rapid and convenient means of meeting lots of members of the opposite sex in a short space of time, and in a safe environment where there's virtually no risk of being openly rejected. The typical arrangement for a speed-dating night is that equal numbers of young men and women gather in a hall, and each of them has, say, a three-minute conversation with each member of the opposite sex. After each encounter both parties fills out their "score card," putting a tick beside the other person's name if they want to see them again, and a cross if they're not interested. At the end of the evening the organizers collate all the results, and if two people happen to tick each other they're given each other's contact details.

In addition to observing how the participants behaved during their speed dates, I was keen to find out a) what they thought of each other, and b) what they thought their dates thought about them. So after they'd completed each date, we asked each of them to complete their scorecard, but also to indicate whether they thought the other person had put a tick opposite their name to indicate that they wanted to see them again. The findings that emerged showed that the men who took part were far less discerning and far less accurate than the women.

When we looked at the scorecards, we found that the men had ticked twice as many people as the women—showing that women are much more selective about whom they'd like to see again.

When we looked at how many people each person thought had ticked them, we found that men's estimates were 50 percent higher than those of the women.

Women were also a lot more perceptive than the men—almost half of the men over-estimated the number of women who'd ticked them, whereas not one of the women who took part over-estimated how many men fancied them.

Several factors have a bearing on these findings. One is that the men were obviously far less discriminating (some of the men, for example, eagerly ticked every woman they met!); another is that the women were more judicious about which men they'd like to see again. It's quite possible that the men simply misconstrued the friendly behaviour of the women as an expression of romantic interest. It's also possible that while the women were being flirtatious, they simply thought they were being charming, and that's why the men got so confused. Either way, the end result was that men thought they were getting the thumbs-up from women, who were actually giving them the thumbs down.

Posture Tells

The postures that a man and a woman adopt when they meet for the first time often reveal their hidden feelings for each other. For example, if the woman folds her arms and coils her legs together it's very unlikely that she's about to run headlong into an affair. On the other hand, if the man sits with his legs apart and leans his body toward the woman it shows that he finds her attractive and is trying to impress her. Open postures are generally associated with positive, accepting attitudes, whereas closed postures are linked to guarded and negative ones.

Posture switching is another matter altogether. For example, when a woman repeatedly crosses and uncrosses her legs in the presence of a man, she's doing more than alternating between closed postures— she's actually drawing attention to her legs. Her motive for doing this is usually unconscious. There are times, however, when it's deliber- ate—like the famous scene in *Basic Instinct*, where the character played by Sharon Stone crosses and uncrosses her legs to draw attention to the fact that she's not wearing anything underneath. Most of the cases where women cross and uncross their legs in the presence of a man are far less dramatic than this, and a lot of the time the man isn't even aware of what's happening. Nevertheless, the way that a woman pos- itions and moves her legs is always very informative, and the postures that the man adopts are equally telling.

Leg Tells

Women also try to make themselves attractive to men by emphasizing the length of their legs, relative to the rest of their body—trying, in this respect, to make themselves look more like a Barbie Doll. The reason why men find long legs sexy is that when girls go through puberty they have a growth spurt and this results in their legs looking pro- portionately longer than the rest of their body. At this stage in their development girls become women and start to get noticed by men. It's this youthful phase in their lives that women try to recover when they attempt to make their legs look longer.[20]

Women can employ three strategies to accentuate the length of their legs: 1) wear high heels; 2) wear a bathing suit or gym kit with a "high leg"—this makes a woman's legs look longer by creating the illusion that they begin at her hips; and 3) walk on tiptoe. Walking on tiptoe works best when women aren't wearing any shoes, and it's a sure sign that they find someone attractive. Take the case where a good-looking man arrives at a house party and several people, including the host and hostess, are sitting around the swimming pool in their bathing suits. The hostess notices the man arriving, so she gets up and goes to greet him. But notice that she's not walking flat-footed—she's moving toward him on tiptoes. And to make sure that nobody thinks she's behaving strangely, she makes a show of dodging the wet patches by the side of the pool. Observing this little scene we can see that the hostess wants everyone to think that she's trying not to slip on the puddles. But the real reason is that she's trying to impress the guest—by walking on tiptoe she's discreetly trying to make her legs look longer, and herefore herself more youthful.

In addition to increasing the apparent length of a woman's legs, high heels also arch her back. This arching of the back is similar to "lordosis" in the animal world. In certain animal species lordosis acts as a sexual releaser—female hamsters and guinea pigs, for example, will arch their back to show a male that they are sexually receptive. When a woman sticks out her bottom and arches her back it has the same arousing effect on a man—that's why "girlie magazines" are full of pictures of women in this pose. When a woman finds a man attractive she sometimes reveals her feelings by arching her back. This may occur while she's standing up, sitting down, or leaning forward and supporting her weight on the table. The action may be almost imperceptible, but it shows that she's sexually attracted to him.

Spatial Tells

The way that a man and a woman arrange themselves spatially says a lot about what each of them is hoping to achieve, and about which stage they have reached in their relationship. As a rule, the closer people are to each other physically, the closer they are emotionally, and possibly sexually too. This also applies to how directly or obliquely they orient their bodies toward each other. During the early stages of courtship both individuals need to treat the other person's space with caution and respect, making sure not to move in close before the other person has given them clearance. One move that people use to gauge the other person's reactions is the "quick-step."

The last time I saw the quick-step used the sequence went as follows: A young man and woman were in conversation, with their bodies attentively oriented toward each other. They were standing some distance apart, with a large patch of no man's land between them. After a few minutes, and while she was still talking, the young woman took a big step forward, completed what she was saying, and then took an equally big step backward, ending up where she'd started. Although the man wasn't consciously aware of what was happening, his response was right on cue—he started to talk and as he did so, he stepped right into the middle of the space she had just vacated. He had now become much more animated. Suddenly it was apparent that he found her attractive. What had clearly happened was that by stepping into no man's land the woman had taken the initiative and produced a very powerful approach tell. By stepping back she had invited him to advance toward her, and without being fully aware of what was happening, he had happily obliged—she had created a vacuum in the space between them, and he had unwittingly been drawn into it.

Watching this exchange, it appeared that neither the woman nor the man realized what was happening. She didn't know that she was using the quick-step or that her movements would have the desired effect on him. Equally, he didn't realize that her actions had controlled his, just as much as if she were a puppeteer and he were a puppet. I was also struck by the remarkably simple way that she had managed to move the relationship on to the next phase—by getting him to step forward she had completely changed his attitude and encouraged him to see that the situation was now full of promise.

Locomotor Tells

Walking style also plays a part in courtship—especially in the early stages when people are making snap judgments about each other. In modifying their gait to impress members of the opposite sex, women tend to accentuate their female characteristics. One way they do this is by rolling their hips. Another is by swinging their arms further back as they walk, and by turning their arms outward in order to emphasize the fact that women's arms are more "supinated" than those of men. Men who wish to emphasize their masculinity tend to do the opposite—they swing their arms across their body and further up in the front, and they rotate their wrists inward in order to stress the fact that men's arms are more "pronated" than those of women.

Head Tells

In the early stages of courtship people often go to extraordinary lengths to make themselves appealing and to put the other person at ease. Several head signals help to further these aims:

The Nod. Women are often very attentive listeners, nodding their head and encouraging men to keep talking—and in many cases regretting it afterward!

The Hair-flick. The hair-flick sometimes serves as an approach tell. And in the later stages of courtship it provides women as well as men with a subtle way of displaying their youth and appearing more attractive.

The Head Cant. As we have already seen, when the head is tilted to one side the person looks helpless and appealing. The origins of head-canting can be traced to the way that babies rest their head on their parent's shoulder, and the fact that tilting the head to one side exposes a vulnerable part of the body, the neck. The head-cant is an ideal courtship signal because it sends a message of appeasement—it's a way of saying to the other person, "Look, I trust you so much that I'm prepared to expose a really vulnerable part of my body to you." A related appeasement gesture, often used by young women, is the "shoulder hop," which is performed by raising and lowering the shoulders very quickly, and sometimes by raising the eyebrows and smiling at the same time.

The Neck Show. In addition to the head-cant, other "vulner-ability displays" involving the neck are used as come-ons. In one the chin is raised slightly; in another the head is turned so that the other person gets an unobstructed view of the neck. Both these actions fall into the category of *show tells*—actions that are designed to expose a vulnerable or particularly appealing part of the body. A similar effect is achieved when people touch their neck. A woman who's attracted to a man may lightly run her fingers along her neck, thereby drawing his attention to her vulnerability and ultimately to her suitability as a partner. This action falls into the category of "pointers"—that is, instances where people use a hand or a finger to draw attention to a part of their body. Another example of a show tell is the "exposed wrist display," where the arm is positioned so that the inside of the wrist is presented to other people. This, like the "neck-show," involves a vulnerable part of the body. When a woman draws attention to her neck or her wrists she's usually unaware of what she's doing. Likewise, even if the man responds posi-tively, he's unlikely to be able to describe what she's done or what it is about her that he finds so attractive.

The neck-show. By exposing her neck, Marilyn Monroe makes herself look vulnerable and sexy. Here, too, she uses other "come-ons": The *Hooded Eyes Look* and the *Parted-lips Pose* suggest that she's in the throes of sexual ecstasy.

Eye Tells

The crucial role that the eyes play in courtship has long been recognized. Writing in the early seventeenth century, Robert Burton called the eye "a secret orator, the first bawd, the gateway of love." He referred to the eyes as "the shoeing-horns" and "the hooks of love," pointing out that by simply looking at each other, lovers are able "to understand one another's meanings, before they come to speak a word."[21]

Psychologists have discovered that when people meet for the first time they often reach a decision about each other within a matter of a few seconds, and frequently before the other person has had a chance to say anything. These "snap judgments" are therefore often based on visual information.[22] What's more, people will often cling to their snap judgments, even in the face of disconfirming evidence. During courtship the participants use their eyes to "assess" and "express"—in other words, to see how the other person is behaving and responding, as well as to convey information about their own needs, intentions and feelings. The expressive role of the eyes is evident in a number of signals:

The Eye-puff. One way people make themselves irresistible is by enlarging their eyes. This is especially noticeable in women. An almond-shaped face, a small chin, rounded cheeks, a pert nose and large eyes are all part of the so-called "baby face"— those innate releasers that make us feel protective toward babies.[23] By enlarging her eyes when she's with her lover, a woman makes herself look defenceless, which in turn makes her lover feel more protective toward her. He too can achieve this effect with the eye-puff.

The Dipped Head. When she's looking at her lover, one of the ways a woman can make her eyes look bigger is by lowering her head. This creates a foreshortened effect, so that her chin appears to be smaller, while the top of her face, including her eyes, seems to be bigger. But there's also another principle at work. Because children are shorter, they sometimes look at adults out of the top of their eye sockets. When a woman lowers her head while looking at her lover it automatically makes her seem much smaller, and therefore more in need of protection. The fact that lowering of the head is associated with submission is another reason why women are more likely to dip their head when they're flirting with a man.[24] Ruth Campbell and her colleagues at University College London have also found that individuals who are photographed looking down are seen as more feminine.[25]

Dilated Pupils. When people become aroused—either pleasantly or otherwise—their pupils tend to dilate. However, people can't consciously control the size of their pupils, and they have no way of knowing how large or small their own pupils are. People are generally more attracted to individuals with large pupils than to those with constricted pupils, although they are seldom aware of the role that pupil size plays in their preferences. But there are individuals who know about pupil dilation and who use it to gauge other people's moods. For example, it's reported that in pre-revolutionary China, jade sellers used to watch the pupils of their customers so that they could see if they liked a particular piece of jade or were happy to pay the asking price.[26] In the sixteenth century, Italian women used a tincture of belladonna to dilate their pupils. Belladonna (which means "beautiful woman" in Italian) contains atropine, which dilates the pupils, making the person look more aroused and therefore more attractive.

The Sideways Look. This is done by looking at someone while one's head is turned away. The sideways look conveys two opposing messages—the directed gaze signals approach, while the averted head signals avoidance. The tension between approach and avoidance is partly what gives the sideways look its appeal—it's what makes the person who is performing the sideways look appear so interesting and attractive. This is especially the case when the look is combined with a smile to create a "turn-away smile." The other factor behind the gesture's appeal is the implicit suggestion that the person is turning back. When a woman looks at a man with her head averted he's inclined to get the feeling that she has stopped what she was doing in order to look at him. He might even imagine that the sight of him was so arresting that the woman's head didn't have time to catch up with her eyes! Women mostly use the sideways look, although men do employ it with the same coquettish effect. But there's something else worth noting. When a woman gives a man a sideways look, she occasionally does so by glancing at him over a slightly raised shoulder. By enlisting her shoulder in this way, the woman subtly highlights a feature of her body that happens to possess the same soft, rounded contours as her breasts and buttocks. When it's performed in this manner, a woman's sideways look is much more than just a look—it instead becomes a potent means of hinting at more interesting parts of her body.

Hooded Eyes. The hooded look is achieved by lowering the upper eyelids, raising the eyebrows slightly, and holding this expression for a while. The effect of this is to narrow the eyes, making them look like "bedroom eyes," and to increase the distance between the eye and the eyebrow, which is one of the things that happens when people try to appear submissive. In a sense the hooded look offers the best of both worlds, because in addition to making the person appear submissive it also gives them a rather knowing and mysterious look, as if they were harbouring some secret. This, however, is not the only explanation. Paul Ekman has suggested that the reason why hooded eyes are so seductive is that they reproduce the expression that appears on people's faces just before they have an orgasm.[27] Whether or not this is true, it is certainly the case that the hooded-eyes gesture is used more by women than by men—most of the time in earnest, but sometimes in jest. It was very popular during the age of the silent screen, when it became the hallmark of actresses like Greta Garbo, who sometimes combined it with the sideways look. Marilyn Monroe was also very keen on the hooded-eyes gesture, which she often combined with the "parted-lips pose." In this pose the jaw is relaxed and the lips are separated, as if they were inviting a kiss. With the lips parted and the eyes half-closed, a woman certainly looks like she's in the throes of sexual ecstasy. Men find this combination of tells seductive because it hints at the pleasure that they could induce in the woman if only they were given a chance.

Touching Tells

Courtship is associated with various kinds of touching. These include people touching themselves, touching the other person and occasions when they touch or manipulate objects.

Self-touching. People touch themselves for all kinds of reasons when the atmosphere is sexually charged. As we have seen, when people feel anxious or self-conscious they often produce "adaptors" by touching their face or rubbing their arm in order to comfort themselves. People also touch themselves as a way of drawing attention to a particular part of their body. Consider a young man and woman who are out on a date in a restaurant. While the young man is talking, the young woman is leaning forward with the palms of her hands supporting her chin and her fingers wrapped around her cheeks. She's doing a "face frame"—using her hands as a picture frame to define the image that she wants him to focus on. While the young man is talking he absentmindedly combs his fingers through his hair. This action is a "pointer" because, even though he doesn't know it, its purpose is to alert his date to his fine head of hair, and to set her thinking about what it would be like to run her own fingers through it. Pointers do two things: they draw someone's attention to a part of the body and they raise the issue of what it would be like to do to someone what they're doing to themselves. All this occurs outside conscious awareness—neither the person who produces the pointer nor the person to whom it's addressed are likely to recognize what's actually happening. In the early days, if you'd watched Hugh Grant on screen you'd have notice that he often produced a sheepish grin while running his hand through his hair. The ostensible purpose of the grin was to suggest that he was feeling embarrassed, and that's why he was running his hand through his hair. In fact, the sheepish grin was a facial decoy—it was designed to obscure the fact that he was touching his hair because, deep down, he wanted viewers to admire it.

Other Touching. As we saw earlier, although women tend to call the shots in courtship, it's typically the man who touches the woman first. That's usually because the woman has indicated that she's ready to be touched; she has, in effect, given the man the green light. The touching that takes place during the early stages of courtship is very different from the touching that occurs during the later stages, both in terms of who's likely to initiate it and what form it takes. In loving relationships women tend to get touched more than men. That's partly because women have a lower touch threshold than men and are therefore more sensitive to touch.[28] This difference emerges soon after birth. Partly for this reason, girls usually show more enjoyment of touch than boys, and this leads to their being touched more by their parents. But in addition to being more sensitive to touch, and appreciating it more, women also regard touch as more meaningful. For them, touch is an important sign of love and affection, whereas for some men it's sometimes more of a means to an end.

Object Touching. People who are courting often reveal their feelings toward each other by the way they manipulate objects. In a restaurant, for example, the way a woman caresses her wine glass or runs her fingers up and down its stem may reveal her intentions toward the man she's dining with. Equally, the way the man reaches across the table, picks up the woman's car keys, and starts to play with them offers strong proof that he wants to possess some part or all of her. Watching what people do to objects often shows what they would like to do to each other.

Smoke Signals

Up until a few years ago a woman who took out a cigarette at a social gathering could reasonably expect a man to offer her a light. The ritual of lighting a woman's cigarette still provides men and women with an opportunity to exchange courtship signals—the man can position his body and the lightor to convey his interest, and he is able to check her out at close quarters while she's busy lighting her cigarette. For her part, the woman can reciprocate by lightly touching his hand, ostensibly to steady herself but really so that she can make physical contact. She can also show her interest in the man by disengaging slowly and looking him in the eye for longer than normal when she thanks him. The elegance of this ritual is that it enables people to exchange suggestive signals very rapidly and with all the ambiguity that courtship requires.

Generally speaking, the courtship signals that men and women exchange are based on the secondary sexual characteristics that distinguish them. Individuals who want to attract members of the opposite sex do so by emphasizing and exaggerating these differences, while people who wish to discourage attention do so by downplaying and disguising them. It's the same with courtship and smoking. A woman who wants to emphasize her femininity usually does so by accentuating the smoking style of women— by holding the cigarette between her extended forefinger and middle finger, positioning it toward the end of her fingers, pointedly exposing her wrist, and smoking slowly. Men react unconsciously to these smoke signals—they know there's something sexy about the woman who's producing them, but they can't explain why they find her so attractive.

Smoking is seen as sexy for several reasons. Firstly, because smoking wasn't traditionally part of the female role, women who smoked were regarded as sexually liberated. This was very noticeable in the 1920s, when young "flappers" scandalized society by taking up the smoking habits of men, and doing it in public! Although this association probably no longer holds, lots of men believe that a woman who smokes is sexier than one who doesn't. Then there's the phallic symbolism of cigarettes and cigars, and the strong connection between smoking and sex, with cigarettes playing a central role immediately prior to sexual foreplay and immediately afterward in the post-coital smoke.

The act of smoking surreptitiously raises the issue of seduction. "We must not forget," said Jean Cocteau, "that a pack of cigarettes, the ceremony of taking one out, igniting the lighter, and the strange cloud which surrounds us, have seduced and conquered the world." Whenever smokers light up, they show themselves to be seduced. By smoking suggestively, they can also be seductive. The languid, unhurried way that the cigarette is raised to the mouth and held between the lips, the way the smoke is savoured and dispelled from the mouth—all of these movements are reminiscent of the acts of love. Although people don't realize it, they often draw conclusions about how someone is likely to behave in bed from the way they smoke a cigarette. That's why flirtatious smoke signals are so successful—they suggestively shape people's impressions of each other without them knowing.

Talk Tells

Men and women often worry about what they're going to say to each other when they first meet because they know that it can have a big impact on what happens next. Men put a lot of effort into pick-up lines.[29] But because women have heard most of them before, and aren't terribly impressed with the new ones, men's opening gambits often fall flat. Men also make a lot of effort in other ways—lowering the pitch of their voice to make them sound more masculine and speaking quietly so that the conversation feels more intimate. Lowering the voice is probably a good idea because women are attracted to men with deep voices—or at least they are when they hear them on the tele-phone, imagining that they're tall and heavily muscled. In this respect, voice quality is actually a dishonest signal because it's an unreliable indicator of body size and it's fairly easy to fake. However, it is a fairly honest signal of dominance and sexual drive, because men with deep voices have higher levels of testosterone. Consequently, women who think that a man with a deep voice is big and muscular are likely to be disappointed, while those who expect him to be dominant and sexy are likely to have their expectations pleasantly confirmed.[30]

During the early stages of courtship men tend to ply women with compliments. Joan Manes and Nessa Wolfson, who analyzed compli-ments in great detail, discovered that three-quarters of them include the word *you* —which is hardly surprising—and that a third include the word *nice*.[31] The formulaic nature of most compliments makes them very easy to compose and equally easy to comprehend. Most people are skeptical about compliments, but this doesn't stop people using them, and it certainly hasn't reduced their effectiveness.

Another thing that works is self-disclosure. Relationships between women are often characterized by intense disclosure—female friends will often know everything there is to know about each other's past, not to mention the intimate details of their sex life. A man knows where his best friend works, which team he supports, and who he's sleeping with, but his friend's emotional life is probably a complete mystery.[32] Many women live in hope of finding a man who enjoys self-disclosure as much as she does—who wants to curl up with her on the sofa and talk about his emotions. In fact, women frequently complain that the men they're dating spend an awful lot of time talking about themselves and the things that interest them, and very little time discussing mat-ters that are of interest to others, unless they happen to be other men. Their big lament, which is usually justified, is that men simply don't ask them questions. If there's one thing that women find attractive in a man it's sufficient curiosity to ask a woman about herself, to show her that he's listening and that he's interested in what she has to say.

One way men try to distinguish themselves from women is in terms of emotionality. Men often take pride in the fact that they don't wear their emotions on their sleeve, while at the same time they're keen to criticize women for being so ready to show their feelings. Whether there actually are differences between the sexes according to how intensely they feel certain emotions is a moot point, but what seems to be beyond doubt—in our society at least—is that women are more emotionally expressive then men.[33] Lots of men make the mistake of seeing this as a sign of weakness, and yet, paradoxically, they find themselves drawn toward women who're emotionally expressive.

When I was studying speed dating a few years ago, I noticed that several of the women who became popular with the men were unusually expressive. During the brief conversations with their "dates" their facial muscles were constantly on the move. One moment they were smiling, the next they appeared amused or puzzled, and when their date said something that was designed to impress, they immediately produced the requisite expression of glee or surprise. This ability to perform a broad range of facial expressions, and to make them appropriate to what's happening at the time, is a seriously undervalued skill. Women who possess this "facial facility" can't help but make a positive impression, and that's because they're sending three messages: 1) they're exposing their empathic side; 2) they're creating a mutual bond of emotional understanding; and 3) they're emphasizing their reproductive value as potential parents who would obviously be sensitive to the emotional needs of their children. There is, however, no reason to assume that facial facility is the sole preserve of women. Men have all the facial equipment they need to display a wide range of appropriate facial expressions, although in doing so they usually run the risk of behaving unconventionally. That said, it's worth noting that, during the early stages of a relationship, men will occasionally adopt some of the interpersonal techniques of women—they'll ask lots of questions, listen intently, become more emotionally expressive and even talk about their feelings. Women who've been exposed to this approach often complain that this seldom extends into their relationship—that once the man starts to feel secure, he reverts to type, stops asking questions and becomes emotionally illiterate.

Laughter Tells

Because language is our crowning glory there's every reason to expect that an ability to speak clearly will be fairly high up in the list of things that men and women look for in a partner. Recent research shows that it's only men who place a premium on finding an articulate companion. Women—possibly because they know it's expecting too much—don't go looking for a mate with linguistic skills. They're much more impressed with other qualities, like a man's sense of humour.

Laughter isn't exactly an aphrodisiac, but it is a vital ingredient in cementing relationships. The research on laughter shows that when men and women are together, it's the women who do most of the laughing.[34] When women are asked what they look for in a man they usually say that they want a guy who likes a good laugh—but what they're really looking for is a man who makes *them* laugh. Robert Provine has pointed out that the aim of men is to make women laugh, not to laugh or be amused themselves. From a woman's point of view, it doesn't matter very much whether the man is given to laughter—what is important, however, is that he passes the "laughter test" by making *her* laugh.[35]

In a research study by Karl Grammer and Irenäus Eibl-Eibesfeldt in Germany, conversations were recorded between pairs of young men and women who had met for the first time. The researchers found that the more a woman laughed during the meeting, the keener she was to meet the man again, regardless of how often he had laughed. For the men, however, it was the other way around. They were keen to get together again with the woman if they'd managed to make her laugh; their enthusiasm for another meeting had nothing to do with how much they personally had laughed.[34]

When a man and a woman meet for the first time, the likelihood of them forming a relationship is not predicted by the total amount of laughter they generate, nor by how much the man laughs—it's predicted by the amount of laughter the woman produces. There are several explanations for this. Laughter reduces the potentially threatening nature of an encounter between a man and a woman—the woman feels that if the man is capable of being amusing then he can't be much of a threat. It might also be that the biochemical changes brought about by laughter act as a form of foreplay—in other words, women want a man who's prepared to tickle her fancy, while men want a woman who wants her fancy tickled and clearly enjoys it. Finally, there's Provine's explanation in terms of the relationship between laughter and status. He suggests that "the desire by women for men who make them laugh may be a veiled request for dominant males. Men who pass the audition for dominance are acknowledged with women's laughter."[35]

We don't normally consider laughter in this light. That's because we perceive people who try to make others laugh as creators of fun and levity, not as individuals who are trying to enhance their own status. I remember a situation many years ago, not long after my wife and I had met, when we spent the evening with another guy and his girlfriend. During the evening the guy switched to a comedy routine, putting on funny voices and pulling faces. Both of the girls were in stitches, but I wasn't amused at all. Later, when we were driving home my future wife said how much she'd enjoyed herself and how amusing she'd found the other guy. I said I didn't find him in the least bit funny. Of course, what I'd failed to recognize is that, by amusing the girls, he'd become more dominant. I was busy complaining that his sense of humour was infantile. I didn't realize that I was feeling grumpy and aggressive because he'd used laughter to elevate his own importance in the eyes of the two girls, and, in the process, to reduce mine.

Compatibility Tells

When people meet for the first time, they employ a mixture of come-ons, hang-ons and put-offs. When things are going well between them, most of the signals consist of come-ons. When there's doubt about the progress of the relationship the hang-ons increase in number, and when the relationship is going nowhere the put-offs start to take over. Monika Moore has made a special study of the put-offs used by women, or what she calls "rejection signals."[38] These include facial gestures like yawning, frowning and sneering, as well as headshaking and manual gestures like putting her hands in her pockets or crossing the arms. All of these signals are used to deter the man, and to show him that the woman isn't interested in taking things any further.

Courting couples often reveal their compatibility through their movements and postures. There is a strong tendency for individuals who like each other, or who feel some rapport, to coordinate their movements and to match their postures. Studies of "interactional synchrony" have shown that people who are on the same wavelength are more likely to synchronize their actions, and vice versa.[39] With our restaurant couple, for example, the man might take a drink from his glass and the woman might respond by wiping the corners of her mouth with her napkin. A few moments later she might lean on the table, and he might respond by moving his chair. What makes the interaction synchronous is the underlying rhythm of the man's and woman's activities—it's not essential that they copy each other, only that they integrate their separate contributions into the same balletic performance. There are occasions, however, when courting couples perform the same actions. Studies of "postural matching" show that the closer two people are emotionally, the more similar the postures they adopt. This works in both directions—not only do people adopt similar postures when they feel more rapport, but they also feel greater rapport after they have assumed the same posture.[40] Individuals don't make a deliberate, conscious decision to copy each other. Rather, it's a matter of these processes occurring spontaneously and unconsciously, so that even after people have assumed the same posture they're not aware of what they've done.

One reason why postural matching occurs during courtship is that certain postures are linked to certain emotions, so that when two people adopt the same posture they are more likely to experience the same feelings.[41] This relationship between posture and mood is very basic. For example, people who are hypnotized and instructed to experience a particular feeling are much more likely to comply if they are placed in a posture that is conducive to that feeling. If they're put into a posture that's inconsistent with that feeling, they may not experience it fully, or even at all. The same kind of relationship that exists between posture and emotion also occurs in everyday life. People who copy the postures of others are in a much better position to empathize with them than those who adopt very different postures. Women, it appears, have a much stronger need for postural matching than men. Geoffrey Beattie discovered, for example, that male–female and female–female pairs assume the same posture more than half the time, but that in male–male pairs the individuals only adopt the same posture for about a quarter of the time that they're together.[42] Men, it seems, are less inclined to match each other's postures. Women, on the other hand, like to copy the person they're with, regardless of whether it's a man or a woman.

If postural matching provides a measure of a couple's compatibility, it's equally true to say that its opposite, postural mismatching, offers an index of a couple's incompatibility. One of the first symptoms of trouble in a relationship is the tendency of individuals to adopt very different postures when they're together. Even when the postures are similar, they may be diametrically opposed, so that instead of facing toward each other, the two people face away from each other. The way that people use their eyes is equally telling. Think of that famous occasion when Prince Charles and Princess Diana were photographed sitting in the back of a car, just before it was announced that they were going to separate. Both of them had a rather studied, sombre countenance, but even more revealing were their postures and their gaze—each of them was oriented away from the other, and their eyes studiously avoided each other's. The rejection signals were flying in both directions.

In contrast to the signs that a relationship is disintegrating, there are tells that show when someone is deeply in love. These include distraction, lack of concentration, sighing, stuttering, and an inability to sleep, eat or drink. The symptoms of love and influenza are often similar—sensations of hot and cold, a lack of energy and an overpowering desire to go to bed. Lovesickness also exhibits some of the symptoms of Obsessive Compulsive Disorder—one-track thinking, strong preoccupations, fixation with routines and the knowledge that one is behaving irrationally but can't do anything about it.

Infidelity Tells

There are four main types of infidelity. The first involves nothing more than a shared intimacy between two people where at least one of them is married or in a stable relationship. These mental acts of unfaithfulness are often conducted on the phone or by email. Although they don't have a physical component, they can sometimes be just as dangerous as a sexual affair, especially when they generate strong attachments. The second type is the "one-night stand," where two people have a brief fling but don't consolidate the relationship. The third involves an extended affair that lasts for a few weeks or months. The fourth consists of a long-term relationship; for example, between a married man and his mistress.

Subterfuge is the essence of infidelity. People will go to enormous lengths to cover their tracks, create credible alibis and conceal their actions. In spite of their best efforts, however, they invariably leave a trail of tells behind them. These include changing an established routine, uncharacteristic irritability, concern about their weight or appearance, vagueness, anonymous phone calls and an apparent loss of interest in sex. Of course many of these symptoms may appear for other reasons, so people who suspect their partner need to be doubly sure that what they see as the signs of infidelity aren't simply the projections of their own insecurity and jealousy.

Possessive Tells

People use a variety of strategies to retain their mate—these are what zoologists call "mate guarding" or "mate retention" tactics. Mate-guarding tactics fall into two broad categories: those that are directed at the mate, and those that are addressed to potential rivals. Those directed at the mate include positive overtures, like displays of affection, gifts, promises and declarations of love. They also include "threats," "teases" and "put-downs." Threats are warnings to the mate about what will happen if they're unfaithful, while put-downs, otherwise known as "gaslighting," are ways of reducing a mate's self-esteem to the point where they don't feel worthy of anybody else's affection.

Teases involve flirting with other people in public so that one's mate feels jealous and more possessive.

Men apparently use threats and put-downs more than women, while women use teases more than men. Men are also more likely to resort to mate-guarding techniques if their female partner is young and attractive, and therefore seen as more desirable by other men. In extreme cases they may even try to reduce her chances of meeting any potential male rivals. Women's mate-guarding tactics may include keeping rivals at bay as well as being especially affectionate and attentive toward their partner. Both men and women who're worried about their partner being poached will often make an extra effort to look attractive and healthy.[43]

Strategies that are directed at the mate tend to be private in nature. Those that are targeted at potential rivals are much more public. They include "resource signals"—in other words, displays of wealth that try to persuade potential rivals that they don't have what it takes to compete, as well as "threats" intended to scare them off. "Ownership signals" are the most common, and in some ways the most interesting of the mate retention tactics, because people aren't always aware of using them. Most ownership signals involve physical proximity—they create the impression that two people are emotionally close because they're physically close. For example, a man who puts his arm around his wife's waist, or his hand on her shoulder at a party, sends two messages: privately he reassures his wife and publicly he tells everyone that she belongs to him. The wife who removes a piece of lint from her husband's jacket, or who adjusts his tie, sends out the same messages of reassurance and ownership.

People also show that they are together by putting their arms around each other, linking arms or holding hands while they're walking along. The sociologist Erving Goffman called these actions "tie-signs."[44] He argued that their main function was to show that the people concerned are connected, hence "tied," to each other. One revealing feature of an established relationship is whether the two people remain in physical contact while they're walking, and if they do, how they actually do it. Although hand-holding appears to be a fairly symmetrical activity, one person needs to have their hand in front, while the other person has to take up the back position. With a married couple, for example, it's usually the husband who assumes the "front hold" and the wife who has the "back hold." It isn't clear whether this happens because men are taller or because they prefer to lead from the front. When the wife takes up the front hold position, it's usually because she's taller than her husband and therefore finds the back hold uncomfortable. If she's shorter, it's usually because she likes to be in charge—even at the cost of some physical discomfort to her and her husband. A good example of this occurred at the inauguration of George W. Bush in 2001. After the ceremony was over, Bill and Hillary Clinton started leaving. The two of them were walking along hand in hand, with Bill looking composed and very much in control, and Hillary looking supportive. However, if you'd looked at them more closely, you'd have noticed that Hillary had the "front hold," while Bill had the "back hold"— an arrangement that could not be explained in terms of their height. It showed that at that precise moment it was Hillary who was in charge, not Bill.

Human courtship, like that of other animals, consists of a series of stages, starting with the first meeting and progressing through to intercourse and the establishment of some kind of relationship.[45] The transition from one courtship stage to the next is inextricably bound up with tells that take the form of invitations to move to the next stage of intimacy. A woman might orient her body toward a man to show him that she's approachable, or a man might brush the hair from a woman's face to show that he wants to kiss her. The way that individuals respond to these overtures decides whether the courtship is going to proceed to the next phase, or whether it's going to get stuck or unwind altogether. What's critical in this whole process, of course, is the way that people read each other's tells. It's not enough for the participants to notice each other's tells—they also need to decode them correctly. People make two errors when they interpret *courtship tells*. One is to err on the side of caution, to "mentally minimize" the tell by assuming that the other person's gestures of affection don't mean anything. The other error is to "mentally expand" the tell by interpreting friendly behaviour as a sign of romantic or sexual interest. As we've seen, men are much more likely to mentally expand women's tells. Women, as a result, are often left wondering how the man got the idea that they were so keen, and doubting their ability to send the right message. The ideal situation would be one where men and women didn't mentally minimize or expand each other's tells. But given the need for understatement and subtlety, which are essential to courtship, this is all very unlikely.

Signs of Trouble

In principle, we should be able to gauge whether a marriage or partnership is going to last, simply by looking at the tells that the two people produce when they're in each other's company. The evidence from psychology is that long-term relationships between men and women are more likely to succeed if the two people come from roughly similar backgrounds, share the same values and have similar expectations for their relationship. As we saw earlier, evidence from observational studies show that the way people express their feelings for each other can have a dramatic effect on how long they remain together. The relationship expert, John Gottman, has discovered several behaviours that predict whether a marriage is likely to withstand the tests of time.[46] One of the most powerful predictors, he found, is contempt—if the husband or wife adopts a dismissive, scornful attitude toward their spouse, there's a strong possibility that their marriage is heading for the rocks. There are several behavioural predictors of a relationship's resilience, the most important being "attentiveness," "synchrony" and "connection."

> **Attentiveness.** This forms the very foundation of successful relationships—it's the way that two people are focused on each other's current and future needs, and it's often revealed by how they gaze at each other, monitor the environment and keep in contact through touch. The importance of gaze is linked to the elementary functions it performs—namely,

expressing affection, monitoring the other person and, in rare cases, regulating their behaviour. It follows that if two people look at each other less, they automatically reduce their ability not only to show how much they value and care for each other but also to find out what their partner is doing or feeling, and to respond appropriately. In that famous photograph of Charles and Diana, taken not long before the royal couple got divorced, we find them in the back seat of a car, both looking away from each other. This image is a prototypical expression of gaze avoidance, but far less striking instances of inattention can be equally damaging to a marriage. For example, in the early days of their relationship, Donald Trump was very attentive toward Melania, creating space for her to speak and watching her appreciatively. In recent years, however, things have almost been the exact opposite. In fact, there have been times when Trump and Melania have been together, and he has appeared not to notice her presence and behaved as if she weren't even there. We saw this very clearly when Trump and Melania made their first official visit together to the White House and the Obamas were waiting to greet them. Trump, we noticed, alighted from the limousine and strolled toward the Obamas, leaving his hapless wife trailing behind, making it look like he'd completely forgotten her. Not long after this, a similar incident occurred at Trump's inauguration. After he'd completed his address to the nation, Trump turned around to face Melania and she responded with a big smile. But as Trump turned back toward the audience, Melania's smile suddenly disappeared and was replaced by a look of utter dejection. Close inspection of what happened revealed that Trump wasn't trying to connect with Melania at all—he was targeting his daughter, Ivanka, instead. Singling out his daughter was understandable, but doing so without attempting to connect with his wife was hardly conducive to a happy marriage.

Synchrony. The animal world contains countless instances where males and females pair up and then go through a courtship dance, which enables them to appraise each other's fitness and capacity for coordination, and at the same time bonds them closer together. Exactly the same thing happens during human courtship, with two people exploring whether they're able to get in tune with each other. How successful they are at synchronizing their movements and activities provides important clues to how well they're coordinated emotionally. We find this, for example, when two people are walking in step with each other or are carefully timing their contributions during a conversation. There's also the matter of how they respond to each other's overtures. For example, when one person makes a move toward the other, does he or she accept the implicit invitation, or do they ignore or reject it? A simple action, like the way two people kiss, for example, can tell us a lot about their relationship. For a shared lip-kiss to work, it's vital that both parties are geared up for what's about to happen, and this will invariably depend on the intention signals they've already produced, and whether these have been noticed and properly interpreted. Then there's the crucial matter of timing. It's probably no exaggeration to say that a lovers' kiss requires all the complex coordination of a moon landing—both parties have to know when to make their first move and how fast or slow to advance, so that their lips meet up exactly at the right moment. All things being equal, couples who manage this are much more likely to form a stable bond, whereas those who struggle to coordinate their efforts are probably heading for disappointment. In the realms of love and attraction, little things like this can take on huge significance.

Connection. When we watch famous couples at public events or on the red carpet, it's very tempting to speculate who has a stable partnership and who is probably going to break up soon. Several things can help us come to a more informed conclusion. One of these is the "cut-out principle" mentioned earlier—namely the mental experiment where, having conceptually removed one member of a couple from the scene, we ask ourselves whether the other person appears to be alone. If the answer is "yes," it means that the two people aren't physically connected; if the answer is "no," it suggests that they are physically connected to each other. Then there's the issue of posture—are the two people oriented toward or away from each other, and in which direction are different parts of their body leaning? Also, are their actions, postures and facial expressions different, and what does each person's facial expression tell us about what they're feeling? In making these sorts of judgments, it's worth looking out for tie-signs and mate-guarding: Are the two people physically connected to each other, and if so, how? Are one or both of them showing signs of protecting or "owning" their partner? When examining the protective or helpful overtures individuals make toward their partner, it's important to watch how the partner responds. For example, back in 2021, when Justin and Sophie Grégoire Trudeau received their first COVID-19 vaccinations, Justin went first, and while he was having his injection Sophie reassuringly held his hand. When it was Sophie's turn, Justin stretched out his hand, offering to hold hers, but she immediately swatted it away, showing that she was quite content to manage on her own. At the time, Sophie's behaviour could have been seen as just another example of the everyday rough-and-tumble of married life. But since the Trudeaus announced their separation in 2023, it's been worth looking back and considering whether Sophie's rejection of Justin's invitation was actually an early indication of her unfolding desire to manage her own life, unencumbered by Justin's solicitous overtures. When marriages and romantic partnerships collapse, our first thought is to search for an explanation in things that have happened recently. Often, however, the causes of relationship breakdown go back some way, and we'd be in a much better position to understand them if we kept our eyes on the early tells.

11. Lying Tells

A lot of the things that we say to other people aren't true—they're fibs, fudges, fabrications, falsehoods and barefaced lies. It's been estimated that we lie to a third of the people we meet each day. Lying is especially common when people are trying to impress each other, and that's why it's so prevalent in dating and courtship. Robert Feldman at the University of Massachusetts found that 60 percent of the people who took part in one of his studies lied at least once during a ten-minute meeting, and that most of them told two or three lies in that time.[1]

Research on lying shows that there is no difference in the numbers of lies told by men and women, but that there are differences in the sorts of lies they tell—men are more likely to produce lies that are designed to make them look impressive, while women are more likely to tell lies that are intended to make other people feel good.[2] Women are generally more inclined than men to express positive opinions, both about the things they like and the things they dislike. Consequently, when women are faced with the possibility of upsetting someone—for example, when they're given a present they don't want—they're more likely to try to protect the other person's feelings by telling a white lie.

Some people consider lying to be a crime, regardless of how big or small the lie is and what effect it has, while others feel that certain lies are legitimate, possibly even necessary. For example, when a woman asks her husband whether he likes her new hairstyle, she's usually inviting him to say something complimentary rather than to give an honest opinion. The husband who makes the mistake of telling his wife that he doesn't like her new hairstyle is probably asking for trouble. So is the wife who offers her husband less than fulsome praise when he asks her what she thinks about his performance on the sports field, or the speech he gave at the office party. Lying lubricates interpersonal relations; without lies our social life would soon grind to a complete halt.

People differ enormously in their propensity to lie. At one extreme are the "George Washingtons," who model themselves on the American president who could not tell a lie; while at the other extreme are the "Machiavellis," who take their cue from the Florentine statesman who advocated lying as a legitimate means of achieving one's goals. People who score high on measures of manipulation are more likely to tell lies, and not to feel bad about it. The same is true of people who are highly expressive and sociable. People who frequently lie tend to be very popular—probably because their ingratiating lies endear them to others.[3] Con artists, hoaxers and politicians have to be accomplished liars; in fact an ability to project an image of honesty, without feeling any sense of guilt about it, is an essential feature of their role. Sales people also need this ability. Bella DePaulo from the University of Virginia performed an experiment with sales personnel who were required either to lie or to tell the truth.[4] When she examined their actions and speech she couldn't find a single difference between those who were telling the truth and those who were lying.

Detection Tells

Although lies form a large part of our exchanges with other people, we're actually not very good at telling whether someone is deceiving us or telling the truth. This isn't for lack of evidence, because 90 percent of lies are accompanied by tells which, like a burglar's fingerprints, leave behind traces of deception.[5]

People often pride themselves on their ability to detect if someone is telling them a lie, especially when that person happens to be someone whom they know well. How often have you heard a mother announce that her children could never lie to her because she "knows them too well" or a young man claim that his girlfriend could never pull the wool over his eyes because he can "see right through her"? In fact the research on lie detection suggests that both the mother and the young man are probably mistaken, because people only detect about

54 percent of the lies they're exposed to, a figure not significantly different from what you'd expect by chance.[6] It's also been discovered that as people get to know each other better their ability to detect each other's lies doesn't improve—it sometimes gets worse![7]

One reason for this is that as people get to know each other well, they become more confident in their ability to detect each other's lies. However, their accuracy doesn't necessarily increase—it's usually just their confidence that grows. Moreover, when people get to know each other well, they're more likely to allow their emotions to get in the way of their diagnostic skills, and this reduces their ability to detect each other's lies. Finally, as each person gets to know what type of evidence of deceit the other person is looking for, they're able to modify their behaviour to reduce the chances of detection.

There are several reasons why people are so bad at detecting lies:

Blissful Ignorance. Even when there are clear signs that someone is lying, they may go unnoticed, not because people are insensitive to these signs, but because they don't want to admit to themselves that the other person is lying. One of the main reasons why individuals believe other people's lies is because they want to believe them, with the result that they end up as co-conspirators in their own deception. Con artists understand this principle completely, and they make a point of telling people what they want to hear.[8] The desire not to discover the truth is also found in politics. British Prime Minister Neville Chamberlain is best remembered for the way he was deceived by Adolf Hitler. When Chamberlain returned from Germany in 1938, brandishing a signed agreement with Hitler, he declared that Hitler was a man to be trusted. At the time there was evidence that Hitler intended to invade Czechoslovakia, but Chamberlain chose to ignore this evidence—had he acknowledged what was happening it would have jeopardized his attempts to secure peace.[9] People have all kinds of motives for ignoring the fact that someone is lying to them. A wife may choose to fool herself that her husband isn't having a serious affair because she's convinced herself that he'll soon lose interest in the other woman. Equally, parents may overlook the fact that their child is taking drugs because they don't want to have to deal with the problem.

Threshold Settings. Individuals' assumptions about the prevalence of lying can affect their ability to spot liars and truthtellers. People who are very trusting and who therefore don't expect others to deceive them are prone to set their detection threshold very high. As a result they are likely to identify the truthtellers quite accurately but not the liars. Highly suspicious people have the opposite problem—because they set their threshold too low, they inadvertently identify most of the liars, but fail to spot the truthtellers. Police officers are a good example of the second type because they tend to set their lie detector threshold so low. The only reason why they are successful at spotting liars is because they think everyone is lying![10]

Gut Feelings. There are two ways of identifying a liar: by looking out for clues to deception or by relying on one's intuition. It has recently been discovered that people who use their gut feelings are less accurate in detecting liars than those who try to base their decisions on the evidence.[11] Indeed, when it comes to detecting deceit, intuition is usually more of a hindrance than a help.

Multiple Causes. People often make the mistake of thinking that specific actions are clues to deception, and not to anything else. It is sometimes assumed, for example, that people who touch their nose while they're talking are automatically telling a lie—that the gesture is a sign of lying, and nothing else. These assumptions overlook the fact that actions and utterances may sometimes provide clues to deception, while on other occasions they may provide clues to states of mind that have nothing to do with deception. People who rely on the polygraph lie detector often make this mistake. The polygraph measures respiration, heart rate and palmar sweating— all of which are indicators of arousal. When people become anxious, their breathing rate increases, their heart rate goes up and their palms start to sweat more profusely. When people are lying they often become anxious, and their anxiety can be detected by the polygraph. However, there are times when people become anxious without lying, just as there are cases where people lie without experiencing any anxiety at all.

Looking Elsewhere. People also fail to detect lies because they're looking for clues in the wrong place. Where people look is usually determined by what they believe are the giveaway signs of lying. If you ask people how they can tell if someone is lying to them, they usually mention shifty eyes or the way people fidget with their hands. Other signs of dishonesty mentioned include smiling, rapid blinking, long pauses and talking too fast or too slow. Some of these behaviours have in fact been found to be clues to deception, but many are not. When Robert Krauss and his colleagues at Columbia University in New York compared the signs that people use to detect lying with those that are actually associated with lying, they discovered very little overlap.[12]

Eye Tells

Most people believe gaze aversion is a sign of lying. They assume that because liars feel guilty, embarrassed and apprehensive, they find it difficult to look their victim in the eye, and they therefore look away. This theory is widespread—in a study covering seventy-five countries and forty-three different languages, it was found to be prevalent all over the world.[13] However, this idea that liars avert their gaze is not supported by the facts. Firstly, patterns of gaze are quite unstable— while some liars avert their eyes, others actually increase the amount of time they spend looking at the other person. Secondly, because gaze is fairly easy to control, liars can use their eyes to project an image of honesty. Knowing that other people assume gaze aversion to be a sign of lying, many liars do the exact opposite—they deliberately increase their gaze to give the impression that they're telling the truth. So if you want to know if someone's lying to you, don't limit your attention to shifty eyes—also look out for those moments when the other person is gazing at you more intently than usual!

Then there's the issue of gaze direction. Since the 1970s, Neuro-Linguistic Programming (NLP) has been offering to help people understand themselves and how they process information, as well as how to spot if someone is lying, based on their eye movements. According to the exponents of NLP, if someone looks up to their right while they're speaking, it shows that they're lying; whereas if they look up to their left it indicates that they're being truthful. A few years ago, British psychologist Richard Wiseman and his colleagues put this to the test by observing the eye movements of people who were lying or telling the truth, and they found that there was no association between what people did with their eyes and whether they were lying or being truthful.[14] It would certainly make the detection of deception much easier if there were such an association, but eye movements appear to be a lot more complex; and, anyway, once you know what people are looking for, it's fairly easy to fake.

Another supposed sign of lying is rapid blinking. It's true that when we become aroused or our mind is racing, there's a corresponding increase in our blink rate. Our normal blink rate is about twenty blinks per minute, but it can increase to four or five times that figure when we feel under pressure. When people are lying, they frequently become aroused, and when liars are concocting a story or searching for an answer to an awkward question, their thought processes speed up. In this kind of situation you might expect their blink rate to go up. In fact, what appears to happen is that while people are lying their blink rate drops slightly, but as soon as they've finished lying it increases above their normal resting blink rate.[15] This suggests that if you want to use blink rate to determine whether someone is lying, you should focus on what happens after the person has spoken, not while they're actually speaking. However, we shouldn't forget that there are times when people have a very high blink rate, not because they're lying, but because they're under pressure. Also, there are times when liars show quite normal blink rates.[16]

Body Tells

Fidgeting and awkward hand movements are also thought to be signs of deceit—the assumption being that when people are lying they become agitated and this gives rise to nervous movements of the hands. As we mentioned earlier, there is a class of gestures called "adaptors," which consists of actions like stroking one's hair, scratching one's head or rubbing the hands together. When people tell lies they sometimes feel guilty or worried about being found out, and these concerns can cause them to produce adaptors. This tends to happen when the stakes are high or when the liar isn't very good at being deceptive. Most of the time the exact opposite happens. Again, because liars are worried about revealing themselves, they tend to inhibit their normal gestural habits. As a result, their actions are likely to become more frozen, not more animated![17]

Movements of the hands, like those of the eyes, tend to be under conscious control, and that's why the hands aren't a reliable source of information about lying. There are other parts of the body, however, which are also under conscious control but, because they're overlooked and neglected, often prove to be a very useful source of clues about deception. Research on lying shows that when people are asked to tell a lie they tend to produce more giveaway signs in the lower part of their body, rather than in the upper part. When video recordings of these people are shown to other people who are required to judge whether they are lying or telling the truth, the judges are more accurate if they are exposed to recordings of the lower part of the body.[18] Clearly there is something about the legs and feet that shows them to be an underrated source of information about lying. It seems that liars focus their efforts at concealment on their hands, arms and face, because they know that's what other people will be watching. Because their feet feel remote, liars don't bother about them—but it's often tiny adjustments of the legs and feet that betray them.

Nose Tells

One gesture that reveals a lie is the "mouth-cover." When this happens it's as if the liar were taking precautions to cover up the source of their deception, acting on the assumption that if other people can't see their mouth then they won't know where the lie has come from. Mouth-covering actions can range from full-blown versions where the hand completely covers the mouth, to gestures where the hand supports the chin or a finger surreptitiously touches the corner of the mouth. By placing a hand on or near the mouth, a liar behaves like a criminal who can't resist the temptation to return to the scene of their crime. Just like the criminal, the hand lays itself open to detection—at any moment it could become apparent to others that the act of touching the mouth is an attempt to conceal a lie.

There is, however, a substitute for touching the mouth, which is touching the nose. By touching their nose the liar experiences the momentary comfort of covering their mouth without the risk of drawing attention to what they're really doing. In this role, nose-touching functions as a substitute for mouth-covering—it's a *stealth tell* because it looks as if someone is scratching their nose, but their real intention is to cover their mouth.

Another school of thought says that nose-touching is a sign of deceit quite separate from anything to do with the mouth. One proponent of this idea is Alan Hirsch who, together with Charles Wolf, has done a detailed analysis of Bill Clinton's grand jury testimony in August 1998, when the president denied having had sex with Monica Lewinsky.[19] They discovered that while Clinton was telling the truth he hardly touched his nose at all, but that when he lied about his affair with Monica Lewinsky, he touched his nose roughly once every four minutes. Hirsch called this the "Pinocchio syndrome," after the fictional character whose wooden nose becomes longer every time he tells a lie. Hirsch suggested that when people lie their nose becomes engorged with blood, and that this produces a sensation that is alleviated by touching or rubbing the nose.

There are at least two arguments against the Pinocchio syndrome. One is that nose-touching may simply be a symptom of anxiety rather than a sign of deceit. The other is that when people lie they often feel apprehensive and fearful about being found out, and that these emotions are associated with the blood draining away from the face—in other words, with vasoconstriction rather than vasodilation. This is the view of Mark Frank of Rutgers University.[20] Frank also points out that experimental research on lying has not shown nose-touching to be a common sign of deceit. Of course it's quite possible that nose-touching does not emerge in laboratory settings, where the stakes are low and the price that people pay if they are exposed as a liar is not terribly high. It's also feasible that nose-touching isn't a sign of deceit for everyone—it might simply be the trademark tell of some people, including Bill Clinton.

Finally there's the possibility that nose-touching has nothing at all to do with deceit or with anxiety, but that it's an unconscious form of rejection. Ray Birdwhistell considered that when one person rubs their nose in the presence of another, it reveals the first person's dislike of the second.[21] As he put it, the "nose rub among Americans is as much a sign of rejection as the word 'No!'" Given this interpretation, Bill Clinton's nose-touching before the grand jury might be seen as an expression of his deep antipathy toward his interrogators, rather than a clue to the fact that he was lying to them.

Surrounding this debate remains the unresolved question of what we mean when we say that someone is lying—is it that we know them to be lying, or do they have to believe that they're not telling the truth? As Mark Frank has pointed out, this issue is highly pertinent to the case of Bill Clinton and his testimony during the Lewinsky affair. Some people argue that Clinton knew that he was lying, but others insist that, given his definition of sex and the way he constructed his evidence, he wasn't lying at all. So do people who have to persuade themselves that they're not lying behave any differently from those who start out with the conviction that they're telling the truth? That's an interesting question.

The mouth-cover. This is an important lying tell. When he testified to the Grand Jury during his impeachment trial, Bill Clinton repeatedly touched his mouth. Other lying tells, also seen here, include excessive sweating, restrained movement of the hands and increased levels of gaze.

Masking Tells

When someone knowingly tells a lie they have to hide two things: the truth and any emotions that might arise out of their attempts at concealment. The emotions that liars feel are generally negative—like guilt or fear about being found out. But liars can also experience the thrill of pulling the wool over other people's eyes—what Paul Ekman has called "duping delight."[22] When people tell small, innocuous lies they don't usually feel any negative emotions at all. However, when they're telling big lies and there's a lot at stake, they often experience very powerful negative emotions that need to be concealed if the lie is to remain hidden. A negative emotion can be concealed by turning away the head, by covering the face with the hands, or by masking it with a neutral or a positive emotion. The strategies of turning away and covering the face don't always work because they tend to draw attention to what the liar is trying to conceal. Masking, on the other hand, enables liars to present an exterior that isn't necessarily connected with lying.

The most commonly used masks are the "straight face" and the "smile." The straight face requires the least effort—in order to mask their negative emotions all the liar needs to do is put their face into repose. The smile is potentially more effective as a mask because it suggests that the person is feeling happy and contented—in other words, experiencing emotions that one doesn't normally associate with lying.

Smiling Tells

Of all the facial expressions, smiling is probably the easiest to produce. It's also disarming, as it makes other people feel positive and less suspicious about the liar. Smiling appeals to liars because most people aren't very good at spotting the difference between a genuine and a false smile, and as a result they tend to take smiles at face value. People can usually identify "blended smiles," which display negative emotions. They find it very easy, for example, to spot a "miserable smile," where the inside edges of the eyebrows are raised and the corners of the mouth are either pulled up or slightly lowered. But people are notoriously bad at detecting false, unblended smiles, and that's why these are used to mask the negative emotions associated with lying.[23]

If you ask people how to spot a liar they often mention smiling. They'll tell you that when someone is lying they're more likely to use a smile to mask their true feelings. However, research on lying shows that it's the other way around—people who are lying smile less than those who are telling the truth. What appears to be happening is that liars occasionally adjust their behaviour so that it's the opposite to what everyone expects liars to be doing. This doesn't mean that liars have abandoned smiling—it simply shows that they smile less than people who are telling the truth. When dissemblers do smile they often produce counterfeit smiles, which aren't necessarily detected by the people at whom they're directed. There are several identifying features of counterfeit smiles:

Duration. Counterfeit smiles are sustained for much longer than genuine, heartfelt smiles.

Assembly. Counterfeit smiles are "put together" more rapidly than genuine smiles. They are also dismantled more quickly.

Location. Counterfeit smiles tend to be confined to the lower half of the face, whereas genuine smiles involve the muscles that pull up the corners of the mouth as well as the muscles that tighten up around the eyes and pull the eyebrows down slightly. Counterfeit and genuine smiles are controlled by different parts of the brain—voluntary centres produce counterfeit smiles, while genuine smiles are produced involuntarily.

Symmetry. Genuine smiles appear on both sides of the face, whereas counterfeit smiles sometimes appear more strongly on one side of the face (usually the right side). That's because the neural pathways associated with voluntary and involuntary facial expressions are different. If you see a symmetrical smile it could be either genuine or false, but if you come across a lopsided smile there's a good chance that it's false.

Although symmetrical and lopsided smiles are quite different to look at, we tend to react to lopsided smiles as if they were genuine. That's because, most of the time, we're unconcerned about the authenticity of smiles—provided other people smile at us, we don't much care what kind of smile we're being offered.

Micro-tells

When people try to mask their emotions their face receives two opposing sets of instructions—while involuntary processes in the brain are instructing the face to show their true feelings, voluntary processes are instructing the face to display the masked expression. For masking to work, voluntary processes need to gain the upper hand so that the person's real emotions remain hidden. Successful masking depends on several factors, including the sheer ability to mask one's emotions, and the strength of the emotion that's being suppressed. When an emotion is very strong it can sometimes overwhelm attempts to suppress it, with the masked expression giving way to the real emotion. There are times, however, when the real emotion momentarily breaks through, and the masked expression then reinstates itself immediately. These glimpses of people's real feelings are called "micromomentary expressions" or *micro-tells*.[24] They are extremely fast and short-lived—typically less than a second! People don't realize it when they produce micro-tells, and the vast majority don't notice it when they're exposed to them. However, people like the police can be trained to spot and interpret them.

When people lie they sometimes produce micro-tells that reveal their true feelings. A person might, for example, be telling a story about how they managed to fight their way out of a burning building, giving the impression that they were completely in command during the incident. While they're telling the story their face remains composed. But all of a sudden their expression changes to one of fear, and then immediately switches back to its normal composure. If you were watching this and you didn't know about micro-tells, you probably wouldn't notice what had happened, and you almost certainly wouldn't spot the brief exposure of fear. To the trained observer this micro-tell would be a useful source of information about the person telling the story—it would show that they're trying to give the impression of being in control, but that during the incident they actually experienced a great deal of fear. Exactly why they felt fearful is something that might need to be pursued.

Because micro-tells are completely involuntary they are rather like traitors—without our knowing it, they betray what we're thinking, but only to those who understand what they mean. Mark Frank and Paul Ekman have claimed that these fleeting glimpses of people's real emotions can be a valuable tool in the detection of deceit. However, the evidence on this issue is far from equivocal. It's been found, for example, that the actual length of microexpressions is critical, because liars and truthtellers can be distinguished on the basis of some microexpressions but not others. It's also been argued that microexpressions are not the best way to identify liars, not least because of the uncertain relationship between the emotions that liars experience and those that they express. Although microexpressions have attracted a great deal of media and commercial interest, the fact that they occur so rarely means that we can't afford entirely to rely on them for clues to lies and deception.[25]

The way that people react when they are no longer required to convince others that they're telling the truth can also provide subtle clues to deceit. For example, most travellers passing through customs have nothing to fear because they don't possess any contraband. The smuggler, on the other hand, needs to keep up the pretense of appearing normal, and usually manages to carry it off. What often distinguishes the smuggler as they walk through customs is the muscular tension in their body. Because it's not apparent how they normally walk, these tensions aren't always easy to spot. What is noticeable, however, is what happens when the smuggler has gone past the customs officials. It's at this point, when there's nothing more to worry about, that the smuggler is likely to relax their body and to produce a *tension release tell*. The change that occurs is seldom dramatic—it sometimes involves a slight lowering of the shoulders—but it's possible to detect. The fact that someone relaxes soon after they've passed through customs suggests that they might have something to hide. Inevitably, there are some people who feel tense about going through customs even when they've got nothing to hide, and who are therefore likely to exhibit the same tension release tell as the guilty smuggler. This only goes to show that while tells are highly informative, they don't always offer a perfect guide to what is happening in people's heads.

Talking Tells

Most people believe that liars give themselves away by what they do rather than what they say or how they say it. In fact, it's the other way around—the best indicators of lying are to be found in people's speech rather than in their bodily behaviour. Aldert Vrij from Portsmouth University has suggested that when people try to catch liars they pay too much attention to their non-verbal behaviour and not enough to speech.[26] This, he points out, is reflected in the tendency to overestimate the chances of detecting deceit by watching someone's behaviour, and to underestimate the chances of catching liars by listening to what they say.

Several features of talk provide clues to lying. Some involve the verbal content of what people say, others the way that people articulate what they're saying.

> **Circumlocution.** Liars often beat about the bush. They tend to give long-winded explanations with lots of digressions, but when they're asked a question they're likely to give a short answer.[27]

> **Outlining.** Liars' explanations are painted with broad brush-strokes, with very little attention to detail. There's seldom any mention of time, place or people's feelings. For example, a liar will tell you that they went for a pizza, but they probably won't tell you where they went or what kind of pizza they ordered. When liars do provide details they are seldom in a position to elaborate on them. So if you ask a liar to expand on their account, it's very likely that they'll simply repeat themselves. When a truth-teller is asked the same question, they usually offer lots of new information.

> **Smokescreens.** Liars often produce answers that are designed to confuse—they sound as if they make sense, but they don't. Examples of remarks that don't make sense include Bill Clinton's famous response during the Paula Jones harassment

case, when he was asked about his relationship with Monica Lewinsky and answered, "That depends on what the meaning of 'is' is." Another example is the justification that ex-mayor of New York City David Dinkins gave when he was accused of failing to pay his taxes: "I haven't committed a crime. What I did was fail to comply with the law."

Negatives. Political lies are frequently couched in the form of a denial—remember Bill Clinton's famous denial "I did not have sexual relations with that woman, Miss Lewinsky." When a politician denies that he is going to introduce a new measure, like raising taxes, you can usually take this as a sign that the measure is about to be introduced. As Otto von Bismarck said, "Never believe anything in politics until it has been officially denied." Liars are more likely to use negative statements. For example, during the Watergate scandal, President Nixon said "I am not a crook." He didn't say "I am an honest man."

Word Choice. Liars make fewer references to themselves—they use words like *I, me* and *mine* less frequently than people who are telling the truth. Liars also tend to generalize by making frequent use of words like *always, never, nobody* and *everyone*, thereby mentally distancing themselves from the lie.

Disclaimers. Liars are more likely to use disclaimers such as "You won't believe this," "I know this sounds strange, but…" and "Let me assure you." Disclaimers like these are designed to acknowledge any suspicion the other person may feel in order to discount it.

Formality. When people are telling the truth in an informal situation they are more likely to use an elided form—for example, they'll say *don't* instead of *do not.* However, someone who's telling a lie in the same situation is more likely to say *do* *not* instead of *don't*. That's because people become more tense and formal when they lie.

Tense. Without realizing it, liars tend to increase the psychological distance between themselves and the event they're describing. As we've seen, one way they do this is by their choice of words. Another is by using the past tense rather than the present tense.

Speed. Telling a lie requires a lot of mental work because, in addition to constructing a credible account, the liar needs to keep the truth separated from the lie. This places demands on the cognitive capacities of the liar, which in turn can slow them down. That's why people pause before producing a lie, and why lies tend to be delivered at a slower pace than the truth—unless, of course, the lie has been carefully rehearsed, in which case there should be no difference in speed.

Pauses. Liars also produce more pauses between their words and sentences, and some of these pauses are filled with speech disfluencies like *um* and *er*. The cognitive work involved in producing a spontaneous lie also gives rise to more speech errors, slips of the tongue and false starts, where the person starts a sentence and then abandons it for another sentence.

Pitch. The pitch of someone's voice is often a very good indicator of their emotional state because when people get upset the pitch of their voice starts to rise. Emotions are closely connected to vocal pitch, and the changes that occur when people become emotional are very difficult to mask or conceal. Although increases in pitch are fairly consistent, they are sometimes quite small, and it is usually necessary to have heard someone speaking in other situations before one can decide whether the pitch of their voice has risen.

High-stakes Lies

Most psychological studies of lying have consisted of carefully controlled experiments, where volunteers have been invited to either lie
or tell the truth, during which their behaviour has been monitored.
It's easy to understand the attraction of doing experiments, because
in addition to randomizing participants to different treatment conditions, they provide standardization and, most important of all, certainty about whether people are lying or telling the truth. As many
psychologists recognize, the downside of experiments is that they
don't necessarily reflect what happens outside the laboratory, where
the stakes of lying are often high, and where there can sometimes be
enormous rewards, as well as punishing consequences, for lying or
concealing the truth. To address this issue, some experimental psychologists have tried to increase the stakes—for example, by offering
financial rewards to participants who're able to lie successfully. Other
psychologists have focused their attention on high-stakes, real-life
cases where there's firm evidence that people have been telling lies.
Cheating in sport is one area where studies have been conducted; serious crime is another.

Cheating in Sport

Probably the most famous—or rather, infamous—cases of lying in
sport are those involving Marion Jones and Lance Armstrong. In 2007,
Marion Jones, the much-garlanded track-and-field winner of several
Olympic and World Championship medals, confessed to taking performance-enhancing drugs, admitted the error of her ways and asked
for forgiveness. Up to that point, whenever she appeared at a press
conference, Jones had resolutely denied taking drugs. However, close
examination of her behaviour on one of those occasions revealed a
cluster of lying tells, including raised eyebrows, a tilted head and a tight
clamping of the mouth as she completed her denial. The mouth-clamp
was particularly informative because it showed that Jones was clamping her lips together so as to ensure that she didn't say anything that
might incriminate her.

A similar clamping of the mouth was also in evidence on several occasions when Lance Armstrong, the disgraced US cyclist and seven-time winner of the Tour de France, denied ever having taken performance-enhancing drugs. Eventually Armstrong was exposed, and he confessed to these crimes, but not before he'd produced a series of well-orchestrated denials. During his denials, Armstrong showed himself to be a persuasive communicator. However, to trained eyes it was clear that he was lying. Not only did he repeatedly refer to himself in the second or third person—a classic means of putting distance between oneself and the events in question—but he also employed a number of "time wasters," like smiling or laughing, which enabled him to delay answering difficult questions. Eventually, after he'd admitted taking drugs, Armstrong tried to give the impression that he wanted to be candid and upfront. But even during his famous, supposedly confessional interview with Oprah Winfrey, he continued to keep his cards close to his chest, clamping his mouth to ensure that he didn't say too much, and showing signs that he was irritated by some of Oprah's questions. Instances of this kind of "push-back," where someone becomes annoyed or angered by probing or accusing questions, are often a clue to deception—they're a means of discouraging the interviewer from probing further.

Serious Crimes

People who have committed serious crimes often try to cover their tracks by going public and pleading for help. For example, a man who's murdered his wife and disposed of the body may inform the police that she's gone missing and then appear on television in order to make a public appeal for information about her whereabouts. Unfortunately, such cases are a lot more common than we imagine. Macabre and disturbing as they are, they provide psychologists with a rare opportunity to explore high-stakes lies in real-life settings. This type of research is normally performed by getting hold of cases where "deceivers" (people who've murdered or hidden another person) and "truthtellers" (those whose friends or relatives have genuinely gone missing) have made public appeals or appeared on television, and then comparing them in terms of what they say, their speech style and their nonverbal behaviour. One such study, conducted by Clea Wright Whelan and her colleagues, gathered recordings of deceivers and truthtellers from the United States, Canada, United Kingdom and New Zealand.[28] It showed that deceivers often attempt to distance themselves from what's happened and from others, whereas truthtellers usually make an effort to connect with the people to whom they're appealing. As a result, deceivers will frequently look less intensely at the people they're addressing, which of course is the opposite of what happens in low-stakes lying. This reversal of looking habits is probably due to the fact that truthtellers are more eager to engage their audience and therefore spend more time looking at them. There are also giveaways in the verbal content of people's appeals. Truthtellers, for example, talk about their failure to understand how anyone could ever abduct or harm the person they know, whereas deceivers aren't mystified at all because they know what's happened. There are even instances where deceivers will give themselves away by using words that show they're fully aware their loved one is already dead.

A similar study, conducted by Leanne ten Brinke and Stephen Porter, showed that deceivers tend to use fewer words than truthtellers.[29] This of course conforms to one of the guiding principles of lying, which is that the best way to avoid saying the wrong thing is to say as little as possible. This study also focused specifically on the facial expressions of individuals who'd pleaded for information about their missing relatives and loved ones. Here it was found that deceivers seldom enlist the muscles of the forehead or those around the mouth, which are associated with genuine facial expressions of grief. Compared to truthtellers, they're also inclined to smile inappropriately and not to activate the muscles around the eyes, which are the hallmark of a genuine smile. Deceivers who plead with the public for help may occasionally be able to muster a passable performance. But in spite of their best efforts, those regions of their brain that are responsible for spontaneous displays of emotion continue to remain inactive, exposing them not only as bad actors but also as liars.

Several years ago when I was presenting a TV program about lying, we decided to include a few documented cases where people were responsible for the death of their partner—including one where a woman had murdered her fiancée in a parked car and then blamed it on an enraged driver. There was also a famous case where a mother had abducted and hidden her daughter and then claimed she'd gone missing. In each of these cases, the perpetrator lied in front of the TV cameras while asking for help and offering a dubious explanation for their behaviour. In the program I tried to show how certain behaviours, which are easily overlooked, can actually serve as important clues to deception. One of these was how liars use their hands to disguise their thinking—how, in some instances, they literally conceal their hand by ensuring that their palm, or their whole hand, remains hidden. Other notable giveaways include narcissism and "duping delight," where liars gain a private thrill, either from becoming the focus of other people's attention or from pulling the wool over their eyes.

When people lie, they often experience strong emotions that give rise to various behaviours that threaten to give them away. The three main emotions are fear, guilt and duping delight. For example, people who're lying may show facial signs of fear because they're worried about what will happen if they're found out. Equally, they may look guilty because deep down they believe that it's unethical to deceive people, or they may show signs of "duping delight" because they're secretly enjoying the experience of fooling others and taking them for a ride. Whether or not these emotions become evident will ultimately depend on the circumstances in which the deception takes place, what kind of people the liars are, and the anticipated costs and benefits of being found out or escaping detection. The relationship they have with those whom they're deceiving may also shape their emotions. Liars are much more likely to feel guilty when they're deceiving someone who trusts them; they're more likely to feel fearful if someone is in a position to punish them; and they're more likely to experience duping delight if they feel that lying to someone will help them to settle a score or make them feel better about themselves.

As we know, telling lies isn't necessarily motivated by the prospect of personal gain—in many instances it's simply an exercise in agency, a case of doing something that's challenging or socially sanctioned. Lying to others usually entails the risk of being found out, but it also promises the clandestine reward of knowing that one is capable of hoodwinking others. People who've committed serious crimes probably have an even greater need for duping delight. They invariably feel threatened by the apparatus of the law and by an inquisitive media. Because they're relatively powerless, they've got very little to lose and a lot to gain by confounding those who might expose them or bring them to justice. Getting their kicks from fooling others remains one of the few sources of excitement available to inveterate liars.

There is a lot of talk nowadays about actions that are supposedly associated with lying—people will tell you that if someone scratches their nose or responds to a question by looking to the right, then it proves that they're telling a lie. None of this is true—there are no individual behaviours to show that someone is lying. They may show that someone is in a state of conflict, under the influence of strong emotions or trying to cover up their feelings of discomfort, but it doesn't follow that they are therefore telling a lie. As Paul Ekman has remarked, "There is no sign of deceit itself—no gestures, facial expression, or muscle twitch that in and of itself means that a person is lying."[30] Another authority on lying, Bella DePaulo, echoes this opinion when she points out that behavioural and speech indicators have a "problematic association" with deception: "They correlate with deception, but not perfectly."[31]

Although there is no guaranteed method of detecting lies, you can do certain things to increase your chances of spotting a liar:

- To detect a lie successfully you need to set your criteria so that they're neither too high nor too low. That way you'll avoid concluding that nobody ever lies, or that everybody lies all the time.

- Where possible, the actions that someone performs while they're supposedly lying should be compared with how they behave when they're telling the truth.
- To be a good lie detector you should also concentrate on behaviours that fall outside conscious control or that the people you're observing are likely to ignore.
- Given the opportunity, it's advisable to focus your attention on what people say and how they say it, rather than on what they do.
- It's important to work out whether the lie is likely to be spontaneous or rehearsed, and whether it's a high-stakes or a low-stakes lie. When the stakes are low or the lie has been rehearsed, the task of detecting the lie is much more difficult.
- To spot a lie you should always focus on a broad range of behavioural and speech clues. If you think you can spot a liar on the basis of a single clue, you're deceiving yourself.

12. Foreign Tells

When people speak the same language it's often very difficult to tell where they come from simply on the basis of their vocabulary, grammar or accent. However, there is sometimes a "shibboleth," a test that shows where they come from. The word *shibboleth* is mentioned in the Book of Judges in the Old Testament. After the Ephraimites had been defeated in battle by the Gileadite army, they tried to sneak back across the River Jordan. The Gileadites, who wanted to make sure that none of them escaped, stopped every man who was trying to cross the river and asked him if he was an Ephraimite. If he said "no," he was asked to say *shibboleth*, which was the Hebrew word for "river." Gileadites pronounced the word *shibboleth*, but Ephraimites said *sibboleth*. Anyone who pronounced the word with an initial *sh* was spared; those who used *s* were immediately executed.

Talk Tells

Fortunately, there are other ways of identifying people's nationality with less bloody consequences. Europeans often have difficulty telling Canadians and Americans apart. But there are some giveaway pronunciations that enable them to spot a Canadian. Canadians, for example, tend to pronounce words like *shout* and *about* as "shoot" and "aboot," while Americans are inclined to pronounce *house* as "hayouse."[1] Americans are likely to greet you with "It's a great day." Canadians, on the other hand, are more likely to say "It's a great day, eh?" While the Americans opt for an upbeat, declarative form, the Canadians prefer to phrase their statements as questions.

Although Australians and New Zealanders have no trouble telling each other apart, outsiders often find it very difficult to distinguish them because they sound so similar. However, there are differences between Australian and New Zealand English. Some of the differences are in vocabulary—New Zealand English, for example, has borrowed many more words from the indigenous Maori people than Australian English has from the Aborigines. There are also differences in the pronunciation of certain vowels. Australians pronounce words such as *air* and *ear* differently, whereas New Zealanders pronounce both as *ear*. There are also instances where the New Zealanders make distinctions but the Australians don't—Australians, for example, pronounce *moan* and *mown* the same, whereas New Zealanders distinguish the two by pronouncing *mown* as *mow-an*. But the big difference is in the way they pronounce "i." New Zealanders pronounce *bat* as *bet, bet* as *bit,* and *bit* as *but.* The English talk of "fish and chips." The Australians, on the other hand, elongate the vowel and talk about "feesh and cheeps," while the New Zealanders, who like to turn "i" into "u," talk about "fush and chups."[2]

Action Tells

Shibboleths can also take the form of actions. To identify someone's nationality it's sometimes enough to watch their table manners. The English, for example, will normally eat with the fork in their left hand and the knife in their right, cutting the food with the knife and transferring it to their mouth with their fork. Americans also hold the fork in their left hand and the knife in their right—but only while they're cutting up their food. As soon as the food has been cut up, they put the knife to one side, shift the fork to their right hand, and use their right hand to transfer the food to their mouth. In Canada the convention is again quite different. The Canadians only resort to their knife when the situation demands it; otherwise they're happy to dispose of the knife and to use the fork to cut up the food and to transfer it to their mouth.

Where people come from is also indicated by tiny gestures, like the way they signal "yes" and "no" with their head. The most common head signals for "yes" and "no" are the nod and the headshake, respectively—in the nod the head is moved up and down, and in the shake it's rotated from side to side. The "nod–shake" code is found all around the world, but it's by no means the only one. The Greeks and Turks, for example, use the "dip–toss" code, where the head is dipped down for "yes" and tossed sharply upward for "no." The "head-toss," as it's called, is often accompanied by closed eyes, raised eyebrows and a click of the tongue. The remnant of the "dip–toss" code may be found in southern Italy and Sicily, having been introduced to the region by the ancient Greeks when they set up trading posts there during the second millennium BC.[3]

If you visit Rome today, you'll find that the Romans use the "nod–shake" code. However, if you travel 200 kilometres south, to Naples, you'll enter a region where the locals use the nod for "yes" and either the headshake or the head-toss for "no."[4] The head-toss consists of a single upward movement of the head, which could easily be confused with a brief nod that begins with an upward movement. In order to avoid this confusion, southern Italians initiate their head-nod with a downward movement. In this respect they're similar to the Greeks, who use a single, downward movement of the head for "yes." Because their nod doesn't conflict with any other signals, northern Italians don't have to worry about whether to begin their nods with an upward or a downward movement. In fact, when we look more closely, we find that northerners initiate their nods in either direction.[5] So if you want to play the role of Professor Henry Higgins and identify where Italians come from, you can simply watch how they signal "yes" with their head. If they start with a downward movement they could be either from the north or the south. But if they start with an upward movement, they're almost certainly from the north.

Greeting Tells

The way that people greet each other also provides clues to where they come from. The handshake, for example, can differ cross-culturally in terms of who uses it, the situations where it's employed, how long the hands are clasped, how vigorously the hands are pumped, and in many other ways. Handshakes in Africa are often executed with a very light grip, and they can extend for several minutes while the participants exchange niceties and make enquiries about each other's relatives. West African handshakes often include embellishments, like a click of the fingers as the hands are released.[6] It's possible that the constant elaboration of handshaking practices in African-American communities owes something to the central role that handshaking plays in West African societies.

Although the English have helped to export the handshake to other parts of the world, during the seventeenth century the handshake, or handclasp, was used exclusively for sealing agreements.[7] It was only later that it became a greeting and started to spread to other countries. According to Theodore Zeldin, author of *The French*, the handshake was exported from England to France, where it became known as "le handshake."[8] Today the French have a very strong attachment to the handshake. While British colleagues might shake hands when they arrive at work, their French counterparts are likely to shake each other's hand several times during the same day. The Russians also shake hands with the same person several times a day, and so do the Italians and the Spaniards. The British and the Germans, on the other hand, tend to confine themselves to one handshake on meeting and another on parting—if in fact they ever shake hands at all.

There are also differences in the way that the handshake is executed. The French, for example, tend to produce a single, determined pump of the hand, whereas the Italians are inclined to draw out the handshake by holding on to the other person's hand. The social rules governing who should shake hands with whom also differ from one country to the next. In France people shake hands regardless of their sex, while in Britain that's also the case in the sphere of business. However, in social settings in Britain handshaking is more likely to occur between two men than between a man and a woman or two women. Because the British tend to see the handshake as being somewhat formal, in social gatherings you'll often find men and women who've just been introduced going for a non-contact greeting, and much the same applies between women.

When people perform a non-contact greeting, they often accompany their verbal salutations with a slight dip of the head. The British have developed their own version, which is the "head-cock." This is performed by shifting the chin to one side while the top of the head is lowered—in other words, by dipping and twisting the head at the same time. This greeting often mystifies visitors to Britain, who wonder what it could conceivably mean. Its origins are rather obscure. It is possible that the head-cock emerged from the practice of tugging the forelock, a submissive gesture used during medieval times. It's also possible that the head-cock originated from the now defunct practice of doffing or touching the hat. Winking is another possible source, because it often involves an involuntary tilt of the head to one side. The collusive message conveyed by winking is also to be found in the head-cock. Finally, the head-cock may be a hybrid gesture—a cross between the head-dip and head-canting, both of which, as we saw earlier, are signals of submissiveness.

Another form of greeting that varies cross-culturally is the kiss. The practice of kissing a lady's hand has all but disappeared, but before the Second World War it was used extensively throughout Europe, especially in countries like Poland and Hungary, which once formed part of the Austro-Hungarian Empire. If you find a man kissing a woman's hand nowadays, the chances are he's joking around. If he's serious he probably has some connection with continental Europe.

Cheek-kissing varies geographically in terms of the number of times people kiss each other on the cheek. Scandinavians tend to make do with a single kiss, while the French go in for the double kiss. The Dutch and the Belgians often employ a multikiss, with at least three separate kisses. In all these countries kissing is a standard feature of the greeting ritual. As a result everyone knows how many kisses to expect and which cheek to kiss first. In countries like Britain, Australia, Canada and the United States—where greeting practices are in the process of evolving—there is often a lot of fumbling and bumping of noses when people try to greet each other with a kiss. These problems aren't so critical for the Welsh or the Irish because historically Celtic communities have been quite uncomfortable about social kissing.[9]

Hugging is another practice that is on the increase—partly because the hug has shed its political connotations and been accepted as something that men can do to express their affection toward each other. But there are still enormous cultural differences in people's attitudes to hugging. Edmund Hillary tells the story that when he and Tenzing Norgay reached the peak of Everest they stood there facing each other, elated at being the first people to have climbed the world's highest mountain. In Anglo-Saxon fashion, Hillary extended his hand to congratulate Tenzing. Tenzing ignored the hand, flung his arms around Hillary and embraced him.[10] That was the proper way to celebrate their achievement!

Face Tells

Nationality is sometimes revealed in facial expressions. Research by Paul Ekman and his colleagues shows that facial expressions that depict the basic emotions—like happiness, sadness, fear, surprise, disgust and anger—are recognized throughout the world, suggesting that the relationship between these emotions and their facial expressions is innate.[11] There are cultural differences, however, in the conventions governing the expression of emotions, as well as differences in how frequently they are displayed, where and to whom they are displayed, and the detailed expression of these emotions. Ray Birdwhistell has observed that smiling in the United States is much more frequent above the Mason-Dixon line than it is below the line, leading him to conclude that smiling means different things to people in the northern and southern states.[12] Of course it doesn't follow that people who smile more are necessarily happier, or that smiling has a different meaning for them than it does for people who smile less. What it does suggest, however, is that the conventions governing smiling, or the expression of happiness, may differ between communities.

This is borne out by Henry Seaford's research on facial expressions in Virginia. Seaford studied historic portraits and photographs in yearbooks. When he compared his Virginia material with material from Pennsylvania, he found a "facial dialect" in Virginia.[13] This consisted of several expressions, including an "orbicular clamp" and a "purse-clamp." In both these expressions the muscles above and below the mouth are tightened and this clamps the lips together. In the "purse-clamp" the muscles at the side of the mouth are also tightened, so that the lips become clamped and pursed together at the same time. Seaford observed that, since people from the British Isles colonized Virginia, the facial expressions of Virginians may have descended from expressions that were once found in Britain.

The English have a long reputation for being cold and unemotional. They are also reputed to have a "stiff upper lip." This is generally intended to refer to the stoical character of the English, but it could equally apply to their facial habits. When they smile the English are much more likely to keep their teeth hidden, and to pull the corners of their mouth sideways rather than up. When the face is in repose, there is also a tendency for the English to purse their lips. This goes back to the sixteenth century, when a small mouth was considered to be desirable. We can see this very clearly in Holbein's portraits of Henry VIII, and more strikingly in his wedding portrait of Jane Seymour, where the King and his future Queen are shown with tightly pursed lips.[14]

Facial habits too are shaped by language. French, for example, is articulated very differently from other languages. Visitors to France often remark on the unusual way that the French move their mouth, and particularly the way they protrude their lips, when they are talking. According to Theodore Zeldin, this is because the French language has more sounds that require the rounding of the lips than other languages. "Nine out of the sixteen French vowels," he tells us, "involve strong lip-rounding, compared to only two out of the twenty English vowels. (Germans have five lip-rounding vowels.) The degree of lip-rounding in French is moreover greater because vowels following consonants often have to be prepared before the consonant is uttered."[15]

Related observations have been made about the German language. Robert Zajonc and his colleagues were interested in the idea that different speech sounds differentially affect blood flow to the brain and that this may affect people's mood. To test this they asked a group of German-speakers to read out a story that either had a lot of "ü" sounds or very few "ü" sounds.[16] Participants who read the story with lots of "ü" sounds were found to have hotter foreheads; they also rated the protagonist in the story less positively. The authors of the study took these findings as support for the notion that "ü" sounds affect blood flow to the brain, which in turn affects mood.

Although this particular effect has not been replicated, psychologists have discovered that mouth postures can affect people's moods in other ways. For example, people who are asked to hold a pencil between their teeth while they're looking at cartoons (and who therefore inadvertently replicate the extended mouth posture of a smile) are likely to rate the cartoons as funnier than people who hold the pencil either between their lips or in their hand. This study supports the "facial feedback theory"—the idea that people's moods can be shaped by the facial expressions that they adopt.[17]

Conversation Tells

Countries differ widely in their enthusiasm for conversation. The French have always struck the English as overly garrulous. "A Frenchman," declared Dr Johnson, "must be always talking, whether he knows anything of the matter or not; an Englishman is content to say nothing, when he has nothing to say." The Italians also have a reputation for being talkative, and so do the Irish. At the opposite extreme are the Finns and the northern Swedes, who are happy to enjoy the presence of others without saying a word.

The Finnish attachment to silence is also evident in the way they organize their conversations. Although the Finns have a wide range of vocal signals they can use as back-channel when they're in the listener role, they prefer to use visual signals, like nods, to encourage the speaker and to show that they understand what the speaker is saying. This avoidance of audible back-channel ensures that the only person who's vocalizing is the person who's occupying the speaker role. It also has the effect of making Finnish conversations sound rather stilted and one-sided—something that foreigners, who are used to giving and receiving audible back-channel, often find rather uncomfortable. This is reinforced by the fact that Finnish conversations have very few interruptions. Consequently, when foreigners talk to a Finn they often get the impression that the Finn doesn't really want the floor, that they're not being attentive and that they're not really interested.[18]

The same could hardly be said of the foreigner's experience in Italy, where conversation is more of a free-for-all. In Italy conversations often take on the appearance of a contest, especially where friends are concerned. In these cases the speaker will often fix their eyes on the listener while the listener looks away. This, of course, is the opposite of what we find in other countries, where the listener looks more intently at the speaker than the speaker does at the listener. In an Italian conversation it's not unusual to find the listener looking around, affecting an air of boredom, while the speaker is constantly moving around so that they're positioned in front of the listener while using their hands to try to capture and hold the listener's attention.

Turn-taking in Italy is based on what I call the "conch shell model"—named after the famous scene in William Golding's *Lord of the Flies*, where a group of English schoolboys are marooned on an island.[19] At their first meeting on the island all the boys start to talk at once, so they make a rule that from that point on only one person will be allowed to speak at a time—the boy who is holding the large conch shell that was found on the beach. Conversations between Italians of similar social status usually conform to the conch shell model, not because the Italians want to eliminate overlap talk—there's very little chance of that—but because the person who has his hands in the air is deemed to be the speaker.[20]

In Italy a speaker who wants to retain their role needs to ensure that their hands are in the air, and that they are gesticulating and holding the other person's attention. The listener, on the other hand, doesn't produce a lot of back-channel, partly because the speaker doesn't need that much encouragement to keep talking, and partly because the listener is less keen about remaining in the role, and therefore is less interested in offering the speaker a lot of support. Here, the listener often withholds his approval by looking away while the other person is talking. This can sometimes create a rather theatrical spectacle, where the speaker is in hot pursuit, trying to ensnare the listener with wild gesticulations, while the listener refuses to ratify the speaker by giving the speaker their undivided attention. To show that they intend to continue, the speaker needs to keep their hands up and to ensure that the listener doesn't get their hands up and thereby lay claim to the speaker role. When I first visited Italy I was struck by how often people would touch each other while they were talking. When two people were talking and the speaker touched the listener on the arm, I assumed that they were being affectionate. What I'd failed to notice was that these are "controlling touches." They're not intended to reassure the listener—they're designed to hold the floor by making sure that the listener can't get their hands up!

Conversation tells. Italians tend to use their hands to hold the other person's attention and to retain the speaker role during conversations.

When Italians want to relinquish the speaker role, they simply lower their hands. This shows that they no longer wish to continue talking. The other termination signal that speakers use is a shrug of the shoulders, which is very similar in meaning to such expressions as "I don't know" that speakers elsewhere sometimes use to relinquish the floor. Listeners who want to take the floor can do so either by interrupting the speaker or by grabbing the speaker's arm, pulling it down, and getting their own gesticulating hands into the air. The listener who wants to signal that they have no desire to take over the speaker's role can do so by keeping their arms folded or by placing their hands behind their back. This serves as an "unintention display"—it shows that the listener is not in a position to start talking. After all, how could they if their hands are hidden?

Hand Tells

Someone's nationality can often be identified at a distance, simply by observing how they use their hands. That's partly because some nations gesticulate more than others.

If there were a league table for expressive use of the hands, the Italians would win. The identification of Italy with wild gesticulation goes back a long way. In 1581 the author of *A Treatise of Daunces* noted that "The Italian in his . . . speeche . . . intermingleth and useth so many gestures, that if an Englishman should see him afar off, not hearing his words, [he] would judge him to be out of his wit, or else playing some comedy upon a scaffold." By contrast, the author observed, a German preaching from a pulpit would look as though he was physically paralyzed.[21]

We tend to assume that nations that gesticulate a lot have always been animated, and that nations that gesticulate very little, like the English, have always been reticent and undemonstrative. This isn't entirely correct. It's generally accepted, even by the English themselves, that they are not a particularly expressive people and they don't go in for elaborate displays of gesticulation. However, there was a time when gesture played a much more prominent role in their lives. A thorough knowledge of posture and gesture was a requirement for all Elizabethan actors, and Shakespeare's plays are full of references to expressive postures and movements of the hands. Hogarth's drawing of scenes from English life show that gesticulation was also popular during the eighteenth century, and that it was not restricted to specific sectors of society. The "grand manner" of oratory, which appeared in Parliament and the pulpit in the nineteenth century, also relied on extravagant use of the hands. It was during this period, however, that a more demure style of social behaviour started to become fashionable, and the English began to lose interest in gesture.[22]

Historically the French have moved in the opposite direction. The French are enthusiastic gesticulators, but this wasn't the case during the sixteenth century. We're told that before Catherine de Medici of Florence arrived in France to marry Henry II, French courtiers made very little use of gesture, regarding the spectacle of flailing arms as rather common and vulgar. By the Restoration, however, the French had joined the ranks of the gesticulating nations, and they have remained there ever since.

If you compare an Italian with a Frenchman, you'll notice that their expressive gestures differ in several ways. First of all, the Italian moves his hands around much more than the Frenchman. What's more revealing, however, are the positions that the fingers assume while the hands are gesticulating. As a rule the French tend to use more open postures of the hand, while the Italians show a preference for "precision grips," where the thumb and forefinger, for example, are pressed against each other, or the tips of all five digits are joined together. Another clue to nationality is to be found in the rhythm of gesticulation—French movements tend to be more languid and even-paced, whereas Italian gesticulation is more staccato and varied in its pace. Then there's the geometry of gesticulation—in other words, the space through which the hands move when they're gesticulating. Here we find that the French tend to confine their movements to the hands and forearms, while the Italians enlist the upper arms as well. As a result, Italian gestures are more expansive and expressive.

Another group that gesticulates a lot but doesn't use expansive movements are Eastern European Jews. David Efron, who completed a special study of gesture in New York City before the Second World War, noticed that when people from Eastern European Jewish communities gesticulate they tend to keep their elbows tucked in and their arms close to their chest—the hands are always busy but they are never far from the body.[23] This, Efron suggested, is the gestural style of an oppressed people—they want to connect with each other, but they're worried about lowering their defences. The hands reach out, but the arms and elbows wait in reserve, protecting the body from attack. In contrast to the restricted, almost apologetic circumference of Jewish gesticulation, Italian gestures are wide-ranging. Because the elbows aren't tucked in, the hands are free to make long excursions away from the body, and the performance is therefore much more spectacular.

There are also national differences in the meanings that people attach to certain gestures. The "thumbs-up" gesture, which most people recognize as a sign of approval or good luck, doesn't always have positive connotations. In Greece, and in parts of Australia where there are large Greek communities, the thumbs-up gesture is an insult. It's an emasculatory gesture, rather similar in meaning to the middle finger gesture, and it's often associated with the expression "Sit on this!" It is worth remembering this if you're planning to spend some time in Greece.[24] Whatever you do, don't present the locals with a raised thumb—they might not like it at all!

Another gesture open to misinterpretation is the famous Greek insult, the *moutza*. This is performed by splaying the fingers and presenting the palm of the hand to the person whom you want to insult. The *moutza* owes its origins to the ancient Byzantine practice of dragging chained criminals through the streets while the local populace picked up dirt and rubbish and thrust it into their faces. Fortunately this demeaning practice has long since disappeared, but the *moutza* lives on as a highly charged insult, often accompanied by expressions like "Take five!" or "Go to hell!" Of course to foreigners the *moutza* looks like an innocent presentation of five fingers, so it's liable to be interpreted as a gesture for the number 5. This is reputed to have happened several years ago when the English football club Nottingham Forest were playing a Greek club in Athens.[25] The sports correspondent for a British newspaper reported that young Greek fans had approached the coach that was transporting the English players, and that they had indicated with their hands what they thought the final score for the match was likely to be—five–nil! What the poor journalist had failed to realize was that this was a deep insult, not some pre-match prediction.

A similar misunderstanding could occur with the famous V-for-Victory gesture. This is performed by separating the index and the middle fingers, keeping the rest of the hand in the shape of a fist, and presenting the palm of the hand toward the other person. In most countries the position of the palm doesn't matter, and the Victory gesture can be performed with the palm facing either forward or back. However, in countries like Greece and the United Kingdom, the position of the palm is crucial. In Greece there is a miniature version of the *moutza* where just the index and middle fingers are extended, with the palm facing forward. This insulting gesture is sometimes accompanied by the expression "Take two!" or "Go halfway to hell!" Just like the Churchillian V-sign for Victory, the miniature *moutza* is performed with the palm facing forward. That's why, in order to avoid any confusion, the Greeks perform their Victory gesture with the palm facing backward. This gesture, however, is identical to the famous insulting V-sign of the British. When the British want to insult each other, they make a V-sign with the palm facing backward. The fact that the Britons and the Greeks have chosen the same gestures to convey very different messages can easily lead to international misunderstanding—when a Greek performs a palm-back V-sign they think they're signalling Victory, but the British person thinks the Greek is being insulting, whereas with the palm-front V-sign the situation is reversed. Here the Briton thinks they're signalling Victory, but the Greek thinks that the Briton's being insulting.[26]

Some gestures are confined to one country, others to a specific region within a country. There are also gestures that span several countries—like drinking gestures. When people offer you a drink by miming the act of drinking, you can often tell where they come from simply by looking at how they arrange their fingers. People from beer-drinking countries like Britain, Germany, Holland and Belgium tend to wrap their fingers around an imaginary beer glass with the four fingers curled and facing the thumb. People from vodka-drinking countries like Russia, Ukraine and Poland use a gesture that mimics the shape of a short vodka glass. Here the first and second fingers are placed opposite the thumb, and the hand is rapidly tilted once or twice to simulate the act of pouring the contents down the throat. People from wine-drinking countries like France, Italy and Spain usually mimic a wine bottle by forming their hand into a fist, extending the thumb, and pointing it toward their mouth. This gesture is sometimes performed by raising the hand above the mouth so that the neck of the "bottle" faces downward. This, of course, mimics the old practice of drinking from a leather bottle, where the bottle was held above the head and the wine was squirted into the mouth. It is therefore very likely that the wine-drinking gesture is a "relic tell"—in other words, a gesture that owes its origins to an ancient practice that has since become extinct.

A comparison of nationalities shows that some gesticulate more than others, and that they fall into three broad groups. In the first group are the Nordic peoples—the Swedes, Finns, Norwegians and Danes— who make very little use of gesticulation and who, compared with other countries, are gesturally illiterate. This category also includes the Japanese, Koreans and Chinese, all of whom make very little use of gesticulation. The second group includes the British, Germans, Dutch, Belgians and Russians, who use gesture in moderation. People who fall into this category tend only to use their hands when they become excited, when they need to communicate over long distances, and when they feel the need to threaten or insult each other. The third group of nations includes the Italians, French, Greeks, Spaniards and Portuguese. It also includes South American nations like the Argentinians and Brazilians, who have been heavily influenced by the Italians, the Spanish and the Portuguese. These three groupings work fine for countries that are culturally uniform or have a dominant cultural group. The scheme works less well with multi-ethnic countries like Canada because some ethnic groups within the country are more gesturally expressive than others. This shows that culture often plays a much bigger part than nationality in shaping people's behaviour.

Some tells are universal, others are local. Universal tells spring from the common biology that people share with each other—the wide-eyed facial expression of fear, for example, is an innate feature of our human make-up, and that's why it's found on every continent. However, some tells are extremely widespread, not because they're innate, but because they've been copied and borrowed by people all around the world. The fact that in almost every country young people wear baseball caps has nothing to do with biology—it's simply part of fashion culture. Then there are local tells, which are confined to specific groups of people. These too owe their existence to cultural invention, and that's why they're much more susceptible to change than tells that are biologically programmed. It's sometimes quite difficult to distinguish universal from local tells, and in the absence of evidence to the contrary we may assume that the meanings we attach to certain actions are similar to the meanings that people in other parts of the world attach to those actions. But, as we have seen, there are numerous cases where people in different parts of the world use the same or similar actions to convey very different meanings. When we overlook this fact it's very easy for international misunderstandings to occur. While some of these misunderstandings may be amusing and insignificant, others may have far-reaching consequences.

13. Business Tells

Tells play a vital role in the world of business. They're at the very heart of people's self-presentations and their attempts to appear leaderlike, committed, trustworthy or personable, and they also constitute an important basis for the inferences that people in the workplace draw about each other. In this chapter we're going to explore some of the revealing ways that tells—both deliberate and unconscious—contribute to the successful exercise of leadership, as well as to persuasive selling and the effective conduct of remote business meetings.

Leadership Tells

Discussions about whether someone has the necessary qualities to be an effective leader tend to focus on internal, psychological attributes. Are they, for example, a person of vision, do they have a sense of purpose, or do they possess the right values? However, leadership doesn't just entail the ideas, principles and feelings that people carry around in their heads; it's also intimately connected with outward appearances—how someone comes across in terms of their looks, their actions, utterances and speech style. It's to these external features that people react, both within and outside an organization, drawing conclusions about what the person in question is really like, what drives them, and, ultimately, whether they have the qualities needed to be a good leader.

When deciding if someone has leadership potential, five topic areas or facets need to be addressed:

1. **Authority.** Does the person look, behave and sound like a leader? Do they exude authority and have a commanding

presence? Does it look like they deserve to occupy a leader-ship position?

2. **Engagement.** Does the person connect with other people? Are they approachable, friendly, personable, empathic, encouraging and supportive?

3. **Confidence.** Is the person self-assured? Does he or she show self-belief and a calm capacity to handle and find solutions to difficult challenges?

4. **Competence.** Are they good at the job? Do they display a thorough grasp of the business? Do they have the necessary operational, technical and managerial skills?

5. **Kudos.** Does the person have an established and well-deserved reputation as a leader? Are they respected and admired for their achievements?

Noticeably, these five facets tend to elicit quite different emotional responses from those who report, either directly or indirectly, to a leader with these qualities. Authority, for example, can sometimes arouse apprehension or fear, whereas engagement usually leads to affection. Competence and confidence, on the other hand, are most likely to arouse admiration, while kudos tends to give rise to feelings of respect.

Although all five facets are desirable in a business leader, it's not unusual to find people rising to positions of power even when they're sorely lacking one or more of these facets. When this happens, their success as a leader is likely to depend on how well they embody those facets that they do possess, as well as the trade-off that takes place between them, and how relevant these facets are to a particular leadership role. It's very obvious that the five facets don't always correlate with each other. A highly competent CEO, for example, doesn't always have complete confidence in their skill set, and it's also not uncommon to find notoriously incompetent managers who've deluded themselves into thinking that they've got what it takes to be an effective leader.[1]

Authority vs. Engagement

As we saw in our discussion of politicians, those people who acquire positions of power often have to decide between producing dominance tells or friendly tells. A similar dilemma confronts business leaders, who may have to choose between emphasizing their authority at the expense of engagement, or vice versa. Ideally, business leaders should be in a position to emphasize both authority and engagement, but this is often very difficult to achieve, not least because so many of the behaviours that signal engagement—like smiling and attentiveness—are also used to communicate submissiveness, which naturally has the unfortunate effect of undermining any attempts to appear authoritative.

Business leaders can attempt to outwardly display their authority in several ways:

Comportment. Standing tall, occupying more than one's fair share of territory, invading other people's personal space without being invited to do so, either explicitly or otherwise, assuming postures that appear to enlarge the body or which signal threat, and adopting asymmetric and/or relaxed poses.

Face. Adopting unsmiling, and even impassive facial expressions that give an impression of seriousness, distance and a reluctance to engage.

Gaze. Resorting to visual dominance by being attentive toward the other person while one is speaking but relatively inattentive when holding the floor.

Gestures. Executing emphatic and symmetrical gestures, and/or large gestures that extend out and away from the body, employing hand postures that communicate superiority, strength, agility and decisiveness.

Touch. Using touch as a status reminder by reserving the right unilaterally to pat and socially touch one's subordinates while indicating that they don't have the right to reciprocate.

Talk. Taking the initiative and dominating conversations, expressing strong opinions, challenging other people's points of view, talking over other people and discouraging them from interrupting you.

Voice. Speaking slowly and fluently, with minimal speech disfluencies, while lowering the pitch of one's voice in order to sound more substantial.

Time. Using the medium of time to signal status, keeping other people waiting, arriving late and then leaving early, peremptorily and without any parting ceremony. Otherwise, moving slowly to create an illusion of bulk, and to show that one's own time is much more important than that of others.

Equally, there are several ways that business leaders can attempt to convey messages of engagement with others:

Comportment. Using open postures and facing orientation to signal inclusiveness and a desire to engage while avoiding defensive postures that might suggest a reluctance to connect with others.

Face. Employing full- and half-smiles to announce one's friendly intentions and willingness to connect with others, tilting the head to one's side to appear unthreatening, being attentive to the other person, nodding approvingly and using animated facial expressions to show that one is impressed.

Gaze. Avoiding any hint of visual dominance by ensuring that one is paying full attention to the other person while they're speaking, even if it means reduced focus on the other person while one is holding the floor.

Gestures. Using modest but nevertheless enthusiastic gestures that stay close to the body while employing open and inviting hand postures to publicize one's willingness to engage.

Touch. Using affectionate and supportive social touch to cement relationships while encouraging others to engage in reciprocal touch.

Talk. Contributing to conversations while enabling the other participants to take their turn and express their point of view, observing the unwritten rules of turn-taking, not talking over the other participants and protecting them from being talked over by other people.

Voice. Speaking at a normal pace, neither too fast nor too slow, while increasing the breathiness of one's voice so as to sound warm and approachable.

Time. Respecting other people's time by not keeping them waiting, arriving on time and not leaving early, using requisite parting rituals to demonstrate that you've enjoyed meeting the other person and look forward to seeing them again.

Over the past fifty years or so the business world has witnessed a marked shift in leadership style, with CEOs and managers becoming less concerned about signalling authority and much more concerned about engagement. National and cultural differences in what's expected of bosses are still in evidence, and factors like the size of an organization and the sector in which it operates can also determine the leadership style that bosses choose to adopt.[2]

However, this doesn't alter the fact that all bosses continue to be confronted with an age-old puzzle, namely to what extent should they try to come across as powerful and dominant, or as someone who's approachable, supportive and consultative? Faced with this dilemma, there's been a growing tendency for business leaders to move away from a macho, self-aggrandizing style of leadership and to embrace a style that's inclusive, democratic and transformational. Nowadays, there's much more emphasis on listening to what the rank-and-file members of an organization have to say, and making them feel that they've got skin in the corporate game. Effective business leaders are more likely to focus on the organization's wider responsibilities, to nurture talent, and to talk about the organization's mission and achievements in terms of "we" rather than "I." In spite of this groundswell shift, it's still possible to find some leadership styles in places where you'd least expect them.

Divergent Styles

Several years ago, I presented a television program about "power tells." In the search for suitable locations to record people exercising their authority, the program director arranged for the film crew and me to spend a day aboard a Royal Navy destroyer, and another day tailing one of the top executives of Microsoft. In these settings, my task was to look out for and comment on the power play. Since the command structure of the navy is famously hierarchical, we'd reasonably assumed that the Royal Navy destroyer would be full of power tells. In contrast, knowing that Microsoft prides itself on having a flat, egalitarian management structure, we anticipated that there'd be hardly any power tells there at all. How wrong one can be!

While standing on the bridge of the destroyer observing the captain interacting with his officers, I was taken aback by how few power tells there were on display. None of the officers appeared to be showing any overt signs of respect or deference toward the captain. In fact, there was hardly anything in their demeanour to suggest that the captain was in charge or that they were taking orders.

The situation at Microsoft could hardly have been more different. There, a business meeting was about to take place between the heads of several European divisions and their overall boss, based in the United Kingdom. During the meeting, whichever way one turned, power tells were on display. For example, when the European heads arrived and shook hands with the boss, virtually all of them gave a slight dip of the head, an action that the boss never performed once. The fact that this subtle dip of the head was never reciprocated shows it to be a status marker; in other words, an action that subordinates perform for their superior, but one that their superior pointedly doesn't perform for them. It's interesting to note that dipping the head in this manner is something that we humans share with our evolutionary cousins, the chimpanzees—when low-ranking chimpanzees encounter the alpha member of the troop, they're quick to show their acceptance of their lowly position by "bobbing" their head up and down.

During the Microsoft meeting, there were also repeated examples of non-reciprocated touch. For example, when the opportunity arose, the overall boss would gently pat various members of his management team on the back or shoulder. As we noted in an earlier discussion, pats like these pretend to be fraternal, but their true purpose is to serve as "status reminders," and that's why they're seldom reciprocated in this context. On one occasion, when one member of the team did reciprocate, the boss immediately responded by coming back with a double pat—clearly, his way of upping the ante and making sure that he got in the last touch!

In the corporate world, the success or failure of the person in charge can often be gauged by observing how subordinates respond to the boss's power displays. The main purpose of power displays is to elicit complementary behaviour from subordinates or, at the very least, to discourage them from engaging in mimicry—a manager might try to make himself look bigger, for example, in order to persuade his staff to make themselves look smaller or, failing this, not to copy him. At the Microsoft meeting, the boss produced a number of power gestures during his talk. These included certain pointing gestures, chopping gestures and what we previously referred to as "knuckle displays"—in other words, gestures that pretend to emphasize what's being said but that are actually disguised ways of exposing the hard, threatening features of the hands, as opposed to the soft, inviting palms.

While the boss was giving his talk, all the European heads were respectfully giving him their full attention—nobody, for example, was gazing around the room or surreptitiously checking their mobile phone. I also noticed that most of them were touching their mouth— sometimes with their hand supporting their chin, occasionally with their index finger resting on their lips. At first glance these actions look like nothing more than polite gestures of attentiveness, but their real purpose is to show the boss that the person touching their mouth has no intention of trying to take over the speaker role, while at the same time subtly restraining themselves from doing so. In this situation, face-touching, and especially mouth-touching, can be seen as a stealth tell—an action that professes to send one kind of message, while actually sending another.

Once we'd finished filming on the Royal Navy destroyer and at the Microsoft meeting, the difference between these two scenes became starkly evident. I'd expected to find many more power tells in the Navy, but in fact it was the other way around—there were very few to be seen on the destroyer, but the Microsoft meeting was teeming with them. That's because there isn't such a pressing need for power tells in a hierarchical organization like the Navy, where interactions are largely dictated by rank and where everyone knows their place. But in an organization with a flat structure, like Microsoft, things are potentially much more fluid. Here, the boss needs to keep reminding everyone that they are the one who's in charge, while subordinates need to keep reminding the boss that they don't represent a threat to his or her authority.

Presence Tells

There are at least two good reasons why demeanour plays such a crucial role in leadership. One is that dominant behaviours have very deep evolutionary roots—a legacy that we share with our distant, non-human ancestors and to which we respond instinctively and often unknowingly. The other reason, of course, is that physical messages about ascendency are implicit—unlike verbal claims to authority, they're much more difficult to repeat and therefore to challenge.

It's long been recognized that people who occupy powerful leadership positions tend to assume postures that increase their apparent size. In recent years this has led psychologists to enquire whether the reverse might also be true—that by actively adopting assertive postures ordinary people would show signs of becoming physiologically and psychologically more powerful, which in turn would predispose them to behave more authoritatively. To address these questions, three American social psychologists—Dana Carney, Amy Cuddy and Andy Yap—conducted a rather ingenious experiment, where they invited participants to their lab and then helped them individually to adopt either one of two "high-power" poses or one of two "low-power" poses for the duration of one minute.[3] The high-power poses were sitting on a chair with the legs extended while the feet resting on a table, with both hands supporting the back of the head, and standing and leaning forward with one's hands splayed on the top of the table. The two low-power poses were sitting with one's knees fairly close together, looking down, with the clasped hands resting on the lap, and standing with the legs crossed and the arms wrapped around the chest.

Before assuming one of the poses, the participants provided saliva samples, and they repeated the same process afterward. This provided pre- and post-measures of testosterone and cortisol, as well as evidence of how much the levels of these hormones had changed as a result of adopting one of the poses. Testosterone was measured to assess how dominant and assertive the participants had become, while cortisol was measured to see whether they felt more or less stressed after adopting one of the poses. After they'd completed the posing, participants were asked to rate how powerful they felt, and they then took part in a short gambling game to gauge how risky they'd become as a result of assuming certain poses.

The results of the experiment revealed that participants who'd adopted high-power poses not only felt more powerful afterward, they also showed increased levels of testosterone and lower levels of cortisol, and on the gambling game their behaviour was noticeably riskier. The experiment claimed to provide evidence for "postural feedback"—demonstrating that when people adopt high-power poses, even for a short duration, it makes them feel more powerful, while at the same time impacting their hormonal system and modifying their subsequent behaviour. In other words, the effect of the poses wasn't restricted to changing how people felt about themselves—it also made them physiologically more assertive and less anxious.

The "power pose" experiment was published in 2010, and it was greeted with an enormous wave of public interest. Amy Cuddy's highly successful TED talk, based on the experimental findings, was watched almost 70 million times on YouTube, making it the second most viewed YouTube clip of all time. Very soon, business trainers and executive coaches all around the world were espousing "power posing" as an instant means of enhancing one's confidence, and a number of British politicians started striking power poses whenever they appeared in public—inspired, one suspects, by the quick-fix nature of the exercise and its promise to make them look more imposing.

Power posing. Psychologist Amy Cuddy demonstrates how to adopt a high-power pose with legs straight, feet apart and hands on the hips.

Since this experiment was published, several attempts have been made to replicate the findings, but with mixed results. While subsequent studies provided strong support for the finding that adopting high-power poses, as opposed to low-power poses, makes people feel more powerful, the earlier findings regarding testosterone and cortisol did not prove to be as replicable.[4] It's also been pointed out that the original experiment failed to include a "control condition," where participants would have adopted neutral poses that were neither high-power nor low-power. To the uninitiated, this criticism might appear to be nothing more than a silly little niggle about experimental design and therefore hardly worth considering, but it's actually quite important because, with an appropriate control condition included, it should in principle be possible to determine how much of the differences between high-power and low-power poses are due to each of these separately. When a neutral control condition was included in subsequent replications, it was discovered that, where a sense of feeling powerful is concerned, most of the difference between high-power and low-power poses was due to low-power poses. In other words, it's not so much that high-power poses increase people's sense of feeling powerful but rather that low-power poses decrease those feelings.[5]

This finding is very much at odds with how the results of the original experiment were presented, where a bright spotlight was trained on the lasting benefits of assuming high-power poses, with low-power poses warranting hardly any mention at all. When the findings of the initial study became widely known, the exclusive focus was on looking more commanding. If, for example, you were about to give a business presentation or to be interviewed for a job, you were advised to set aside a few minutes beforehand and to prepare yourself by standing with your legs wide apart—admittedly a quick fix but nevertheless a sure way to boost your confidence! However, as follow-up studies have now shown, there isn't a lot to be gained by standing with your legs far apart and your arms akimbo, or leaning forward with one's hands splayed on a desk, but there's a lot to lose by sitting with one's hands folded on one's lap and looking down or standing with crossed legs and wrapping one's arms around one's chest. The accumulated evidence from power pose studies therefore draws us toward a counter-intuitive conclusion, namely that if we want to persuade ourselves and others that we possess leadership qualities, then our main investment should be on not appearing or sounding powerless rather than on trying to look and sound powerful.

Is It All About Size?

Some psychologists have suggested that there's an essential difference between "power poses," where the body is made to look bigger by extending the arms and legs outward, and "prestige," where the body is made to look upright and taller.[6] Aside from this, several important insights can be gained by taking a closer look at the poses that were used in the original "power pose" experiment.

According to the authors, their express purpose for selecting the two high-power poses was that the poses increase the apparent size of the person performing each pose, which is why they labelled them "expansive poses." In contrast, their reason for selecting the two low-power poses was that they appear to make the person performing these poses look smaller, hence the reference to them as "contractive poses." The main focus of the experiment was therefore on what happens when people make themselves look bigger or smaller—does it impact on their hormones, make them feel more or less powerful and modify their subsequent behaviour?

There are some interesting things to note about the four poses that were used in the original experiment. The first is that they vary in terms of their inherent dynamism. Typically someone who's sitting, looking down, with their hands folded on their lap comes across as looking static, with no suggestion that they're about to get up and do something different. The same can be said of someone who's standing with their legs crossed and their arms wrapped around their chest. As we've already noted, this "scissors stance" leg posture can reasonably be read as an "unintention display," in other words, as an indication that the person who's striking this pose has no intention of moving away. So if the two low-power poses are essentially static, what about the two high-power poses? Well, when we see someone standing with their feet apart and their arms akimbo, we don't necessarily get the impression that they're about to engage in some other activity, which means that this particular pose can rightly be regarded as static too. However, this certainly doesn't apply to someone who's leaning forward with their hands splayed on the top of a table. Here, if only because of the intrinsic tension in the posture, the person looks as if they're poised and ready to do something different. Unlike the other three poses, the pose with the person leaning forward is replete with "action imminence"—even though the pose is frozen in time, it contains the strong suggestion that the person is physically in transition, that they're on the verge of doing something different.

But there's something else that potentially separates the four poses. When someone strikes a dominant or a submissive pose, their actions have been shown to elicit a complementary response from other people present—specifically, with people producing submissive poses when someone adopts a dominant pose or, alternatively, producing dominant poses in response to a submissive one.[7] Although there's complementarity in both cases, it's very likely that high-power poses have a much stronger effect on how other people respond, covertly as well as overtly. Whether people realize it or not, when someone assumes a dominant posture in their presence, it places demands on them to react—should they, for example, continue as normal, be more submissive or try to appear dominant too? It seems that while both high- and low-power poses have a capacity for "altercasting"—literally, casting another person in a certain role—there's a marked difference between the two types of pose, because with low-power poses it's a matter of inviting someone to adopt a complementary role, whereas with high-power poses it's a case of coercing them to do so.[8]

All of this suggests that high- and low-power poses don't just differ according to how large or small they make someone appear—they also vary according to how much action imminence they exhibit and the nature of the altercasting they exert over other people. This naturally begs the question whether experimental effects, which have thus far been attributed solely to apparent differences in physical size, might actually be partially or wholly due to factors like action imminence and altercasting. Could it be that people who assume low-power poses end up feeling less empowered than those who adopt high-power poses, simply because their body postures feel less dynamic and/or because they sense that their actions don't have as much impact on other people?

Powerless Tells

In order to look and sound like a business leader, it's important to avoid producing submissive signals and inadvertently giving the impression of being powerless. Broadly speaking, these signals take the form of "powerless actions" or "powerless speech." Powerless actions might include the following:

Posture. Poses that make us look smaller or less active, or that invite others to feel and appear superior, convey a message of subordinacy. Defensive poses, which give the impression that we're preparing to be attacked, are also to be avoided.

Head Movements. Tilting or canting the head to one side is a submissive posture because it makes us look shorter, reduces our apparent readiness to act and, more importantly, exposes the neck, which is a highly vulnerable part of the body. Also, nodding the head, either repeatedly or vigorously, when listening to someone speaking, can give the impression that we are totally in agreement with that person, and/or that we have no desire to question what they're saying or to contradict them.

Visual Subordinacy. In conversations, the natural instinct of subordinate individuals is disproportionately to increase the amount of time they spend looking at someone who's speaking, relative to how much they look at that person while they themselves are holding the floor. One way for leaders to avoid giving this impression is to reverse the process somewhat, by spending disproportionately more time looking at the other person while they themselves are speaking and less while they're listening, thereby borrowing some of the unconscious style that's so often exhibited by people who wield power.

Self-touching. Subordinate individuals and people who're unsure of themselves are inclined to touch their face, particularly when they're listening to what someone else has to say. There are several reasons why people touch their face in this kind of situation—these include seeking self-comfort, hiding part of the face, positioning the hand defensively close to the face, or indicating that one has no desire to take over the speaker role. It follows therefore that not touching your face when you're involved in a conversation naturally helps to reduce the chances of others deciding that you're powerless, uncertain or lacking in confidence.

Note-taking. Leaders who are chairing meetings tend to take notes sparingly, if at all. That's partly because conscientious note-taking makes one look subordinate—think, for example, of those obsequious generals surrounding Kim Jong-un, the leader of North Korea, who furiously record everything he has to say. Also, if you're busy taking notes during a meeting, you're unlikely to spot when it's a good time to chip in and therefore far less likely to make an active contribution to the proceedings.

Excessive Smiling. Smiling performs a broad range of functions, with one of its roles being to serve as an appeasement signal—in other words, to demonstrate that the person who's smiling has friendly intentions and isn't a threat. One way that people try to make themselves look less subservient is by reducing their smiling or by ensuring that their smiles don't blend with extraneous facial expressions of fear or apprehension, which might lead others to infer that they're unsure of themselves. There are, however, certain mitigating circumstances where reduction of smiling is no longer required. For example, although Nelson Mandela was a big smiler, nobody ever thought that his smiles had anything to do with appeasement. That's because Mandela was universally recognized as a man of principle who'd been prepared to spend twenty-seven years in prison for his political beliefs, and who therefore had absolutely no reason to try and appease anyone. Consequently, his smiles were invariably seen as a reflection of his pleasure and his desire to engage, and nothing to do with appease-ment. This shows how our reading of other people's expres-sive behaviours can so readily be influenced by what we know and expect of them. In Mandela's case, his reputation and the high regard in which he was held overrode the interpretations that would normally be applied to his actions had they been performed by someone else. This mitigating feature of smiling may help to explain why men smile less as they ascend the corporate ladder, whereas female leaders who become CEOs continue to smile as much as they did when they first entered the world of business. Maybe the kudos that senior women have gained by the time they become CEOs is sufficient to off-set any need to reduce their smiling.

In addition to nonverbal signs of powerlessness, there are also verbal ones. Over the years students of language have identified what they call "powerless speech"—that is, speaking styles that makes people sound subordinate, weak, tentative and ineffectual.[9] It's reported that people who produce powerless speech are less likely to be appointed to positions of authority and less likely to be respected, promoted or to persuade others. The defining features of powerless speech are as follows:

Hesitation. Speech hesitation is characterized by the use of filled pauses (where the pause contains expressions like *um, well,* and *er*) and unfilled pauses (where there's silence during the pause). It's been found that filled pauses are linked to anx-iety. If you use them consistently, they could suggest to others that you haven't worked out what you going to say and/or that you're unsure of your own opinions.

Tag Questions. These consist of questions that are tagged onto the end of a statement, like "That's the solution, don't you think?" or "That's what we could do—right?" Tag questions suggest uncertainty and a tendency to defer to others. The net effect is to leave others thinking that you don't really have any confidence in your own opinions.

Hedges. These involve the use of words that reduce the certainty of a statement—for example, *kind of, sort of, probably, some of, generally, may, might* and *could*. If you use them extensively, they're likely to give other people the impression that you're not entirely convinced about what you're saying.

Disclaimers. Disclaimers include expressions like "This might not be the best idea, but…," which suggests to others that the person is unsure about the value of their contribution.

Clearance. When you begin your contribution with a statement like "Can I just say this?", it makes it sound like you're searching for permission to say something. It has the effect of immediately putting you in a rather subordinate position.

Voice. In the process of modifying their voice, people can very easily come across as subordinate. As we saw earlier, people who are in positions of power tend to speak more slowly and to lower the pitch of their voice, whereas individuals who feel unsure of themselves often do the opposite—they raise their pitch and start to gabble.

Self-handicapping. This involves attempts to persuade others that you don't possess the skills needed to perform a given task. Imagine that you and several other people form part of a large team, about to embark on a specific business project, when one of the new members says "I'm not really very good at this." By saying this, they're effectively putting out a request to the other team members, inviting them to relax their judgment and, in this case, to lower their criteria for what they would otherwise consider to be an acceptable contribution to the project. This might give the person a pass in the short term, but in the long term the others may come around to the opinion that the person in question is simply not up to scratch. There are other reasons why the new team member might say "I'm not really very good at this." One is an attempt to disarm other people's envy about their position or abilities, while at the same time indicating that they aren't competitive or self-satisfied. Another reason is to try and appear suitably modest. This is fine when everyone around knows that the person in question has all the skills that are needed for the job. In other words, false modesty, which isn't modesty at all, only works properly if other people know you're being modest. Because, if they don't, they might very easily take you at face value and draw their own conclusions. The problem with putting oneself down—even well-meaningly or jokingly—is that other people might take you at your word and decide not to take you seriously. False modesty needs a touch of irony; it requires that when you deny having certain talents, everyone around is fully aware that you do have them. But self-handicapping isn't only strategic. There may be instances where you genuinely believe that you're not up to the job, even though there's ample evidence to the contrary. Here, you may try to deflect praise for a job well done, even redirecting all the praise to others. You might even attribute your success, which they they you richly deserve, to luck or good fortune, rather than to your own talents or hard work. Whether conscious or not, self-handicapping remarks like these can very easily lead other people to conclude that you don't really have what it takes to be successful. These sorts of remarks can therefore make you sound powerless.

Women Leaders

Women leaders often find it extremely difficult to perform their role, especially in business organizations that have traditionally been male-dominated. This is due to widespread and entrenched archaic assumptions about the characteristics needed to be a good leader, most of which—surprise, surprise!—are generally assumed to involve assertive, supposedly masculine qualities. Stereotyping and gender bias are rife in the business world, creating barriers for women who are trying to climb the corporate ladder. Not only do women have a tough time being hired into leadership positions, but they also face challenges in retaining their authority. Women have to contend with prejudicial attitudes about their suitability for leadership positions from men and, oddly, from women too. When they do acquire positions of power, things don't necessarily become easier, because women have to work much harder than men to earn and retain the respect of other people in the organization, and they're constantly having to prove themselves—something that male leaders have to contend with far less frequently. People are more ready to attribute the successes of women leaders to luck and good fortune rather than to talent and hard work, and when things do go wrong, women's errors are often explained in terms of their gender rather than the demanding circumstances they've had to face. Insecurity can also play a part, because even when high-flying women have absolutely no reasons for doubting their own abilities, it appears that they're much more susceptible to "imposter syndrome" than high-flying men.[10]

The difficulties women leaders encounter would be laughable if they weren't so tragic. Rather ironically, women are often better equipped for positions of power than their male counterparts. They might not always have the same amount of experience, but women leaders tend, on the whole, to be smarter as well as more democratic, collaborative and sensitive to the needs of other people. Temperamentally, they're often better equipped to being in charge.[11]

In addition to the obstacles placed in their way, aspiring female leaders need to resolve other difficult matters. All leaders, regardless of sex, need to decide what kind of corporate persona they're going to adopt. Should they, for example, attempt to dominate the scene or try to come across as more engaging? Of course, this dilemma is also experienced by male leaders, but cultivating a leadership persona is a lot less fraught for men than it is for women leaders, largely because it's considered to be natural for male leaders to be authoritative and for female leaders to be engaging. It's probably fair to say that while male leaders who adopt a supposedly more feminine style of leadership are seldom penalized for their efforts, women leaders who try to adopt a supposedly more masculine style of leadership can very quickly meet with resistance, both from women and men. Women leaders who are assertive, or who try to lay down the law at work, are often seen as "pushy" or "bitchy," whereas their male counterparts who do very much the same thing are lauded for being "visionary" and "far-sighted." In their attempts to fashion an acceptable and effective persona, female leaders should be aware that the success of their attempts to appear authoritative could depend on whether those attempts are verbal or nonverbal. It's been found, for example, that women leaders who produce verbal displays of dominance tend to be disliked by other people, whereas those who produce physical displays of dominance—like taking up more space, staring at other people, possibly smiling less—find it much easier to assert their power while at the same time remaining liked.[12] Clearly, the success of women leaders' efforts to project their corporate persona is likely to depend on the medium through which they choose to do so.

Then there are the specific elements of behaviour and speech that women leaders resort to when communicating with others. Women have a much stronger tendency to employ subordinate behaviours than men—behaviours like head-canting, self-touching and excessive smiling. To appear more leaderlike, women leaders need to eliminate, or at the very least reduce, these habits from their behavioural repertoire. It's also well established that women, women leaders included, are much more likely to incorporate features of powerless speech into their talk, making a lot more use of hedges and disclaimers, for example, and trying to seek clearance for their opinions. Here again, eliminating or reducing the frequency of these verbal items from their utterances is definitely something worth considering. Making these changes might not make them seem more powerful, but it will definitely make them look and sound less powerless.

It's worth noting is that while there's been a swing away from autocratic leadership and toward more engaging styles of business leadership, the golden mean—the sweet spot for managerial effectiveness, if you will—is bound to lie somewhere between the two extreme styles of leadership. Autocratic styles of leadership, devoid of any engagement, invariably prove to be unworkable—certainly in the modern, Western world, where employees, quite rightly, object to being pushed around and not being listened to. The opposite extreme, where leaders focus exclusively on being engaging, is equally dysfunctional, simply because being a leader requires the exercise of some authority. In this connection, Slovakian commentator Slavoj Žižek has claimed to have identified what he calls the "postmodern boss" or "friendly boss." His complaint is that bosses who fit this description don't really want to be in charge; instead, they devote their efforts to being especially nice to those below them and doing their best not to give any instructions. With leaders dodging their responsibilities and subordinates being denied proper guidance, the result is typically one of confusion and frustration.

Selling Tells

Face-to-face selling comes in all shapes and sizes—ranging from the classic doorstep encounter, where someone is trying to offload brushes, dusters and other household goods, all the way through to, say, a glittering automobile showroom, where the salesperson skilfully guides a prospective customer through the various features and benefits of the models on display. While sales transactions may differ according to what's being sold and their degree of subtlety, they all involve a pitch of sorts, with the salesperson making a special effort to encourage a sense of trust and to allay any fears that they might be pulling the wool over the customer's eyes.

To achieve these goals and conclude a sale, sellers usually have to rely on certain persuasive strategies:

PRESENTING
Sellers need to present themselves as relatively normal individuals so that they don't raise suspicions about their motives or intentions. This

is usually helped by dressing appropriately and by looking neat and tidy. In this way, they are able to demonstrate that they are not a maverick, and that they're prepared to make a special effort on the customer's account. In the process of presenting themselves, the salesperson needs to come across as business-like, trustworthy and relaxed, as well as friendly but not overly familiar. Appearing relaxed is important because it suggests confidence in oneself, the organization and what's being offered to the customer. At the same time, appearing agreeable is important because it provides the basis for a relationship of sorts between seller and customer.

PITCHING

Unless the customer knows exactly what they want, the salesperson usually needs to articulate the virtues of what they're selling, highlighting its merits and possibly its affordability. And, if necessary, disparaging the competition. In most sales transactions, it's not feasible for the salesperson to offer an exhaustive description of the goods or services on offer, but they do need to give the impression that they're covering features the customer considers to be vital to their decision about whether or not to go through with the purchase.

GAMING

In order to allay any fears that the customer is being taken for a ride, it's necessary for the seller to frame the transaction as a particular kind of game. Too often customers perceive sales transactions as a "zero-sum game"—in other words, as an event from which only one person, in this case the seller, emerges as the winner and where they themselves end up as the loser. To counter this perception of inequity, the seller needs to frame the ongoing transaction as a "non-zero-sum game"— an event where both the customer and the seller end up as deserving winners. There are, however, some instances where sellers manage to successfully frame their sales transaction as a zero-sum game. In a fruit-and-vegetable market, for example, it's not uncommon to hear the stallholder brandishing their wares while loudly lamenting the fact that their price is so low that they're virtually giving them away.

The topsy-turvy message here is that it's the unfortunate seller, not the buyer, who's about to end up as the loser.

RELATING

The success of a sales pitch often depends on the establishment of a degree of rapport between the prospective customer and salesperson, with most of the effort of course coming from the salesperson. The reason behind this is that customers, either knowingly or unwittingly, prefer to do business with someone they like, or with whom they feel some kind of affinity, rather than with someone about whom they feel indifferent. But a warm relationship doesn't only serve to create a positive glow around the sales transaction itself—it also provides the customer with a ready means of rationalizing their purchase after the event. In other words, if you feel that you've connected with someone who's just sold you something, you're much more likely to feel that you've made the right decision.

Sellers have numerous strategies at their disposal when it comes to building real or illusory relationships with prospective customers:

Ice-breaking. Using polite and engaging small-talk to help form a bond.

Demeanour. Adopting warm and friendly facial expressions and behaviour to encourage feelings of affinity.

Posture. Facing the other person and using open rather than closed postures to signal one's social accessibility.

Matching. Copying the postures and actions of the prospective customer as a way of suggesting that you're both on the same wavelength. When using this ploy, it's essential to ensure that the customer isn't alerted to it, so matching needs to be performed with subtlety. It also needs to be restricted to affiliative or neutral behaviours, because if you copy someone who, for example, is behaving dominantly, your actions are very unlikely to have the intended effect of bringing the two of you closer together.

Discretion. Resisting the temptation to express controversial views about politics, religion or social affairs.

Enquiry. Asking the prospective customer what they're looking for so that you can adapt your pitch to suit the customer's motives and preferences.

Attention. Demonstrating through body movements and speech that you are attentive and interested in what the prospective customer has to say, while using reflection and asking thoughtful questions to show understanding and appreciation.

Elevation. Employing subtle ingratiation techniques, like agreement, compliments and flattery to boost the prospective customer's sense of self and to increase the shared feel-good factor.

INCLUDING

When dealing simultaneously with two or more potential customers, it's vital that the seller spends some time looking at each of the people present—naturally when listening, but especially when speaking. Focussing one's attention on a single customer—say, the most senior person present—can turn out to be highly insensitive, causing those who've been overlooked to take offence. Some years ago, a banker friend of mine told me that he'd been at a meeting where an external consultant had pitched an idea to him and his boss, and that the consultant had spent the entire meeting addressing and looking at his boss, ignoring him altogether. My friend admitted that he felt so snubbed by this behaviour that when his boss asked him afterward what he thought of the meeting, he deliberately gave the consultant's proposal the thumbs down. Sellers who focus all their attention on the person who makes the final decision can very easily upset the other people present who feel that they're being treated as if they're invisible. In addition to causing offence, this misplaced behaviour can also lead to a loss of business.

INVOLVING

By building rapport with prospective customers, sellers are able to foster an impression or an illusion of familiarity and closeness, which in turn helps to redefine the transaction and make it seem less like it's devoted exclusively to selling. In fact, there's a strong, often unconscious, motivation for sellers to make it look like they're purely in the business of outlining options, offering disinterested advice and even doing the prospective customer a friendly favour—all of which is designed to dispel any suspicion that they're hunting down and preying upon the potential customer.

This is neatly illustrated in Daniel Pink's book *To Sell Is Human*, where he describes an intriguing study conducted by Kimberly Elsbach and Roderick Kramer.[13] These researchers spent several years immersed in the super-charged world of Hollywood pitches, observing and analyzing how people went about trying to persuade studio executives to take up their ideas for films and TV series, and why some pitches succeeded while others failed. The central finding that emerged was that the success of a pitch depended not so much on sellers' one-sided attempts to convince executives, but on the extent to which they gave executives a chance to become involved, to contribute their ideas and to gain a feeling of ownership over the project under discussion. This process of actively involving the buyer can also be a means of indirectly encouraging buyers to sell to themselves.

When buyers are cast in the passive role of listening to a pitch, they're simply exposed to the seller's blandishments. But when they're given a chance to offer their own opinions and ideas, not only do they become more actively involved, they also hear what they themselves have to say and are therefore more likely to be persuaded about the merits of a proposed project, which is partly, if not largely, of their own making. A similar principle of involvement is evident in the sales strategy of posing rhetorical questions. It's been found, for example, that pitches which include rhetorical questions—in other words, which invite prospective customers to become mentally active agents—are much more likely to have a successful conclusion.

The powerful effects of giving customers an opportunity to voice positive opinions and form favourable impressions about what's on offer can also be found in the seemingly innocent behaviour of restaurant waiters. We're all familiar with the situation where we're seated in a restaurant, we've ordered our meal and are half way through it, when the waiter returns and inquires how things are going. Unless the meal we've ordered falls dismally short of our expectations—and we're bold enough to say so—our natural instinct is to be vaguely complimentary. Social pressure encourages us to be compliant, to respond to the waiter's query with a statement like "Fine, thank you." Even when we're not entirely happy with what we've been served, we might react this way because we don't wish to fully engage with the waiter, but we feel the need to save their face or we don't want to defy convention by appearing churlish. In the process of saying that everything's fine, not only do we provide the waiter with a welcome endorsement, but we also hear ourselves voicing a favourable opinion, which, to reduce any cognitive dissonance we might experience, is likely to subtly improve our view of the meal we've ordered. So next time a waiter comes over and asks if you're enjoying the food, remind yourself what's really happening: while the waiter thinks that they are merely being polite and solicitous, their true purpose, even if they don't realize it, is to get you to say something that's likely to enhance your enjoyment of the meal you've ordered.

INFLUENCING

Psychologists have identified a whole raft of persuasive techniques that are relevant to selling. Probably the best-known of these is the so-called "foot-in-the-door technique," which involves getting someone to agree to a small request so that later on they're more amenable to a bigger request (one they probably wouldn't have agreed to if it had been put to them initially). This compliance strategy seems to work on several levels—not only by establishing a working relation-ship between the prospective customer and the salesperson, but also by luring the prospective customer into a psychological state where the second request seems close enough to the first, not to be rejected. It's also worth noting that getting someone to agree to a small request shifts them psychologically into a "yes mode," where they're prone to be more helpful and compliant. That's why a salesperson's first move is often to ask you a series of questions that you're most likely to answer in the affirmative—it's their guileful method of coaxing you into "yes mode" so that your critical faculties are temporarily blunted and your impulse to help comes to the fore.

Then there's the "door-in-the-face technique," which is basically the mirror-image of the foot-in-the-door technique. Here the sales-person starts with a big request that, once rejected, is then followed up with a smaller and ostensibly more appropriate request. This strategy operates on two levels, namely offering relief and providing flattery. The salesperson relieves the prospective customer of any concern that they're about to be confronted with an even more outlandish request (which they'd have to turn down) while at the same time flattering the customer into believing that they've forced the salesperson to make a much more reasonable follow-up request.

TIMING

One of the ways that sellers put pressure on prospective customers is by telling them that the deals on offer are time-limited. In other words, if the customer doesn't cough up and make their purchases now, then they won't be able to do so later. This particular strategy works in at least three ways: 1) by reducing the amount of time that prospective customers have to carefully examine what's on offer; 2) by forcing the customer to make hurried, often ill-considered decisions; and 3) by activating FOMO, the fear of missing out. People with a strong desire to avoid regret, who cherish the opinions of others, and who don't mind being pushed around tend to be more susceptible to time-limited selling.

ACTIVATING

People who make a living from selling are often aware of the various reasons why prospective customers resist what's on offer, and in some cases they've evolved sales techniques to try and overcome this resistance. Saving is a good case in point, because people often need a lot of persuasion to make investments and put money aside for the future. That's largely because saving involves deferral of benefits—in other words, when we save, we automatically sacrifice the chance of spending money today so that we can enjoy the benefits of spending more money later on. All saving therefore involves what psychologists call "intertemporal choice"—choosing between consumption at different times. Psychologists have discovered that one reason why people find it so hard to save is that the indeterminate benefits of consuming in the future often appear less attractive than the more certain benefits of consuming now.

But there's another big reason why people find it hard to save: they don't or can't relate to their futures selves. This is borne out by a fascinating study where people were placed in an fMRI scanner and asked to think about: a) themselves now, b) themselves in the future, c) a total stranger now, and d) a total stranger in the future. When the neurological evidence was examined, it was found that the brain activity involved in thinking about their future self was less similar to their present self than the activity involved in thinking about a total stranger.[14] This explains why people's relationships to their future self are likely to impact on activities like saving—if you think of your future self as being more similar to a stranger than to your present self, there's much less reason to put money aside for a rainy day. In this context, saving is rather like giving your money to a complete stranger instead of enjoying it yourself now.

Activating a certain mindset or a novel way of seeing the world or oneself can often make it much easier for sellers to influence the behaviour of prospective customers. For example, psychologists have discovered that when people are shown digitally aged photographs of their own face—in other words, images of how they're likely to appear in a few decades time—they're more inclined to recognize the continuity between their present and future selves, and consequently they're a lot more ready to invest money in a saving account.[15] People may be persuaded to save by examining a balance sheet projection of their finances; but bringing them face-to-face with their future self can potentially have an even greater impact on the immediate actions they undertake to safeguard their future.

SELECTING

Most prospective customers prefer to be treated as individuals and, if possible, exclusively. That's one of the reasons why premier hotels and expensive boutiques make a point of remembering the names of their clientele, knowing their quirks and treating them with respect, if not affection. The evidence suggests that prospective customers are especially motivated by the belief that what they're being offered isn't available to everyone else—in other words, that it's an exclusive offer and they're therefore being treated as someone who's special. This was certainly the approach of Victor Lustig, the infamous con artist who "sold the Eiffel Tower" in the 1920s. He pulled off his daring scam by forging documents, inviting wealthy scrap metal merchants to a meeting in a smart Paris hotel, and informing them that he'd chosen them specially because they were "honest businessmen." In a single stroke, Lustig was able to give the impression that integrity was vitally important to his business dealings while flattering the assembled merchants by leading them to believe that what they were being offered was highly exclusive.

When it comes to being selective, the unequalled maestro—certainly in modern times—was fraudulent financier Bernie Madoff. After he'd created an asset management business valued at over 60 billion dollars, it was discovered that Madoff had actually been running a massive, highly successful Ponzi scheme. This enabled him to offer his clients eye-watering returns on their investments—not because he was some investment guru, but because he was illicitly using the money provided by new clients to pay enormous dividends to his existing clients. Madoff knew that his Ponzi scheme would eventually run out of road and come crashing down, but there were a few people, excluding some prominent banks, who suspected him of foul play. In fact, at the height of the scheme, hundreds of wealthy individuals were eager to hand their money over to Madoff, blinded no doubt by the extraordinary returns he was offering. Here, Madoff proved to be a pass master, because instead of opening the gates and allowing just anybody to join his scheme, he made it clear to everyone that he was extremely selective. This made membership even more desirable, with people clamouring to get on to his books. At the time, Madoff happened to be a member of the highly exclusive Palm Beach Country Club. Since this was widely known, a long line of super wealthy people thought nothing of paying the $300,000 fee to join the club—not, you understand, so they could enjoy its lounges or sporting facilities, but solely to increase their chances of casually bumping into Bernie Madoff and being invited to join his exclusive asset management scheme.

Online Tells

Everyone recognizes that conducting a business meeting with someone online is not the same thing as meeting that person face-to-face. Exactly how similar or different these encounters are for you will depend on a variety of factors, like how acquainted you and the other person are with online meetings and whether your respective experiences have been positive or negative. There are a number of reasons why online or virtual meetings generally feel strange. One is that each person attending the meeting is located in their own tiny video tile; another is that the participants appear on our screens side by side and/ or stacked unnaturally on top of each other. The sensation that we have of other people online is therefore very different from how we experience them face-to-face. In addition, virtual meetings don't offer what psychologists call "immediacy"—the multi-sensory feeling that someone is in your immediate presence.

Part of our discomfort about virtual business meetings can be attributed to the fact that our brains are hard-wired for face-to-face interaction—it's what we experience from the moment we're born, enabling us to become expert practitioners in face-to-face interactions even though we're not necessarily aware of the interpersonal skills we've acquired. When we're in someone else's immediate presence our brain is, relatively speaking, in its comfort zone because it's processing information that it's used to dealing with. Virtual meetings, on the other hand, present the brain with new and unusual challenges so it has to invest extra effort to make sense of what's happening, giving rise to what psychologists are calling "Zoom fatigue," where long hours of virtual interaction are much more exhausting than the equivalent amount of time spent talking to people face-to-face.[16]

But there's another important feature of online meetings—namely the fact that we see ourselves on screen alongside the other person or persons taking part. This of course isn't something we experience when we meet people face-to-face, where we don't have the faintest clue what we look like or how other people see us. If you were meeting someone face-to-face and you discovered that a mirror was positioned so that you could see yourself all the time, you'd find the situation very bizarre indeed, and yet this is almost a standard feature of virtual meetings.

This ability to see yourself and others on screen at the same time is what psychologists call the "rear-window phenomenon," and it can give rise to all kinds of problems. One is the irresistible urge to keep checking your appearance and, in some cases, to compare it to that of others (or even to try and improve your appearance by resorting to a "touch-up" option). It's also been discovered that looking at yourself in the mirror doesn't help, even for short periods of time, because it can make you unnecessarily critical of your own appearance. Seeing oneself online all the time can also give rise to a condition called "the imaginary audience," where we delude ourselves into believing that the other people in an online meeting are watching our every move.

During online meetings it's advisable not to worry too much about how you look or to imagine that the other people present are constantly assessing your appearance. After all, there's a good chance that they're spending the time looking at themselves! It's also worth noting that when we're engaged with people online, we need to be slightly more emphatic with our body language. Marshall McLuhan made the interesting point that television is what he called a "cool medium"—in other words, it dampens down and reduces the immediate impact of the visual message. This being the case, we need to compensate for the coolness of onscreen meetings by injecting a bit more energy into our communications in order to get them across.

Online Best Practice

When taking part or organizing online meetings, the following procedures are worth adopting:

Preparation. Virtual meetings require noticeably more preparation than face-to-face meetings, so make sure that you're positioned in front of a neat, professional-looking background, that your laptop is fully charged, that extraneous computer programs are closed, and that you've lined up any material you want to share with others. If you're the host, assign a password and enable the waiting room function so that you can control who enters and lock the meeting after everyone's arrived.

Camera. Position your camera at eye level so that you're not looking up or down at the other person or people on the call. Also position yourself so that you're in the centre of the frame, neither too close nor too far away from the camera. Employ a good lighting system and make sure that the lighting is in front of you. If it's behind you, you're likely to appear in silhouette, with the result that the others won't be able to see your face or your facial expressions.

Notes. Try not to take notes on your laptop during the meeting, and if you must take notes, do so sparingly on a notepad. If you need to consult notes during the meeting, it's often a good idea to pin them on a board beside the camera, roughly at eye level. That way you should be able to read them while making minimal movements of your head and eyes.

Gestures. During an online meeting, it's fine to use expressive hand gestures to accompany what you're saying, but make sure that they appear within, rather than outside, your camera frame.

Eye Contact. If you want to give other people the impression that you're looking directly at them, look into the camera rather than at the person or people on the screen. This poses a slight problem, because on the one hand you want to appear attentive, while on the other you'll want to take the opportunity to watch the others and see what they're doing. One way to resolve this dilemma is to alternate between these two strategies.

14. Tell-tales

You're going to work in the morning. You walk out the front door, you get in your car, you drive through the traffic, you park the car and walk into the building. The person in reception greets you as you enter and you say hello back. You go up to your office and sit down. Your assistant comes in, says good morning and hands you your mail. You say good morning and thank them, and then they leave. You're ready to start the day.

You're obviously an observant person because on your way to work you spotted things that very few people would have noticed. You saw that the clock face on the railway station had been changed, that the flag at City Hall was flying at half-mast, and that the lanes in the car park have been given a new coat of paint. But you missed several things. You didn't notice, for example, that the person in reception, whose face is normally beaming, could only manage a lopsided smile this morning, or that your assistant, who's been with you for twelve years, had bags under their eyes. How were you to know that the person in reception had been to the dentist earlier this morning, and that your assistant had been up all night because the baby couldn't get to sleep?

There are several reasons why you failed to spot these telltale signs. Like most other people, you're quick to notice changes to your physical environment but slow to spot changes in the people around you. It's not that these people are unimportant—in fact they mean a lot to you. It's just that you've come to take them for granted. You're comforted by the knowledge that they don't change, and that—like the characters in the film *Groundhog Day*—they're always there, doing the same thing day after day.

This is all linked to what psychologists call "change blindness." Change blindness takes several forms, one of which is the inability to notice how people have changed. In a clever experiment conducted by Daniel Simons and Dan Levin at Harvard, the experimenter approached strangers on the campus and innocently asked them for directions.[1] Imagine for a moment that you're one of the unsuspecting subjects who took part in the experiment. You're walking across the campus when a stranger approaches you and asks you for directions. While you're talking to him, two workmen walk between you and the stranger, carrying a large wooden door. Naturally you feel irritated by this interruption, but after the workmen have moved on you continue giving directions to the stranger. When you've finished, the stranger thanks you and informs you that you have just taken part in an experiment. "Did you notice anything different after the two men passed by with the door?" he asks. "No," you reply, "I didn't notice anything at all." He then explains that he's not the same man who initially approached you for directions. The original man walked off behind the door, leaving the present man behind in his place to continue the conversation! At this point the first man walks over and joins you. Looking at the two of them, standing there together, you can see how very different they are. Not only do they differ in height and build, but they're also dressed differently and have very different voices.

If you'd behaved this way, you wouldn't have been alone, because more than half of the people who took part in the experiment failed to notice the difference between the two men. After the workmen had disappeared and the switch had taken place, the subjects continued to give directions as though nothing unusual had happened. This experiment shows that while we think we notice what's happening around us, a lot of the time we don't. Not only are we oblivious to the changes that take place in people's appearance, but we're also insensitive to the words, gestures and expressions they use. But it goes further, because in addition to suffering from "change blindness," we're also afflicted with *tell blindness*.

There are three reasons why we don't notice tells. The first is a "failure of observation"—we simply don't pay enough attention to what people say and do. The second is a "failure of recognition"—we may notice that people are behaving in certain ways, but we don't recognize their actions as being informative. The third is a "failure of interpretation"—we recognize that there's something informative about someone's behaviour, but we can't see what it reveals about them; in other words, we can't read the tells. These failures can be remedied by developing what Charles Darwin called the "habit of minute observation"—watching people closely, paying attention to details, comparing people in different situations, and basing our conclusions on what we observe about people rather than what they inform us about themselves.

When we're looking out for tells, there are several principles that we need to follow. These form the basis of *telleology*.

Look for Multiple Tells. It's often tempting to draw inferences about people on the basis of a single tell—especially when you're trying to decide whether someone is lying or telling the truth. This temptation should always be resisted, because the strength of tells is always in direct proportion to their number—the more tells someone displays, the more certain you can be about what they're thinking or feeling.

Don't Jump to Conclusions. It's also tempting to assume that tells always reveal the same things about people. Unfortunately that's not always the case, because a tell can sometimes convey quite different meanings. For example, if you were to meet someone with sweaty palms you'd probably conclude that they were nervous about something. But you could be wrong—the person might have hyperhidrosis, a genetic condition that has nothing to do with anxiety. The moral here is that you should always make your inferences conditional until you've had a chance to check them out.

Compare People with Themselves. In order to interpret someone's tells it's sometimes necessary to compare that person in several different settings, rather than to compare them with lots of other people in one setting. For example, if you arrived at a party and your host greeted you effusively, you'd want to know whether you'd been singled out or if everyone was getting the same treatment. To find out, you'd need to watch how your host greets other guests—in other words, you'd have to compare them with themselves. That way you'd be able to find out whether your host was especially pleased to see you, or whether they're equally enthusiastic about everybody.

One reason why we're so blind to *tells* is that they seem so small and insignificant. We're so busy concentrating on what people are saying to us that we fail to notice their choice of words, the inflection of their voice, and the way they move their hands and feet. One of the most important lessons to emerge from telleology is the fact that, where tells are concerned, size doesn't matter. In fact, it's often the tiny, almost imperceptible actions that provide clues to people's thoughts and personality. This is most noticeable in situations where people act unintentionally and where they aren't aware of their actions. As Arthur Schopenhauer pointed out, "It is with trifles, and when he is off guard, that a man best reveals his character."

It was attention to detail that formed the basis of Sherlock Holmes's legendary ability to understand people's motives and to solve mysteries. "You know my method," said Holmes. "It is founded upon the observance of trifles." His advice was "Never to trust general impressions—but concentrate upon the details."[2] It's often in their tiny tells and in the minutiae of their unintended actions that people are most revealing about themselves—in slips of the tongue, minuscule hand movements, and the fleeting, almost tachistoscopic micro-tells that flicker across their face when they're trying to conceal their true feelings.

Telleology promises to play an increasingly important role in forensic science. In the old days the only tools available to a detective were his keen senses. There have been enormous changes since Sherlock Holmes looked out of his window, noticed how a woman hesitated before crossing the road, and informed Dr. Watson that "oscillation upon the pavement always means an *affaire du coeur*."[3] Although today's detectives recognize the need for a trained eye, their task is made easier by the opportunity to record people's actions, to view them repeatedly, and to subject them to detailed analysis. A good example is John Napier's analysis of the famous cinefilm of "Bigfoot," where he was able to show that the style of walking was entirely humanoid.[4]

Whether we like it or not, we're all involved with tells—there's no escaping them. Cascades of tells are produced whenever we interact with other people, and even when we remain silent in their company. Some of these tells are under our control—they're the ones that we use to present a particular image of ourselves. But there are also tells that we cannot control, like blushing and pupil dilation, as well as tells that we can control but don't, like preening, posture matching and certain facial expressions. As we noticed earlier, there are differences in how we relate to unintended tells, because while we may be painfully aware of the fact that we're blushing, there's no way we could know that our pupils are dilated; we are only ever aware of the treachery of our cheeks, never that of our pupils. Equally, while we are quite capable of positioning our limbs or moving our hands in ways that are designed to create a certain impression, we often fail to consciously control these features of our behaviour, allowing them instead to reveal moods and thoughts that we might otherwise wish to keep hidden.

Although we're often blind to other people's tells, this doesn't mean that we're unaffected by them. In recent years psychologists have discovered that features of their social environment can unconsciously shape people's moods. For example, Sheila Murphy and Bob Zajonc found that people's moods are affected very differently, depending on whether they are exposed to a smiling or a scowling face. In both instances, their subjects were only exposed to these faces for four milli-seconds, which was too short for them to be aware of what they had seen.[5] Ulf Dimberg and his colleagues at Uppsala University have gone one step further by showing that our facial responses are influenced by other people's facial expressions, even when we're unaware of what they're doing with their face. Dimberg and his colleagues placed elec-trodes on their subjects' faces and then exposed them to subliminal images of smiling, angry or neutral faces.[6] They found that subjects were more likely to frown when they were presented with an angry face, and more likely to raise the corners of their mouth when they were exposed to the smiling face, even though they were completely unaware that they'd seen a face.

These studies suggest that other people's tells can affect us in ways of which we are entirely unaware. They also raise the possibility that the way we respond to other people has more to do with the tiny, almost subliminal features of their demeanour than to the gross, more obvious aspects of their behaviour. I was very struck by this when I watched Bill Clinton address the Labour Party Conference in Blackpool, back in October 2002. At the time Tony Blair was having trouble persuading Labour members that it would be necessary for Britain to support the United States if it decided to go to war against Iraq, and it was thought that Bill Clinton would be able to bring the doubters into line behind Blair. The speech was vintage Clinton—he flattered the delegates, exposed both sides of the argument and showed that he was fallible. But more importantly, he interspersed his remarks with Clintonian tells—that upward-looking smile, the magisterial wave, the carefully timed hesitations to remind everyone that politics was about making tough decisions. When he said that war is indiscriminate—"I do not care how precise your bombs and your weapons are, when you set them off innocent people will die"—he did his trademark lip-bite tell, reminding the gathering that he was someone who could very easily be overwhelmed by his feelings. At the end of the speech there was thunderous applause. When conference members were interviewed on TV afterward, they were all ecstatic—MPs of every political hue said that Clinton was on their side. There was of course no mention of the various oratorical devices that he'd used, even though it was these devices that had electrified the conference rather than anything Clinton had said. The delegates thought they were responding to his arguments, but they weren't. They were reacting to the tells that he had produced, those little signals that he'd marshalled to show that he was thoughtful and sensitive, a man of political conviction with strong emotions. It was the tells—the medium, not the message—that had won the day.

In the first chapter we saw that the word *tell* comes from poker, where it's used to describe any action or speech mannerism that reveals what kind of hand someone is holding or the strategy they're using. The ensuing chapters have shown that the notion of tells isn't exclusive to the game of poker, and that it can profitably be applied to a wide range of everyday pursuits. Poker is like life in some respects, and different in others. Part of the similarity lies in the fact that we need to conceal our thoughts, feelings and intentions from others, just as poker players need to keep their hand and their motives hidden.

The other similarity lies in individuals' attempts to understand each other, and to use their observations as a guide to what other people are thinking. When you're playing poker there are two sources of information about the kind of hand another player is holding—one is the cards you're holding, and the other is the way the other person is behaving. The trouble with the latter is that there's no way of knowing whether the inferences you draw about the other person's hand are based on what they're failing to conceal or what they are doing in order to deceive you. In many respects, life's the same—it's not always clear whether the conclusions we draw about other people are based on actions that they can't control or actions that they've deliberately produced in order to mislead us. In poker this conundrum is solved by comparing the various hands that a player has with the way that they behave during each round. Although life isn't neatly parcelled into discrete deals, it's still possible to link individuals' circumstances to the way they behave, and in this way to identify their tells.

When you're playing poker with someone for the first time there's no way of knowing what their tells are—the only thing you can do is assume that the common tells apply to them as much as they do to anyone else. After watching another player for several rounds, it should be possible to identify their signature tells. The same thing applies outside the game of poker—it takes several occasions to recognize the distinctive features of someone's behaviour and to link these to what they're feeling. In the meantime we can always resort to our knowledge of common tells in order to work out what that person is probably thinking or feeling.

The study of tells promises to enrich our lives in many ways. By focusing our attention on the tiny details and transient aspects of other people's behaviour we're exposed to the enormous complexity of our social world, and this can only encourage us to be more sensitive toward other people. Observing other people's tells also turns our attention back on ourselves—it sensitizes us to our own behaviour and helps us to recognize that while we are using other people's tells to draw inferences about them, they're doing exactly the same thing to us. In addition, the study of tells is potentially liberating because it reveals how people try to manipulate others and how they give themselves away; being armed with these insights helps to protect us from the dangers of being manipulated ourselves. Finally, the study of tells invites us to see the world differently, and to recognize that people are constantly conveying information about themselves in the form of tells. Unpacking these tells enables us to read their minds and to understand them more fully.

Acknowledgements

I would like to thank my wife, Jill, and my daughters, Katie and Clementine, for their patience and loving support, without which this book would not have been possible. Thanks are also due to my agent, Caradoc King, for his advice and encouragement, to Martha Lishawa, Linda Shaughnessy and Rebecca Percival at United Agents, to Brenda Kimber, Marianne Velmans and Sheila Lee at Doubleday, and especially to Brad Wilson at Collins, along with Canaan Chu and Tracy Bordian, for all the help and support they have given me. In addition I would like to express my gratitude to my brother, Tony, and his wife, Julia, for their encouragement over the years, as well as to the following friends and colleagues for their valuable help and suggestions: Suzie Addinell, Simon Andreae, Max Atkinson, Rad Babic, Geoffrey Beattie, Steven Beebe, Susan Beebe, Giovanni Carnibella, Mike Christie, Alberta Contarello, Tina Cook, Patrick Corr, Paul Ekman, Bridget Farrands, Rob Farrands, Norma Feshbach, Seymour Feshbach, Mark Frank, Adrian Furnham, Tim Gardam, Doris Ginsburg, Gerry Ginsburg, Fergus Gleeson, Peter Henderson, Tim Horner, Diana Ivy, Brett Kahr, Christine Kuehn, Mansur Lalljee, Roger Lamb, Ian Livesey, Peter Marsh, Marie O'Shaughnessy, Sophie Ratcliffe, Monica Rector, Rachel Reeves, Bryan Richards, Dunja Sagov, Sandra Scott, Barry Shrier, Caroline Simmonds, Frank Simmonds, Mary Sissons Joshi, Charles Smith, Mike Smith, Michael John Spencer, Oliver Spiecker, Martine Stewart, Michael Stewart, Paddy Summerfield, Gaby Twivy, Paul Twivy and Peter van Breda. Finally I would like to record my special thanks to Peter du Preez, Michael Argyle and Desmond Morris, who taught me so much of what I know and encouraged my interest in human behaviour.

Notes

1. Tells

1. Caro, M. (1994) *The Body Language of Poker: Caro's Book of Tells*. Secaucus, NJ: Carol Publishing Group.
2. Haggard, E. A., and Isaacs, K. S. (1966) "Micromomentary facial expressions as indicators of ego mechanisms in psychotherapy." In L. A. Gottschalk and H. Auerbach (eds), Methods of Research in Psychotherapy. New York: Appleton-Century-Crofts; Pan, H., Xie, L., Wang, Z., Liu, B., Yang, M., & Tao., J. (2021). Review of micro-expression spotting and recognition in video sequences. Virtual Reality & Intelligent Hardware, 3(1), 1–17; Zhang, H., Yin, L., and Zhang, H. (2023) "A review of micro-expression spotting: Methods and challenges." Multimedia Systems, 29, 1897–1915.
3. Hess, E. (1975) *The Telltale Eye*. New York: Van Nostrand Reinhold.
4. Ekman, P., and Friesen, W. (1969) "Nonverbal leakage and clues to deception." *Psychiatry*, 32, 88–106.
5. Freud, S. (1905) "Fragments of an analysis of a case of hysteria." *Collected Papers*, Vol. 3. New York: Basic Books (reprinted 1959).
6. Ro, K. M., Cantor, R. M., Lange, K. L., and Ahn, S. S. (2002) "Palmar hyperhidrosis: evidence of genetic transmission." *Journal of Vascular Surgery*, 35(2), 382–86.
7. Dryden, J., and Clough, A. H. (eds) (1902) *Lives of Noble Grecians and Romans*, Vol. 3. Boston: Little, Brown.
8. Bulwer, J. (1644) *Chirologia; or the Natural Language of the Hand*. London.
9. Mahl, G. F., Danet, B., and Norton, N. (1959) "Reflections of major personality characteristics in gestures and body movements. Research Report to A.P.A. Annual meeting." Cited in B. Christiansen (1972) *Thus Speaks the Body*. New York: Arno Press.
10. LaFrance, M. (1985) "Postural mirroring and intergroup relations." *Personality and Social Psychology Bulletin*, 11(2), 207–17; Bernieri, F., and Rosenthal, R. (1991) "Interpersonal coordination: Behavioural matching and interactional synchrony." In R. S. Feldman and B. Rime (eds), *Fundamentals of Nonverbal Behavior*. Cambridge: Cambridge University Press; Chartrand, T. L., and Lakin, J. L. (2013) "The antecedents and consequences of human behavioral mimicry." *Annual Review of Psychology, 64*, 285–308; Farley, S. D. (2020) "Introduction to the spe-

cial issue on nonconscious mimicry: History, applications, and theoretical and methodological innovations." *Journal of Nonverbal Behavior*, 44(1), 1–4.

11. Provine, R. R. (1996) "Contagious yawning and laughter: Significance for sensory feature detection, motor pattern generation, imitation, and the evolution of social behavior." In C. M. Heyes and B. G. Galef (eds), *Social Learning in Animals: The Roots of Culture*. New York: Academic Press.

12. Krebs, J. R. and Dawkins, R. D. (1984) "Animal signals: mind-reading and manipulation." In J. R. Krebs and N. B. Davies (eds), *Behavioral Ecology: An Evolutionary Approach*. Sunderland, MA: Sinauer.

13. Gottman, J. M., and Silver, N. (1999) *The Seven Principles for Making Marriage Work*. New York: Crown Publishers.

14. Davis, J. I., Senghas, A., Brand, F., and Ochsner, K. N. (2010) "The effects of BOTOX injections on emotional experience." *Emotion*, 10(3), 433–40; Havas, D. A., Glenberg, A. M., Gutowski, K. A., Lucarelli, M. J., and Davidson, R. J. (2010) "Cosmetic use of botulinum toxin-a affects processing of emotional language." *Psychological Science*, 21(7), 895–900; Baumeister, J. C., Papa, G., and Foroni, F. (2016) "Deeper than skin deep: The effect of botulinum toxin-A on emotion processing." *Toxicon*, 118, 86–90; Coles, N. A., Larsen, J. T., Kuribayashi, J. and Kuelz, A. (2019) "Does blocking facial feedback via Botulinum Toxin injections decrease depression? Critical Review and meta-analysis." *Emotion Review*, 11(4), 294–309.

2. Dominant Tells

1. Kalma, A. (1991) "Hierarchisation and dominance assessment at first glance." *European Journal of Social Psychology*, 21, 165–81.

2. Cassidy, C. M. (1991) "The good body: When big is better." *Medical Anthropology*, 13, 181–213; Ellis, L. (1994) "The high and the mighty among man and beast: How universal is the relationship between height (or body size) and social status?" In L. Ellis (ed.), *Social Stratification and Socioeconomic Inequality*, Vol. 2, Westport, CT: Praeger.

3. Gunnell, D., Rogers, J., and Dieppe, P. (2001) "Height and health: Predicting longevity from bone length in archaeological remains." *Journal of Epidemiology and Community Health*, 55, 505–7.

4. Ellis, B. J. (1992) "The evolution of sexual attraction: Evaluative mechanisms in women." In J. H. Barkow, L. Cosmides and J. Tooby (eds), *The Adapted Mind: Evolutionary Psychology and the Generation of Culture*. New York: Oxford University Press; Pawlowski, B., Dunbar, R., and Lipowicz, A. (2000) "Evolutionary fitness: Tall men have more reproductive success." *Nature*, 403 (6766), 156; Stulp, G., Simons, M. J., Grasman, S., and Pollet, T.V., (2017) "Assortative mating for human height: A meta-analysis." *American. Journal of Human Biology*, 29(1), e22917; Pisanski, K., Fernandez-Alonso, M., Díaz-Simón, N., Oleszkiewicz, A.,

Sardinas, A., Pellegrino, R., et al. (2022) "Assortative mate preferences for height across short-term and long-term relationship contexts in a cross-cultural sample." *Frontiers in Psychology*, 13:937146.

5. Tremblay, R. E., Schaal, B., Boulerice, B., Arseneault, L., Soussignan, R. G., Paquette, D., and Laurent, D. (1998) "Testosterone, physical aggression, dominance, and physical development in early adolescence." *International Journal of Behavioral Development* 22(4), 753–77.

6. Cassidy, C. M. (1991) "The good body: When big is better." *Medical Anthropology*, 13, 181–213; Case, A., and Paxson, C. (2008) "Stature and status: Height, ability and labor market outcomes." *Journal of Political Economy*, 116(3), 499–532; Thompson, K., Portrait, F., and Schoonmade, L. (2023) "The height premium: A systematic review and meta-analysis." *Economics and Human Biology*, 50:101273.

7. Hensley, W. E. (1993) "Height as a measure of success in academe." *Psychology: A Journal of Human Behavior*, 30(1), 40–6.

8. Weisfeld, G. E., and Beresford, J. M. (1982) "Erectness of posture as an indicator of dominance or success in humans." *Motivation and Emotion*, 6(2), 113–31; Weisfeld, G. E., and Linkey, H. E. (1985) "Dominance displays as indicators of a social success motive." In S. L. Ellyson and J. F. Dovidio (eds), *Power, Dominance, and Non-verbal Behavior*. New York: Springer Verlag.

9. Riskind, J. H. (1983) "Nonverbal expressions and the accessibility of life experience memories: a congruence hypothesis." *Social Cognition*, 2(1), 62–86; Riskind, J. H. (1984) "They stoop to conquer: Guiding and self-regulatory functions of physical posture after success and failure." *Journal of Personality and Social Psychology*, 47(3), 479–93.

10. Lott, D. F., and Sommer, R. (1967) "Seating arrangement and status," *Journal of Personality and Social Psychology*, 7(1), 90–5; Sommer, R. (1969) *Personal Space*. New York: Prentice-Hall.

11. Schnurnberger, L. (1991) *40,000 Years of Fashion: Let There Be Clothes*. New York: Workman Publishing; Glover, M. (2019). *Thrust: A Spasmodic Pictorial History of the Codpiece (Ekphrasis)*. New York: David Swirner Books.

12. Spicer, J. (1991) "The Renaissance elbow." In J. Bremmer and H. Roodenburg (eds), *The Cultural History of Gesture*. Cambridge: Polity Press.

13. From the English edition of Desiderius Erasmus' *De Civilitate Morum Puerilium* (1532), translated by Robert Whitinton (1540) and cited by Joaneath Spicer (1991), ibid.

14. Mueller, U., and Mazur, A. (1997) "Facial dominance in Homo Sapiens as honest signalling of male quality." *Behavioural Ecology*, 8, 569–79; Mazur, A., and Booth, A. (1998) "Testosterone and dominance in men." *Behavioral and Brain Sciences*, 21, 353–98.

15. Keating, C. F. (1985) "Human dominance signals: The primate in us." In S. L. Ellyson and J. F. Dovidio (eds), *Power, Dominance, and Non-verbal Behavior*. New York: Springer Verlag.

16. Keating, C. F., Mazur, A., and Segall, M. H. (1981) "A cross-cultural exploration of physiognomic traits of dominance and happiness," *Ethology and Sociobiology*, 2, 41–8.

17. Tiedens, L. Z. (2001) "Anger and advancement versus sadness and subjugation: The effect of negative emotion expressions on social status conferral." *Journal of Personality and Social Psychology*, 80(1), 86–94.

18. Dabbs, J. M. (1992) "Testosterone, smiling and facial appearance." *Journal of Nonverbal Behavior*, 21, 45–55. *See also* Mazur, A., and Booth, A. (1998) "Testosterone and dominance in men." *Behavioral and Brain Sciences*, 21, 353–98.

19. Schniter, E. (2000) "The evolution of yawning: Why do we yawn and why is it contagious?" MA thesis, Department of Anthropology, University of Oregon; Guggisberg, A.G., Mathis, J., Schnide, A., and Hess, C. W. (2010) "Why do we yawn?" *Neuroscience & Biobehavioral Reviews*, 34(8), 1267–76; Norscia, I., and Palagi, E. (2011) "Yawn Contagion and Empathy in *Homo sapiens*." *PLoS ONE*, 6(12): e28472; Poole, K. L., and Henderson, H. A. (2023) "Social cognitive correlates of contagious yawning and smiling." *Human Nature*, November, 1–19.

20. Schino, G., and Aureli, F. (1989) "Do men yawn more than women?" *Ethology and Sociobiology*, 10, 375–8.

21. Ridgeway, C. L., Berger, J., and Smith, L. (1985) "Nonverbal cues and status: An expectation states approach." *American Journal of Sociology*, 90(5), 955–78; Schwartz, B., Tesser, A., and Powell, E. (1982) "Dominance cues in nonverbal behavior." *Social Psychology Quarterly*, 45(2), 114–20.

22. Kalkhoff, W., Thye, S. R. and Gregory, S. W. (2017) "Nonverbal adaptation and audience perceptions of dominance and prestige." *Social Psychology Quarterly*, 80(4), 342–354; Dippong, J. (2020) "Status and vocal accommodation in small groups." *Sociological Science*, 7, 291–313. *See also* Bilous, F. R., and Krauss, R. M. (1988) "Dominance and accommodation in the conversational behaviours of same and mixed-gender dyads." *Language and Communication*, 8(3/4), 183–95.

23. Ohala, J. J. (1994) "The frequency code underlies the sound-symbolic use of voice pitch." In L. Hinton, J. Nichols and J. J. Ohala (eds), *Sound Symbolism*. Cambridge: Cambridge University Press.

24. Krebs, J. R., and Dawkins, R. D. (1984) "Animal signals: Mind-reading and manipulation." In J. R. Krebs and N. B. Davies (eds), *Behavioral Ecology: An Evolutionary Approach*. Sunderland, MA: Sinauer; Collins, S. (2001) "Men's voices and women's choices." *Animal Behavior*, 60, 773–80.

25. Elliot, A. J. (1981) *Child Language*. Cambridge: Cambridge University Press.

26. Pemberton, C., McCormack, P., and Russell, A. (1998) "Have women's voices lowered across time? A cross-sectional study of Australian women's voices." *Journal of Voice*, 12(2), 208–13.

27. Henley, N. (2001) "Body politics." In A. Branaman (ed.), *Self and Society*. Malden, MA: Blackwell.

28. Chance, M. R. A. (1967) "Attention structure as the basis of primate rank orders." *Man*, 2(4), 503–18, reprinted in M. R. A. Chance and R. R. Larsen (eds) (1976) *The Social Structure of Attention*. London: Wiley.

29. Strongman, K. T., and Champness, B. G. (1968) "Dominance hierarchies and conflict in eye contact." *Acta Psychologia*, 28, 376–86; Argyle, M., and Cook, M. (1976) *Gaze and Mutual Gaze*. Cambridge: Cambridge University Press; Rosa, E., and Mazur, A. (1979) "Incipient status in small groups." *Social Forces*, 58, 18–37; Webbink, P. (1986) *The Power of the Eyes*. New York: Springer Verlag.

30. Ellyson, S. L., Dovidio, J. F. and Fehr, B. J. (1981) "Visual behavior and dominance in women and men." In C. Mayo and N. M. Henley (eds), *Gender and Nonverbal Behavior*. New York: Springer Verlag; Dovidio, J. F., and Ellyson, S. L. (1982) "Decoding visual dominance: Attributions of power based on relative percentages of looking while speaking and looking while listening." *Social Psychology Quarterly*, 45(2), 106–13.

31. Mehrabian, A. (1969) "Significance of posture and position in the communication of attitude and status relationships." *Psychological Bulletin*, 71(5), 359–72.

3. Submissive Tells

1. Darwin, C. (1872) *The Expression of the Emotions in Man and Animals*. London: John Murray.

2. Efron, D. (1942) *Gesture and Environment*. New York: Kings Crown Press.

3. Brault, G. J. (1963) "Kinesics and the classroom: Some typical French gestures." *The French Review*, 36, 374–82.

4. Gilbert, P. (2000) "Varieties of submissive behavior as forms of social defense: Their evolution and role in depression." In L. Sloman and P. Gilbert (eds), *Subordination and Defeat: An Evolutionary Approach to Mood Disorders and Their Therapy*. Mahwah, NJ: Erlbaum.

5. Collett, P., and Contarello, A. (1987) "Gesti di assenso e di dissenso." In P. Ricci Bitti (ed.), *Communicazione e Gestualità*. Milano: Franco Angeli; Collett, P. (1993) *Foreign Bodies: A Guide to European Mannerisms*. London: Simon & Schuster.

6. Goffman, E. (1976) "Gender advertisements." *Studies in the Anthropology of Visual Communication*, 3, 69–154, reprinted as Goffman, E. (1979) *Gender Advertisements*. New York: Harper & Row; Morris, D. (1979) *Manwatching: A Field Guide to Human Behaviour*. London: Jonathan Cape; Regan, J. M. (1982) "Gender displays in portrait photographs." *Sex Roles*, 8, 33–43; Halberstadt, A. G. and Saitta, M. B. (1987) "Gender, nonverbal behavior, and perceived dominance: a test of a theory." *Journal of Personality and Social Psychology*, 53, 257–72; Wilson, A., and Lloyd, B. (1990) "Gender vs. power: Self-posed behavior revisited." *Sex Roles*, 23, 91–8.

7. Costa, M., Menzani, M., and Ricci Bitti, P. E. (2001) "Head canting in paintings: An historical study." *Journal of Nonverbal Behavior*, 25(1), 63–73.

8. Chance, M. R. A. (1962) "An interpretation of some agonistic postures: The role of 'cut-off' acts and postures." *Symposium of the Zoological Society of London*, 8, 71–89.

9. Bradley, M. M., Moulder, B., and Lang, P. J. (2005) "When good things go bad: The reflex physiology of defense." *Psychological Science*, 16, 468–73.

10. Zebrowitz, L.A. (1997) *Reading Faces: Window to the Soul?* Boulder, CO: Westview Press.

11. Hall, J. A., Smith LeBeau, L., Gordon Reinoso, J., and Thayer, F. (2001) "Status, gender, and nonverbal behavior in candid and posed photographs: A study of conversations between university employees." *Sex Roles*, 44, 677–91; Hall, J. A., Carter, J. D., Jimenez, M. C., Frost, N. A., and Smith LeBeau, L. (2002) "Smiling and relative status in news photographs." *Journal of Social Psychology*, 142, 500–10.

12. Van Hooff, J. A. R. A. M. (1972) "A comparative approach to the phylogeny of laughter and smiling." In R. A. Hinde (ed.), *Nonverbal Communication*. Cambridge: Cambridge University Press.

13. Hecht, M., and LaFrance, M. (1988) "License or obligation to smile: The effect of power and gender on amount and type of smiling." *Personality and Social Psychology Bulletin*, 24, 1326–36; LaFrance, M., and Hecht, M. A. (1999) "Option or obligation to smile: The effects of power and gender on facial expression." In P. Philippot, R. S. Feldman and E. J. Coats (eds), *The Social Context of Nonverbal Behavior*. Cambridge: Cambridge University Press.

14. Duchenne de Boulogne, G. (1862) *Mécanisme de la physionomie humaine*. Paris: Jules Renard (reprinted in English as *The Mechanism of Human Facial Expression*, edited and translated by R. A. Cuthbertson, Cambridge, Cambridge University Press, 1990).

15. Cashdan, E. (1998) "Smiles, speech and body posture: How women and men display sociometric status and power." *Journal of Nonverbal Behavior*, 22(4) 209–28; LaFrance, M., and Hecht, M. (2000) "Gender and smiling: A meta-analysis of sex differences in smiling." In A. H. Fisher (ed.), *Gender and Emotion*. Cambridge, Cambridge University Press, 1990; Hall, J. A., Carney, D. R., and Murphy, N. M. (2002) "Gender differences in smiling." In M. H. Abel (ed.), *An Empirical Reflection on the Smile*. New York: Edwin Mellen Press.

16. Dabbs, J. M. (1992) "Testosterone, smiling and facial appearance." *Journal of Nonverbal Behavior*, 21, 45–55.

17. Darwin, C. (1872) *The Expression of the Emotions in Man and Animals*. London: John Murray.

18. Ricks, C. (1974) *Keats and Embarrassment*. Oxford: Clarendon Press.

19. Leary, M. R., Britt, T. W., Cutlip, W. D., and Templeton, J. L. (1992) "Social blushing." *Journal of Personality and Social Psychology*, 112(3), 446–60; Crozier, W. R. (2006). *Blushing and the Social Emotions: The Self Unmasked*. Basingstoke: Palgrave Macmillan.

20. Halberstadt, A., and Green, L. R. (1993) "Social attention and placation theories of blushing." *Motivation and Emotion*, 17(1), 53–64; De Jong, P. J. (1999)

"Communicative and remedial effects of social blushing." *Journal of Nonverbal Behavior*, 23(3), 197–217.

21. Smith, W. J., Chase, J., and Lieblich, A. K. (1974) "Tongue showing: A facial display." *Semiotica*, 11, 201–246.

22. Dolgin, K. M., and Sabini, J. (1982) "Experimental manipulation of a human nonverbal display: The tongue show affects an observer's willingness to interact." *Animal Behaviour*, 30, 935–6; Jones, N., Kearins, J., and Watson, J. (1987) "The human tongue show and observers' willingness to interact: Replication and extensions." *Psychological Reports*, 60, 759–64.

23. Kendon, A. (1975) "Some functions of the face in a kissing round." *Semiotica*, 15, 299–334.

24. Festinger, L., and Carlsmith, M. (1959) "Cognitive consequences of forced compliance." *Journal of Abnormal and Social Psychology*, 58, 203–10.

25. Jones, E. E. (1964) *Ingratiation*. New York: Appleton-Century-Crofts; Gordon, R. A. (1996) "Impact of ingratiation on judgments and evaluations: A meta-analytic investigation." *Journal of Personality and Social Psychology*, 71(1), 54–70; Stengel, R. (2000) *You're Too Kind: A Brief History of Flattery*. New York: Simon & Schuster.

26. Judge, T. A., and Bretz, R. D. (1994) "Political influence behavior and career success." *Journal of Management*, 20(1), 43–65.

27. Colman, A., and Olver, K. R. (1978) "Reactions to flattery as a function of self-esteem: Self-enhancement and cognitive consistency theories." *British Journal of Social and Clinical Psychology*, 17(1), 25–9.

4. Conversation Tells

1. Walker, M. (1982) "Smooth transitions in conversational turn-taking: Implications for theory." *Journal of Psychology*, 110, 31–7.

2. Sacks, H., Schegloff, E., and Jefferson, G. (1974) "A simplest systematics for the organization of turn-taking in conversation." *Language*, 50, 696–735; Beattie, G. (1983) *Talk: An Analysis of Speech and Non-verbal Behaviour in Conversation*. Milton Keynes: Open University Press.

3. Yngve, V. J. (1970) "On getting a word in edgewise." *Papers from the 6th Regional Meeting of the Chicago Linguistic Society*, Chicago: Chicago Linguistic Society.

4. Meltzer, L., Morris, W. N., and Hayes, D. (1971) "Interruption outcomes and vocal amplitude: Explorations in social psychophysics." *Journal of Personality and Social Psychology*, 18, 392–402.

5. Anderson, K. J., and Leaper, C. (1998) "Meta-analyses of gender effects on conversational interruptions: Who, what, when, where and how." *Sex Roles*, 39(3/4), 225–52.

6. Tannen, D. (1981) "New York Jewish conversational style." *International Journal of the Sociology of Language*, 30, 133–49.

7. Kendon, A. (1967) "Some functions of gaze-direction in social interaction." *Acta*

Psychologia, 26, 2–63; Argyle, M., and Cook, M. (1976) *Gaze and Mutual Gaze*. Cambridge: Cambridge University Press; Beattie, G. (1978) "Sequential temporal patterns of speech and gaze in dialogue." *Semiotica*, 23(1/2), 29–52.

8. Harrigan, J. A., and Steffen, J. J. (1983) "Gaze as a turn-exchange signal in group conversations." *British Journal of Social Psychology*, 22(2), 167–8; Kalma, A. (1992) "Gazing in triads: A powerful signal in floor apportionment." *British Journal of Social Psychology*, 31, 21–39.

9. Duncan, S. (1972) "Some signals and rules for taking speaking turns in conversations." *Journal of Personality and Social Psychology*, 23(2), 283–92.

10. Caspers, J. (2000) "Looking for melodic turn-holding configurations in Dutch." *Linguistics in the Netherlands 2000*, Amsterdam: John Benjamins; Wichmann, A., and Caspers, J. (2001) "Melodic cues to turn-taking in English: evidence from perception." In J. van Kuppeveldt and R. Smith (eds), *Proceedings of the 2nd SIGdial Workshop on Discourse and Dialogue*. Aalborg, Denmark.

11. Walker, M., and Trimboli, C. (1983) "The expressive function of the eye flash." *Journal of Nonverbal Behavior*, 8(1), 3–13.

12. Scheflen, A. E., and Scheflen, A. (1972) *Body Language and Social Order*. Englewood Cliffs, NJ: Prentice-Hall; Scheflen, A. (1973) *How Behavior Means*. New York: Gordon & Breach.

13. Sebba, M., and Tate, S. (1986) "You know what I mean? Agreement marking in British Black English." *Journal of Pragmatics*, 10, 163–72.

14. Commins, S. (1935) *The Complete Works and Letters of Charles Lamb*. New York: Modern Library.

15. Feldman, S. (1959) *Mannerisms of Speech and Gestures in Everyday Life*. New York: International Universities Press; Weintraub, W. (1989) *Verbal Behavior in Everyday Life*. New York: Springer Verlag.

16. Weinstein, E. A. (1966) "Toward a theory of interpersonal tactics." In C. Backman and P. Second (eds), *Problems in Social Psychology: Selected Readings*. New York: McGraw-Hill.

17. Lakoff, G. (1973) "Hedges: A study in meaning criteria and the logic of fuzzy concepts." *Journal of Philosophical Logic*, 2, 458–508; Schiffrin, D. (1988) *Discourse Markers*. Cambridge: Cambridge University Press; Holmes, J. (1990) "Hedges and boosters in women's and men's speech." *Language and Communication*, 10(3), 185–205.

18. Malmstrom, J. (1960) "*Kind of* and its congeners." *English Journal*, 44, 288–90.

19. Holmes, J. (1986) "Functions of *you know* in women's and men's speech." *Language in Society*, 15, 1–22.

20. Lockard, J. S., Allen, D. J., Schiele, B. J., and Wiemer, M. J. (1978) "Human postural signals: Stance, weight-shifts and social distance as intention movements to depart." *Animal Behaviour*, 26, 219–24.

21. Wildeblood, J., and Brinson, P. (1965) *The Polite World*. London: Oxford University Press; Rockwood, J. (1992) *The Craftsmen of Dionysus: An Approach to Acting*. New York: Applause Books.

5. Greeting Tells

1. Kendon, A., and Ferber, A. (1973) "A description of some human greetings." In R. P. Michael and J. H. Crook (eds), *Comparative Ethology and Behavior of Primates*. New York: Academic Press.

2. Wildeblood, J., and Brinson, P. (1965) *The Polite World*. London: Oxford University Press; Rockwood, J. (1992) *The Craftsmen of Dionysus: An Approach to Acting*. New York: Applause Books.

3. Bulwer, J. (1644) *Chirologia: or the Natural Language of the Hand*. London.

4. Frumin, I., Perl, O., Endevelt-Shapira, Y., Eisen, A., Eshel, N., Heller, I., Shemesh, M., Ravia, A., Sela, L., Arzi, A., and Sobel, N. (2015) "A social chemosignaling function for human handshaking." *eLife*, 4, e05154.

5. Doran, G. D. (1998) "Shake on it." *Entrepreneur Magazine*, July.

6. Givens, D. (1977) "Greeting a stranger: Some commonly used nonverbal signals of aversiveness." *Semiotica*, 19(1/2), 13–28; Hall, P. M., and Hall, D. A. S. (1983) "The handshake as interaction." *Semiotica*, 45(3/4), 249–64.

7. Collett, P. (1983) "Mossi salutations." *Semiotica*, 45(3/4), 191–248.

8. Chaplin, W. F., Phillips, J. B., Brown, J. D., and Clanton, N. R. (2001) "Handshaking, gender, personality, and first impressions." *Journal of Personality and Social Psychology*, 79(1), 110–17.

9. Stephanopoulos, G. (1999) *All Too Human: A Political Education*. New York: Little, Brown.

10. Goffman, E. (1971) *Relations in Public*. Harmondsworth: Penguin; Greenbaum, P. E., and Rosenfeld, H. M. (1980) "Varieties of touch in greetings: Sequential structure and sex-related differences." *Journal of Nonverbal Behavior*, 5(1), 13–25; Ocklenburg, S., Packheiser, J., Schmitz, J., Rook, N., Güntürkün, O., Peterburs, J., and Grimshaw, G. M. (2018) "Hugs and kisses: The role of motor preferences and emotional lateralization for hemispheric asymmetries in human social touch." *Neuroscience and Biobehavioral Reviews*, 95, 353-360; Packheiser, S., Rook, N., Dursun, Z., Mesenholler, J., Wenglorz, A., Güntürkün, O., and Ochlenburg, S. (2019) "Embracing your emotions: Affective state impacts lateralization of human embraces." *Psychological Research*, 83, 26–36; Dueren, A.L., Vafeiadou, A., Edgar, C., and Banissy, M.J. (2021) The influence of duration, arm crossing style, gender and emotional closeness on hugging behaviour. *Acta Psychologica*, 221, 103441.

11. Collett, P. (1993) *Foreign Bodies: A Guide to European Mannerisms*. London: Simon & Schuster.

12. Erasmus, D. (1540) *Opera Omnia*, 9 vols. Basle.

13. Gunturkun, O. (2003) "Human behaviour: Adult persistence of head-turning asymmetry." Nature, 421, 711; Chapelain, A., Pimbert, P., Aube, L., Perrocheau, O., Debunne, G., Bellido, A., and Blois- Heulin, C. (2015) "Can population-level laterality stem from social pressures? Evidence from cheek-kissing in humans." *PLoS One*, 10.

14. Bakken, D. (1977) "Saying goodbye: An observational study of parting rituals." *Man–Environment Systems*, 7, 95–100; Summerfield, A., and Lake, J. A. (1977) "Nonverbal and verbal behaviours associated with parting." *British Journal of Psychology*, 68, 133–6; Albert, S., and Kessler, S. (1978) "Ending social encounters." *Journal of Experimental Social Psychology*, 14, 541–53.

15. Knapp, M. L., Hart, R. P., Friedrich, G. W., and Shulman, G. M. (1973) "The rhetoric of goodbye: Verbal and nonverbal correlates of human leave-taking." *Speech Monographs*, 40, 182–98.

6. Political Tells

1. Araujo, R., Ferreira, J. J., Antonini, A., and Bloem, B. R. (2015) "'Gunslinger's gait': A new cause of unilaterally reduced arm swing." *British Medical Journal*, Dec 14; 351:h6141.

2. Henton, C. G., and Bladon, R. A. W., (1985) "Breathiness in normal female speech: Inefficiency versus desirability." *Language and Communication*, 5, 221–7; W. Hardcastle and J. Laver (eds) (1995) *The Handbook of Phonetic Sciences*. Oxford: Blackwell.

3. Klofstad, C.A. (2016) "Candidate voice pitch influences election outcomes." *Political Psychology*, 37(5), 725–738; Klofstad, C. A. (2017) "Looks and sounds like a winner: Perceptions of competence in candidates' faces and voices influences vote choice." *Journal of Experimental Political Science*, 4(3), 229–240.

4. Masters, R. D. (1988) "Nice guys don't finish last: Aggressive and appeasement gestures in media images of politicians." In M. R. A. Chance and D. R. Omark (eds), *Social Fabrics of the Mind*. Hove: Lawrence Erlbaum.

5. Chance, M. R. A. (1962) "An interpretation of some agonistic postures: The role of 'cut-off' acts and postures." *Symposium of the Zoological Society of London*, 8, 71–89.

6. Atkinson, M. (1986) *Our Masters' Voices: The Language and Body Language of Politics*. London: Methuen.

7. Harris, S. (1991) "Evasive action: How politicians respond to questions in political interviews." In P. Scannell (ed), *Broadcast Talk*. London: Sage.

8. Bull, P., and Mayer, K. (1993) "How not to answer questions in political interviews." *Political Psychology*, 14(4), 651–66; Bull, P. (1998) "Political interviews: Television interviews in Great Britain." In O. Feldman and C. De Landtsheer (eds), *Politically Speaking*. Westport, CT: Praeger.

9. Bull, P., and Mayer, K. (1988) "Interruptions in political interviews: A study of Margaret Thatcher and Neil Kinnock." *Journal of Language and Social Psychology*, 7(1), 35–45.

10. Beattie, G. (1982) "Turn-taking and interruption in political interviews: Margaret Thatcher and Jim Callaghan compared and contrasted." *Semiotica*, 39(1/2),

93–114.

11. Schegloff, E. A. (1989) "From interview to confrontation: Observations on the Bush/Rather encounter." *Research on Language and Social Interaction*, 22, 215–40.

7. Royal Tells

1. Nicolson, H. (1968) *Diaries and Letters, 1945–1962,* edited by N. Nicolson, London: Collins.
2. Lacey, R. (1977) *Majesty: Elizabeth II and the House of Windsor.* London: Hutchinson.
3. Provine, R. R. (2000) *Laughter: A Scientific Investigation.* London: Penguin.
4. Castiglione, B. (1528) *Libro del Cortegiano.* Venice (translated by Sir Thomas Hoby as *The Book of the Courtier.* London, 1561).
5. Naunton, R. (1641) *Fragmenta Regalia* (reprinted in H. Walpole (ed.), *Paul Hentzner's Travels in England.* London, 1797).
6. Hoggart, S. (1986) "Caribbean Queen." In T. Grove (ed.) *The Queen Observed.* London: Pavilion Books.
7. Tooley, S. A. (1896) *The Personal Life of Queen Victoria.* London: S. H. Bousefield.
8. Windsor, E. (1987) *Wallis and Edward: Letters 1931–1937: The Intimate Correspondence of the Duke and Duchess of Windsor,* edited by M. Bloch. Bath: Chivers.
9. Henley, N. (2001) "Body politics." In A. Branaman (ed.), *Self and Society.* Malden, MA: Blackwell.
10. Windsor, E. (1951) *A King's Story: The Memoirs of H.R.H. the Duke of Windsor.* London: Cassell.
11. Bloch, M. (1973) *The Royal Touch: Sacred Monarchy and Scrofula in England and France,* translated by J. E. Anderson. London: Routledge & Kegan Paul.
12. Holden, A. (1979) *Charles: Prince of Wales: A Biography.* London: Little, Brown.
13. Mehrabian, A. (1969) "Methods and designs: Some referents and measures of nonverbal communication." *Behavioral Research Methods and Instrumentation,* 1, 203–7; Beebe, S. S., Beebe, S. J., and Redmond, M. V. (2002) *Interpersonal Communication: Relating to Others.* Boston: Allyn & Bacon.
14. Montagu, A. (1971) *Touching: The Human Significance of the Skin.* New York: Columbia University Press.
15. Darwin, C. (1872) *The Expression of the Emotions in Man and Animals.* London: John Murray.

8. Anxiety Tells

1. Marks, I. M., and Nesse, R. M. (1994) "Fear and fitness: An evolutionary analysis of anxiety disorders." *Ethology and Sociobiology,* 15, 247–67.
2. Christiansen, B. (1972) *Thus Speaks the Body.* New York: Arno Press; Fried, R.,

and Grimaldi, J. (1993) *The Psychology and Physiology of Breathing: In Behavioral Medicine, Clinical Psychology and Psychiatry*. New York: Plenum.

3. James, W. (1980) *The Principles of Psychology*, 2 vols. New York: Henry Holt.

4. Perera, J. (1988) "The hazards of heavy breathing." *New Scientist*, 3 December, 46–8.

5. Reich, W. (1949) *Character Analysis*. New York: Farrar, Strauss & Giroux; Lowen, A. (1958) *Physical Dynamics of Character Structure*. New York: Grune & Stratton.

6. Lowen, A. (1958) *Physical Dynamics of Character Structure*. New York: Grune & Stratton.

7. Middlemist, R. D., Knowles, E. S., and Matter, C. F. (1976) "Personal space invasion in the lavatory: Suggestive evidence for arousal." *Journal of Personality and Social Psychology*, 33, 541–6.

8. Hinde, R. (1982) *Ethology: Its Nature and Relations to Other Sciences*. Oxford: Oxford University Press.

9. Ekman, P., and Friesen, W. A. (1969) "The repertoire of nonverbal behavior: Categories, origins, usage, and coding." *Semiotica*, 1, 49–98.

10. Waxer, P. (1977) "Nonverbal cues for anxiety: An examination of emotional leakage." *Journal of Abnormal Psychology*, 86, 306–14; Daly, J. A., Hogg, E., Sacks, D., Smith, M., and Zimring, L. (1983) "Sex and relationship affect social self-grooming." *Journal of Nonverbal Behavior*, 7, 183–9; Shreve, E. G., Harrigan, J. A., Kues, J. R., and Kagas, D. K. (1988) "Nonverbal expressions of anxiety in physician–patient interactions." *Psychiatry*, 51 (4), 378–84; Kenner, A. N. (1993) "A cross-cultural study of body-focused hand movement." *Journal of Nonverbal Behavior*, 17(4), 263–79; Morris, D. (1994) *Bodytalk: The Meaning of Human Gestures*. New York: Crown Publishers; Pang, H.T., Canarslan, F., and Chu, M. (2022) "Individual differences in conversational self-touch frequency correlate with state anxiety." *Journal of Nonverbal Behavior*, 46, 299–319.

11. Harrigan, J. A., and O'Connell, D. M. (1996) "How do you look when feeling anxious?" *Personality and Individual Differences*, 21(2), 205–12. *See also* Leventhal, H., and Sharp, E. (1965) "Facial expressions as indicators of distress." In S. Tomkins and C. Izard (eds), *Affect, Cognition and Personality*. New York: Springer Verlag.

12. Milgram, S. (1974) *Obedience to Authority*. New York: Harper & Row.

13. Farabee, D. J., Holcom, M. L., Ramsey, S. L., and Cole, S. G. (1993) "Social anxiety and speaker gaze in a persuasive atmosphere." *Journal of Research in Personality*, 27(4), 365–76.

14. Stern, J. A. (1992) "The eye blink: Affective and cognitive influences." In D. G. Forgays, T. Sosnowski and K. Wrzesniewski (eds), *Anxiety: Recent Developments in Cognitive, Psychophysiological and Health Research*. Washington: Hemisphere.

15. Spille, J. L., Grunwald, M., Martin, S., and Mueller, S.M. (2021) "Stop Touching Your Face! A systematic review of triggers, characteristics, regulatory functions and neuro-physiology of facial self touch." *Neuroscience and Biobehavioral Reviews*, 128, 102–116; Zhang, N., Jia, W., Wang, P., King, M-F., Chan, P-T.,

and Li, Y. (2020) "Most self-touches are with the nondominant hand". *Scientific Reports*, 10, 10457.

16. Bell, C. (1847) *The Anatomy and Philosophy of Expression, as Connected with the Fine Arts*. London: John Murray.

17. Jackson, D. D. (1985) "From the lungs to larynx to lip, it's jitter, shimmer and blip." *Smithsonian*, 6 (July), 78.

18. Ellgring, H., and Scherer, K. R. (1996) "Vocal indicators of mood change in depression." *Journal of Nonverbal Behavior*, 20(2), 83–110.

19. Siegman, A. W. (1987) "The telltale voice: nonverbal messages of verbal communication." In A. W. Siegman and S. Feldstein (eds), *Nonverbal Behavior and Communication*. Hillsdale, NJ: Erlbaum; Siegman, A. W., and Boyle, S. (1993) "Voices of fear and anxiety and depression: The effects of speech rate and loudness on fear and anxiety and depression." *Journal of Abnormal Psychology*, 102(3), 430–7.

20. Murray, D. C. (1971) "Talk, silence and anxiety." *Psychological Bulletin*, 75, 244–60; Rochester, S. R. (1973) "The significance of pauses in spontaneous speech." *Journal of Psycholinguistic Research*, 2, 51–81.

9. Sports Tells

1. Papineau, D. (2017). *Knowing the Score: How Sport Teaches Us About Philosophy*. New York: Basic Books; Kniffin, K. M., and Palacio, D. (2018) "Trash-talking and trolling." *Human Nature, 29*(3), 353–69; Duncan, S. (2019) "Sledging in sport—Playful banter, or mean-spirited insults? A study of sledging's place in play." *Sport, Ethics and Philosophy*, 13(2), 183–97; Johnson, C. and Taylor, J. (2020) "More than bullshit: Trash talk and other psychological tests of sporting excellence." *Sport, Ethics and Philosophy*, 14(1), 47–61.

2. Joseph, S., and Cramer, D. (2011) "Sledging in cricket: Elite English batsmen's experiences of verbal gamesship." *Journal of Clinical Sport Psychology, 5*, 237–51; Lawless, W. and Magrath, R. (2021) "Inclusionary and exclusionary banter: English club cricket, inclusive attitudes and male camaraderie." *Sport in Society*, 24(8), 1493–1509.

3. Ring, C., Kavussanu, M., Al-Yaaribi, A. Tenenbaum, G., and Stanger, N. (2019) "Effects of antisocial behaviour on opponent's anger, attention, and performance." *Journal of Sports Science*, 37(8), 871–77; McDermott, K. C. P., and Lachlan, K. A. (2021) "Emotional manipulation and task distraction as strategy: The effects of insulting trash talk on motivation and performance in a competitive setting." *Communication Studies, 72(5)*, 915–36.

4. Webster, G. D., DeWall, C. N., Xu, Y., Orozco, T., Crosier, B. S., Nezlek, J. B., Bryan, A. D., and Bator, R. J. (2021) "Facultative formidability: Physical size shapes men's aggressive traits and behaviors in sports." *Evolutionary Behavioral Sciences*, 15(2), 133–58.

5. Land, M. and McLeod, P. (2001) "From eye movements to actions: How batsmen hit the ball." *Nature Neuroscience*, 3,134–45.

6. Güldenpenning, I., Kunde, W., and Weigelt, M. (2017) "How to trick your opponent: A review article on deceptive actions in interactive sports." *Frontiers in Psychology, 8,* Article 917; Panten, J., Loffing, F., Baker, J., and Schorer, J. (2019) "Extending research on deception in sport: Combining perception and kinematic approaches." *Frontiers in Psychology, 10,* Article 2650.

7. Dawkins, R., and Krebs, J. R. (1978) "Animal signals: Information or manipulation?" In J. R. Krebs and N. B. Davies (eds), *Behavioural Ecology. An Evolutionary Approach.* Oxford: Blackwell, 282–309; Stuart-Fox, D. (2005) "Deception and the origin of honest signals." *Trends in Ecology and Evolution, 20*(10), 521–23; Pentland, A. (2010). *Honest Signals: How They Shape Our World.* Boston: MIT Press.

8. Jackson, R. C., Warren, S., and Abernethy, B. (2006) "Anticipation skill and susceptibility to deceptive movement." *Acta Psychologica,123*(3), 355–71; Brault, S., Bideau, B., Kulpa, R., and Craig, C.M. (2012) "Detecting deception in movement: The case of the side-step in rugby." *PLoS ONE,* 7(6): e37494.

9. Buckolz, E., Prapavesis, H., and Fairs, J.H. (1988) "Advance cues and their use in predicting tennis passing shots." *Canadian Journal of Sport Sciences, 13(1),* 20–30; Panten, J., Loffing, F., Baker, J., and Schorer, J. (2019) "Extending research on deception in sport: Combining perception and kinematic approaches." *Frontiers in Psychology, 10,* Article 2650.

10. Müller, F., Jauernig, L., and Cañal-Bruland, R. (2019) "The sound of speed: How grunting affects opponents' anticipation in tennis." *PLoS ONE,* 14(4): e0214819.

11. Kunde, W., Skirde, S., and Weigelt, M. (2011) "Trust my face: Cognitive factors of head fakes in sports." *Journal of Experimental Psychology: Applied,* 17(2), 110–27; Polzien, A., Güldenpenning, I., and Weigelt, M. (2021) "A question of (perfect) timing: A preceding head turn increases the head-fake effect in basketball." *PLoS ONE,* 16(5): e0251117; *See also* Sebanz N., Shiffrar M. (2009) "Detecting deception in a bluffing body: The role of expertise." *Psychonomic Bulletin and Review,*16(1),170–75.

12. Morris, P.H., and Lewis, D.F. (2010) "Tackling diving: The perception of deceptive intentions in association football (soccer)." *Journal of Nonverbal Behavior, 34,* 1–13.

13. Dessing, J. C., and Craig, C. M. (2010) "Bending it like Beckham: How to visually fool the goalkeeper." *PLoS ONE,* 5(10): e13161.

14. Lyttleton, B. (2015) *Twelve Yards: The Art and Psychology of the Perfect Penalty Kick.* London: Penguin; Memmert, D. and Noel, B. (2020) *The Penalty Kick: The Psychology of Success.* Maidenhead: Meyer and Meyer.

15. Miller, C. (1996). *He Always Puts It to The Right.* London: Orion; Avugos, S., Azar, O.H., Sher, E., Gavish, N., and Bar-eli, M. (2020) "The right-oriented bias in soccer penalty shootouts." *Journal of Behavioural and Experimental Economics, 89,* 101546; Pereira, M. R., and Patching, G. R. (2021) "Goal side selection of penalty shots in soccer: A laboratory study and analyses of men's World Cup shoot-outs." *Perceptual and Motor Skills.* 28(5), 2279–2303; Avugos, S., Azar, O. H., Sher, E., Gavish, N., and Bar-Eli, M. (2023) "Detecting patterns in the behaviour of goalkeepers and kickers in the penalty shootout: A between-gender

comparison among score situations." *International Journal of Sport and Exercise Psychology*, 21(2), 196–216.

16. Masters, R. S. W., van der Kamp, J., and Jackson, R. C. (2007) "Imperceptibly off-centre goalkeepers influence penalty-kick direction in soccer." *Psychological Science*, 18, 222–23; Noël, B., van der Kamp, J., and Memmert, D. (2015) "Implicit goalkeeper influences on goal side selection in representative penalty kicking tasks." *PLoS One*,10(8):e0135423. *See also* Weigelt, M., Memmert, D., and Schack, T. (2012) "Kick it like Ballack: The effects of goalkeeping gestures on goal-side selection in experienced soccer players and soccer novices." *Journal of Cognitive Psychology*, 24, 942–56.

17. Savelsbergh, G. J., Van der Kamp, J., Williams, A. M., and Ward, P. (2005) "Anticipation and visual search behaviour in expert soccer goalkeepers." *Ergonomics*, 48(11–14),1686–97; Jordet, G., and Smeeton, N. J., and Williams, A. M. (2012) "The role of movement exaggeration in the anticipation of deceptive soccer penalty kicks." *British Journal of Psychology*, 103(4), 539–55; Lopes, J. E., Jacobs, D. M., Travieso, D., and Araújo D. (2014) "Predicting the lateral direction of deceptive and non-deceptive penalty kicks in football from the kinematics of the kicker." *Human Movement Science*, 36, 199–216.

18. Jordet, G., and Hartman, E. (2008) "Avoidance motivation and choking under pressure in soccer penalty shootouts." *Journal of Sport & Exercise Psychology*, 30(4), 450–57; Zheng, R., van der Kamp, J., Miller-Dicks, M., Navia, J., and Savelsbergh, G. (2023) "The effectiveness of penalty takers' deception: A scoping review." *Human Movement Science*, 90, [103122].

19. Furley, P., Dicks, M., Stendtke, F., and Memmert, D. (2012) "'Get it out the way. The wait's killing me.' Hastening and hiding during soccer penalty kicks." *Psychology of Sport and Exercise, 13*(4), 454–65.

20. Kraus, M. W., Huang, C., and Keltner, D. (2010)T"actile communication, cooperation, and performance: an ethological study of the NBA." *Emotion.* 10(5), 745–49.

21. Kneidinger, L. M., Maple, T. L., and Tross, S. A. (2001) "Touching behavior in sport: Functional components, analysis of sex differences, and ethological considerations." *Journal of Nonverbal Behavior*, 25(1), 43–62.

22. Matsumoto, D., and Willingham, B. (2006) "The thrill of victory and the agony of defeat: Spontaneous expressions of medal winners of the 2004 Athens Olympic games." Journal of Personality and Social Psychology, 91(3), 568–81; Matsumoto, D., and Hwang, H. S. (2012) "Evidence for a nonverbal expression of triumph." Evolution and Human Behavior, 33(5), 520–29; Hwang, H. C., and Matsumoto, D. (2014) "Cultural differences in victory signals of triumph." Cross-Cultural Research: The Journal of Comparative Social Science, 48(2), 177–91.

23. Šebesta, P., T ebický, V., Fialová, J., and Havlí ek, J. (2019) "Roar of a champion: Loudness and voice pitch predict perceived fighting ability but not success in MMA fighters." *Frontiers in Psychology*, 10, 859; Raine, J., Pisanski, K., Bond, R., Simner, J., and Reby, D. (2019) "Human roars communicate upper-body strength

more effectively than do screams or aggressive and distressed speech." PLoS ONE, 14(3), Article e0213034.

24. Moll, T., Jordet, G., and Pepping, G. J. (2010) "Emotional contagion in soccer penalty shootouts: Celebration of individual success is associated with ultimate team success." *Journal of Sports Sciences*, 28(9), 983–92.

25. Morris, D. (2019). *The Soccer Tribe*. New York: Rizzoli.

26. Cialdini, R. B., Borden, R. J., Thorne, A., Walker, M. R., Freeman, S., and Sloan, L. R. (1976) "Basking in reflected glory: Three (football) field studies." Journal of Personality and Social Psychology, 34(3), 366–75.

27. Medvec, V. H., Madey, S. F., and Gilovich, T. (1995) "When less is more: Counterfactual thinking and satisfaction among Olympic medalists." *Journal of Personality and Social Psychology*, 69(4), 603–10; Hedgcock, W. M., Luangrath, A. W., and Webster, R. (2021) "Counterfactual thinking and facial expressions among Olympic medalists: A conceptual replication of Medvec, Madey, and Gilovich's (1995) findings." Journal of Experimental Psychology: General, 150(6), e13–e21.

28. Tracy, J. L., and Matsumoto, D. (2008) "The spontaneous expression of pride and shame: Evidence for biologically innate nonverbal displays." *Proceedings of the National Academy of Science USA*, 19;105(33), 11655–11660; Matsumoto, D., and Willingham, B. (2009) "Spontaneous facial expressions of emotion of congenitally and noncongenitally blind individuals." Journal of Personality and Social Psychology, 96(1), 1–10; Hwang, H. C., and Matsumoto, D. (2014) "Dominance threat display for victory and achievement in competition context." Motivation and Emotion, 38(2), 206–14.

29. Panten, J., Loffing, F., Baker, J., and Schorer, J. (2019) "Extending research on deception in sport: Combining perception and kinematic approaches." Frontiers in Psychology, 10, Article 2650.

30. Haselhuhn, M. P., Ormiston, M. E., and Wong, E. M. (2015) "Men's facial width-to-height ratio predicts aggression: A meta-analysis." *PLoS ONE*, 10(4): e0122637; Geniole, S. N., Denson, T. F., Dixson, B. J., Carré, J. M., and McCormick, C. M. (2015) "Evidence from meta-Analyses of the facial width-to-height ratio as an evolved cue of threat." *PLoS ONE*,10(7): e0132a26.

31. T ebický, V., Havlí ek, J., Roberts, S. C., Little, A. C., and Kleisner, K. (2013) "Perceived aggressiveness predicts fighting performance in Mixed-Martial-Arts fighters." *Psychological Science*, 24(9), 1664–72; Little, A. C., T ebický, V., Havlí ek, J., Roberts, S. C., and Kleisner, K. (2015) "Human perception of fighting ability: Facial cues predict winners and losers in mixed martial arts fights." Behavioral Ecology, 26(6), 1470–75; T ebický, V., Fialová, J., Stella, D., Coufalová, K., Pavelka, R., Kleisner, K., Kuba, R., Št rbová, Z., and Havlí ek, J. (2019) "Predictors of fighting ability inferences based on faces." Frontiers in Psychology, 9, Article 2740.

32. Kraus, M. W., and Chen, T.-W. D. (2013) "A winning smile? Smile intensity, physical dominance, and fighter performance." Emotion, 13(2), 270–79.]

10. Sexual Tells

1. Eibl-Eibesfeldt, I. (1971) *Love and Hate: The Natural History of Behavior Patterns.* New York: Holt, Rinehart & Winston; Morris, D. (1971) *Intimate Behaviour.* London: Jonathan Cape; Singh, D., and Young, R. K. (1995) "Body weight, waist-to-hip ratio, breasts, and hips: Role in judgments of female attractiveness and desirability for relationships." *Ethology and Sociobiology*, 16, 483–507; Furnham, A., Dias, M., and McClelland, A. (1998) "The role of body weight, waist-to-hip ratio, and breast size in judgments of female attractiveness." *Sex Roles*, 3/4, 311–26.

2. Lloyd-Elliott, M. (1995) *Secrets of Sexual Body Language.* London: Hamlyn.

3. Buss, D. (1994) *The Evolution of Desire.* New York: Basic Books. *See also* Walter, K. V., et al. (2020) "Sex differences in mate preferences across 45 countries: A large-scale replication." *Psychological Science, 31*(4), 408–423.

4. Guttentag, M., and Secord, P. (1983) *Too Many Women? The Sex Ratio Question.* Beverly Hills: Sage Publications.

5. Anderson, J. L., Crawford, C. B., Nadeau, J., and Lindberg, T. (1992) "Was the Duchess of Windsor right? A cross-cultural review of the socioecology of ideals of female body shape." *Ethology and Sociobiology*, 13(3), 197–227; Pettijohn, T. F., and Jungeberg, B. J. (2004) "Playboy playmate curves: Changes in facial and body feature preferences across social and economic conditions." *Personality and Social Psychology Bulletin*, 30(9), 1186–97.

6. Perper, T. (1985) *Sex Signals: The Biology of Love.* Philadelphia: ISI Press; Perper, T. (1989) "Theories and observations on sexual selection and female choice in human beings." *Medical Anthropology*, 11(4), 409–54.

7. Burton, R. (1621) *The Anatomy of Melancholy.* Oxford: Henry Cripps.

8. Birdwhistell, R. (1970) *Kinesics and Context.* New York: Ballantine.

9. Moore, M. M. (1985) "Nonverbal courtship patterns in women: Context and consequences." *Ethology and Sociobiology*, 6, 237–47.

10. Wiley, R. H. (1991) "Lekking in birds and mammals: Behavioral and evolutionary issues." *Advances in the Study of Beha*vior, 20, 201–91.

11. Krebs, J. R., and Dawkins, R. D. (1984) "Animal signals: Mind-reading and manipulation." In J. R. Krebs and N. B. Davies (eds), *Behavioral Ecology: An Evolutionary Approach.* Sunderland, MA: Sinauer.

12. Grammer, K., Jutte, A., and Fischmann, B. (1997) "Der Kampf der Geschlecter und der Krieg der Signale." In B. Kanitscheider (ed.), *Liebe, Lust und Leidenschaft: Sexualität im Spiegel der Wissenschaft.* Stuttgart: Hirzel; Penton-Voak, I. S., Perrett, D. I., Castles, D. L., Kobayashi, T., Burt, D. M., Murray, L. K., and Minamisawa, R. (1999) "Menstrual cycle alters face preferences." *Nature*, 399, 741–2.

13. Walsh, D. G., and Hewitt, J. (1985) "Giving men the come-on: Effect of eye contact and smiling in a bar environment." *Perceptual and Motor Skills*, 61, 873–4.

14. Moore, M. M. (1985) "Nonverbal courtship patterns in women: Context and consequences." *Ethology and Sociobiology*, 6, 237–47.

15. Kleinke, C. L. (1986) "Gaze and eye contact: A research review." *Psychological Bulletin*, 100(1), 78–100; Lizuka, Y. (1992) "Eye contact in dating couples and unacquainted couples." *Perceptual and Motor Skills*, 75, 457–61; Grammer, K., Krück, K., Juette, A., and Fink, B. (2000) "Non-verbal behavior as courtship signals: The role of control and choice in selecting partners." *Evolution and Human Behavior, 21*(6), 371–390.

16. Walsh, D. G., and Hewitt, J. (1985) "Giving men the come-on: Effect of eye contact and smiling in a bar environment." *Perceptual and Motor Skills*, 61, 873–4.

17. Givens, D. B. (1978) "The nonverbal basis of attraction: Flirtation, courtship, and seduction." *Psychiatry*, 41, 346–59; Givens, D. B. (1983) *Love Signals: How to Attract a Mate*. New York: Crown.

18. Grammer, K., Krück, K., Juette, A., and Fink, B. (2000) "Non-verbal behavior as courtship signals: The role of control and choice in selecting partners." *Evolution and Human Behaviour*, 21, 371–90.

19. Abbey, A. (1987) "Misperceptions of friendly behavior as sexual interest: A survey of naturally occurring incidents." *Psychology of Women Quarterly*, 11(2), 173–94; Shotland, R. L., and Craig, J. M. (1988) "Can men and women differentiate between platonic and sexually interested behavior?" *Social Psychology Quarterly*, 51(1), 66–73; LaFrance, M., and Vial, A. C. (2016) "Gender and nonverbal behavior." In D. Matsumoto, H.C. Hwang and M.G. Frank (eds), *APA Handbook of Nonverbal Communication*. Washington, DC: APA; Place, S. S., Todd, P. M., Penke, L., and Asendorpf, J. B. (2009) "The ability to judge the romantic interest of others." *Psychological Science, 20*(1), 22–26; Brandner, J. L., Pohlman, J., and Brase, G. L. (2021) "On hits and being hit on: Error management theory, signal detection theory, and the male sexual overperception bias." *Evolution and Human Behavior*, 42(4), 331–42; Ruckel, L. M., (2022) "'She wants me, she wants me not': Individual differences in attachment, rejection sensitivity, and self-esteem and men's perception of women's sexual interest." *Personality and Individual Differences*, 196, 111733; Ivy, D. K., and Wahl, S. T. (2014) *Nonverbal Communication for a Lifetime*. Dubuque, IA: Kendall Hunt.

20. Morris, D. (1977) *Manwatching: A Field Guide to Human Behaviour*. London: Jonathan Cape.

21. Burton, R. (1621) *The Anatomy of Melancholy*. Oxford: Henry Cripps.

22. Ambady, N., Hallahan, M., and Conner, B. (1999) "Accuracy of judgments of sexual orientation from thin slices of behavior." *Journal of Personality and Social Psychology*, 77, 538–47; Ambady, N., LaPlante, D., and Johnson, E. (2001) "Thin slice judgments as a measure of interpersonal sensitivity." In J. Hall and F. Bernieri (eds), *Interpersonal Sensitivity: Measurement and Applications*. Hillsdale, NJ: Lawrence Erlbaum.

23. Berry, D. S., and McArthur, L. A. (1985) "Some components and consequences of a babyface." *Journal of Personality and Social Psychology*, 48, 312–23; McArthur, L.

Z., and Berry, D. S. (1987) "Cross-cultural consensus in perceptions of babyfaced adults." *Journal of Cross Cultural Psychology*, 18, 165–92.

24. Eibl-Eibesfeldt, I. (1971) *Love and Hate: The Natural History of Behavior Patterns.* New York: Holt, Rinehart & Winston.

25. Campbell, R., Wallace, S., and Benson, P. J. (1996) "Real men don't look down: Direction of gaze affects sex decisions on faces." *Visual Cognition*, 3(4), 393–412.

26. Hess, E. (1975) *The Telltale Eye.* New York: Van Nostrand Reinhold; Aboyoun, D. C., and Dabbs, J. M. (1998) "The Hess pupil dilation findings: Sex or novelty?" *Social Behaviour and Personality*, 26(4), 415–19.

27. Paul Ekman, personal communication.

28. Montagu, A. (1971) *Touching: The Human Significance of the Skin.* New York: Columbia University Press; Lockard, J. S., and Adams, R. M. (1980) "Courtship behaviors in public: different age/sex roles." *Ethology and Sociobiology*, 1, 245–53; McCormick, N. B., and Jones, A. J. (1989) "Gender differences in nonverbal flirtation." *Journal of Sex Education and Therapy*, 15(4), 271–82.

29. Perper, T. (1985) *Sex Signals: The Biology of Love.* Philadelphia: ISI Press; Murray, T. E. (1985) "The language of singles bars." *American Speech*, 60(1), 17–30.

30. Krebs, J. R., and Dawkins, R. D. (1984) "Animal signals: Mind-reading and manipulation." In J. R. Krebs and N. B. Davies (eds), *Behavioral Ecology: An Evolutionary Approach.* Sunderland, MA: Sinauer; Dabbs, J. M., and Mallinger, A. (1999) "Higher testosterone levels predict lower voice pitch among men." *Personality and Individual Differences*, 27, 801–4; Collins, S. (2001) "Men's voices and women's choices." *Animal Behaviour*, 60, 773–80.

31. Manes, J., and Wolfson, N. (1980) "The compliment formula." In F. Coulmas (ed.), *Conversational Routine.* The Hague: Mouton. *See also* Herbert, R. K. (1990) "Sex-based differences in compliment behaviour." *Language in Society*, 19, 201–24; Holmes, J. (1995) *Women, Men and Politeness.* London: Longman.

32. Dindia, K., and Allen, M. (1992) "Sex differences in self-disclosure: A meta-analysis." *Psychological Bulletin*, 112, 106–24.

33. Grammer, K. (1990) "Strangers meet: laughter and non-verbal signs of interest in opposite-sex encounters." *Journal of Nonverbal Behavior*, 14(4), 209–36.

34. Fischer, A., and LaFrance, M. (2015) "What drives the smile and the tear: Why women are more emotionally expressive than men." *Emotion Review*, 7(1), 22–29.

35. Provine, R. R. (2000) *Laughter: A Scientific Investigation.* London: Penguin.

36. Grammer, K., and Eibl-Eibesfeldt, I. (1990) "The ritualization of laughter." In W. A. Koch (ed.), *Natürlichkeit der Sprache und der Kultur.* Bochum: Brockmeyer.

37. Provine, R. R. (2000) *Laughter: A Scientific Investigation.* London: Penguin.

38. Moore, M. M. (1998) "Nonverbal courtship patterns in women: rejection signalling—an empirical investigation." *Semiotica*, 118(3/4), 201–14.

39. Grammer, K., Krück, K. B., and Magnusson, M. S. (1998) "The courtship dance: Patterns of nonverbal synchronization in opposite-sex encounters." *Journal of Nonverbal Behavior*, 22(1), 3–27.

40. Bernieri, F. J., and Rosenthal, R. (1991) "Interpersonal coordination: behavior matching and interactional synchrony." In R. S. Feldman and B. Rime (eds), *Fundamentals of Nonverbal Behavior*. Cambridge: Cambridge University Press.

41. LaFrance, M. (1979) "Nonverbal synchrony and rapport: Analysis by the cross-lag panel technique." *Social Psychology Quarterly*, 42, 66–70; Bavelas, J. B., Black, A., Lemery, C. R., and Mullett, J. (1987) "Motor mimicry as primitive empathy." In N. Eisenberg and J. Strayer (eds), *Empathy and Its Development*. Cambridge: Cambridge University Press; Bernieri, F. (1988) "Coordinated movement and rapport in teacher–student interactions." *Journal of Nonverbal Behavior*, 12, 120–38; Dijksterhuis, A. (2000) "Automatic social influence: the perception—behavior link as an explanatory mechanism for behavior matching." In J. Forgas and K. D. Williams (eds), *Social Influence: Direct and Indirect Processes*. Philadelphia: Psychology Press.

42. Beattie, G. (1988) *The Candarel Guide to Beach Watching*. Hove: Rambletree.

43. Buss, D. M., and Shackelford, T. K. (1997) "From vigilance to violence: Mate retention tactics in married couples." *Journal of Personality and Social Psychology*, 72, 346–61; Buss, D. (2000) *The Dangerous Passion: Why Jealousy Is as Necessary as Love and Sex*. London: Bloomsbury; Lindová, J. (2022) "Mate Retention." In T. Shackelford (ed), The *Cambridge Handbook of Evolutionary Perspectives on Sexual Psychology* (Cambridge Handbooks in Psychology, pp. 343–73). Cambridge: Cambridge University Press; Mogilski, J. K., and Shackelford, T. K. (2023) "Mate guarding and partner defection avoidance." In V. G. Starratt (ed), *The Oxford Handbook of Evolutionary Psychology and Romantic Relationships*. New York: Oxford University Press; Klein, W., Li, S., and Wood, S. (2023) "A qualitative analysis of gaslighting in romantic relationships." *Personal Relationships*, 1–25.

44. Goffman, E. (1971) *Relations in Public*. Harmondsworth: Penguin.

45. Givens, D. B. (1983) *Love Signals: How to Attract a Mate*. New York: Crown; Perper, T. (1985) *Sex Signals: The Biology of Love*. Philadelphia: ISI Press.

46. Gottman, J. M., and Silver, N. (1999) *The Seven Principles for Making Marriage Work*. New York: Crown Publishers; Gottman, J. M. (2015) *Principia Amoris: The New Science of Love*. Routledge/Taylor & Francis Group.

11. Lying Tells

1. Feldman, R. S., Forrest, J. A., and Happ, B. R. (2002) "Self-presentation and verbal deception: Do self-presenters lie more?" *Basic and Applied Social Psychology*, 24(2), 163–70.

2. DePaulo, B. M., Epstein, J. A., and Wyer, M. M. (1993) "Sex differences in lying: how women and men deal with the dilemma of deceit." In M. Lewis and C. Sarrni (eds), *Lying and Deception in Everyday Life*. New York: Guilford Press; DePaulo, B. M., Kashy, D., Kirkendol, S. E., Wyer, M. M., and Epstein, J. A. (1996) "Lying in everyday life." *Journal of Personality and Social Psychology*, 70(5), 979–95; Feldman,

R. S., Forrest, J. A., and Happ, B. R. (2002) "Self-presentation and verbal deception: Do self-presenters lie more?" *Basic and Applied Social Psychology*, 24(2), 163–70.

3. Feldman, R. S., Tomasian, J. C., and Coats, E. J. (1999) "Nonverbal deception abilities and adolescents' social competence: Adolescents with higher social skills are better liars." *Journal of Nonverbal Behavior*, 23(3), 237–49; Kashy, D., and DePaulo, B. M. (1996) "Who lies?" *Journal of Personality and Social Psychology*, 70(5), 1037–51.

4. DePaulo, P. J., and DePaulo, B. M. (1989) "Can attempted deception by salespersons and customers be detected through nonverbal behavioral cues?" *Journal of Applied Social Psychology*, 19, 1552–77.

5. Ekman, P. (2001) *Telling Lies*. New York: W. W. Norton.

6. Bond, C. F., and DePaulo, B. M. (2006) "Accuracy of deception judgments." *Personality and Social Psychology Review*, 10(3), 214–234.

7. McCormack, S. A., and Parks, M. R. (1990) "What women know that men don't: Sex differences in determining the truth behind deceptive messages." *Journal of Social and Personal Relationships*, 7, 107–18; Millar, M. G., and Millar, K. (1995) "Detection of deception in familiar and unfamiliar persons: The effects of information restriction." *Journal of Nonverbal Behavior*, 19(2), 69–84.

8. Burton, S. (2000) *Impostors: Six Kinds of Liar*. London: Viking.

9. Ekman, P. (2001) *Telling Lies*. New York: W. W. Norton.

10. Vrij, A. (2001) *Detecting Lies and Deceit*. Chichester: John Wiley.

11. Seager, P. (2001) "Improving the ability of individuals to detect lies." Unpublished Ph.D. thesis, University of Hertfordshire.

12. Krauss, R. M. (1981) "Impression formation, impression management, and nonverbal behaviors." In E. T. Higgins, C. P. Herman and M. Zanna (eds), *Social Cognition: The Ontario Symposium*, Vol. 1. Hillsdale, NJ: Erlbaum. *See also* Vrij, A., and Semin, G. R. (1996) "Lie experts' beliefs about nonverbal indicators of deception." *Journal of Nonverbal Behavior*, 20, 65–80; Anderson, D. E., DePaulo, B. M., Ansfield, M. E., Tickle, J. J., and Green, E. (1999) "Beliefs about cues to deception: Mindless stereotypes or untapped wisdom." *Journal of Nonverbal Behavior*, 23, 67–89; Vrij, A. (2001) *Detecting Lies and Deceit*. Chichester: John Wiley.

13. The Global Deception Research Team (2006) "A world of lies." *Journal of Cross-Cultural Psychology*, 37(1), 60–74.

14. Wiseman, R., Watt, C., ten Brinke, L., Porter, S., Couper, S.L., and Rankin, C. (2012) "The eyes don't have it: Lie detection and neuro-linguistic programming." *PLoS One*. 2012;7(7):e40259

15. Leal, S., and Vrij, A. (2008) "Blinking during and after lying." *Journal of Nonverbal Behavior*. 32(4), 187–94.

16. Vrij, A. (2001) *Detecting Lies and Deceit*. Chichester: John Wiley.

17. Vrij, A., and Fisher, R. P. (2020) "Unraveling the misconception about deception and nervous behavior." *Frontiers in Psychology*. 11: 1377.

18. Ekman, P., and Friesen, W. V. (1969) "Nonverbal leakage and clues to deception." *Psychiatry*, 32, 88–106.

19. Hirsch, A. R., and Wolf, C. J. (1999) "A case example utilizing practical methods for detecting mendacity." AMA Annual Meeting, Washington, DC [Abstract], NR505: 208; Hirsch, A. R., and Wolf, C. J., (2001) "Practical methods for detecting mendacity: A case study." *Journal of the American Academy of Psychiatric Law*, 29(4), 438–44.

20. Davis, K. (1999) "Clinton and the truth: On the nose?" *USA Today*, 19 May, 4; Dribben, M. (2002) "In your face." *The Philadelphia Inquirer*, 19 October.

21. Birdwhistell, R. (1955) "Do gestures speak louder than words?" *Collier's*, 4 March, 56–7.

22. Ekman, P. (2001) *Telling Lies*. New York: W. W. Norton.

23. Ekman, P., Friesen, W. V., and O'Sullivan, M. (1988) "Smiles when lying." *Journal of Personality and Social Psychology*, 54, 414–20; Ekman, P. (2001) *Telling Lies*. New York: W. W. Norton; Frank, M., Ekman, P., and Friesen, W. (1993) "Behavioral markers and recognizability of the smile of enjoyment." *Journal of Personality and Social Psychology*, 64(1), 83–93.

24. Haggard, E. A., and Isaacs, K. S. (1966) "Micromomentary facial expressions as indicators of ego mechanisms in psychotherapy." In L. A. Gottschalk and A. H. Auerbach (eds), *Methods of Research in Psychotherapy*. New York: Appleton-Century-Crofts; Ekman, P., and O'Sullivan, M. (1991) "Who can catch a liar?" *American Psychologist*, 46, 913–20.

25. Frank, M. G., and Ekman, P. (1997) "The ability to detect deceit generalizes across different types of high-stake lies." *Journal of Personality and Social Psychology*, 72, 1429–39; Matsumoto, D., and Hwang, H.C. (2018) "Microexpressions differentiate truths from lies about future malicious intent." *Frontiers in Psychology*. 9:2545; Burgoon, J. K. (2018) "Microexpressions are not the best way to catch a liar." *Frontiers in Psychology*. 9:1672; Porter, S., and ten Brinke, L. (2008) "Reading between the lies: Identifying concealed and falsified emotions in universal facial expressions." *Psychological Science*, 19, 508–514.

26. Vrij, A. (2001) Ibid.

27. Anoli, L., and Ciceri, R. (1997) "The voice of deception: Vocal strategies of naïve and able liars." *Journal of Nonverbal Behavior*, 21(4), 259–84.

28. Wright Whelan, C., Wagstaff, G., and Wheatcroft, J. (2013) "High-stakes lies: Verbal and nonverbal cues to deception in public appeals for help with missing or murdered relatives." *Psychiatry, Psychology and Law*. 21, 523–37.

29. Porter, S., and ten Brinke, L. (2010) "The truth about lies: What works in detecting high-stakes deception?" *Legal and Criminological Psychology*, 15(1), 57–75; ten Brinke, L., Porter, S., and Baker, A. (2012) "Darwin the detective: Observable facial muscle contractions reveal emotional high-stakes lies." *Evolution and Human Behavior*, 33(4), 411–16; ten Brinke, L., and Porter, S.B. (2012) "Cry me a river: Identifying the behavioral consequences of extremely high-stakes interpersonal deception." *Law and Human Behavior*, 36 6, 469–77.

30. Ekman, P. (2001) *Telling Lies*. New York: W. W. Norton.
31. DePaulo, B. M. (1994) "Deception." In T. Manstead and M. Hewstone (eds), *Blackwell Encyclopaedia of Social Psychology*, pp 164–8. Oxford: Blackwell.

12. Foreign Tells

1. 1 Chambers, J. (1973) "Canadian rising." *Canadian Journal of Linguistics*, 18, 113–35; Penner, P., and McConnell, R. (1980) *Learning English*. Toronto: Gage Publishing.
2. Bell, A. (1997) "The phonetics of fish and chips in New Zealand: Marking national and ethnic identities." *English World-Wide*, 18(2), 243–70; Scott, A. W., and Starks, D. (2000) " "No-one sounds like us?" A comparison of New Zealand and other southern hemisphere Englishes." In A. Bell and K. Kuiper (eds), *New Zealand English*. Wellington: Victoria University Press.
3. Collett, P., and Contarello, A. (1987) "Gesti di assenso e di dissenso." In P. Ricci Bitti (ed), *Communicazione e Gestualità*. Milano: Franco Angeli; Collett, P. (1993) *Foreign Bodies: A Guide to European Mannerisms*. London: Simon & Schuster.
4. Morris, D., Collett, P., Marsh, P., and O'Shaughnessy, M. (1979) *Gestures: Their Origins and Distribution*. London: Jonathan Cape.
5. Collett, P. (1993) *Foreign Bodies: A Guide to European Mannerisms*. London: Simon & Schuster.
6. Collett, P. (1983) "Mossi salutations." *Semiotica*, 45(3/4), 191–248.
7. Bulwer, J. (1644) *Chirologia: or the Natural Language of the Hand*. London.
8. Zeldin, T. (1988) *The French*. London: Collins Harvill.
9. Collett, P. (1993) *Foreign Bodies: A Guide to European Mannerisms*. London: Simon & Schuster.
10. Hillary, E. (1999) *View from the Summit*. London: Doubleday.
11. Ekman, P. (1982) *Emotion in the Human Face*. Cambridge: Cambridge University Press.
12. Birdwhistell, R. (1970) *Kinesics and Context*. New York: Ballantine.
13. Seaford, H. W. (1981) "Maximizing replicability in describing facial behavior." In A. Kendon (ed.), *Nonverbal Communication, Interaction, and Gesture*. The Hague: Mouton.
14. Collett, P. (1993) *Foreign Bodies: A Guide to European Mannerisms*. London: Simon & Schuster.
15. Zeldin, T. (1988) *The French*. London: Collins Harvill.
16. Zajonc, R. B., Murphy, S. T., and Inglehart, M. (1989) "Feeling and facial efference: Implications of the vascular theory of emotions." *Psychological Review*, 96, 395–416.
17. Strack, F., Martin, L., and Stepper, S. (1988) "Inhibiting and facial conditions of the human smile: A nonobtrusive test of the facial feedback hypothesis." *Journal of Personality and Social Psychology*, 54, 768–77. *See also* Cappella, J. N. (1993) "The facial feedback hypothesis in human interaction: Review and speculation."

Journal of Language and Social Psychology, 12, 13–29; McIntosh, D. N. (1996) "Facial feedback hypothesis: Evidence, implications, and directions." *Motivation and Emotion*, 20, 121–47.

18. Lehtonen, J., and Sajavaara, K. (1985) "The silent Finn." In D. Tannen and M. Saville-Troike (eds), *Perspectives on Silence*. Norwood, NJ: Ablex.

19. Golding, W. (1954) *Lord of the Flies*. London: Faber & Faber.

20. Collett, P. (1993) *Foreign Bodies: A Guide to European Mannerisms*. London: Simon & Schuster.

21. Anon. (1581) *A Treatise of Daunces*. London.

22. Efron, D. (1942) *Gesture and Environment*. New York: Kings Crown Press.

23. Efron, D. (1942) Ibid.

24. Morris, D., Collett, P., Marsh, P., and O'Shaughnessy, M. (1979) *Gestures: Their Origins and Distribution*. London: Jonathan Cape.

25. Collett, P. (1982) "Meetings and misunderstandings." In S. Bochner (ed.), *Cultures in Contact*. Oxford: Pergamon.

26. Collett, P. (1993) *Foreign Bodies: A Guide to European Mannerisms*. London: Simon & Schuster.

13. Business Tells

1. Furnham, A. (2003) *The Incompetent Manager: The Causes, Consequences and Cures of Managerial Failure*. London: John Wiley.

2. Collett, P. (1998) "Contrasting styles in international management research," *Journal of Managerial Psychology*, 13(3/4), 214–24.

3. Carney, D. R., Cuddy, A. J. C., and Yap, A. J. (2010) "Power posing brief nonverbal displays affect neuroendocrine levels and risk tolerance." *Psychological Science*, 21, 1363–69.

4. Ranehill, E., Dreber, A., Johannesson, M., Leiberg, S., Sul, S., and Weber, R. A. (2015) "Assessing the robustness of power posing: No effect on hormones and risk tolerance in a large sample of men and women." *Psychological Science, 33*, 1–4; Loncar, T. (2021) "A decade of power posing: Where do we stand?" *The Psychologist*, 8 June; Körner, R., Röseler, L., Schütz, A., and Bushman, B. J. (2022) "Dominance and prestige: Meta-analytic review of experimentally induced body position effects on behavioral, self-report, and physiological dependent variables." *Psychological Bulletin*, 148(1–2), 67–85.

5. Elkjær, E., Mikkelsen, M. B., Michalak, J., Mennin, D. S., and O'Toole, M. S. (2022) "Expansive and contractive postures and movement: A systematic review and meta-analysis of the effect of motor displays on affective and behavioral responses." *Perspectives on Psychological Science, 17*(1), 276–304.]]

6. Witkower, Z., Tracy, J. L., Cheng, J. T., and Henrich, J. (2020) "Two signals of social rank: Prestige and dominance are associated with distinct nonverbal displays." *Journal of Personality and Social Psychology, 118*(1), 89–120; Körner,

R., Schütz, A. (2022) "Poses and Postures as Status Displays." In: Shackelford, T. K., Weekes-Shackelford, V. A. (eds) *Encyclopedia of Evolutionary Psychological Science*. Springer, Cham. https://doi.org/10.1007/978-3-319-16999-6_3870-1

7. Tiedens, L. Z. and Fragale, A. R. (2003) "Power moves: Complementarity in dominant and submissive nonverbal behavior." *Journal of Personality and Social Psychology*, 84(3), 55868.]]

8. Weinstein, E.A., and Deutschberger, P. (1963). "Some dimensions of altercasting." *Sociometry*, 26(4), 454–66.]]

9. Fragale, A. R. (2006) "The power of powerless speech: The effects of speech style and task interdependence on status conferral." *Organizational Behavior and Human Decision Processes, 101*(2), 243–61.

10. Pinker, S. (2008) *The Sexual Paradox*. New York: Scribner.

11. Eagly, A., and Carli, L. L. (2007) *Through the Labyrinth: The Truth About How Women Become Leaders*. Boston: Harvard Business School Press. Rode, D. L. (2017) *Women and Leadership*. Oxford: Oxford University Press.

12. Williams, M.J. and Tiedens, L.Z. (2016) "The subtle suspension of backlash: A meta-analysis of penalties for women's implicit and explicit dominance behavior." *Psychological Bulletin*, 1432(2), 165–97.

13. Pink, D. (2012) *To Sell Is Human*. London: Canongate; Elsbach, K. D. and Kramer, R. M. (2003) "Assessing creativity in Hollywood pitch meetings: Evidence for a dual-process model of creativity judgments." *Academy of Management Journal*, 46(3), 283–301; Elsbach, K. D. (2003) "How to pitch a brilliant idea." *Harvard Business Review*, 81(9), 117–23.

14. Ersner-Hershfield, H., Wimmer, G. E. and Knutson, B. (2009) "Saving for the future self: Neural measures of future self-continuity predict temporal discounting." *Social Cognitive and Affective Neuroscience*. 4(1), 85–92.

15. Hershfield, H. E., Goldstein, D. G., Sharpe, W. F., Fox, J., Yeykelis, L., Carstensen, L. L., and Bailenson, J. N. (2011) "Increasing saving behavior through age-progressed renderings of the future self." *Journal of Marketing Research, 48*, S23–S37.

16. Bailenson, J. N. (2021) "Nonverbal overload: A theoretical argument for the causes of Zoom Fatigue." *Technology, Mind, and Behavior, 2*(1); Shockley, K. M., Gabriel, A. S., Robertson, D., Rosen, C. C., Chawla, N., Ganster, M. L., and Ezerins, M. E. (2021) "The fatiguing effects of camera use in virtual meetings: A within-person field experiment." *Journal of Applied Psychology, 106*(8), 1137–55.

14. Tell-Tales

1. Simons, D., and Levin D. (1998) "Failure to detect changes to people during a real-world interaction." *Psychonomic Bulletin & Review*, 5, 644–9.

2. Truzzi, M. (1973) "Sherlock Holmes: applied social psychologist." In M. Truzzi (ed.), *The Humanities as Sociology*. Columbus, OH: Charles E. Merrill.

3. Doyle, A. C. (1891) "A case of identity." In W. S. Baring-Gould (ed.) (1967), *The Annotated Sherlock Holmes*. New York: Clarkson N. Potter.

4. Napier, J. R. (1973) *Bigfoot: The Yeti and Sasquatch in Myth and Reality*. London: E. P. Dutton.

5. Murphy, S. T., and Zajonc, R. B. (1993) "Affect, cognition, and awareness: Affective priming with optimal and suboptimal stimulus exposures." *Journal of Personality and Social Psychology*, 64, 723–39.

6. Dimberg, U., Thunberg, M., and Elmehed, K. (2000) "Unconscious facial reactions to emotional facial expressions." *Psychological Science*, 11, 86–9.